THE POLITICAL ECONOMY OF CHANGE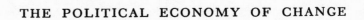

THE POLITICAL ECONOMY OF CHANGE

BY WARREN F. ILCHMAN
AND NORMAN THOMAS UPHOFF

UNIVERSITY OF CALIFORNIA PRESS
BERKELEY, LOS ANGELES, LONDON • 1971

University of California Press
Berkeley and Los Angeles, California

University of California Press, Ltd.
London, England

Copyright © 1969, by
The Regents of the University of California

Second Printing, 1971
First Paperback Edition, 1971
ISBN: 0-520-01390-5 cloth
       0-520-02033-2 paper
Library of Congress Catalog Card Number: 71-81743
Printed in the United States of America

12-5-74

*Dedicated to
Men of Knowledge
and Men of Public
Action*

DAVID E. APTER

MARVER H. BERNSTEIN

KENNETH E. BOULDING

A. H. HANSON

MARION J. LEVY, JR.

W. ARTHUR LEWIS

B. S. RAGHAVAN

FREDERICK L. SCHUMAN

DONALD C. STONE

ALBERT WATERSTON

*With appreciation for their work and friend-
ship, which have encouraged us to address
ourselves to the problems treated in this book.*

PREFACE

If on August 3, 1966, the New York *Times* had reported that a team of six political scientists was flying to Nigeria to advise Colonel Yakubu Gowon, newly installed leader of the Nigerian Military Government, who would have cared? Political scientists might have wondered whether their colleagues on this mission were behaviorists or institutionalists, functionalists or theorists; whether any were students of ideology, political parties, political culture, or public administration. Nigerians might have wondered skeptically who was going to foot the bill. Friends of Nigeria would probably have confided to themselves the hope that the visitors would not make things worse than they were already. Any concern would have been alleviated by the assumption that advice tendered by the visitors would not be taken seriously. All three sets of probable reactions to our hypothetical news item disturb us greatly. We think many political scientists share our feeling that the discipline of political science fails both to fulfill its own intellectual standards of rigor and cogency and to meet the standards of utility and relevance set by others. We hope that such political scientists and the others who look to our discipline for guidance will find merit in this book.

This is in several ways a preliminary book. It is preliminary in that the perspective it offers on political and economic activity can, through subsequent scholarship, be greatly refined and expanded to provide more sophisticated and relevant knowledge about achieving men's goals. Moreover, it is preliminary as a statement of our intention to undertake—with others, we hope—such a task. This book is also a respectful protest against the present "state of the arts" for studying developing nations and the policy choices leaders in such nations must make. It is respectful as a protest because we appreciate the difficulty of making scholarship relevant to public action and because we recognize that many previous works by scholars have paved the way for this venture. At the same time, it is a protest against the failure of scholars in the non-economic social sciences to transcend typologies and *ex post facto* analysis and fasten their attentions upon the achievement and improvement of public purposes; it is also a protest against the failure of economists to understand their subject in its political environment.

We present in the following pages a new version of an old subject— political economy. It is our hope that this version will prove useful to those concerned with improving public choices. At a time when people in communities everywhere confront problems of great magnitude and complexity, we need not be devotees of the state to recognize the importance of finding and improving the means whereby men can best combine their resources and ideas for working out urgently needed solutions. Nor are we unduly harsh if we say that social scientists have generally neglected their responsibility to participate in this task.

Indicative of this neglect is the fate of the formal study of political economy. The editors of the new *International Encyclopedia of the Social Sciences* (1968) fail to include an entry on Political Economy or even to consider this field of study specifically among the various schools of economic thought. (On the other hand, the editors of *Webster's New Third International Dictionary* trace the evolution of the term "political economy" from the eighteenth century—"[a] branch of the art of government concerned with directing governmental policies toward promotion of the wealth of the government and of the community as a whole"—to the twentieth century—"a modern social science dealing with the interrelationship of political and social processes.") Of course, the theoretical and practical difficulties inherent in the study of political economy are many, especially in comparison with more conventional approaches in economics and political science. Fewer simplifying assumptions are permissible in political economy. The development of theory is more inextricably linked with the empirical world and all of its vagaries and intractabilities. Value judgments and ethical problems abound, and are made more complicated when collective rather than individual choices are involved. Perhaps another factor has contributed to the decline in intellectual interest in political economy. Practitioners of politics and government have so often defaulted on their promises to create a better life for others that it is not surprising that many expect the "good life" to be achieved more readily through private than through public choices. We are grateful that, despite the difficulties of formal analysis and the possibilities of abuse by officeholders and aspirants, a few hearty social scientists have persevered in the study of public policies.

We approach the issues and application of political economy chiefly through the discipline of political science, though we are students of economics and sociology as well. Because our version of political economy differs in many respects from the traditional one, some may think a different designation preferable. We are aware that we do not always use economic terms as economists do, but our underlying concerns remain the concerns of the early political economists. We want to determine what relationship between those in authority and those subject to it is likely to be most productive for the community. We also seek to determine what courses government must follow to see that the resources of a community are used most economically and effectively to achieve the goals set for that community. Some political scientists have worked to elucidate the political dimensions of economic choices, but our approach tries to expand the limits of analysis to deal with problems of allocation and productivity in all spheres of public choice, not just the economic sphere. Thus we find political economy an appropriate if not an unambiguous designation for our analytical approach.

A model of politics, not a theory of politics, is developed in this book. One cannot ask: "Is it true?" Rather, one must ask: "Does it give insights into political phenomena?" or "Does it provide analytical power for making evaluations and predictions?" We would like to think of our model as one for persons who are tired of models. The recent proliferation of models and nomenclature in political science has yet to yield substantial results. We would hope that political scientists will be persuaded not to elaborate any more models until the empirical test of utility is applied to existing approaches. We are quite willing to stake this model's longevity on its empirical results. Mr. Uphoff has already found the model valuable in his study of the utilization of external economic assistance to promote economic, social, and political development in Ghana. At present Mr. Ilchman is in India preparing a political economy study of the educated unemployed.

As a focus for exposition, we have chosen the perspective of statesmen in developing countries. Despite initial appearances, however, the book is not about Colonel (now General) Gowon of Nigeria. We chose to begin our book with a discussion of Gowon because the situations and choices he had to confront at the time we began writing this book made more real to us the need for a different kind of political science. Although our exposition deals primarily with the needs and aims of political leaders in authority, the model of political economy has no conservative bias. To the extent that it illuminates the political process, it is as relevant to a Che Guevara as to an Eduardo Frei. We could have dealt more explicitly with the choices and strategies of anti-statesmen or of particular sectors such as peasants or civil servants, yet the book is already longer than we would have liked. (Indeed, in the final draft we omitted one whole chapter dealing with political solvency and stability.) Thus, we must rely on the reader's ingenuity and thoughtfulness for many applications, extrapolations, and extensions of the model.

There are many persons to whom we are deeply grateful for assistance in developing our ideas. The model received its most extensive use and criticism in graduate and undergraduate seminars, first at the Center for Development Economics at Williams College and then in the Department of Political Science at the University of California, Berkeley. In four years, over one hundred and fifty young scholars improved our formulations and tested our conclusions. We are deeply indebted to our colleagues and friends: Robert Biller, Carolyn Elliott, Ernst Haas, Alice Stone Ilchman, Todd R. LaPorte, G. Bingham Powell, Carl G. Rosberg, Richard N. Rosecrance, Bernard B. Schaffer, Arthur Stinchcombe, and Aaron Wildavsky. Miss Lee Goldberg, our editor, worked valiantly to save our readers from the barbarous onslaught of our social science prose. To her we are enormously grateful. Mr. Ilchman expresses his appreciation to the Rockefeller Foundation, and especially to Kenneth Thompson, for making possible both his original travel to various developing countries and the leisure to think about a social science more useful to policy studies. Mr. Uphoff expresses his appreciation to Frederick Harbison and to Education and World Affairs for the opportunity to work in Nigeria during part of 1966 and to see how great was the "social science theory" gap, even in comparison with the admittedly large resource gap.

We also wish to acknowledge the assistance of the Institute of International Studies of the University of California, and especially that of Miss Helen Rudy and Mrs. Marjorie Short, in preparation of the manuscript. By acknowledging our many sources of assistance, encouragement, and helpful criticism, we do not wish to implicate any of them in what may be found to be transgressions against social science or logic. Perhaps more than is necessary for most authors, we must take full responsibility for any of the book's shortcomings.

Warren F. Ilchman
Norman Thomas Uphoff

CONTENTS

ANALYTICAL TABLE
OF CONTENTS

THE POLITICAL ECONOMY
OF CHANGE

I

WHY POLITICAL ECONOMY?

And we are on the eve of a search for rational choice models of political growth—an approach which may make political theory more relevant to public policy. Like the authors of the *Federalist Papers*, contemporary political theorists are inescapably confronted with problems of how resources may be economically allocated to affect political change in preferred directions. The justification for this quest for an allocation-of-resources theory of political development is not only its relevance to central concerns of public policy, but its uses as a test of the validity and power of our theories. It forces us to place our bets, set the odds, and confront straightforwardly the issue of the kind of prediction which is possible in political science.

Gabriel A. Almond [1]

CONSIDER THE SITUATION OF COLONEL YAKUBU GOWON. What would a political scientist have advised this young African leader who on the first of August, 1966, accepted leadership of the National Military Government of Nigeria? The problems confronting Gowon were typical of those prevalent in most developing countries. He faced the challenges of achieving political stability and national unification, sustaining economic and social development and national independence, accommodating conflicting group demands, and reducing tension among regions and classes. It was the agglomeration of these problems that made Gowon's position precarious and made the welfare of millions of Nigerians hang in the balance. Could a political scientist have improved upon the choices Gowon made to resolve these various issues?

For Gowon, the distinction of being both the youngest head of state in Africa and head of the largest African country could hardly compensate for

[1] Almond (1966:877). References cited are listed on pp. 287–302 according to author and date.

the host of difficulties and demands he faced in trying to hold Nigeria together and lead it toward economic, social, and political development. Before the coup that put him in power, Colonel Gowon had been highly
regarded by his military colleagues for his intelligence, ambition, and good
sense. In fact early in July of 1966, it had been rumored that if the progressive young army officers were to oust their older and undynamic commander, Major-General Aguiyi-Ironsi, Gowon would be their choice as a
successor.[2] Circumstances, however, were to prevent Gowon from assuming authority with a mandate for reform backed by army power. On July
29, Nigeria was convulsed by the second bloody military coup within the
year. This coup was not directed against civilian politicians, but rather split
the army itself. Mutinous Northern troops rebelled against their Southern
officers, seized control of Lagos, capital of Nigeria, and Ibadan, capital of
the Western Region, and "decapitated" the Military Government by as-
sassinating Ironsi and the Military Governor of the West.

The young Hausa majors from the North who masterminded the coup
and who held three-fourths of Nigeria under threat of military violence demanded that the North be allowed to secede from the rest of Nigeria on
favorable terms which included guaranteed right of access to the sea and a
share of the revenues from the oil mined in the Eastern and Midwestern
Regions. After two days of talks with Brigadier Ogundipe, Ironsi's second-in-
command, with Colonel Gowon, then Army Chief of Staff, and with several top civil servants, the mutineers were convinced that unilateral secession would not be in the best interests of the North. The rebels reluctantly
agreed to drop their demand for secession, provided leaders from all parts
of Nigeria would begin full-scale consultations to determine the most acceptable form of association for the regions.

For the regions of Nigeria to function together as one country, if only on
an interim basis, a new head of government was needed. The National
Military Government, though its numbers were depleted, still held nomi-

[2] On January 15, 1966, progressive young army officers had toppled the Federal Nigerian government in a coup that ended five years of independent civilian
rule. The coup, however, did not put the younger officers in authority. Surviving civilian politicians called on General Ironsi, the commander of the army, to
form a military government. Though the rebel officers pledged their support,
the government was not entirely united. Ironsi's slowness to undertake radical
constitutional, political, and economic reforms led to dissatisfaction among the
younger officers and members of the more progressive civilian sectors, most of
whom were Southerners. Yet Ironsi knew the stiff opposition such reforms
would receive from Northerners and was not prepared to use coercion to back
up any far-reaching restructuring of the Nigerian polity. The reforms he did an-
nounce between April and July were not approved of by most Northerners, and
in May there was retaliatory violence against Southerners living in the North.

nal authority. Brigadier Ogundipe was unacceptable to the mutineers because he was a Westerner who besides had little taste or temperament for politics. Thus Gowon, a popular officer and a Northerner, though neither of the Hausa tribe nor the Moslem religion as were the rebel leaders, was the logical successor to Ironsi. On August 1, Colonel Gowon announced in a radio broadcast to the nation that he had been elected by a "majority of the Supreme Military Council" to head the Military Government. He declared that he would reverse all measures taken by the Ironsi regime toward a unitary government. He called on the soldiers to return to their barracks and announced that consultations with regional leaders would begin in order to determine the best form of association for Nigeria. Finally, he asked Nigerians to remain calm and to give him their support.[3] Although he did not say so, he knew that the Northerners who then dominated the army had chosen him to preside over the dissolution of his country.

Colonel Gowon, however, was a nationalist. He did not intend to let Nigeria fall apart into separate and feuding pieces if he could by his efforts avert such dissolution. Surely as astute and ambitious a leader as Gowon must have been nearly overwhelmed by the dismal gap between his nominal authority as Supreme Commander of the National Military Government and his actual power to direct events. A host of decisions confronted him: How could he best maintain his shaky grip on authority? How could he prevent his faction-torn country from breaking up into three, four, or more sovereign and antagonistic states? How could he restore some degree of national unity to Nigeria and re-embark the country on its course of development?

HOW COULD COLONEL GOWON BEST CHOOSE AMONG ALTERNATIVE COURSES OF ACTION?   How should he assess the costs and benefits of alternative policies? How could he use the meager resources at his disposal—some legitimacy, limited authority, sparse information, a certain amount of economic resources, and an uncertain capacity for coercion—to bring about a measure of political stability and to effect desired short-run changes in the political environment? How could he use or reshape the institutions at hand to minimize losses in national progress and create momentum for long-term development? The following choices, among others, confronted Colonel Gowon: [4]

(1) What role should Gowon assign to the army? Should he try to re-

---

[3] The text of Gowon's speech is given in "Return to Civil Rule Soon," *Daily Times* (Lagos), August 2, 1966.

[4] We consider here only the problems facing Gowon in his first months of office before the crisis of Biafran secession. We assume that under certain conditions the secession could have been avoided.

build it? It had been torn apart by two fratricidal purges and was perhaps more capable of contributing to the killing and chaos than of halting it. Should he repatriate all army personnel to their region of origin? After the coup Hausa soldiers had sporadically lynched Ibos in Lagos and elsewhere in the West. Repatriation of all soldiers would reduce incidents of violence, but would at the same time remove from Lagos those Northern Tiv soldiers who provided Gowon's personal security and constituted his main direct source of power.[5]

(2) Should Gowon move quickly to restore civilian rule, which had been abrogated by the military in January? Could civilian leaders hold the country together and restore peace? Perhaps the politicians might provide the needed conciliatory and pragmatic leadership, but their sectionalist bias and frequent venality had occasioned the first coup and might again plague Nigeria.[6]

(3) Should Gowon grant more influence to the traditional leaders of Nigeria? In the absence of party politics, these leaders were the only effective representatives of the people. But they too stood for the ethnic loyalties and jealousies that had brought Nigeria to the brink of self-destruction.

(4) What should Gowon do if Northern soldiers and civilians in Kano and other Northern cities continued to massacre their Ibo neighbors? The government of Eastern Nigeria estimated that between the end of July and the end of September 7,000 Easterners were killed in the North, many thousands more were wounded, and over a million were forced to return to the East. This killing made reconciliation between the East and North much more difficult to achieve and greatly reduced Gowon's ability to work

[5] Gowon did, in fact, call for repatriation of army personnel, but without success. Northern troops in Lagos and the West did not want to give up their position of strength; those in the North were reluctant to let Eastern soldiers return home, for these soldiers might form the nucleus of an eastern army that could be used offensively or defensively against a Northern army. Although some repatriation did take place, it was by no means complete.

[6] Gowon promised to restore civilian rule, but cited no definite time. During his first week of rule, he gained great popularity among Southerners by releasing Chiefs Awolowo and Enaharo, leaders of the opposition to the previous civilian regime. Both had been convicted in 1963 for allegedly plotting to overthrow the regime unconstitutionally. To gain some measure of immediate support, he also released dozens of politicians who had been jailed after the January coup pending a thorough investigation of all allegations of graft and corruption against them. Although evidence of incredible audacity and graft had been accumulated since January, each politician had some local base of support that Gowon hoped to tap to gain at least short-term stability for his regime.

out a political solution. Yet he had almost no force at his disposal that he could dispatch to ensure the security of non-Northerners.

(5) What should Gowon do if the East or North announced secession? Each was attempting to goad the other into leaving the Federation first so that the other would bear the onus for breaking up the country. Could or should Gowon call in Commonwealth, OAU, or United Nations forces to hold the country together?

(6) Should Gowon try to use the police once the army had plunged into disorder? Although its membership was mostly Ibo, the police seemed to support Gowon and maintained a high degree of order during the military disturbances. Yet because of their ethnic origin, Ibos on the force remained subject to appeals from the East.

(7) How could Gowon finance central government operations if deprived of tax and oil revenues from the regions? Colonel Ojukwu, Military Governor of the East, had cut off payments of oil royalties because he did not recognize Gowon as legitimate successor to Ironsi. Could or should money be borrowed internally or from abroad, or should force be used to keep the regions sending revenues to Lagos?

(8) Should Gowon have economic planners continue work on a new development plan to commence in 1968, though no one knew what form the country would have when the existing plan expired? What could Gowon do about the suspension of governmental and private foreign aid to Nigeria and the precipitous decline in private foreign and domestic investment?

(9) Should Gowon concentrate his efforts on rallying the intellectual elite in support of his government, or should he concentrate more on reaching the masses by appealing to values in their traditional culture?

(10) Should Gowon undertake a national tour to preach a secular gospel of nationalism and national unity? Might a pan-Africanist ideology lead Nigerians to subordinate tribal allegiances to a broader racial and cultural union where pan-Nigerianism had failed?

(11) Should Gowon take over all communications media? Should he attempt, despite constitutional difficulties, to alter the school curricula to inculcate nationalism? Should he organize youth brigades to bring together young persons of different tribes to work in projects for the national benefit?

WHAT COULD A POLITICAL SCIENTIST ADVISE COLONEL GOWON? Could a political scientist, drawing on the propositions of his discipline, offer any better advice to Colonel Gowon than could a shrewd politician or an experienced journalist on the scene? We fear not. Without wishing to gainsay the contributions of many political and social scientists, we believe that contemporary political science fails especially when it is expected to deal with the problems of choice confronting statesmen like Gowon.

Why is this the case? A major reason is the perspective adopted by today's social scientists, a perspective quite removed from the process of choice or the ramifications of concrete political activity. Macro-analytical approaches, which view society and the polity in global terms, cannot handle choices made by the statesman and other political activists.[7] This inability to deal with choice is inherent in some of the assumptions underlying these approaches. Analyses based on systems or structural-functional models impose criteria for political action that are not necessarily those of the regime or of political actors. These analyses also fail to illuminate the costs and consequences of concrete, short-term political activity. Many macro-analytical approaches require "total knowledge" of a system to make judgments about its parts. For the most part, they treat government as a dependent variable or as a function of the rest of the system. While functional or systems theorists may insist that a regime can pursue goals independently without regard for the demands made by others, they do not and cannot specify the conditions under which regimes act as independent variables in the political process, or explain how, if a regime's leaders desire to realize the goals of others, they can realize these goals most effectively.[8] We wish to have a political science that at the least can do the latter!

Similar problems are presented by other approaches, especially those that treat political and social phenomena as functions of stages or levels of development. Most familiar among these is the analysis of "ideal types" or of dichotomous characteristics of societies considered "traditional" or "modern." The typological approach has an ancient and honorable lineage which includes scholars like Tönnies, Durkheim, Maine, and Weber. Its influence has been strengthened as the pattern variable analysis proposed by Talcott Parsons has been adopted by other political and social scientists.[9] However, by analyzing societies in terms of traits presumed charac-

[7] Among the most influential and important works in political and social science dealing in terms of systems or functional analysis we would include Parsons (1951); Levy (1952); Easton (1953), (1957), and (1965); Almond (1960); and Deutsch (1963).

[8] The importance of politics as an independent variable is convincingly illustrated by Paige (1966). More extensive critiques of the various models and approaches have been offered by Huntington (1965), Pye (1965), and Diamant (1966).

[9] Parsons' set of dichotomous pattern variables, used to distinguish between more traditional and more modern societies, can be found in Parsons (1951:58–

teristic of the extremes of conceptualized continua, little can usefully be said about the political, social, and economic relationships in societies that do not correspond to these ideal types or in societies that may deviate from the ideal type in differing respects and degrees.[10] Furthermore, typological analyses are not explanatory and have not dealt systematically with problems of causation. They all too often treat modernization as a determinate process leading to institutions, norms, and behavior of the sort found in western industrial societies. This evolutionary or teleological bias, though often only implicit, is misleading because of the differences that exist and will continue to exist between various societies and polities.[11]

Insofar as typological analyses consider the development problems and choices facing a statesman at all, their suggestions involve politically irrelevant time periods and are thus productive only of despair for the policymaker who takes them seriously. Colonel Gowon would have found small consolation in the assurance that advancing differentiation would probably usher in a new Nigeria eventually marked by achievement, universalistic and affectively neutral norms, and functionally specific institutions. Nor

67) and Parsons and Shils (1951: Chap. I). These variables have been used by a number of political scientists. See Almond (1960); Riggs (1957); and Riggs (1964), which adds the type of "transitional" society. Marion Levy's work on modernization and the structure of societies goes well beyond the pattern variable analytical approach by describing "relatively non-modernized" and "relatively modernized" types of societies, but it still has the weaknesses of typological comparative analysis when it comes to judging policy choices and alternatives. See Levy (1966).

[10] This criticism applies with particular force to the kind of analysis employed by Lipset which uses empirical variables, to be sure, but which treats political democracy and stability as a function of socio-economic variables rather than as a result of political choices and values. See Lipset (1960: Chap. II). A more interesting use of such indicators, which, however, is still not useful in determining the optimal use of scarce resources, can be found in Deutsch (1961).

S. N. Eisenstadt is an important contributor to the analysis of modernization as a process. However, the weakness of the kind of analysis he employs lies in his concern for modal patterns of development without examining or proposing conditions that cause or require variations in patterns and policy. Eisenstadt takes note of this deficiency, but to our knowledge has not elaborated his analysis beyond ideal-typical statements. See especially Eisenstadt (1961). The most explicit and best treatment of modernization as a process *between* the poles of traditional and modern industrial society is given by Apter (1965). Though suggestive in many respects, this study is still constrained by the use of typological methods. Apter himself states (1961:89n) that he regards typological analysis as probably "the most primitive form of scientific work."

[11] Black (1966); see Chapter IV, pp. 95–96.

would it have helped him to be told that "transitional" periods are difficult and unavoidable. What he needed was assistance in shaping productive, constructive policies of the sort normally employed by statesmen.

While we have just stated that it is difficult, if not impossible, to find in much of contemporary political and social science an understanding of political choice that relates to politically relevant time periods, we do not, however, mean to imply that no interest has been shown in the problems of policy. Various political and social analyses of nation-building have been made which seek to identify the requisites for the status and functions of a nation-state.[12] Unfortunately, such analyses provide little assistance in setting priorities if and when all desirable actions and policies cannot be undertaken together. Nor do they ascertain in non-tautological terms when a requisite is satisfied.[13] A variation on the nation-building approach is the consideration of psychological or behavioral variables instead of, or in addition to, institutional factors. Studies that follow psychological or behavioral lines, such as studies of political culture, may give policy-makers a better understanding of public propensities and probable public responses to decisions. These studies, however, are limited to an auxiliary role in any effort to improve the efficiency of political choices, since they have not yet reliably established predictable connections between attitudes and actions or between motivation and behavior.[14]

Probably the most advanced theoretical model proposed to date is that of Almond and Powell.[15] Understandably, this model comes closest of any

[12] Some of the better works of this type are Bendix (1964) and Emerson (1960). Emerson's essay on nation-building in Africa (1963) and the other essays in Deutsch and Foltz (1963) are also representative of this analytical approach.

[13] A cogent critique of this and other approaches is made by Huntington (1965), who makes a useful effort to determine criteria for setting priorities for government investment decisions. His criterion of "institutionalization" has merit, but treats a restricted range of choices.

[14] The most notable are Almond and Verba (1963) and Pye (1962). In these studies political attitudes are usually diverse and are often inconsistent. What actions emerge from the welter of attitudes are probably more attributable to particular circumstances or stimuli than the political culture approach would assume. Holt and Turner (1966:31) suggest, for example, that Pye's analysis of the psychological factors affecting the Burmese could have led him to find character traits exactly the opposite of those he reports.

[15] Almond and Powell (1966). Although our model of political economy uses many of the same terms and concepts as that of Almond and Powell, ours is derived from economic theory, whereas theirs comes from what they call a division of powers model, augmented, to be sure, by many aspects of structural-functional analysis.

to achieving Almond's goal of a "rational choice model of political growth." It focuses on the capabilities that enable a political system to perform its functions in response to demands from the public or abroad, or enable it to carry out its own objectives. While the model could be more successful than previous models have been in assisting political leaders in developing countries to make choices among policy alternatives, its instruments for action are basically role differentiation and cultural secularization. Unfortunately, these are rather blunt and awkward instruments for affecting or controlling change. Nor does the model suggest with the specificity a policy-maker needs how or how much a given capability should be expanded.[16]

For the reasons suggested above, we think that contemporary political and social science can provide little guidance in the conduct of politics. It does little good to analyze situations in terms of output failure, particularistic versus universalistic values, mobilization versus reconciliation systems, systems requisites, prismatic traps, political culture, or extractive capabilities if these concepts cannot be usefully applied to real situations like Colonel Gowon's and if they offer no reliable means for making predictions and setting priorities. To the extent that political and social science are indeed scientific and concerned with real problems, their practitioners should be able to make useful evaluative and predictive statements about alternative courses of action for the statesman. If such statements about the outcome of political actions in particular situations cannot now be made, this situation is due only in part to a lack of information. The more significant cause is, we think, inadequate understanding and conceptualization of political processes.

What is needed are some way of assessing the comparative efficiency of policy alternatives and some means of formulating priorities. The statesman must make his choices under the discipline and penalties of the scarcity of resources. He cannot undertake all the actions that might appear wise, and he must be able to decide wisely within the range of alternatives open to him. Thus to further his policy objectives, he needs to know *how much* of *what* resources can best be used *when*. Each course of action involves political, social, and/or economic costs. He must determine the relative benefits of each. How might a political scientist help a statesman such as Colonel Gowon to choose among the various courses open to him or to

---

[16] Almond and Powell (1966:194). We are not certain that their model can accomplish as much as it claims, but such criticism will also be made of our model. We feel, however, that the model we elaborate will deal more usefully with concrete choices.

alter the courses available to him? How would a political scientist conceptualize and analyze the resources involved in different policy alternatives in order to arrive at some judgment about priorities, taking into account relevant costs and benefits? The inability of political and social scientists to answer questions such as these is, we think, unfortunately clear.

WHAT CAN ECONOMISTS ADVISE ABOUT POLITICAL CHANGE AND DE-
VELOPMENT?   If political and social scientists can provide little assistance
in making rational choices about the use of a polity's scarce resources, we
might be led to think that economists could be more helpful. The economist's central concern is, after all, the efficient use and optimum allocation
of resources. However, an examination of major economic strategies for
growth—the "big push" balanced growth strategy, the unbalanced growth
strategy, and the model of capital formation through use of unlimited supplies of labor—not just in terms of their economic merits, but in terms of
their social, political, and administrative requirements, suggests that economists can at present offer little better guidance to the statesman.[17]

Each strategy requires a certain type of regime to implement it. The balanced growth strategy, in which a comprehensive set of complementary investments must be made in a coordinated fashion to provide the level and
composition of demand necessary to make each of them profitable, can
only be adopted by a regime that has a considerable amount of resources
and control over both public and private enterprise. This regime must have
central planning and a means of persuasion, inducement, or coercion to secure compliance. The regime must also have a high degree of unanimity
among its intellectual, bureaucratic, and military elites, or alternatively
must have the strong support of a closely-knit business sector. Only such
leadership and power could secure the complete cooperation necessary for
the massive coordinated investment program required by the strategies of
Rosenstein-Rodan and Nurkse. Yet the regime that has such leadership
and power, despite Rosenstein-Rodan's intention to the contrary, would be
authoritarian.

The unbalanced growth strategy proposed by Hirschman directs government to make those selected "unbalancing" investments in social overhead
capital or directly productive activities that will create pressures for further
private and/or public investment. In addition, government may subsidize
those private entrepreneurs who make strategic unbalancing investments.

[17] The first strategy has been proposed by Rosenstein-Rodan (1943) and
Nurkse (1957: Chap. I), the second by Hirschman (1958), and the third by
Lewis (1954a) and Nurkse (1957: Chap. II). For a more detailed analysis of
these three strategies, see Ilchman and Bhargava (1966).

This strategy requires that the regime be sympathetic to the interests and activities of private entrepreneurs, or presumably to those of foreign investors. For this reason, it cannot be taken seriously by socialistically-inclined regimes or by regimes in countries where private business has low status.

The model elaborated by Lewis or the scheme suggested by Nurkse may apply to a regime that has complete state ownership of the means of production or to a government dominated by the business sector. In the Lewis model, economic growth depends on the reinvestment of profits from the capitalist sector, which in turn depends on relatively low wage levels stemming from an unlimited supply of labor. Thus the regime run according to this strategy must keep wage levels low in order to sustain economic development. In Nurkse's plan the regime puts unemployed persons to work constructing capital such as roads, dams, and irrigation canals. In either plan the regime must be willing to use coercion, as the point of both plans is to minimize the money returns to labor, which from an economist's point of view is "free" because of its redundancy. Neither model, nor that of balanced growth, can afford to be libertarian in its political orientation, and it is likely that a moratorium on political opposition would be desired by those in authority.[18]

In all three strategies the interests of the urban working class and the peasantry are given short shrift. Yet any regime that relies on a broad membership base, with many sectors able to make effective demands on

[18] Lewis proposes the alternative of capital formation through credit creation. Because of the availability of unemployed labor resources, output and capital may be increased by this measure with only short-term inflation. Lewis, who is more in the tradition of political economy than are most other economic strategists, makes clear that there are political consequences to the redistribution effects of inflation. Farmers, workers, pensioners, landlords, or creditors may have their situations worsened as a result of capital formation through credit creation. However, Lewis concludes that if inflation is short-lived, being self-extinguished as output increases, the adverse effects would only be temporary.

Lewis suggests that many governments would find it politically easier to develop through credit creation than through taxation or capitalist saving out of profits. Yet he notes that this alternative is not open to many regimes: "In some communities any further inflation of prices would ruin their fragile social or political equilibrium; in others this equilibrium will be destroyed if there is not a sharp increase in output in the near future; and in still others the equilibrium will be ruined either way." Lewis (1954a:423, 431). Although he is sensitive to the political and social consequences of economic policies, Lewis does not explore the political and administrative requirements of a regime that could consider following this strategy.

the regime, could not contain the demands of these classes for higher wages and/or expenditures for social welfare, housing, health, and education. The regime adopting any of these strategies must thus be able to prevent the broad mass of the public from influencing allocative decisions, all the more difficult if private entrepreneurs or business interests are particularly favored with subsidies and profits while other sectors have restricted incomes and are beset with heavy taxes. These strategies assume either that the rural and urban working populations will be docile enough to accept this situation or that the regime will be able to maintain a condition of stability through the use of coercion. However, growing income disparities, regressive taxation, and suppression of the right of labor organization would probably not be accepted for long without unrest and thus would necessitate increasing expenditure for social welfare and/or coercion. In addition, regional imbalances not remedied by the optimal investment pattern of the balanced growth strategy would be a source of discontent.

Apart from their economic merits, all of these strategies impose severe political requirements on any regime, limiting its freedom of action and creating conditions for discontent at the same time that they close off channels for expression of dissatisfaction. When investment is channeled into capital infrastructure or directly productive activities rather than into housing, health, or education, and when the benefits from economic development are apportioned in an unequal manner, social grievances and political problems are magnified. These strategies also impose high administrative requirements on any regime that would undertake them. We do not mean to imply that economic development can take place without political conflict, social tensions, and administrative overload. Rather we suggest that pursuing an economic strategy without consideration of the concommitant political, social, and administrative requirements is unwise and perhaps impossible. Economic development is a difficult and usually a slow process. Some investment strategy may accelerate (without easing) the task, but that strategy will most probably be some combination of suboptimizing investment decisions. Any regime wishing to remain in authority, unless it is prepared and able to use coercion broadly and effectively, will have to calculate the political and social costs of economic plans and proposals. Economists can suggest how to use scarce economic resources most efficiently if they have adequate, reliable data—a proviso seldom satisfied in developing countries. They cannot, however, include non-economic resources or goals.

A statesman cannot wish away the non-economic requirements or consequences of economic strategies. For this reason, he is not interested in freeing the economic market from impingements of status, authority, or coercion for the sake of economic efficiency or optimality. His world seldom permits the luxury of *ceteris paribus* or *mutatis mutandis* assumptions. The resources economists treat are too narrowly conceived to satisfy the needs of the statesman in a developing country. The costs and benefits that economists might calculate for Colonel Gowon in Nigeria would at best represent an economic optimum, not a political or social optimum. Perhaps more important, economists' recommendations would probably not survive the crossfire of political and social struggles.

Colonel Gowon's problem was only partially one of allocation. The supply of resources at his disposal was meager to the point of regime bankruptcy. To stay in authority and to advance Nigeria's development he needed to enlarge the amount of resources at his command. His tasks were to increase the flow of resources to the regime from the sectors, to accelerate the generation of resources by the regime itself, and to improve the degree of efficiency with which resources were used to achieve his objectives. Political scientists and other social scientists do not yet have analytical tools for dealing with problems of political productivity. Economists can analyze production and make comparisons, but only of economic resources.

The problem of political production that Colonel Gowon faced is not unique to the situation in Nigeria after the 1966 coups. It is the major political problem of governments throughout Africa, Asia, and Latin America. Thus it should be the major concern of any political and social scientist who seeks to understand and aid in alleviating the problems of developing countries. Concepts, propositions, and theories less abstract than those derived from macro-analytical, typological, or nation-building approaches are needed to make social science relevant to the problems of new nations. Unless political scientists can deal specifically with the production and management of political and other resources, they will be able to do little more than write conceptually and typologically elegant political histories of development. The political process in developing countries will go on with minimal understanding by or assistance from social and political scientists.

WHAT KIND OF SOCIAL SCIENCE MODEL IS NEEDED FOR POLITICAL RELEVANCE? The kind of model needed to understand and meet the needs of developing countries must be able to transcend typological analysis. This kind of analysis has attempted to isolate and integrate the most salient features of politics into analytical frameworks, but it neither explains behavior nor informs choices. Political science must go beyond this rudimentary stage of theoretical development if it is to avoid further analytical immobility. To overcome the deficiencies of typological analysis, political scientists must be able to treat politics as *process*. Efforts have been made along these lines; however, in our opinion, they have not been satisfactory.[19] We believe that the model we have constructed provides a useful basis for dealing with politics as process, so that political choice and change can be analyzed in dynamic terms for any type of system.

We are prepared to argue for policy-oriented analysis, free from assumptions of equilibrium or predetermined development. We are afraid that the political scientist's inability to assist in productive policy-formation in developing countries has led to a preoccupation with economic judgments and proposals. By now it is clear that the problems of developing countries persist in spite of, or perhaps in part because of, analysis and prescriptions that are primarily or solely based on economic considerations. We wish to see political science address itself—again—to these problems by dealing seriously with questions of public policy. In attempting to evaluate policy alternatives, we must remember that like economic analysis, political analysis in developing countries has limited information or data to work with. Constructing a general equilibrium analysis for such nations is an unmanageable and perhaps an impossible task. Thus political scientists must be able to make reasonably reliable partial analyses, working from *ceteris paribus* assumptions whenever necessary. The more information that is available, the more reliable and valid the conclusion should be, but lacking complete information, an analytical model for developing countries must be in a position to "economize" on its information requirements.

We would expect such a model to be able to treat inputs of economic, social, and psychological information in a useful way so that policy choices could take into account all available relevant knowledge. The model must thus be able to integrate pertinent theory and findings of the other social sciences. It is clear that no adequate model can be narrowly disciplinary in dealing with the problems of developing countries. A political scientist cannot understand or usefully analyze politics if he conceives of it narrowly

[19] For example, Truman (1951). See also Jacobson (1964). Lacking an adequate framework for the analysis of political processes, students of comparative politics will be as limited in their analysis and relevance to policy as economists who can only compare economic systems in terms of types—capitalism, socialism, communism, and so forth. The strength of economic analysis lies in the fact that the tools it provides for dealing with economic processes and productivity enable economists to treat all concrete systems in comparable terms. The factors of economic production—land, labor, and capital—are combined and utilized in quite the same way in communistic as in capitalistic economies. Comparative political analysis will be grossly limited until it can deal similarly with the factors of political production in any political system.

and has only one disciplinary string to his bow. At the same time, the uniqueness and pre-eminence of politics must not be submerged in the borrowings from other disciplines. The problem is one of preserving this uniqueness and pre-eminence while at the same time drawing into the analysis those elements of conceptualization and empirical work from other disciplines that make the political process more intelligible and subject to deliberate direction.

A model of politics should not impose a logic external to the system and its participants. It must operate within the assumptions of the polity it is analyzing. This statement is not an espousal of ethical neutrality, but rather a disavowal of ethnocentrism. It is essential to minimize intellectual prejudice in dealing with situations that are and will remain quite different from our own. Finally, to be operational, a model must be able to deal with useful time periods of the stateman's own choosing and must introduce more rigorous and unambiguous means of measuring and comparing his policy alternatives.

Despite the shortcomings of their development strategies, economists have produced the most rigorous and precise discipline in the social sciences. Their analyses of value, exchange, efficiency, and productivity are, we believe, relevant to the formulation of the "allocation-of-resources theory of political development" for which Almond has called. In our model we have tried to develop a rigor and precision similar to that of economics in order to deal with the production and allocation of political resources. Working from assumptions and concepts akin to those of economics, it should be possible for us to compare the costs and benefits involved in alternative courses of action, to weigh marginal utility and productivity, to develop political investment strategies realistically based on analyses, and to determine opportunity costs and political profitability. Our aim may appear grandiose or overly ambitious, yet we believe that if political science does not reach this new stage of development it will become an increasingly irrelevant factor in the advance of knowledge and welfare.[20]

[20] As William C. Mitchell (1967) has shown, there is increasing interest among political scientists in the utilization of economic concepts in the study of politics. Though formerly an advocate of political sociology, Mitchell now sees greater utility in economic assumptions and modes of analysis when dealing with the phenomena of political life. James S. Coleman, one of the most discerning students of politics in developing countries, has also recently pointed out ways in which an analytical perspective combining political and economic approaches would make social science more relevant and rigorous with respect to developing areas. See Coleman (1967).

HOW HAVE POLITICAL AND SOCIAL SCIENCE CONTRIBUTED TO SUCH A
MODEL? Our model of political economy is not an eclectic synthesis
of various concepts and propositions. It has a coherence and logic of
its own which is in large part derived from economic theory. However, the
analytical base of our model owes much to the work of Almond, Apter,
Easton, and Parsons. Others, Deutsch, Eisenstadt, and Huntington, for example, have developed concepts of analysis similar to ours. While we do
not justify our own work on the grounds that others have already proven
the validity or utility of some of the various elements of the model we propose, we recognize that social science is a collective endeavor and that
progress arises from sequential and/or parallel development of concepts
and formulations. Political economy is a logical outgrowth of many contributions to social science in the following areas:

The State as an Organization. Before the work of Easton, Almond,
Parsons, and Deutsch, the state was viewed essentially as a distributive
arena. These scholars contributed a new view of the state as an organization interacting with those persons, groups, and other organizations that
constitute its environment. According to this new view, the state is capable
not only of allocating, but of producing such products as political stability,
participation, or maximum feedback.[21] The work of Easton and others
provided a much needed antidote to exaggerated notions of state sovereignty and preoccupation with institutional descriptions. It made clear that
the state depends on the inputs of others, for which inducements, in particular, authoritative decisions, must be offered. Thus discussions of sovereignty, obligations, and rights gave way to analyses of demands, supports,
outputs, and feedback.

Easton's analysis proceeded from the idea that political community is
based on a political division of labor that establishes authority roles.[22] This
new view of authority and the conception of legitimacy consequent upon it
are more empirically manageable than were previous views. Easton's focus

[21] Although Easton defined politics as "the authoritative allocation of
values," he did not in his model give the state a special commanding position in
the political process as those political scientists who emphasized sovereignty had
done. Instead, his model considered authority a function of the degree to which
interaction satisfactorily meets the needs and demands of individuals and
groups. See Easton (1965). Though Parsons' structural-functional approach led
him to emphasize equilibrium and pattern-maintenance more than change and
conflicts of interest, his analysis of organizations in general contributes to an
understanding of the state as an organization. See especially Parsons (1956).

[22] Easton acknowledges the work of Deutsch and Ernst Haas in elaborating
this concept. See Easton (1965: Chap. XI).

on authority roles suggests that an examination of the legitimacy status accorded to these roles and their occupants is crucial to an understanding of the dynamics of politics. Such a focus permits definition of the limits of authority in terms of the acceptance authority receives in given areas.[23]

Political Resources. Though still lacking operational rigor, the concept of political resources has more and more come into common use. This concept becomes the central concern of our model, making it possible for us to treat political, social, and economic factors within a common framework of analysis. We use the term "resources" much in the way that Easton uses the term "values," to denote things of economic, social, and political worth. We prefer the former term because it emphasizes the production rather than the consumption aspects of the political process.[24]

S. N. Eisenstadt came close to such a conception of political resources when he wrote that the implementation in developing countries of new programs such as community development and industrialization required:

the effective mobilization of various types of resources . . . [the most important of which were economic, manpower, and educational, but also] political resources of support for the various policies of the new ruling elite. . . . These resources were of a kind not readily available in those countries and their creation, therefore, became as it were, an important task of the new regimes, indispensable for the implementation of the new collective goals which they set themselves.[25]

Eisenstadt writes of the creation of "free-floating" resources through the undermining of traditional authorities and relationships. But, he points out, gaining political support and other resources requires making promises

[23] An interesting adaptation of Parsons' structural-functional analysis was undertaken by William C. Mitchell. Mitchell sees scarcity as the central problem of the polity; conflict is endemic and necessitates authority. The polity, he says, produces power in the form of decisions and policies. The chief inputs are support, demands, and hard resources. Engendering support is the key to mobilizing resources. We find this analysis quite suggestive, but it is limited by its failure adequately to disaggregate inputs and outputs in terms of specific resources. See Mitchell (1958).

[24] Harold Lasswell (1936) treats political values as essentially consumption-oriented. Parsons' use of "resources" in many of his writings treats both production and consumption aspects. Dahl has dealt most specifically with *political* resources (1961). Dahl's use of political resources is discussed in Chapter III, p. 50.

[25] Eisenstadt (1961:25); for a discussion of resources, see also Eisenstadt (1963a).

that many social groups will expect to see fulfilled. Because government needs to use its resources to reward supporters, to maintain its position, and to control various other social forces, it "could easily come to an impasse in which the implementation of the various societal goals—and its own ultimate claims to legitimation—became seriously impeded by the necessity to spend many more of its resources as emoluments for various groups of supporters." [26]

Almond and Powell deal more specifically with the effects of government distribution on the allocation of resources. To them government jobs, taxation, education, regulations on behavior, knighthoods, and medals of honor are values distributed by government that have an effect on the support given to government.[27] Their formulation of resources, however, requires them to focus on extractive capability rather than on the resources themselves.[28] Marion Levy does not discuss resources in the terms we use, but does consider the implications of alternative allocations of status, wealth, power, and responsibility. His analysis shows the relationship between social, political, and economic resources but unfortunately does not explore systematically the process of exchange among them.[29]

Politics as Interaction and Exchange. Accompanying the above-mentioned changes in the orientation of political science has been a new and different approach to social theory that focuses on roles and the interaction between persons and structures rather than on the nature of the structures themselves. Introduced by Parsons with Shils and others, this approach aims at integrating a behavioral dimension into institutional analysis.[30] We have found this approach especially useful because of its

[26] Eisenstadt (1961:26–28).

[27] Almond and Powell (1966:199).

[28] Almond and Powell's treatment of resources is somewhat ambiguous, as this passage illustrates:

> A nation's elite may believe that they can achieve a more stable equilibrium and can better sustain their position through authoritarian repression and symbol manipulation. They may despair of trying to juggle the nation's slender extractive resources so as to satisfy present welfare demands while still investing in economic growth to provide for future demands.
>
> Almond and Powell (1966:212).

Usually Almond and Powell speak of a nation's extractive *capability* to place resources at the disposal of the regime. This perspective leads them to concentrate on capacity or potential rather than on the specific levels of resources available or required, or on how these "slender" resources can be used most effectively.

[29] Levy (1966).

[30] Parsons (1951); Parsons and Shils (1951).

application by Parsons and Smelser to the analysis of economics in terms of social theory. Parsons and Smelser treat the subject matter and theory of economics in terms of social systems. The similarity of analytical structures in sociology and economics when viewed in terms of interaction suggested to them that phenomena of one social science discipline could be understood using the theory and analytical tools of another. They write that the theories and propositions of economics "possess more than economic significance. . . . The peculiarity of economic theory, therefore, is *not* the separate class of variables it employs, but the *parameters* which distinguish the special case or class of cases we call economic in the use of the general variables or social theory from the other important types of special case." [31]

Political exchange is a way of describing the social interaction that takes place in the political sphere. Our conception of political exchange has for the most part been influenced by the body of theory and concepts used by economists, but we find that political exchange is becoming a concern of political scientists as well. It is implicit in Easton's analysis. Deutsch, who draws considerably on Easton, treats the question of exchange more explicitly, though he calls it interchange rather than exchange. Following Parsons' scheme of analysis, he talks of physical flows of goods and services between households, economy, polity, and culture. One of his examples of interchange in the political system is the support extended by households to the rulers "who in turn use this support to make and enforce binding decisions." [32] Deutsch introduces the concept of currency into his model, defining it as a "social mechanism" that makes transactions between units more flexible and general. He also discusses the equivalent of inflation in political exchange.[33] It is interesting to us that Deutsch would use in a model based on cybernetics terms that we derive from economics.

In sociology George C. Homans and Peter Blau have advanced the conception of social life as exchange. We find Blau's discussion of exchange and power in social life especially suggestive, though his model applies primarily to social interaction. Blau examines many of the relationships and problems analyzed in our model of political economy. His conceptions of resources, exchange, marginal utility, elasticity, supply and demand, and

[31] Parsons and Smelser (1956:2, 6).

[32] Deutsch (1963:117–118).

[33] Deutsch writes of citizenship and loyalty as currencies "not immune to disorders resembling severe inflation." He also treats votes as countable currencies, put into the system by extending the franchise to certain groups of citizens. See Deutsch (1963: 118–119).

investment are also very similar to ours. Blau's analysis is quite relevant for considering the behavior of sectors in our model, though it is less applicable to the behavior of the polity as a whole.[34]

Political Enterpreneurship, Infrastructure, and Investment. Our model of political economy makes use of the concept of political entrepreneurship. This concept has already been introduced by others. Eisenstadt, for instance, defines political entrepreneurs as people who are able to mobilize social and political attitudes and activities and integrate them into political organizations and processes according to the premises of modern political and parliamentary institutions.[35] Apter characterizes entrepreneurs as "those who organize a following in order to gain access to state resources." [36] While our usage does not differ substantially from that of Apter and Zolberg, the tangibility of the resources we consider permits a closer comparison of the political entrepreneur with his economic counterpart.

The concept of political infrastructure has also received attention, notably from Eisenstadt and Shils. According to Eisenstadt, this concept includes institutions or patterns of behavior that increase and/or ensure a stable flow of resources to the regime.[37] Huntington, in his thoughtful analysis of infrastructure, advocates the creation of organizations to channel political competition to serve the public interest. These organizations will, he believes, offset the destabilizing and potentially degenerating impact of "mobilization." Huntington tries to specify criteria for measuring "institutionalization" and argues that this effort should have highest priority for the use of a regime's resources. While a broader framework of analysis and comparison is needed before a scheme of priorities can be fixed, Huntington outlines well the need for political infrastructure.[38]

Related to the concepts of political entrepreneurship and political infra-

[34] See Homans (1950) and (1961); Blau (1964); and the imaginative work by Bredemeier and Stephenson (1962). After completing our manuscript, we received the recently published book by Curry and Wade, which is an explicit treatment of political exchange in theoretical terms. The authors believe, as we do, that political exchange is "one of the central ways in which, increasingly, political scientists will come to think about politics" (1968:ix).

[35] Eisenstadt (1961:41).

[36] Apter (1965:70–71). Zolberg also finds the term useful. He writes: "In order to be successful, organizations have to mobilize support from much larger bodies of people and compete with an increasing number of political entrepreneurs drawn into the game once the risks of punishment had practically disappeared and the rewards had become more tangible." Zolberg (1966:19).

[37] See Eisenstadt (1961); also Shils (1961).

[38] Huntington (1965); see also Esman (1966).

structure is the concept of political investment. This concept has been formulated by several political scientists and has incorporated features of economic investment such as the setting of priorities and the calculation of productive consequences. Huntington, for example, would give high priority to building up interest groups, political parties, associations, and the like, and would devote most of a regime's resources to this end. Almond and Powell, on the other hand, would support more diversified investment strategies tailored to the needs of the particular country:

The development strategies which will be appropriate for the new political systems will differ one from the other. These nations will need to take into account their different starting points from both a cultural and structural point of view. The rate of investment in political development will have to reflect differences in resource base, as well as in the ability of these societies and political systems to absorb investment efficiently. Bureaucratic, political-party, interest-group and communications elites cannot be trained over-night.[39]

To Almond and Powell, a strategy of political investment would stress scheduling efforts to solve system development problems. It would include "compensatory investments to cope with the disruptive consequences of modernization processes" and with the consequences of investment in education, industrialization, urban planning, and other "non-political" areas.[40] Although our treatment of investment is somewhat more extensive than theirs and employs terms other than "capabilities," "structural differentiation," or "cultural secularization," their orientation and our own are virtually the same.

Propensities. The behavioral element in our model of political economy is that of *orientations to action.* As used in the work of Parsons and Shils, this term is the sociological equivalent of the economic concept of *propensities.*[41] We have chosen to use the latter term to maintain the consistency of our terminology, but the same principle lies behind both.

[39] Almond and Powell (1966:330) treat state-building and nation-building as other than political investments. In their model those organizations that make possible participation in decision-making are "some form of political infrastructure" (35–37). Our interpretation of what constitutes political investment is less confined.

[40] Almond and Powell (1966:330–331). Their approach requires making what we consider artificial boundary distinctions between the political and the non-political.

[41] Parsons (1951); Parsons and Shils (1951: Chap. I).

Propositions about the behavior of all individuals, of a group of individuals, or of a particular individual may be made and tested empirically. In political economy, as in economics, the analysis of propensities aims at the prediction of behavior. Almond and Verba's study of political cultures and sub-cultures suggests how behavioral propensities might be formulated, although attitudes must also be tested against behavior before reliable statements predicting behavior can be made.[42] Almond and Powell include propensities in their analytical model, treating them as the psychological dimension of the political system that is manifested in the political culture. The kinds of orientations that exist in a population will, they say, have a significant influence on the ways in which the political system works.[43] In our model the term "propensities" describes the behavioral predispositions of groups (sectors), and the term "parameter" describes those behavioral characteristics applying to a population as a whole.

Politics in developing countries has been characterized by Geertz as strongly influenced by "primordial attachments." [44] These attachments must be treated as "givens" in any analysis. Persons in developing countries are often inclined to perceive group interests as paramount, identifying self-interest with the interest of the group, whether the group is based on religion, caste, class, race, tribe, occupation, language, ethnicity, religion, or custom. Persons will usually have a primary attachment to one group and few cross-cutting allegiances.[45] Thus any political model for developing countries must be based on assumptions about political interaction that are different from the atomistic notions of individualistic activity often posited in political analyses.[46] For this reason, our central focus on sectors has special significance and relevance for statesmen of these countries.

Conflict. In reaction to the emphasis on social stability and equilib-

[42] Almond and Verba (1963:31). See also Pye and Verba (1965).

[43] Almond and Powell (1966:50).

[44] Geertz (1963b).

[45] Pye has characterized the pattern of "non-Western" politics as communal: "In the more conspicuous cases the large communal groupings follow ethnic or religious lines. But behind these divisions lie the smaller but often more tightly knit social groupings, which range from the powerful community of Westernized leaders to the social structure of each individual village." He points to the relative stability of political allegiances that results from this communal framework of politics: "Any change in political identification generally requires a change in one's social and personal relationships; conversely, any change in social relations tends to result in a change in political identification." See Pye (1962:16–17).

[46] Along these lines, George Blanksten argues for the "group analysis" approach for an understanding of Latin American politics. See Blanksten (1959).

rium found in functional analysis of society, a few social scientists have tried to formulate alternative models of social interaction.[47] Criticisms have been made of conflict models—they have been charged, for example, with underemphasizing the importance of cooperation in economic, social, and political relations—yet such models frequently reveal more of the important elements in the politics of developing countries than do more conventional models. We find this mode of analysis useful and in the best tradition of social science.

Choice. Social science has increasingly focused on choice as the decisive element in understanding and guiding political change and development. Almond's call for "rational choice models of political growth" reflects this new focus. Concern with choice has also been well articulated by Apter in his analysis of the politics of modernization. Although we do not adopt Apter's model for analysis of normative and structural conditions affecting choice, we nevertheless do try to elaborate on his orientation towards choice. The model of political economy that we propose in the next chapter is concerned, to use Apter's words, with "the improvement of the conditions of choice, and the selection of the most satisfactory mechanisms of choice." [48]

[47] Perhaps the best short statement of this alternative position is presented by Rolf Dahrendorf (1958:115–127); see also Dahrendorf (1959). Coser (1956) formulates empirically testable propositions that if accepted offer considerable predictive power. Though seemingly abstract, these propositions offer more insight into tribal and regional group behavior in Nigeria than do many specific studies of that country. A good summary critique of the tendency in social science to ignore or subsume conflict when analyzing development is presented by Riggs (1968:197–201). His effort to incorporate the effects of conflict into a structural-functional analysis of whole systems, we do not, however, find convincing.

[48] Apter (1965:9–11) defines modernization as basically a non-economic process originating "when a culture embodies an attitude of inquiry and questioning about how men make choices." For him the political system is "a system of choice for a particular collectivity," and government is "the mechanism for regulating choice. Differing political systems will not only embody different ways of choosing but vary in their priorities. Governments will vary in the ways they regulate choice. . . . One of the characteristics of the modernization process is that it involves both aspects of choice: the improvement of the conditions of choice, and the selection of the most satisfactory mechanisms of choice."

II

THE NEW POLITICAL ECONOMY

In framing an ideal, we may assume what we wish, but should avoid impossibilities.

Aristotle, *Politics*

Colonel Gowon and other statesmen, both in authority and out, need help that conventional political science and economics cannot provide. The weaknesses and strengths of these two social sciences are complimentary: in the case of political science, we find an appropriate perspective but improper tools, while in economics we find useful tools but a distorted perspective. We propose a synthesis of the natural advantages of each discipline to provide an appropriate perspective and adequate tools. This we call political economy.

Perhaps the name "political economy" is misleading. In our study we do not employ the term as it was once used. The new political economy we propose is not single-mindedly concerned, as was its forbearer, with increasing the wealth of a nation, though we recognize the importance of such increases. Nor is it preoccupied with the ideal of an autonomous economic sphere and with the consequences of government intervention for production, though it is clearly concerned with the effects of political choices on the production and exchange of goods and services. The new political economy may be described as the analysis of the consequences of political choices that statesmen and other persons make involving the polity's scarce resources. It aims at improving the efficacy of these choices so that desired ends may be better or more economically achieved through political processes. Such analysis must be both projective and evaluative. The political economist attempts to make calculations of the costs and benefits of alternative uses of scarce resources more precise and predictable. By basing his calculations on the objectives and possibilities to be found in a particular political community, he should be able to help statesmen and anti-statesmen to make more productive choices, congruent with their own value commitments and with demands from the political community.

We can clarify the political economist's particular concern with choice by contrasting the orientations of an economist, a political scientist, and a political economist toward crucial issues involving change. The economist usually advances a strategy or policy to achieve a desirable economic end, such as maximum growth of national product, and then asks: "What political arrangement is most conducive to achieving this objective?" or "How can the political impediments to achieving this objective be removed or neutralized?" In like fashion, the political scientist projects some desirable political end, such as complete independence from other nations, and then asks: "What level of economic productivity or what type of ownership of the means of production will best achieve this end?" or "How can the economic impediments to achieving this objective be removed or neutralized?" The political economist, on the other hand, is less one-sided in orientation. Instead of trying to neutralize politics like the economist, he tries to identify the creative possibilities inherent in the political situation and the real political costs involved. Thus he might reverse the economist's question and ask: "Given the resources at the disposal of the regime, now or potentially, what opportunities exist for increasing the production of goods and services in the country?" He might also modify the political scientist's question. Instead of posing the questions implicit in much current literature on political development, the political economist wants to know: "Given the resources of the regime, now or potentially, what political choices are possible and what might be their cumulative effects?" He would point out that to be mindful of Aristotle's dictum on avoiding impossibilities is not simply to accept constraints on choice, but rather to acknowledge and study these constraints in order to change them in desired directions.

In adapting for political economy many of the tools and assumptions of economics, we are departing from a recent tradition of political science the proponents of which have looked toward sociology and psychology. This tradition is not without merit, but its findings have limited utility for the statesman. Economics, on the other hand, is oriented toward policy.[1] The

[1] We should make clear that our interest in economics is due less to the discipline's quantification than to its conceptual rigor. A cogent critique of the limits of quantification in social science is provided in Bernhard (1960:1–5). Bernhard concludes that "if subjects like economics, sociology, political science and psychology are to be predictive sciences, minds must be developed, not just mechanical models—minds as broad and subtle as that of Keynes and others to appraise correctly the significance of the measurable factors and to weigh and

emphasis economists place on choice permits their findings to be applied, with varying degrees of fidelity, to public decisions made tomorrow, next month, next year, or in some humanly comprehendable time period. In their work economists have taken into account the fact that choices are limited by the scarcity of resources, and they have therefore tried to estimate in advance the consequences of alternative strategies. Their assumption of generally predictable behavior, which derives from the social constraint of scarcity, helps them to steer clear of a view of behavior as random and unique, a view that still obfuscates much of political science.[2] Most important, their predisposition for *ex ante* analysis and the quantitative tools and concepts underlying such a predisposition permit them to speak in terms of productivity and to apply the criterion of productivity to alternative choices and strategies. Through the analysis of payments to factors of production, economists are able to link production and distribution and to place questions of allocation in the context of productivity as well as that of welfare.[3]

judge the non-measurable factors." (5). The quotations he presents on this subject are worth citing, for instance this one from Alfred Marshall:

> . . . every economic fact . . . stands in relations as cause and effect to many other facts; and since it *never* happens that all of them can be expressed in numbers, the application of exact mathematical methods to those which can is nearly always a waste of time, while in the large majority of cases it is positively misleading; and the world would have been further on its way forward if the work had never been done at all . . . the longer I live the more convinced I am that—except in purely abstract problems—the statistical side must never be separated even for an instant from the non-statistical . . . the forces of which economics has to take account are more numerous, less definite, less well known, and more diverse in character than those of mechanics; while the material on which they act is more uncertain and less homogeneous (2, 3).

[2] Much of contemporary political science is Baconian in orientation. Like Francis Bacon, political scientists seem to feel that from describing the political universe, a pattern will emerge, and they therefore place a premium on cataloging data and on constructing typologies to encompass data. Early economists, on the other hand, saw good sense in the Newtonian "conservation" assumption about the behavior of the universe and applied a similar assumption to economic behavior. The only political scientists who have adopted the scarcity assumption are those working in the two most advanced sub-fields of the discipline: voting behavior and national security studies.

[3] Numerous attempts have already been made to apply economic theory to politics. Some of the most notable works of this kind are: Downs (1957); Riker (1962); Dahl (1956); Dahl and Lindblom (1953); Buchanan and Tulloch (1962); and Olson (1965). These books undertake a variety of intellectual tasks. We find them of limited utility for application to policy. They too fre-

The Productivity of Politics

Central to the new political economy is the concept of the productivity of politics. While various political and social scientists have become concerned with the productive side of political choices, the majority of political scientists have conspicuously neglected this aspect of choice and have concentrated instead on allocation or distribution. Political scientists who have neglected the productive aspect of politics and concentrated instead on the distributive aspect have by implication considered the production of political resources unimportant. By doing this, they have assumed that persons in authority live in a *mutatis mutandis* world or that political activity resembles a zero-sum game. These assumptions cannot pass most commonsense tests. Such an emphasis on distribution, however, explains at least in part the propensity of political scientists to construct typologies and to be satisfied with relatively static analysis.

As we have already pointed out, the work of conventional economists alone is not sufficient to provide a science of choice that works from a logic of political preferences within a particular community. Economists analyze only goods and services. The statesman is concerned with and responsible for other values as well. Moreover, the maximization of economic values cannot be achieved by using economic resources alone. New status and authority relationships have been identified in the literature on economic development as prerequisites to modification in the modes of production. Indeed, a strategy for economic change cannot help but be a strategy for political change as well. To comprehend these other variables, the new political economy must determine the optimal combinations of resources, available or potential, for achieving those public ends desired by statesmen and others.

The study of political economy is as relevant to the choices made by revolutionaries as it is to those made by the authorities, as relevant to the choices made by various sectors of the population as it is to those made by the government itself, as relevant to choices aiming at political chaos as it is to those that seek to achieve political stability. In our study we are adopting the perspective of the statesman whose task it is to combine various resources into public policies. Our concern is with the productive conse-

quently proceed from unrealistic or unacceptable assumptions, or they are too narrowly concerned with democratic institutions in a Western context to aid a statesman in a developing country.

quences of these policies for the existing and future allocation of status, authority, and economic resources, as well as for the store of resources available to the statesman for future political choices. In other words, political economy combines the economist's interest in productivity with the political scientist's sensitivity to issues of distribution. We believe that both disciplines will benefit from such a union. The resources used in the new political economy share many of the characteristics of resources used in conventional economic analysis. Resources are valued by the regime and the sectors of the polity for themselves and for what they make possible. They may be consumed or used productively. They may be saved, invested, recovered in kind, or lent. Like goods and services, they flow from the activities and attitudes of individuals—members of sectors or of the regime.

POLITICAL MARKETS AND POLITICIZATION.

Political resources and political exchange will be discussed in detail in the following chapters. The conceptions underlying them can be most easily grasped by thinking of society as composed of three markets: the political, the social, and the economic.[4] In each market characteristic values and dispositions are exchanged between persons, between sectors, and between these and the regime. Goods and services are exchanged in the economic market, status in the social market, and authority and legitimacy in the political market. In each market implicit and explicit bargaining goes on, values are determined through the influence of supply and demand, and much exchange is routine. Each participant in a market seeks from others some amount or combination of resources that will satisfy his goals and/or prevent others from achieving opposing goals. Often a participant uses his resources from one market in a second or third market, such as, for example, when status is "purchased" by money or goods.

While the economic market is quite tangible and familiar, it is perhaps more difficult to see how status is exchanged in the social market. In the social market some participants start from an affluent status position, while others have meager status resources. The former are able to accord high or low status to others more effectively than the latter, who operating at a disadvantage can do little to alter the allocation of status. Of all three markets, the political market is the most difficult to comprehend, yet it is the

[4] Our use of markets is figurative only, and we intend no reification of the social and political markets discussed below. It is not necessary to accept our figurative discussion of markets in order to make use of our model of political economy.

most important in terms of its effect on the others. In it the regime or influential sectors exercise authority to alter or uphold allocations in all three markets. Sectors may make exchanges to improve their position in other markets, or conversely, may use resources secured from exchange in other markets to bring about or maintain a particular exchange position in the political market. At the same time, the regime may use the resources available to it to maintain its exchange relationships in the political and other markets or to alter the exchange relationships in other markets. Whenever resources gained in the political market are used to maintain or alter the allocation of resources in the economic and social markets, such exchanges become "politicized" and therefore become part of the study of political economy.

Politicization—the altering of exchange relationships in the economic and social markets, and the penetration of peripheral political markets by national issues—is especially important in developing countries. In these countries governmental planning, both economic and social, can be seen as an attempt to politicize the exchange relationships prevailing in the economic and social markets. Subsidizing a consumer goods industry in the private sector, developing heavy industry in the public sector, consolidating land holdings, replacing the village moneylender with a system of cheap public credit, upgrading the status of women and other disadvantaged groups—all these policies require the use of the polity's scarce resources to bring about desired exchange patterns. The idea of markets helps to illustrate the process of politicization in developing countries and the problems resulting from it.

Like its counterpart, monetization of economic exchange, politicization attempts to escalate participation of certain sectors from the peripheral to national activity. Often regimes choose not to politicize these sectors, preferring to maintain dual political markets that barely interact. In these cases regimes fear a corresponding escalation of demands on already scarce resources or have an ideological preference for excluding from national life those who participate on the traditional subsistence political level. Often, however, the choice is not the regime's to make. Political opponents seek to bring those at the subsistence level into the national political market in order to mobilize enough support to displace the authorities and take over the authority roles for themselves.

Politicization creates serious problems for regimes in developing countries. As the centrality of politics increases, so does the regime's vulnerability. Where disappointments and frustrations were formerly diffused, the process of politicization frequently transfers resentment to the regime. For

the most part, this resentment arises in regimes where the capacity for productive exchange and investment is only rudimentary and where the many
alternatives and desired objectives far outstrip a regime's supply of resources to pursue them. Thus the major problem that statesmen in developing nations must face is that of increasing the volume of political resources at their disposal. On doing so hinge their chances for attaining
their objectives, remaining in authority, and fulfilling their vision of the
good society. Statesmen must therefore set themselves about the tasks of
developing new sources of supply, expending those resources already available, and achieving more efficient and innovative management of existing
resources. To the degree that the new political economy can analyze
choices in the context of the scarcity of resources with a logic approximating that of political activity, it should be of assistance to political actors in
various polities.

POLITICAL RESOURCES AS THE BASES OF POWER.

Each regime is differentially endowed with a supply of resources. Combined in policies, resources are the means by which a regime induces or
coerces compliance in order to implement its objectives for the polity.
Policies of different regimes can be compared over time and among countries on the basis of the comparative efficiency of different combinations of
resources. These resources and their currencies, used or withheld, constitute the regime's factors of political production. According to our model,
those resources held by the regime are economic goods and services, authority, status, information, and coercion. Resources produced by the sectors of the population are economic goods and services, status, legitimacy,
information, and violence. The regime wants or needs some combination
of sector resources to achieve its aims. Resources are desired by the sectors
or by the regime for consumption or for use in acquiring other resources.
We can speak of rich regimes and poor regimes according to the amount
and composition of resources each has at its disposal. Some regimes are dependent on coercion to compensate for little information or devalued
authority; others are so able to allocate status that they may conserve on
other resources when securing compliance.

We think that the analysis of political resources contributes to a resolution of the age-old question of what constitutes power. Each of the resources mentioned above produces a form of power, the amount depending
on relative supply and demand. Goods and services produce economic
power, status yields social power, and authority and legitimacy are the basis

of political power. Information's claim to power is manifested by the adage that knowledge is power, and of course coercion and violence are forms of physical power. All of these resources may be employed in various amounts and combinations by participants in the political market. In an aggregate sense, power is measured by the incidence or degree or compliance with public policies or group demands. A powerful regime is one that can achieve and secure desired behavior from sectors by using the resources, currencies, and threats at its disposal. Thus a regime that is rich in resources is potentially powerful. But a regime poor in resources, in which the leadership deploys those resources it has in innovative and efficient ways to achieve a higher incidence of compliance, is also relatively powerful. We can say then that statesmen are powerful to the extent of their ability to generate political capital and increase its productivity.[5]

Alternative Uses of Political Resources

While it is impossible to simplify the logic of all statesmen into an abstract system, it is possible to suggest the general areas among which statesmen must make choices. In five areas all statesmen must decide whether, on whom, how much, and when to spend their scarce resources. Since their relative importance for any statesman differs, and since each regime will have different emphases and priorities, these areas should be considered without attribution of priorities. The five policy areas are:
  (1) Choices to cope with social and economic change;
  (2) Choices to induce social and economic change;
  (3) Choices to remain in authority in the present;
  (4) Choices to remain in authority in the future;
  (5) Choices to construct political and administrative infrastructure.
Our analysis proceeds with a number of simplifying assumptions: first, the statesman has at his command limited resources, in varying amounts and types, with which to implement choices affecting the character and quality of the polity's collective life; second, as a result of the division of labor that defines authority roles in a society, the statesman alone has the resource of authority at his disposal; third, the statesman wishes to remain in authority; and fourth, the statesman, to realize his valued ends, will make choices that formally aim at increasing the productivity of his political resources.

  [5] "There is, however, no quality of politics that can make men powerful out of relation to their purposes!" This is a modification of Dwight Waldo's paraphrase of Lord Robbins' statement about economics. See Waldo (1948:183–184, 202).

COPING WITH AND INDUCING SOCIAL AND ECONOMIC CHANGE.

The first policy area, choices to cope with social and economic change, includes public decisions to use scarce resources to ameliorate dislocations and, when necessary, to meet the subsequent demands resulting from changes in modes of production, social relations, and styles and places of living. These dislocations and demands may or may not arise from changes induced by government, but their effects cannot be ignored except at some cost to other ends valued by the statesman. Policies to cope with change might include expenditures for housing, urban amenities, population control, price stabilization, land redistribution, and traditional culture. In establishing such policies, the statesman is essentially reacting to problems.

The second area, choices to induce social and economic change, generally involves creative choices. Rather than acting to remedy shifts in the exchange relationships that take place in or between the economic and social markets, the statesman may attempt to use his scarce political resources to bring about new exchange relationships and to alter the means and volume of production. A choice intended to cope with change responds to a clear and present need; a choice intended to induce change is aimed toward a desired future condition or advantage. While the statesman's conception of social and political causality affects all choices, it is more likely to influence his use of resources to induce change.

We are interested in examining the policies adopted in both areas in terms of their effectiveness in achieving intended new relationships, in terms of the opportunity costs of resources used, and in terms of the subsequent effect of such policies on the regime's political capital position. Indeed, the statesman's choices in both areas are often summarized in a nation's social and economic plan. This statement of public intentions includes programs both for coping with problems arising from existing exchange relationships and for bringing about new ones. However, a plan must encompass, at least implicitly, the third and fourth areas of choice as well.

REMAINING IN AUTHORITY IN THE PRESENT AND FUTURE.

Resources may be used to enable the regime to remain in authority in the present or in the future. We must at this point make a distinction between these two objectives. A statesman's choices to ensure the former may not be the same as, and indeed may run counter to, his choices to ensure the latter. In either case we are concerned with the impact of such choices on the regime's capacity to survive. There is a similarity between areas one and three, and areas two and four. Like choices to cope with change, choices to remain in authority in the present are more reactive than creative, as they remedy dislocations arising from changes in the existing terms of political exchange. We cite as possible examples the Indian government's decision to grant statehood to the Naga people or Colonel Gowon's release of many political prisoners from jail. In contrast, choices that aim at clear future objectives and are designed to bring about new, more fruitful political relationships are often creative choices. Examples of choices intended to contribute to future authority might include the Shah of Iran's decision in 1961 to enfranchise women or India's reservation of legislative seats for outcastes and tribal groups. All four areas of choice require the expenditure of scarce resources and bring about new allocations of status, authority, and/or wealth. Each choice can be judged by the criterion of productivity and can be measured in terms of how well it satisfies its intended purpose. For each, a judgment of opportunity costs must be made.

BUILDING POLITICAL AND ADMINISTRATIVE INFRASTRUCTURE.

The final area in which a statesman may choose to spend his scarce political resources is that of political and administrative infrastructure. Although we will discuss this area at length in Chapter VIII, we will merely point out now that such infrastructure includes expenditures to establish, sustain, and strengthen institutions, processes, and values that will economize on political resources in the future or increase their production. To be more specific, political and administrative infrastructure includes political parties, elections, legislatures, local government, bureaucracy, army and police, constitutions, laws, communications networks, women's or youth organizations, trade unions, other mediate groups, education, and ideology. Like its social and economic counterparts, political and administrative infrastructure requires basic investments to make governance more efficient and perhaps more responsive to the governed.

While political processes could go on without expenditures for infrastructure, they would be costly and cumbersome, both for the regime and for the sectors. However, not all infrastructure is created by the regime. Some regimes have natural advantages such as a common language for communication, or inherit from previous regimes institutions such as local government or values such as peaceful resolution of political conflicts. Moreover, some infrastructure, political parties, for example, is created by the sectors, and much of it is liable to be used by persons other than the statesman for purposes of which he may not approve. Like all uses of political capital, expenditures for infrastructure are susceptible to ordinal cost-benefit and alternative use-value calculations.

Every use of resources involves making the distinction between consumption and investment. Staying in authority in the present and coping with social and economic change generally involve the use of political resources for immediate consumption. In most instances necessity gives priority to these choices. On the other hand, witholding resources from consumption in order to employ them in policies that will yield some desired end in the future would be considered investment in political as well as in economic terms. Investing in the development of a future political coalition, a program of new land tenure patterns, or a system of local government entails risks and costs that must be compared with the benefits of present consumption foregone. While the distinction between consumption and investment may not always be clear,[6] political economy will make this distinction on the basis of the length of the projected time horizon and the degree of uncertainty of benefits.

THE NECESSITY OF CHOICE.

The conventional analyses of political, social, and economic development set the use of resources to induce or cope with change or to build infrastructure against the use of resources to maintain the regime in authority. As political economists we do not share the judgment that those political choices that do not further desired social and economic change are necessarily counterproductive, undesirable, major impediments to progress, or short-sighted. Today it seems common for analysts to champion one set of choices and to view all other choices as counterproductive to their preferences. As political economists we do not dispute the likelihood that areas of choice may be mutually exclusive. We refrain, however, from ranking choices without reference to specific contexts. Because we have opted here for the perspective of the statesman, we will accept the statesman's ordering of the choices confronting him and will assume that it is guided by necessity and his values. Our tasks are to assess the probability of his making good his decisions with the means at his disposal, to evaluate the effects of the policies he adopts, and to detail the opportunity costs of different policies.

[6] We are aware of the difficulty of making this distinction in economics, for example, in considering education. See Harbison and Myers (1964: Chap. I); also Schultz (1961).

The statesman is confronted with the necessity to make choices involving the expenditure of resources in the five areas we have delineated. Some regimes need not worry about remaining in authority and can concentrate more resources on policies to induce social and economic change. Other regimes are so near bankruptcy that the only choices open to them are those that can maintain their authority in the immediate present and in the coming year. Still others are so deficient in infrastructure that major amounts of resources must be spent in this area. Each of the choices a statesman makes affects his capacity to make other choices. Many choices bear fruit only after a long period, others in a very short time. Some choices can be described, to use an economic term, as "lumpy"; others entail the problems and opportunities of externalities.

Often a policy for coping with change enhances a regime's capacity to remain in authority in the present. Yet a policy to induce major social and economic changes may make future authority more difficult to maintain. A statesman's choice to remain in authority in the present may impair his regime's ability to survive in the future. Other choices may render useless the infrastructure invested in over the years. Even if scarcity were not the common lot of regimes everywhere, the fact that many policies are incompatible or mutually exclusive would complicate a statesman's choice of strategy. To condemn a statesman for not using the lion's share of his resources for social and economic change is, to our mind, unreasonable. To attribute a statesman's inability to implement his goals to his having fallen into a "prismatic trap" or to a lack of stable identity is to fail to see the impact of necessity on his political life and the dilemma of conflicting goals he faces. We hope that the study of political economy will not only provide a new way of understanding choices, but will also result in greater generosity in passing political judgments.

A regime makes certain choices in response to the demands of sectors and others in response to the felt needs of the statesman. Although it is sometimes difficult to distinguish between these choices in practice, choices for consumption are prompted by demands, while choices for political investment are more frequently motivated by felt needs. Demands are claims made by a sector on the polity's scarce resources, both potential and available. By making demands, a sector seeks to improve its well-being or to affect that of others. A sector may demand economic goods and services, money, participation or influence in authoritative decisions, status and prestige, information, no coercion, or coercion against others. It may also demand that resources be extended or denied to other sectors. Those demands that do not in any way involve the regime are not a part of the study of political economy.

Whether choices are made in response to the felt needs of the statesman or in response to demands arising from the sectors, the condition of
scarcity forces the statesman to choose among alternatives. When dealing
with sectors, he must often make choices in the face of incompatible or
mutually exclusive demands. The statesman cannot meet at the same time
the demands of landless laborers and large landlords, secular nationalists
and ulamas, industrialists and trade-union leaders. Choices will usually
favor one sector and not another because in most cases resources are too
scarce to satisfy all demands.

Conventional economists insist that fewer demands will go unmet if the
economy is made more productive. For this reason, they usually urge the
statesman to give top priority to economic development. They are, to be
sure, partly right in their assumption, but economic productivity will not
satisfy all the demands of the sectors. "The end of ideology" is hardly in
sight. Many of the demands made in developing countries entail the redistribution of status and authority, which are both, by definition, scarce.
Neither can be made plentiful without drastically diminishing its value. A
greater supply of economic goods and services may in some cases make demands for status and authority less intense, but would hardly sanction a
single-minded concern with inducing economic change.

In the face of frequent mutual exclusiveness of demands and the per-
sistent scarcity of resources, the statesman has various options. He may
choose to meet some demands wholly or in part. Some demands he will
ignore or explicitly reject. Sometimes when a demand from the sectors cannot be met, the statesman may seek to substitute resources that he thinks
will be temporarily acceptable; in some situations he may give the sectors
currency as claims on resources in the future. He may employ coercion to
remove the effects of certain demands, or he may institute education to remove the causes. Each option requires the spending of resources now and
in the future. For each, calculations must be made to determine its potential for increasing the total stock of political capital at the disposal of the
regime. Such calculations are the foundations of choice. Given the necessity of choices, the statesman must figure out on whom, how much, in
what combination, when, where, why, and for what return the regime's
scarce political resources should be spent. In our model we try to make the
statesman's calculations explicit, so that political economists may assist him
in making more productive choices.

Before we would attempt to make judgments about a regime's limitations
and possibilities, there are a number of questions that must be answered:

(1) How rich is the regime? In what resources is it presently and potentially richest, and poorest?

(2) How effective are the regime's political institutions in facilitating political capital formation?

(3) How effective are present decisions and policies in improving the regime's resource position?

(4) What entrepreneurial qualities does the statesman possess? Is he capable of finding new sources of supply, of combining resources in novel fashions, or is he particularly efficient in managing what resources he has?

(5) What are the statesman's propensities, values, priorities, and time horizons for public action? How do these affect his choices?

These questions apply to any regime. They lay the foundation for a post-typological social science that is relevant to developing countries.

The Statesman's Political Environment

The statesman's political environment is neither homogeneous nor unstructured. He must deal concretely with different groups and interests in order to achieve his objectives for the polity. Our model of political economy analyzes the statesman's political environment in terms of *sectors*. We define a sector as a group of persons who respond to political issues in a similar fashion. The generally predictable behavior of sectors makes possible calculations about how best to make political plans and investments. It enables the statesman to calculate, for example, the type and extent of infrastructure needed, the chances of inducing change, or the possibilities of building coalitions to remain in authority in the future. The differing responses of sectors to the dislocations of change force the statesman to make choices.

ANALYSIS OF SECTORS.

It is sector resources that by and large permit the regime to remain in authority or bring about its downfall, and it is on the political performance of sectors that the statesman's likelihood of achieving his valued ends depends. It is assumed that the members of a sector seek to maintain or improve their own status and well-being and will act accordingly. Sectors may be formally organized with acknowledged leadership, in which case they have the attributes of collectivities; [7] otherwise they are categorical in char-

---

[7] "A collectivity is a *special type* of social system which is characterized by the capacity for 'action in concert.' This implies the mobilization of the collectivity's resources to attain specific and usually explicit goals; it also implies the formalization of decision-making processes on behalf of the collectivity as a

acter, participating in political claim-making when rewards or losses from the political process warrant their action. Sectors are especially relevant to political economy when they use their resources to change or maintain the existing allocation of values or when they are engaged by the regime to achieve its goals.

The interests sectors promote are many and varied. Sectors may be formed to promote religious, geographic, cultural, social, or purely political interests. A sector may be concerned with a single issue or interest such as the formation of a linguistic state or the protection of landless laborers, or it may be concerned with multiple and perhaps related interests such as regional uplift, protection of the Hindu way of life, and the advancement of minority rights in general. A suggestive inventory of sectors might include feudal landlords, middle peasantry, moneylenders, landless laborers, tenant farmers, priests, teachers, regionalists, feudalists, small businessmen, industrialists, minority-group merchants, military, high-ranking civil servants, other civil servants, intellectuals, moderate industrial workers, radical workers, and pro-Peking Communists. An individual could be a member of more than one of these sectors. However, as group allegiance in developing countries is still relatively undiffused, persons are likely to have a dominant allegiance. We assume that the number of cross-cutting allegiances will increase with social and economic development and differentiation.

Sectors differ not only on the basis of their interests and degree of organization, but also according to their resource position and its composition. Sectors possess, in differing degrees, economic goods and services; information; status for others; legitimacy status for the regime; violence; currencies such as money, support, and allegiance; and threats. One sector, a merchants' association, for instance, might be rich in economic goods but poor in its capacity to perpetrate violence. Another sector, a trade union, for example, might be rich in support (votes) but poor in economic goods and services. Some sectors are relatively wealthy overall; others are relatively poor. Each sector combines its resources and exchanges them to secure its political ends or to prevent others from achieving theirs. The combinations change over time, depending on their success and the supply of and demand for resources.

whole. This explicitness applies both to the legitimation of the rights of specific units to make such decisions and the obligations of other units to accept and act upon the implications of these decisions. The formal organization (e.g., a bureaucracy in the widest sense) is the prototype of such a system." Parsons and Smelser (1956:15).

IDEOLOGIES, PROPENSITIES, AND TIME HORIZONS.

Although a statesman will usually be familiar with the organizations, interests, and resource positions of his society's sectors, he should also be familiar—and often is, in the case of the major sectors—with their ideologies, propensities, and time horizons. Interests are seldom expressed in isolation from other preferences a sector's members might have. Associated with interests are the values, feelings, and notions of political causality that comprise a sector's ideology. An ideology represents the sector's conception of the good society. It contains value judgments about the sector's own role and the roles of others in the prevailing social stratification as well as judgments about current or alternative allocations of resources. Implicit in these value judgments is an ordering of preferences and a "zone of indifference" that delimits the range of actions tolerable to the sector. When a statesman figures that "the intellectuals will be pleased," "the feudal class will be outraged," "this is not crucial to Chinese merchants," or "the unions will never trust us on this decision," he speaks from an understanding of the ideological orientations of the sectors in question. He will adjust his own calculations accordingly.

If, however, the statesman used only his assessment of ideology as a guide, his calculations would be too costly or simply wrong. Ideology provides few explicit clues to the behavior patterns, or propensities, of various sectors. In political economy propensities are the sectors' procedural and resource preferences for political action—not just what is sought, but also how it is sought. The concept of "propensity to save" in economics, for instance, does not suggest why the population saves a certain portion of its income, or for what, or why different sectors save larger or smaller shares. It only describes their differential preference to do so. When the statesman figures that "the military might withhold protection if their perquisites are not increased," "the students will riot if amnesty is not granted to the rebels," "the tenant farmers will follow the advice of their landlords," or "labor will not be patient for gains in income," he is calculating on the basis of propensities.

The following is a partial but representative list of propensities which we will discuss in greater detail in Chapter IV. Each propensity also implies its converse and suggests intermediate positions.

(1) Propensity to demand material gains rather than psychic gains;
(2) Propensity to seek immediately self-interested goals rather than collective goals (or sector goals rather than community goals);

(3) Propensity to seek immediate gratification rather than deferred gratification;
(4) Propensity to use public channels rather than private channels;
(5) Propensity to persist with demands rather than withdraw demands when they are not met;
(6) Propensity to use violence and threats of violence rather than peaceful negotiations;
(7) Propensity to seek direct confrontation rather than action through intermediaries.

For the statesman, a knowledge of the propensities of major sectors is virtually a prerequisite for making efficient choices. Indeed, when new and inexperienced regimes, especially military regimes, take over, the costs of ignorance of sectoral propensities are often all too evident. We believe that the study of political economy can reduce these costs.

Finally, to make effective choices, the statesman must understand the time horizons or time preferences of the various sectors. These are best understood by distinguishing between expectations and aspirations.[8] An expectation has an imperative quality about it and will produce a sense of deprivation in sector members if it is not fulfilled within a defined period of time. An aspiration, on the other hand, is long-term, more wishful than imperative, and produces a sense of disappointment when unfulfilled. Each has different political consequences. The statesman is probably roughly aware of what those consequences might be, for they affect the sequence of his choices. When a statesman claims that "the religious leaders demand immediate action on the educational programs," or that "higher civil servants will endure austerity if a future rise in income is promised," he is speaking from his knowledge of the sector's time horizons. For most developing polities it is perhaps worth noting that the "revolution of rising expectations" is fortunately more of a "revolution of rising aspirations."

STRATIFICATION OF THE POLITICAL COMMUNITY.

Our discussion of sectors may have left the impression that apart from resources and ideology, sectors are otherwise more or less equal in their power to influence the regime. This is not the case. Sectors are stratified, as we have illustrated in Figure 1, into what may be considered five groupings. The first grouping we call the *core combination* (sectors 6, 7, and 8 in

[8] Hoselitz and Willner (1962:363–365).

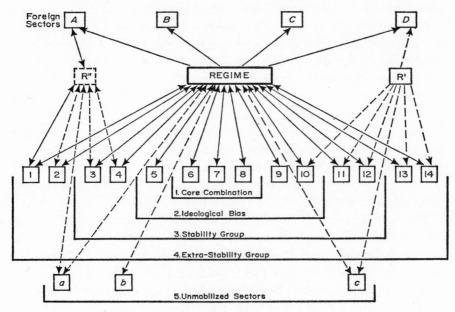

Figure One.

Figure 1). It is an alliance of those sectors that have most influence on public policy and the personnel and goals of the regime.[9] The demands of

[9] The reality of a core combination forming the basis for a regime is widely recognized, though seldom treated analytically. Rupert Emerson, for example, describes changes in the power relations of nineteenth century Japanese and Chinese regimes much in terms of shifting "core combinations" of sectors. His comparison of Chiang Kai-Shek's and Mao Tse-Tung's regimes during the twenties, thirties, and forties, demonstrates, we think, the analytical utility of the core combination concept. See Emerson (1960:263–264).

In his analysis of Italian parties, Giovanni Sartori points to the shifts in the combination of sectors supporting the ruling and opposition parties, especially as different economic, political, and religious issues come to the fore. See Sartori (1966:162). In the same volume, Dankwart Rustow discusses the core combination of Ataturk's regime in Turkey, an alliance of party, armed forces, and bureaucracy. Changes were made, and this combination was extended in the decades that followed. The changes made were reflected in the membership in the Turkish Assembly between 1926 and 1946. See Rustow (1966:121, 131, 133). Richard Pfaff contrasts Ataturk's strategy with the strategy of Reza Shah in Iran. Much of the difference in strategy can be traced to the respective core combinations of each statesman. See Pfaff (1963).

A core combination may be only one sector. Leonard Binder (1965) suggests that there was such a core combination in Egypt after Farouk was ousted by the

these sectors are usually more fully satisfied than the demands of other sectors because the "venture capital" these sectors supplied to the statesman in earlier days now entitles them to "interest." (We add "usually" because many core combinations are fragile alliances, and many of the major demands from the constituent sectors are mutually exclusive.) The core combination enjoys a privileged position vis à vis the regime, but can maintain it only if the regime remains in authority. Thus its various sectors have an interest in keeping the regime's resource position strong. They know that in order to achieve their objectives and to further their ideological preferences, they must in return furnish the regime with some measure of resources and support. A core combination commonly found in developing countries is an alliance of intellectuals, military, and civil servants.

The second grouping we call the *ideological bias*. It includes those sectors such as 5, 9, and 10 whose present and future relationships with the regime are included in the core combination's conception of the good society. Sectors in the ideological bias provide relatively little political capital, and few of their members hold major public positions, though members may often hold symbolic positions. The statesman's priorities are seldom altered by the demands of these sectors. An example of a sector in the ideological bias of a regime might be the middle peasantry in India, highly favored by legislation, but neither conspicuous in high places nor a crucial source of political capital. A core combination lacking cohesion or congruence may try to include mutually antagonistic sectors within the ideological bias. Such might be the case when both agricultural and industrial labor sectors are favored. The issues of inflation, price stabilization, and agricultural production might dissolve the core if conflicting demands could not be satisfied.

The third grouping of sectors, sectors 3, 4, 11, and 12, for example, we call the *stability group*. Here we find acquiescent sectors as well as those whose disaffection could disrupt the stability of the regime. The latter are not favored by the regime in its policies, and their members almost never occupy public positions, except in the opposition. However, as these sectors can easily withold resources, bargaining over their demands is especially common. Political economy may illuminate the strategy of marginal sectors

Revolutionary Command Council. That sectors in the core combination can impose costs on a regime is illustrated by Martin Kilson's discussion of the Sierra Leone People's Party and its dependence on traditional chiefs (1966: 190). Aristide Zolberg also makes this point in discussing why in the Ivory Coast, leadership composed almost entirely of civil servants made the party extremely vulnerable to administrative pressure. See Zolberg (1964a:101).

(such as 3) that threaten and then use violence to press their demands, or the counterstrategy of the regime as it weighs the costs of using different resources, especially coercion, in response to demands from these sectors.

The fourth grouping we call the extremist or *extra-stability group*. To meet the demands of sectors such as 1, 2, 13, and 14, a fundamental change in the kind of choices made by the regime, if not in the regime itself, would be necessary. The regime meets the demands and very often the existence of these sectors with threats of coercion, or with actual coercion. The character of sectors in this group varies with each regime, but we could cite as examples a Moslem Brotherhood or a pro-Peking Communist party. Ironically, last year's proscribed sector occasionally becomes tomorrow's regime.

A fifth and final grouping includes the *unmobilized sectors* such as *a, b,* and *c.* An unmobilized sector is a category of persons who are largely unpoliticized, but who can be considered in sectoral terms because of their potential productive characteristics. Public issues that engage the nation have hardly touched them. Their resources are usually too meager, or the cost of mobilizing their resources is too high, to warrant the expense of involving these sectors in the political process. Landless laborers, unskilled workers, and perhaps even religious ulamas or sadhus commonly fall into this category.

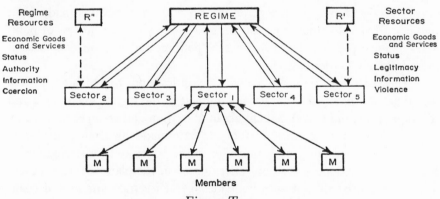

Figure Two.

The relationship of exchange between regime and sectors is shown in Figure 2. Here we find the resources held and sought by both. Our analysis assumes that both will act to maintain and improve their status and well-being, and that choices on the one hand and demands on the other will be backed by the expenditure of scarce resources in hopes of getting favorable returns or keeping exchange patterns from becoming more undesirable.

This exchange relationship pertains to all sectors of the polity, varying, of course, in the composition and amount of resources exchanged. The regime is barraged with demands from all sectors. The statesman has limited resources and many ends he wishes to achieve. When a sector demand and an end of his coincide, so much the better. This coincidence occurs most frequently in the case of sectors in the core combination and the ideological bias. These sectors will seek only marginal changes in allocation, as the prevailing distribution will be more satisfactory to them than it will be to other sectors located more toward the extremes. In the case of these other sectors, especially those in the stability group, compliance with the regime's wishes is usually purchased by satisfying certain of their demands.

We can put forward some general propositions with reference to the schema presented in Figure 1. As one moves from the extremes toward the center, violence and coercion decline as resources used to regulate or achieve demands. Furthermore, as one moves out from the center toward the extremes, sharing of economic resources and authority will decline as means of regulating or satisfying demands of the sectors. When disputes or competition arise between sectors, in most cases the regime will side with the sector nearest the center or will not intervene to protect the one more toward the extremes. In general, those resources most highly valued by the regime will also be those most highly valued by the sectors. Sectors and regime will vie to shift inducements offered and contributions made from resources they value most to resources they value less. The process of political exchange provides the dynamics of politics, and we will deal with it more fully in Chapter IV.

A polity's stratification system and the political ends to which the regime would devote that system are usually implicit in the regime's economic and social plan. Behind this statement about allocation and changes in distribution patterns lies the political plan of the statesman—his strategy for bringing about more productive relationships in the polity and for strengthening his regime's position. Not all objectives stated in the plan will be achieved, and often efforts will not even be made to reach certain announced goals. Scarcity may make some objectives unattainable, or the economic and social plan may diverge from the political plan. Political planning aims at expending given amounts of different resources in certain ways with the hope of increasing the flow of resources at the disposal of the regime. It often involves expenditures to mobilize sectors hitherto not participating in the polity but which can provide net benefits for the regime.

Despite our description so far, political economy is not a closed model. As we show in Figure 1, external governments can be sectors too. The statesman may procure from foreign sources economic resources or force to be used for coercion. The legitimacy status accorded to the regime by international recognition also contributes to the statesman's authority at home. What does he give up in return? Resources may be more plentiful in other political systems, but the limitations of scarcity still apply, and terms of exchange must be fixed by bargaining. Foreign governments may desire status for their country's political or economic system, but they will be more likely to desire influence over authoritative decisions, economic repayment in some form, information, or even restraint from international violence.[10] The statesman combines what resources he has to induce external regimes to comply with his wishes, and the foreign power, to be sure, follows a similar course. The details of international political exchange are not elaborated in this book, but working them out should not be difficult once the model is understood. We suggest in passing that the stratification system we have outlined for domestic sectors could be applied internationally, assuming some nations as allies (core combination), others as preferred but not allied (ideological bias), and so forth.

Uses of the New Political Economy

Among other things, the model of political economy enables us to suggest what constitutes political solvency. Our emphasis on resources permits us to refer to rich regimes and poor regimes, solvent regimes and bankrupt regimes. Without such knowledge we could not begin to help the statesman make choices within the realm of the possible. Solvent regimes, quite simply, are those in which income at least equals expenditures. Despite threats or instances of violence, they are stable regimes, able to deal effectively and efficiently with demands from the sectors. To the extent that these regimes have a surplus of resources, they are able to undertake saving and investment to increase their political capital. Insolvent regimes, on the other hand, are ones in which expenditures exceed income and in which no policy choices are likely to make up the deficit. When a regime faces bankruptcy, it may pursue any of several possible courses of action. It may try to expand infrastructure in order to extract or produce more resources, economize on expenditures, or reduce demands; it may expand the core combination in order to increase the commitment of resources to the regime; it may modify its position in order to establish a new relationship with previously extremist groups; or it may invest in and involve unmobilized sectors,

[10] Foreign aid may be given to gain military allies who will use their armies against a third country.

or borrow from abroad. Each course has its costs. Regimes usually opt for some combination of these strategies.

The new political economy permits a number of definitions of political development, a tribute, perhaps, to its versatility. Political development may, for example, be defined as increasing levels of solvency, though this definition does not distinguish low-expenditure from high-expenditure regimes. Another definition might focus on the increasing capacity to meet and induce changing and expanding demands. A third definition might combine the former two to consider political development in terms of both generating resources and processing demands. A fourth definition might extend political development to cover an increase in the number of political entrepreneurs. The complementary facets of political economy permit various approaches to the analysis of political development, a subject yet to be satisfactorily explained by social scientists. We will not attempt to offer any definitive treatment of this subject, but will leave this to future work.

The model of political economy may be used to analyze any regime at any point in time. Its limitations stem from the data presently available and not, we believe, from its construction. The model does not presume a desired final state and is not confined in scope to treating conditions of equilibrium. Neither does it call for the regime or the sectors to establish an equilibrium situation. Practically, the model can deal with any type of regime. In some systems the core combination may be widened to include the entire polity. The extra-stability group may be enlarged to analyze a beleaguered regime confronting a hostile environment. Totalitarian, authoritarian, liberal, bourgeois, and socialist regimes can all be handled. The number and identity of the sectors is infinitely expandable. While we think our model is especially fruitful for the analysis of developing nations, we believe it is also helpful in understanding more established political communities, their policies, and their sectors. For that matter, since the model draws heavily on organization theory, it might with modifications apply to any organization or community.

Models seem to be of two sorts—those that lead the scholar away from the empirical world and those that make him dig more deeply there. Though our initial presentation of the model in this chapter has had to be general and relatively abstract, the following elaboration and the empirical work that should ensue from it make it clear that our model is one of the latter sort. While it may be premature for us to abandon our four-cell matrices and dichotomous pattern variables entirely, we feel that political economy may not only lead the scholar back to the empirical world, but also might make him more relevant to it.

III

POLITICAL RESOURCES

Conservative [Japanese] leadership made maximal use of the resources that were built into their society—values, institutions and men.

Robert Scalapino [1]

Political leaders in Japan during the period following the Meiji restoration possessed an insight into the nature and utilization of resources that enabled them to achieve their goals of economic and social change while maintaining political stability. Their commonsense understanding of political resources appears to us to have been superior to that possessed by political scientists today. Today's political scientists have failed to find a way to handle the diversity of factors of political production.

The diverse inputs of economic production have for analytical purposes been divided into three categories: land, labor, and capital. These categories, however, are broad enough to include natural resources and raw materials as well as land, high-level management as well as skilled and unskilled labor, and financial assets as well as capital goods. By reducing disparate factors of production into these basic groupings, denominated in terms of money, it becomes possible to speak meaningfully about efficiency of production, optimum production functions, substitutibility, marginal productivity, and so forth. An effective study of political productivity also requires that factors be grouped for purposes of analysis. The categories need to be comparable, though not necessarily similar or homogeneous. We know that at this stage of our thinking, our presentation of the political factors of production will of necessity be elementary; however, we hope that our discussion will open the way for greater refinement.[2]

---

[1] Scalapino (1964:97).

[2] Economics has had the benefit of long study and analysis of its factors of production, yet the classification of factors continues to be debated. Economists

One political scientist, Robert Dahl, has already given serious attention to political resources, but his work has been more descriptive than analytical. In his study of community power in New Haven, Connecticut, he suggests political resources quite similar to those we use, although his methodology and empirical referent differ from ours. He includes social standing (which is similar to our status); cash, credit, and wealth (economic resources); control over sources of information (information); legality and popularity (elements of legitimacy); and control over jobs (related to economic resources and status). He does not regard force as a political resource, perhaps because he is trying to describe domestic American politics. Recent events in American cities, however, suggest that force needs to be considered a political resource. Unfortunately, Dahl regards the exercise of authority more as distributive in the "who gets what when" tradition of Lasswell than as a productive and relatively autonomous factor. Thus he does not consider authority a resource.[3]

In subsequent work Dahl undertakes a somewhat more theoretical discussion of political resources.[4] He talks of the uneven control of resources and the cumulative inequality that results, but still pays little attention to what or which are political resources and why they are so. We feel that while he does consider conflicting and competing aims as normal or basic to the political process, his view of the political community is too simplified. We think that little analytical advantage is gained by differentiating, as Dahl does, between the "powerful," the "power-seekers," the "political strata," and the "apolitical strata," each group regarded as relatively homogeneous. We believe that our model of political stratification can be applied just as appropriately to New Haven as to Nicaragua.

In political economy all resources have their origin in the *activities and attitudes* of members of the political community. They are principally characterized by *scarcity* and *productivity*. Those resources used by the sectors in exchange with the regime or by the regime itself to alter or preserve the allocation of resources in society we term *political resources*. For political economy the definition of politics is analogous to Marshall's delineation

have not agreed, for example, on whether to include technology as a factor. Some would include management or organization or entrepreneurship, though most would not. The importance of a rigorous and discriminating conception of resources is illustrated by the advances in economic analysis stimulated by the distinctions Marshall introduced in the analysis of factors of production. See Parsons and Smelser (1956:26ff). We hope that similar theoretical advances in the analysis of political factors will be made.

[3] Dahl (1961:226–267).
[4] Dahl (1963:15–17, 32–33).

of economics as a discipline concerned with those aspects of men's attitudes and activities that are subject to measurement in terms of money.[5] Political economy is concerned with those aspects of men's attitudes and activities that affect in some way the exercise of, or competition for, authority.

Goods, services, status, or information exchanged between sectors are part of the "private" sphere; only when they involve or affect the regime's resources, in particular its unique resources of authority and coercion, do they become political. Often, to be sure, changes threatened or made in the private sphere incline disadvantaged sectors to seek government support or intervention. When a sector makes a matter "public," the resources used by it and other sectors and those used by the regime are considered political. We would say that economic, social, and other resources become political whenever they affect or involve the exercise of authority, just as whatever is denominated in terms of money becomes "economic."

Uses of Resources

The resources analyzed in the study of political economy have most of the characteristics of those analyzed in the study of economics. Although political resources have both productive and allocative aspects, we consider them primarily as factors of political production. Political resources may be *used* or *saved* by those who produce them and those who receive them. When used, resources may be *spent, wasted, recovered in kind,* or in some cases *lent* or *borrowed.* Those that are saved may under certain conditions be *invested* to increase future production or efficiency. Political resources derive their value from their scarcity and their productivity. Because they yield satisfactions when consumed or can be used to secure other, more valued resources and satisfactions, they are sought by both the sectors and the regime.

We would like to underscore the *instrumental* nature of resources. We speak of resources as though they were valued for themselves, but they are in most instances desired as means to ends. Even goods and services, the most tangible of resources, are means to somatic and psychic satisfactions. Although some persons may prize the mere possession of these resources, this should not disguise the fact that resources are desired for personal satisfactions of one sort of another. We do not intend to probe the

[5] See Parsons and Smelser (1956:13) for a discussion of Marshall's definitions.

extent and bases of such satisfactions. Rather we will be content to deal with the instrumental behavior of acquiring and disposing of resources.

As economists have discovered, not all resources are simply consumed by use. Food when used (eaten) is no more. A machine, on the other hand, when used becomes gradually less efficient in production, and as it wears out (or is surpassed by more productive machinery) we measure its deterioration in terms of *depreciation.* The information represented by a patent is an "input" in the productive process, and it remains constant. If others possess the patent, its value usually declines, but its productivity in terms of volume remains the same. The distinction between more and less exhaustible resources is of critical importance in political economy. In our discussion, we usually speak of resources as though they were "consumed" with use and were not renewable, but this inference is often not exactly correct. To qualify each statement about resource use by saying that some resources are more readily exhausted than others would be too cumbersome. We therefore ask the reader to bear in mind that a less general discussion of resources would discriminate among degrees of exhaustibility.[6]

Political resources are continually exchanged. Exchanges are often voluntary and to the parties' mutual advantage, yet they are sometimes made under duress, without tangible compensation to either party.[7] Those resources gained by exchange may in turn be consumed, saved, invested, or used in production. Well-being may be increased through the exchange of

[6] In place of the usual classification of resources in terms of their exhaustibility, Wantrup suggests that resources be distinguished in terms of non-renewability (stock resources) and renewability (flow resources). This distinction does not imply that renewable resources cannot be used up, but only that with reasonable "management" or "conservation" they need not be reduced. We have not tried to formulate a theory of resources for politics similar to Wantrup's for economics. However, there may be in political exchange a critical zone similar to the one he delineates in economics. In economic analysis the critical zone covers a more or less clearly defined range of rates of use below which a decrease in flow cannot be reversed *economically* under presently foreseeable conditions. Conceivably a range of rates of political expenditure could be outlined below which a decrease could not be reversed *politically.* See Ciriacy-Wantrup (1952: Chap. III). In general, we speak of resources as though they were non-renewable "stock" resources, though it is clear that some political resources, authority and legitimacy in particular, are renewable under conditions of management or conservation and thus belong more to Wantrup's category of "flow" resources.

[7] In his review of Homans' work (1961), Kenneth Boulding suggests that positive reciprocity is not the only basis for exchange. There may be "threat systems" using force and "love systems" based on sacrifice. See Boulding (1962). Exchanges involving negative inducements or unrequited voluntary contributions are basic to our model.

less-valued for more-valued resources. The productivity of resources varies depending upon the uses to which resources are put; therefore, different values will be put on a resource by the regime and the various sectors, depending on the use to which each wishes to put the resource. The differing degrees of utility and productivity of resources give vitality to the political processes of altering or preserving allocations of resources.

Flows of Resources

Like economic goods and services, resources are often more appropriately viewed as a flow than as a stock. The regime and sectors produce goods and services which may be used in the political process or which may be withheld. The statesman makes authoritative decisions expending resources or refuses to do so. Members of the sectors accord legitimacy status to the regime or do not. The regime offers status, esteem, and deference to some sectors and not to others. Sectors may use violence against the regime or other sectors or may conserve this resource. Similarly, the statesman may direct coercion against some sectors or may not. Information may be exchanged by members or authorities of the political community, or withheld. At any one time, for analytical purposes, we treat a quantity of existing resources as given and calculate accordingly, yet in doing so we should not obscure the dynamic or continuous nature of political production and interaction. For the sake of clarity and precision, we speak of an allocation of resources as existing at a given point in time, but allocations change over time as flows change in magnitude and direction. Thus we need to think of the prevailing allocations as cumulative patterns or averages that are altered to the extent that marginal patterns of allocation diverge from them.

Individuals, whose activities and attitudes produce political resources, decide to exchange or withhold these resources on the basis of advantage gained. Advantage may consist of avoiding or minimizing sanctions such as violence or coercion, or may consist of furthering ideological or normative values. In engaging in production and exchange, individuals weigh the value of alternative courses of action in terms of *opportunity costs*—the value attached to benefits foregone or the losses avoided by following one course rather than another. The flow of resources and the relative and absolute changes in resource allocation over time constitute the heart of the political process.

The productivity of resource allocations can be viewed from the perspective of either the regime or the sectors. From the viewpoint of the regime, those patterns of allocation that increase its share of the flow of resources or permit more rapid achievement of its goals will be judged most productive. Yet to the extent that production and exchange by sectors and regime are to mutual advantage and raise the level of resources produced and offered for exchange, the polity as a whole is more productive. The statesman aims at achieving for his regime a profit or surplus resulting from revenue greater than expenditures. Yet both sectors and regime profit from a rising level of political or economic output because the demand for and availability of resources are increased. Political exchange and political resources are the form and substance of the political process and can bring about greater productivity from the point of view of both the regime and the sectors.

Political Currencies

Despite the fact that resources are exchanged continuously and not simply on a barter basis, there is as yet no comprehensive denominator that enables us to compare political resources in absolute terms. We find the idea of *currencies* that facilitate exchange of resources especially useful. A political currency is analogous in function to money in economics: it may serve as a *medium of exchange, a store of value, a standard of deferred payment, a measure of value,* or some combination of these functions. In our model, unfortunately, the last function mentioned is the least concrete.

The denomination of value for political currencies and resources is a matter that we have not resolved. The reader may expect us to present some "gold standard" of value for the sake of empirical analysis, but this we cannot do. We can only suggest the direction in which empirical and theoretical work may lead the study of political economy. Each of the resources—goods and services, status, information, authority, legitimacy, coercion, or violence—gives to its possessor some amount of power. The amount depends on many factors. Simply stated, the power conferred by possessing a certain resource is a function of the extent to which another wishes to have the resource and what it stands for; or, if the resource is negatively valued, as are violence or coercion, power is a function of the extent to which another wishes to avoid receiving the resource. The more another wishes to have or to avoid a resource, the more power he confers on its possessor; if his desire to have or avoid the resource becomes less, the possessor's power is decreased.

Thus power is not simply a matter of resources, but of tastes, preferences, and values as well. This fact makes exchange relationships somewhat volatile, though still governed by the principles of supply and demand interaction and therefore in essence predictable. A single standard of value is not necessary. There is, of course, no absolute standard of value or exchange for economic resources. The gold standard is simply a convention, accepted by many but not all controllers of currency. In political life we can point to several currencies, exchangeable one for another only when mutually agreeable and at a rate mutually acceptable. Economic resources, for example, are denominated in terms of money, or the power to command goods and services. Social power may be judged in terms of the amount of esteem and deference that a man's or group's prestige can claim from others. Power may be the ultimate unit for denominating the value of political resources and their currencies. Those familiar with the literature on power will appreciate why we do not wish at this stage to get tangled in its vagaries and artificialities. Still, we think that a more tangible and measurable concept of power is ultimately essential to political science, and we would hope for the perseverance of some and the patience of many in this endeavor.

Although we are not able to attach cardinal values to given amounts of a resource or currency, ordinal valuation is possible and common. From the viewpoint of a regime or a sector, a given amount of one resource is likely to be valued more than a given amount of another. Relative valuation according to the preferences of a regime or sector, made in terms of marginal utility or marginal productivity, provides means of tangible comparisons.[8] By means of ordinal valuation, the resources involved in public policy can be examined and compared from a practical point of view that embraces the whole range of political resources, including those originally considered social and economic.

[8] Others have also tried a similar approach to valuation. See Parsons and Smelser (1956); Blau (1964); and Homans (1961). Unfortunately, Curry and Wade's book on political exchange was not published until after we had completed our manuscript. We feel that the authors have made a useful contribution to the emerging study of political economy. We chose not to attempt as specific an application of economic theory to problems of comparing political utility as they have attempted with economists' "indifference analysis." Nevertheless, we find their work very helpful and are gratified that their conclusions about the possibilities and limitations of using economic theory for improving political choices are so close to our own. See Curry and Wade (1968:esp. Chap. I.).

Supplies and Demands

The regime and sectors possess and/or produce resources that they utilize to secure desired resources from one another. Our treatment of resources is somewhat similar to Easton's, which focuses on inputs (demands and supports) and outputs. Almond and Powell have expanded upon Easton's framework in an effort to analyze development capabilities and strategies. At the risk of causing some confusion between their model and ours, we cite the categories and examples they suggest for political analysis.[9]

Almond-Powell Classification of
Political Inputs and Outputs

INPUTS-DEMANDS:

(1) Demands for allocations of goods and services: wage and hour laws, educational opportunities, recreational facilities, roads and transport;

(2) Demands for the regulation of behavior: provisions for public safety, controls over markets, and rules pertaining to marriage, health, and sanitation;

(3) Demands for participation in the political system: the right to vote, to hold office, to petition government bodies and officials, and to organize political associations;

(4) Demands for communication and information: affirmation of norms, communication of policy intent, or the display of majesty and power of the political system in periods of threat or on ceremonial occasions.

INPUTS-SUPPORTS:

(1) Material supports: payment of taxes or other levies, and the provision of services such as labor on public works or military service;

(2) Obedience to law and regulations;

(3) Participatory supports: voting, political discussion, and other forms of political activity;

(4) Attention paid to governmental communication, and the manifestation of deference or respect to public authority, symbols and ceremonials.

[9] Almond and Powell (1966:25–27).

OUTPUTS:

(1) Extractions: tribute, booty, taxes, or personal service;
(2) Regulations of behavior;
(3) Allocations or distributions of goods and services, opportunities, statuses, and the like;
(4) Symbolic outputs: affirmations of values, displays of political symbols, statements of policies and intents.

Such a formulation, we think, makes demands from the sectors primary and assigns secondary, if any, importance to the goals and claims of the regime. In our model we consider the demands of the regime to be as important as or more important than those of the sectors. We do so not to give symmetry to the model but to account for the ability of governments to pursue policy objectives and to possess what is commonly called power. Both sectors and regime seek to acquire resources for consumption and for productive purposes. We see the process whereby they increase their respective abilities to achieve goals and satisfy demands not in terms of capabilities, but in terms of resources produced and exchanged.

To give the reader an overview of our political economy approach, it may be helpful to present political resources and currencies in diagrammatic form. The respective objectives of the regime and sectors and the resources each offers as inducements to the other are shown in Table 1. In this table the claims made by sectors are analogous to the demands of Easton's or Almond and Powell's model. The resources offered by the sectors serve the same function as inputs or supports. Those resources offered by the regime may be considered the outputs of the political system. However, we include a fourth set of factors—those resources that the regime needs to pursue *its own* objectives.

In our formulation there are no assumptions of necessary equilibrium or balance, and there is no "black box" converting inputs into outputs. Any resources held by the regime may be exchanged for any others held by sectors, or vice versa. The model sets forth the principal factors of political production. While the reader may think us foolhardy to try to reduce the complexity and incongruities of politics to such a simple model, he should judge our "reductionism" in terms of the means it provides for evaluating political choices, either for the benefit of the statesman, or of the anti-statesman who seeks to replace the statesman in a position of authority.

Political Resources and Regime-Sector Interaction

Regime	Sectors
Seeks: [10]	Seek:
1. To cope with social and economic change	1. To maximize their well-being, status, and authority
2. To induce social and economic change	2. To increase their productive capacity
3. To stay in authority in the present	3. To achieve their respective ideological goals
4. To stay in authority in the future	
5. To build political and administrative infrastructure	
Has and Offers:	Have and Offer:
1. Goods and services, and money	1. Goods and services, and money
2. Status and prestige	2. Status and prestige
3. Information	3. Information
4. Coercion (or no coercion) and threats	4. Violence (or no violence) and threats
5. Authority and influence	5. Legitimacy, and allegiance and support
Needs or Wants:	Need or Want:
1. Goods and services, and money	1. Goods and services, and money
2. Status and prestige	2. Status and prestige
3. Information	3. Information
4. No violence (or violence against others) and threats	4. No coercion (or coercion against others) and threats
5. Legitimacy, and allegiance and support	5. Authority and influence

The Factors of Political Production

ECONOMIC GOODS AND SERVICES.

The most tangible political resources are, of course, economic goods and services. We need say relatively little about them. They flow from the activities of individuals and are initially allocated as payments for the factors of labor, land, and capital used in the process of production. Exchange of

[10] To our view, the five objectives sought by the regime embody and make manifest a regime's ideology. For this reason, we have not included pursuance of ideological goals as a separate objective.

these resources is carried on by barter or through use of the currency of *money*, with rates of exchange set in either case by relative supply and demand. Shifts in prices and in supply and demand may occur with or without government involvement.

The size of the private sphere varies from one community to another. Some part of goods and services will be produced and consumed by the sectors, unaffected by and not affecting the exercise of authority. However, the regime invariably exercises its authority to draw some economic resources from the sectors, either in kind or in money currency. These particular resources are then used by the regime to affect other resource flows. In addition to taxation, various government means for altering the allocation of economic resources are rationing, price controls, excise taxes and tariffs, compulsory deliveries or expropriation, subsidization, and grants. To make and sustain such alterations, the regime uses some of its authority or coercion and must usually invest resources in infrastructure such as bureaucracy and police. We do not assume here that the private sector is the sole source of goods and services. The public sector may control or operate considerable means of production quite apart from its regulation of the private sector. More important, as the government controls the issuance of currency, it may increase its command over goods and services by creating money.[11] If the price level can be maintained, a regime may in effect be producing goods and services for itself at little or no cost to itself by manipulating the money supply.

The particular allocation of economic resources, like that of other resources, has consequences for productivity and future output. Output is distributed as payments to owners of factors of production and is an important incentive to further production. However, sectors have different propensities to consume, save, or invest their income. If those that invest their income productively receive a larger share of output, future production will probably increase. If those sectors that spend all their earnings get more income, aggregate demand is raised and thus investment by others is stimulated. Some sectors will only hoard income or invest it unproductively. If these sectors are significant in the economy of a developing country, they will impede economic improvement. If raising gross national

[11] The currency of money represents generalized claims on economic resources. It is convertible into specific goods and services because of its function as a standard of deferred payment, a medium of exchange, and a measure and store of value. Conversion of money into goods and services is, however, not automatic. If the supply of currency is too great vis-à-vis the resources it makes claims upon, the rate of exchange will be inflated and few if any resources may be gained in return for currency.

product is the statesman's chief concern, he would do well to alter the allocation of income against such sectors to make the economy more productive. If, however, these sectors are politically important to his regime, no preoccupation with reallocation or GNP growth will be feasible. Although the relationship between other resources and currencies is not strictly the same as that between economic resources and the currency of money, the two relationships are analogous. In general, the better we understand the nature, valuation, and exchange of economic resources and currency, the more easily we can conceptualize and analyze the other resources treated in political economy.

STATUS.

As economic goods and services flow from the activities of individuals, status flows from the attitudes of individuals toward social roles and their occupants. Consonant with prevailing norms and values, the attitude of *esteem* and behavior of *deference* are accorded in differing degrees to different roles and persons. Social status relations are organized and summarized in terms of *social stratification*. We define the term "status" in the way that T. H. Marshall defines "social status," as denoting "position in the hierarchy of social prestige." The social resource of status is a composite of personal statuses that represent the rights and duties attached to positions within any structure or organization. An individual has many statuses. He may be doctor, father, councillor, wicket-keeper, church warden, and husband, to use Marshall's examples. "Although these statuses cannot be added up," says Marshall, "they all contribute to the position of the individual [seen in his totality] within the community [conceived as a whole]." [12] The status of a group is naturally altered by changes in the status of its members, who themselves benefit or lose from changes in the status of the group.

The ubiquity of status relationships is evident to students of social interaction.[13] Status produces satisfaction for those individuals and groups that enjoy greater esteem and deference than others. However, status is by nature scarce.[14] The gratifications associated with higher status and the de-

[12] Marshall (1965:227).

[13] Lloyd Fallers attributes this ubiquity to man's common tendency to judge his fellows and himself as more or less worthy in light of some moral standard. See Fallers (1963:162) and (1964). For a more theoretical treatment of the subject of status, see Parsons (1954: esp. 69–72).

[14] Social roles, like political roles, are distinguished in terms of their superiority and inferiority. In his historical analysis of modernization, Cyril E. Black

privations implicit in lower status provide strong impetus for political activity.[15] In developing countries the competition for status is particularly acute because of the changing roles and new roles that accompany development.[16] The most significant shifts from old to new norms of status can be explained by the reduced importance of ascriptive criteria for determining status (family, kinship, and communal ties) and the growing importance of achieved status in occupational roles.[17] New elites often occupy a special position in society and displace other groups. By being able to grant or withhold community services, they anticipate "a share in the respect, wealth and political affairs of the community." [18]

Esteem and deference are for the most part accorded non-politically, that is to say, they are neither directed by nor do they affect the regime. Their accordance is determined by prevailing norms and usages; as these change, the allocation of status is altered. As long as such changes in allocation do not involve authority, they remain within the private sphere. However, because of the unequal economic and political relationships associated with differences in status,[19] changes in the relative status of groups

observes that while there may be a leveling in terms of income, education, and career opportunities, it "is not matched by a similar leveling of social or political roles . . . and one may in fact question whether such distinctions will ever disappear." Black (1966:21).

[15] The differentiation of roles in a society means that the same criteria of worth cannot be satisfied equally by all. The hopes and fears of groups of persons variously placed in the stratification system are expressed in cultural norms. According to Fallers (1963:162–164), persons want higher status but also want to be protected from competition from below. These norms, which contain definitions of excellence as well as judgments about the relative worth of roles and the stratification system as a whole, are a basic part of the ideologies of the different sectors.

[16] Apter considers problems arising from the introduction of "modernizing" roles into developing societies. As he puts it, the existing stratification of status, which constitutes a network of obligation, is ruptured by the impact of these new roles. See Apter (1965:323).

[17] Both Fallers and Apter examine this problem in some detail. Apter is especially concerned with the impact of new occupations associated with science and technology. See Apter (1965: Chap. V) and Fallers (1963).

[18] Liebenow (1956:443).

[19] Fallers notes that in India, "within a local community, members of different castes tended to be bound to one another by obligations to supply mutual though often rather asymmetrical services, assigned in terms of a division of labor by caste." Although this may be an extreme example, it illustrates the relationship between allocation and status, and between status and belief. See Fallers (1963:178). Murray Edelman (1964:16) suggests that myth, under-

usually involve shifts in the allocation of other resources. Hence changes in status affect the allocation of wealth and authority, and usually have concrete political consequences. Conversely, status may be changed by altering the distribution of other resources. If a regime seeks to raise or lower status for a group, it will probably have to make concomitant alterations in the distribution of wealth and authority in order to achieve the desired change in flows of esteem and deference.

Esteem and deference, like goods and services, provide in their consumption aspect personal satisfactions or gratifications. Yet their productivity is more than hedonistic. We cannot understand the striving for status unless we appreciate the advantages possessed by those sectors having high status. The association between status, wealth, and authority is not coincidental. Status may be used to obtain more of other resources. Higher-status sectors, for example, can often get goods and services free or at low prices from lower-status sectors, though their ability to pay is greater than that of the lower-status sectors. In an stable society, higher-status sectors are more likely than lower-status sectors to be immune from violence or coercion. A regime is more likely to respond favorably to a demand for authority or influence from a higher-status sector than to a comparable demand from a lower-status sector.

In developing countries today, higher-status sectors possess many privileges. The exchanges between high- and low-status sectors may take place outside the political or public sphere. At some point, however, the regime, on its own or at the insistence of less privileged groups, may intervene to make such exchanges more "equitable." Kemal Ataturk, for example, passed a law in 1934 requiring uniform use of the titles *bay* and *bayan* ("Mr." and "Miss/Mrs."), thereby eliminating the common forms of address that had distinguished gentlemen and ladies from lower-class men and women.[20] When such actions are taken by a regime, status relationships become politicized.

There are many ways in which a regime can affect the allocation of status. In most developing countries, for instance, completion of education beyond primary school entitles a person to higher status and enables him to earn greater economic rewards. Access to higher education is usually government-controlled, thus permitting the authorities to affect the status

stood generally and generically, accounts for extraordinary privileges or duties, great social inequalities, severe burdens of rank, and so forth.

[20] The limited effectiveness of this measure is discussed in Rustow (1965:181).

of individuals or groups.[21] Similarly, membership in the governing party confers status or prestige, the amount depending on the productivity and scarcity of party membership. Recognition of a minority group's language as "official" will grant that sector increased status. In addition, a regime can bestow awards, knighthoods, medals, and the like on individuals so that they will receive greater esteem and deference.

Examples of political allocation of status are numerous, yet the political importance of such allocations is often underestimated. Some of the most well-known attempts at status reallocation and the use of status to reallocate other resources were made by Stalin's Soviet regime. While it is true that "Stakhanovite" workers received greater monetary emoluments than their less productive fellow workers, their increased earnings were less than their greater output warranted; the "surplus value" was compensated for by the greater esteem and deference they received.[22] Medals for "heroism" reallocated status among and within groups of workers, authors, even mothers. Party membership was a highly selective mechanism for eliciting effort and allegiance in return for status and the income and influence associated with it. To reorder the social stratification of the country at large, party leaders employed ideology.[23] An equally radical attempt at status reallocation was made in Japan after the Meiji restoration. It was decreed that "all are equal under the Emperor." [24] This leveling of status vis-à-vis the Emperor enabled the regime in effect to cancel status differences and then to reissue and allocate status selectively.

In Ghana there has been a similar use of party organization to reallocate status. In 1959, when commemorating the tenth anniversary of the founding of his ruling Convention People's Party, Ghanaian President Nkrumah

[21] For a discussion of education as a determinant of status and prestige in Indonesia, see Fischer (1965:104–105). Coleman (1965: Part IV) describes how the statism of many developing countries leads to greater government control over and manipulation of educational opportunity.

[22] See McClosky and Turner (1960:133, 339); also Fainsod (1963:255).

[23] As economic deprivations such as fines serve as inducements, so also do status deprivations. Status may be lowered by economic penalties. More serious deprivations may result from ideological denunciations of roles and sectors or from humiliation of individuals or groups. Restrictions on various freedoms such as the freedom to move about, to speak, to marry, or to practice religion are impingements on status as much as on behavior. Such restrictions may be threatened or carried out in order to gain an advantage in terms of another's resources. Coercion and violence are resources that a regime or sector may use to effect status reallocation.

[24] Scalapino (1964:105).

emphasized the precedence of the CPP over the government. He announced his intention of "raising the prestige of our Party to its proper
status in our national structure." From that time forth, at all public and
civic functions, members of the CPP Central Committee were to take
precedence over those ministers of government who were not Central
Committee members.[25] Later, as Zolberg comments, "the status of party
officials was visibly reinforced when the regional commissioners were given
ministerial rank and the secretary-general was given the title of ambassador." [26] The pursuit of status in political competition is also illustrated
by Redfield's report of the efforts of the Mexican village Chan Kom to be
recognized as the *municipio* in its area. As a *municipio* Chan Kom would
be entitled to a variety of government services it did not then enjoy. If another village in the area won this status instead, Chan Kom would be less
likely to grow and prosper. To achieve this valued status, Chan Kom citizens showed their support for the regime by forming a local branch of the
ruling PRI party.[27]

It is not easy to distinguish between social status as a group attribute and
the status of individuals that derives from the various positions they occupy. Each contributes to the other, to be sure. We think it useful to analyze the difference in terms of the *prestige* that is conferred upon an individual by identification with a particular group or class. We define prestige
as a social currency that represents a claim on esteem and deference.
Different social statuses confer varying amounts of prestige on their members. Individuals gain prestige from different memberships, activities, and
group characteristics. Thus social status is considered as basically a group
phenomenon valued by individuals for the prestige and other benefits it
gives to members.[28] The distinction between status and prestige is well il-

[25] Zolberg (1966:57).

[26] Zolberg (1966:95).

[27] For the story of Chan Kom and its successes, see Redfield (1950: esp.
18–20).

[28] "Prestige depends on interpersonal recognition of status differentiation,"
write Hugh and Mabel Smythe. It requires "at least one person who claims
deference and another who honors the claim. A person's claim to prestige and
his position in the prestige hierarchy, in general, depend upon the evaluation of
his social function and his behavior by others in the community." See Smythe
and Smythe (1960:7). A more theoretical treatment of prestige is offered by
Parsons and Smelser (1956:51), who discuss the relation between social stratification and a society's value system. They consider respect to be the reward accorded to individuals for conformity with a society's set of values: "In cases
when degrees of this respect are compared with others, we might call it pres-

lustrated by Morroe Berger's discussion of the status of Egyptian civil servants. Objectively, says Berger, the status of civil servants had declined since the Second World War for many reasons, among them notions of democracy, the decline of foreign rule, increases in availability of education, increases in employment opportunities for educated youth, and the relative decline in government salaries.[29] Yet the public continued to hold civil servants in high esteem:

. . . unaware of this change, [the public] still sees the government official as the lofty personage he once was. The civil servant seems to think he is living on accumulated prestige.[30]

Prestige does not serve as a medium of exchange in exactly the way that money does for economic resources, but esteem and deference, the tangible manifestations of status, may be secured with it. Prestige thus serves as a store of value and as a standard of deferred payment of esteem and deference.

We recognize that status is the "softest" of the resources in empirical terms, though this fact in no way detracts from its importance in political exchange. It represents the link in political economy between objective behavior and subjective values and norms. There are several ways of looking at status and prestige, so often bracketed together in common conversation as if there were no distinction between them. One way is to look at status as fixed social capital and prestige as a more liquid social asset. In this sense, we consider status a resource and prestige its currency. It should be possible at some stage empirically to measure status in terms of prestige gradients or units. Even if these measures are relative, they may be given tangibility and precision through the work of sociologists who view social interaction in terms of resources and exchange.[31]

tige." They consider prestige the *output* of the social system, and we agree, though we would not tie it solely to a pattern-maintenance function.

[29] Berger (1957:102–103, 111–113).

[30] Berger (1957:94–95).

[31] We are obviously not sociologists or we would have developed the resource and currency qualities of status and prestige more comprehensively and perhaps more persuasively. We leave considerable scope for refinements and modifications by sociologists interested in problems of social and political interaction. Some sociologists may not agree with our classification of resources. In a book that could be read in political economy terms, Lenski (1966) chooses to regard status and prestige as goals of man along with survival, sustenance, health, creature comfort, affection, and salvation. Money and other forms of wealth, organizational office and other institutionalized roles, and education or training he treats as "instrumental values"—what we consider to be resources. While we

What are commonly called "status symbols" are perhaps more properly regarded as forms of prestige. Titles, material accoutrements, and the like serve as media of exchange, measures of prestige and stores of status, i.e., esteem and deference.[32] Status symbols are certainly subject to inflation and have other characteristics of currency. Only when they have consequences for or are affected by authority, however, are they political. We consider prestige the currency for status and status symbols to be the manifestations of prestige.

We have suggested how status may be allocated for political purposes. Let us suggest means of according prestige. When a statesman praises a group or person, he gives that group or person some amount of prestige; he is stating his willingness to accord esteem and deference to them. However, the amount of esteem and deference that will be generated from the rest of the community will depend in part on the value others attach to the statesman's esteem and deference. If he himself has little prestige, the prestige he gives to others nets them little. The same is true of the denigration of a group or person; its effect will depend on the status and prestige of the person initiating it. A more reliable means of conferring prestige is the designation of eligibility for certain political, social, or economic rewards. For example, conferring the status of "advisor" on a person entitles him to the increased esteem and deference that usually accompany this role. There may be some prestige conferred by giving a person prominence in the mass media. Appointments to a position with greater and more secure economic rewards also has a prestige element, as those who respect possession of wealth and income will give the appointee more esteem and deference.

Growing prestige may be converted into higher status under certain circumstances. Such a conversion takes place, for example, when a merchant class is able to use the prestige derived from its newly acquired wealth to move up the social ladder. Declining prestige usually also leads to a re-ordering of a group within the social stratification system. As a summary of status relationships, the social stratification represents differential flows of esteem and deference within a society. Stratifications may be more or less productive. Some changes may reallocate status in such a way that the flow of resources to the regime is increased. From the regime's point of view,

are pleased to find a number of similarities in analytical perspective between Lenski's work and our own, we would still maintain that status and prestige should be viewed as resources despite their "consumption" aspects.

[32] George Foster observes that "in the modern world, there appears to be a near universal desire to emulate in some degree the behavior of people who occupy a higher position than we do," and that "increased prestige is achieved through acquisition or modification in certain visible symbols such as food, clothing, housing, material items and speech patterns." Foster (1962:147).

such changes are productive. On the other hand, some stratifications yield greater total output of esteem and deference. An egalitarian social revolution, for example, probably not only reallocates status but increases it in the aggregate.[33] The study of political economy seeks to comprehend the politically relevant effects of changing status allocations in a society and the means that bring these effects about.[34]

INFORMATION.

Information stems from the intellectual activity of persons who create or acquire knowledge and transmit it. The activity of communication contributes some "value-added" to this resource. Information violates the law of conservation, since sharing it does not diminish its quantity, though its value may decline as more persons possess it.[35] Information may be an economic or social resource, yielding goods and services or esteem and deference. We consider it here as a political resource, affecting or being affected by the use of authority. Possession of certain information may permit the statesman to achieve certain objectives with less expenditure of resources, or it may facilitate increasing his other resources. Especially productive in political terms is information on others' intentions, their resource positions, and what matters they consider of vital significance or

[33] In such a revolution the status and prestige of the social elite may decline precipitously, but the previously less-privileged come to be regarded with greater respect. The powerful effect of the appellation *citoyen* during the French Revolution we see again in the outpouring of effort elicited by the designations *tovarich* and *compadre*. The total volume of esteem and deference may be radically increased following revolutionary changes in social stratification. Yet at the same time, there is bound to be tension because people would invariably like to be "more equal than others." The striving for relatively greater status and prestige continues to be a driving force, even in nominally egalitarian societies.

[34] Status and prestige are sought by statesmen and other authorities either for personal gratification or for enhancement of their authority. A systematic connection between social status, personal prestige, and political authority is seldom made, though it is apparent that respect for authorities and their offices contributes to compliance with authoritative decisions. We will consider the relationship between respect and compliance when we discuss legitimacy as a resource.

[35] Our thinking about information as a resource has been stimulated by Kenneth Boulding's essay, "Knowledge as a Commodity." Boulding says that knowledge "is clearly related to information which we can now measure; and an economist especially is tempted to regard knowledge as a kind of capital structure, corresponding to information as an income flow." See Boulding (1961:1).

of indifferent importance.[36] Thus from one point of view, the value of information to the stateman or to a sector can be gauged by the saving or increase of resources that results from possessing that particular information. But information held by either the statesman or a sector may be valued by the other for the same reasons. From a second point of view then, the value of information can be gauged in terms of the resources that can be gained by using such information in exchange with others. Information, therefore, may be productive for political purposes either directly or in exchange for other resources.

Obviously not all information has political value. We would say that any information used by the authorities to secure compliance from sectors or by sectors to affect the exercise of authority should be considered political. A regime may often go to great expense to maintain censorship over the flow of information to or between sectors. In attempting to preserve a monopoly on certain information, a statesman may try to keep from the general public information that reflects unfavorably on official actions or plans. If this information were held by other sectors, various costly demands or sanctions would result. Thus information's value may be negative rather than positive.

The importance of secrecy in politics and government becomes clearer when we understand information as a resource. The value of a particular piece of information is crucially affected by whether or not the possessor of that information has a monopoly. Once certain information is shared, its original owner experiences a sharp decrease in control over its use. This is why secrets are usually shared only with persons over whom the original owner can exercise effective sanctions. Fear of such sanctions reduces the likelihood of further divulgence to others. The wider the distribution of information, however, the more cheaply information can be acquired. A monopoly owner of certain information can bargain to get a price approximating the full worth of that information to the purchaser, but when many people have the same information, each may be eager to get what he can for it before another does the same. The price paid must, however, exceed whatever losses might be suffered by the divulging person as a result of sanctions exercised by the original possessor.

[36] Apter treats information as one of the functional requisites of government rather than as a resource, but there are nevertheless many similarities between his consideration of information and our own. For Apter, information is knowledge that permits a regime accurately to predict the consequences of policies. This definition would be applied equally well to sectors, which seek to know in advance the likelihood and consequences of policy choices. See Apter (1965: esp. 237–238).

Means must be found by those in authority to keep themselves informed of the political situation; securing these means may require making certain political investments.[37] Governments value information so highly that they will often expend considerable resources to maintain an intelligence network. Or political leaders will expend considerable effort to maintain informal contacts that yield useful information. Experimentation with policies may be justified within government on the grounds that useful information will be gained.[38] Information is no less valued by members of a sector. Pye's description of the role of information in Burmese politics suggests how a sector may utilize information for political advantage:

The problem of imperfect information in Burmese politics is . . . complicated by the political elite's keen appreciation of the extent to which *information is power*. Indeed, this consideration receives so much attention that Burmese are in constant danger of confusing the fact that they know something that someone else does not with the notion that they have power over that person. Thus information becomes something to be collected and withheld until it can be properly used to advance one's interests, and a mark of political skill is the ability to tell exactly who is in the know with respect to individual pieces of information.[39]

Information that is held and used by the regime to increase compliance with government policies is political, as is that used by the sectors to bargain for intervention of authority to improve their resource position. As Fagen puts it, "members of all structures participate at times in the planned withholding of information," [40] whether for reasons of personal security or advantage. When we speak of the productivity of information in political economy, we are referring to the sense in which information may be used to gain more resources through exchange. In our model we do not suggest any currency for information. Strictly speaking, information is either possessed or not; it has no medium of exchange, store of value, or standard for deferred payment. Moreover, there is no equivalent in politics of the "patent" in economic production, a fact that makes the pursuit and guarding of information more zealous. Perhaps in a sense "rumors" and

[37] See Fagen (1966:116) and Easton (1965:263).

[38] Albert Hirschman has pointed out that in development planning, when communication between decision-makers and those affected by their mistakes is poor, information may still be gained through mistakes, costly as this might be. See Hirschman (1963:242).

[39] Pye (1962:132–133) (italics ours).

[40] Fagen (1966:74).

"leaks" are currencies for political information. Though these may be significant in some situations, we do not analyze their effects in our model.

FORCE.

We think it neither facetious nor cynical to cite Thomas Hobbes' commentary on force as a political resource. Politics, he once suggested, is like a game of cards: the players must agree which card is to be trump. But with this difference, he adds, that in politics whenever no other card is agreed upon, clubs are trumps.[41] This is to be sure an observation rather than a normative statement. Many political leaders have tried to reduce the use of force in political exchange, an effort we think deserving approval. But force will continue to be used by regime and sectors as long as they do not satisfactorily achieve their respective goals using other resources. Eliminating the use of force requires that other resources be more effective for gaining compliance or satisfying demands. As we mentioned earlier, not all exchanges in a political community are voluntary or mutually advantageous. Force or the threat of force often reallocates resources. A regime may resort to expropriation, for example, or it may impose sanctions and deprivations that it will eliminate in return for other resources.

We must first distinguish between force employed by a regime and that used by sectors. Force employed by a regime has the sanction of authority and thus may be considered to some extent legitimate. We call it *coercion*. Force used by sectors without the regime's sanction we call *violence*. It is a matter of definition or philosophical preference whether or not some acts of force by a government may fall outside the bounds of legitimacy and therefore be considered violence rather than coercion. When we use the term "coercion" in this study, we are distinguishing governmental use of force from that which lacks official sanction. The distinction between violence and coercion is not new. Many definitions of the state have been based on the possession of a monopoly on the legitimate use of force, or coercion. Yet it is also clear that violence has been and is significant, in different degrees, in most political communities.

Force is not necessarily productive. In an exchange of sanctions, the collective losses of the parties involved may well exceed the total gains of both parties. The use of force that yields to the stronger party greater benefits than costs in the short run may prove to be costly over a longer period. The stronger party may have to continue to expend force or it may discover that

[41] Hobbes (1862:122). We acknowledge Rustow's discussion of this analogy (1963).

the use of force has made impossible the establishment of more voluntary and mutually beneficial exchange relationships. The net benefits from expending force in the short or long run cannot be determined a priori but must be estimated, usually from past experience. It is possible that a stronger party can by the use of force gain more resources than it loses, even over considerable time. In such situations, coercion or violence may be said to be productive and can contribute to the achievement of political ends as much as any other resource can.[42]

The application of force in political exchange is limited by costs and availability. Regime and sectors are both limited by the availability of men and materials. Furthermore, there may be ideological or psychic costs for both if norms disallow unlimited use of force. Costs from retaliation probably provide the most important check on the use of coercion and violence. Those against whom force is directed may respond with force or other resources to halt the force directed against them. Withholding services or status may avert violence or coercion, or positive inducements may "buy off" the purveyors of force. The productivity of coercion or violence must always be considered *net* of losses incurred.

A regime may use force to compensate for a loss or lack of support or allegiance. It may, for example, rig elections that confer legitimacy on authorities and force persons to vote in them. The anti-statesman too may resort to force to further his ends. He may use terrorism to get votes for his occupancy of a position of authority. Both statesman and anti-statesman may extort from unwilling contributors money needed to maintain a political organization or movement. Conscription into military service or impressment into guerilla forces strengthens the respective abilities of both to use force. In such cases, coercion and violence are spent to be recovered in kind. Both the statesman and anti-statesman may prefer to acquire resources through exchange or voluntary contribution, but exigencies often dictate otherwise.

The sectors need not and frequently do not acquiesce to regime coercion. They may respond with violence. Indeed, some sectors find that violence is the only effective resource they have to press their interests. An example is the use of violence by labor groups in Peru as a means of political bargaining:

[42] In Deutsch's analysis physical force is regarded as a "damage-control mechanism" which may "forestall or stop in its early stages a possible chain reaction of disobedience or defiance." Deutsch suggests that superior force may give a regime "the most primitive kind of political solvency." See Deutsch (1963:122).

. . . demonstrations and the threat of mass violence are an integral part of the system itself, the means by which labor groups bring pressure to bear upon the centralized executive. Utilized in a rational and calculating fashion in the particular circumstances of Peruvian politics, mass violence becomes almost the equivalent of free elections in other political systems—the regularized means by which incumbent elites are threatened with the loss of office if they do not accede to expressed demands of important groups in the populace. Rather than constituting a threat to the system's usual performance, mass violence has become a . . . regularized . . . channel of access. . . .[43]

There are, of course, many ways in which sectors can use violence. Strikes and demonstrations may only contain the threat of violence, but may turn into riots at the slightest provocation. Assassination and sabotage represent more concerted uses of violence, and may turn into guerilla warfare if they spread in scale. As our previous example illustrates, violence may be used quite deliberately for purposes other than the overthrow of a government or an expression of frustration and alienation. Violence may be an established and even stabilizing part of the political process when governed by norms that limit its scale and duration.[44]

As may be evident, *threats* of coercion and violence serve as currencies for force. Threats are media of exchange, stores of value, and standards of deferred payment. They may be inflated and depreciated when they become too numerous in relation to a regime or sector's capacity to back them up with force. It is obvious that coercion and violence are usually negatively valued. Unless courting martyrdom, sectors wish to minimize coercion used against them just as the regime desires to minimize violence directed against it. Yet a sector may wish coercion used against other sectors, or the regime may seek to direct sectoral violence against dissident sectors as a means of punishment or control. In a civil war, the statesman will try to mobilize the sectors' capacity for violence in order to destroy his opponents, who in turn appeal for violence to overthrow the statesman's regime. Those sectors that support the winning side will be able to make claims on the polity's scarce resources as payment for their contribution.

It may be asked whether *non-violence* is a political resource. In our model it is not, though it is a potent political activity when part of a

[43] Almond and Powell (1966:81–82) discussing Payne (1965a); see also Payne (1965b).

[44] Hirschman (1963) discusses the pervasive and accepted use of violence as a political resource in Latin American politics.

political strategy. Non-violence used politically in the manner of Gandhi or Martin Luther King, Jr. represents the *denial and withdrawal of legitimacy*. The significance of this definition and explanation will become clearer after reading our treatment of legitimacy as a resource.[45]

LEGITIMACY.

Since legitimacy differs in some respects from other resources, some persons may dispute our treatment of legitimacy as a resource.[46] We consider legitimacy a resource because of its productive and scarce characteristics. The statesman needs or wants legitimacy because to the extent he has it, he needs to expend fewer other resources to secure compliance with a policy. Thus possession of legitimacy produces other resources at less cost to the regime. Because legitimacy is productive in this way, the statesman will pay sectors for according it to him, his regime, and his decisions. Legitimacy is therefore productive for the sectors as well. Unfortunately for the regime, legitimacy is not a "free good." Legitimacy and its currencies, allegiance and support, commit sectors to surrender resources to the regime, either in the present or in the future. Sectors will not grant legitimacy to the regime unless the regime in turn in some way enhances their well-being, either by augmenting their resource position or furthering their normative and ideological preferences. To acquire and maintain legitimacy the statesman or the anti-statesman must confer benefits of some sort on the particular sector from which legitimacy is sought.

A grant of legitimacy involves opportunity costs for both sectors and regime. A regime that receives legitimacy status from one sector may be unable to receive it from another, antagonistic sector. Or legitimacy acquired on the basis of maintaining peace may preclude legitimacy for waging war. Sectors cannot accord legitimacy or allegiance and support to both the statesman and anti-statesman. Nor can they accord legitimacy to agricultural development but withhold it from, say, land reclamation projects. Legitimacy and its currencies contribute significantly to the achievement

[45] For a discussion of the political uses of non-violence, see Sibley (1963), which contains a number of historical examples of non-violence employed to oppose and nullify regime demands through active refusal to accord legitimacy to those in authority.

[46] In more developed polities, a case might be made for considering legitimacy as political infrastructure, or perhaps as a behavioral parameter. The fact that the line between resource and infrastructure cannot always be clearly drawn should not cause undue concern, since the distinction is ultimately an analytical one.

of the policy ends of both the statesman and his opponents, but can be acquired only by astute relations with the sectors. When legitimacy is lacking, the costs of government or of acquiring authority go up considerably.

The resource of legitimacy is less tangible than other political resources. There is, however, an analogous resource in economics. *Good will* possessed by enterprises is an intangible but valuable asset. It represents excess earning power and derives from the reputation and know-how of an establishment. Frequently it will be based on monopoly power. A quite tangible value is assigned to good will in corporate balance sheets, where it represents the difference between tangible assets on the one hand, and net worth plus liabilities on the other. One explanation of the value of good will is that the firm's product is widely known and preferred.

It is readily apparent that legitimacy depends on the monopoly power derived from occupancy of authority roles, as well as on reputation and political know-how. Legitimacy may be accorded to the authority roles themselves, to their occupants, or to decisions affecting the allocation of specific resources. The statesman's position is strongest if legitimacy is accorded on several or all of these three grounds. Securing compliance with a decision regarded as not legitimate on any of these three grounds will require an expenditure of resources by the statesman equivalent to the expenditure of a private person seeking the same compliance. To the extent that legitimacy is accorded, compliance will be forthcoming with proportionately less expenditure of resources. Perhaps several illustrations will help to clarify our previous discussion.

Taxation is an area in which accordance of legitimacy is quite crucial. Acceptance of the political division of labor generally carries with it some obligation to contribute to the maintenance of the regime. This obligation is not monolithic or unconditional, but is rather specific in degree and area. Some basic level of taxation may be acceptable to a sector without tangible and direct compensation from the regime; the shared benefits of law and order or security from aggression might be regarded as legitimate justifications for payment of taxes. Beyond this level, however, *quid pro quo* benefits must be conferred by the regime in return for increments in taxation. Alternatively, the regime must employ coercion to extract money from the sector.

While legitimacy itself may be difficult to measure, the "excess earning power" that may accrue from occupying authority roles has tangible effects. Suppose, for example, a statesman declares a tax but does not specify its use, nor does he threaten coercion or other sanctions if the tax is not paid. If a sector complies with this tax, we would say that it does so on the basis of the legitimacy it accords to the statesman, his regime, and his "right" to make authoritative allocations of this kind. However, the legitimacy status accorded to the statesman varies from sector to sector and from decision to decision. Since some sectors will not accord legitimacy to the tax edict and will comply only if offered positive or negative inducements, it is probable that the statesman will threaten coercion against *any* sector not paying the tax. It is therefore difficult to determine how voluntary any sector's compliance is. Yet it follows that a sector according greater legitimacy to the statesman and his tax edict than does another sector will consequently pay the tax with fewer inducements than this other sector will.

If legitimacy can be measured, it can be said to be inversely proportional to inducements. The value of the fewer inducements required to secure compliance from the first sector is equal to the greater amount or value of the legitimacy that that sector has accorded to the statesman. In part, the differential in inducements needed to secure compliance from the various sectors may be attributed to different valuations placed on money and on avoiding coercion. However, to explain the differential solely in such terms would be grossly to exaggerate the effects of these valuations. The differential in inducements is best understood by estimating and assessing the value of the differing amounts of legitimacy accorded to the regime and statesman. Certainly the statesman is aware of the differential and seeks as much legitimacy for himself and his decisions as he can get "economically."

Sectoral contributions to the maintenance of a military force provide another illustration of the role of legitimacy in political economy. We might say that the agreement of sectors to support a government engaged in a war abroad amounts to a purchase of security, but this is too simple a statement. The war may not threaten the vital interests of many sectors that nonetheless contribute men as well as money to the war effort. Because these sectors recognize the "right" of the government to wage war and commandeer men and money, they give up these resources to the regime without tangible compensation. If they do not consider the foreign engagement legitimate, resources may still be recruited from them, but only as a result of coercion or other inducements. The more legitimacy that is accorded to the regime and the war it is waging, the less expenditure of other resources will be required to acquire needed money and men.

In many instances a statesman may wish to elicit support by awarding honorific titles to certain prominent members of key sectors. Such honors, however, are not necessarily valued unless they confer esteem and deference from the rest of the community. If sectors consider it legitimate for the regime to grant such awards to individuals, they will not require compensation from the regime for the greater esteem and deference accorded to those honored, even though the according of honors reduces in relative terms their own receipt of esteem and deference. When legitimacy for such awards has not yet been established, the statesman must select initial recipients quite strategically in order to include leaders from all principal sectors. Thus each of the sectors receives a grant of status in return for granting its esteem and deference to all award-winners. In this way the regime gets the sectors to acknowledge the legitimacy of such awards, and hence the reallocation of prestige the awards represent. Once this legitimacy is acknowledged, the statesman may confer awards more restrictively, and no *quid pro quo* will be required to get sectors to grant esteem and deference to persons so honored.

Legitimacy is often analyzed primarily in terms of political norms or values. By regarding *political status* as the basis for the resource of legitimacy, we also include behavioral and structural aspects in our analysis. The political esteem (attitude) accorded to authority roles and their occupants leads to some political deference (activity) toward those in authority and their policies. There is nothing wrong with considering legitimacy primarily in normative terms. Admittedly, by defining legitimacy in terms parallel to those used for considering social status, we must ignore some of the nuances and complexities of legitimacy relationships. But we are prepared to forego these aspects of the study of legitimacy until it can be demonstrated that our approach to the analysis of legitimacy is less operational and less fruitful for prediction than the traditional, more normative approach. What is more, our approach seems worth pursuing because it fits in with some of the recent work in political theory.[47] Following Easton's analysis, we see political roles as differentiated by an explicit or implicit division of political labor.[48] Over time and in comparison with other regimes, a regime and its authority roles may have greater or lesser political status vis-à-vis the rest of the political community, that is, they may receive

[47] Another reason for treating legitimacy in terms of political status is that in many developing countries, social and political status are virtually coterminous. For example, Donald Levine finds "a very tenuous distinction between the occupation of high status on the one hand and the possession of authority on the other, whether the latter be conceived as the legitimated capacity to influence the actions of others or as a legitimate agency for allocating values. Men who possess a good measure of one or more of the qualities for which high status is ascribed in Amhara society—family, age, wealth, ecclesiastical rank, and political rank—are esteemed throughout the society, and their judgments and decisions are binding in their local contexts." Levine (1965:251).

[48] Easton (1965:191–193).

more or less political esteem and deference. The amount of esteem and deference accorded depends on the degree to which the political division of labor is accepted and on the extensiveness of the division—on how many and what kinds of issues are accepted as public or on the geographical areas over which the political division of labor extends. The more areas, substantive and geographical, that sectors think it proper or acceptable for the regime to regulate without giving *quid pro quo* inducements, the more legitimacy a statesman has to draw on in securing compliance from the sectors.

Legitimacy stems from the attitudes of sector members toward the political division of labor and is manifested in their activities of political deference. Like status, legitimacy is thought of as a flow rather than as a stock. Through the medium of political currency, however, claims may be stored. Sectors accord legitimacy or withhold it over time, exchanging it for resources held by the regime. At times those in authority may through coercion secure acknowledgment of the right to make binding decisions. However, conferring benefits usually yields greater political esteem and deference from the sectors. A regime's promotion of such relatively abstract values as national sovereignty, social justice, religious orthodoxy, or ideological rectitude may earn legitimacy from certain sectors. Although abstract, these values should not, however, be regarded as intangible. As goals they represent future commitments of resources that the sectors value and favor. Thus legitimacy, while less tangible than other resources, has quite tangible consequences for political exchange, and the values that prompt sectors to confer legitimacy involve quite tangible resources.

Our treatment of legitimacy as a form of status also suggests the importance of the *political prestige* of leaders, both in and out of office. To the extent that the statesman personally, apart from his role, receives political esteem and deference, he can secure compliance at less cost because of the legitimacy accorded his decisions. Similarly, the anti-statesman may trade on his political prestige to get resources from those sectors that accord esteem and deference to him. Occupancy of a political office that is accorded legitimacy status by the sectors confers political prestige on the incumbent. Yet conversely, the political prestige of the office-holder also affects the legitimacy status of the office. The statesman who acquires much political prestige on the basis of his accomplishments in office usually increases the legitimacy of the office itself, and the reverse is also true. The statesman who fails to acquire prestige may diminish the legitimacy of the office he occupies if the sectors come to put less value on the particular political division of labor.

We would suggest that there are two kinds of political currency associated with legitimacy, *allegiance* and *support*. Allegiance is accorded in differing amounts by different sectors to the authority roles of a regime. It represents a generalized acceptance of the political division of labor. In addition, it serves as a measure and store of political status, and particularly as a standard for deferred payment of political esteem and deference. Although allegiance is generally accorded to regimes, it may be given to an anti-statesman's political movement that aims at transforming the political order and establishing a reformed political community.[49]

The most important and versatile of all political currencies is support, which may be given to political leaders either in or out of office. Support is more than just a currency for legitimacy, in that it may be used by a leader to secure any resource. Indeed, it may be thought of as an IOU. When a statesman holds pledges of support from a sector, he may convert these into legitimacy for his decisions or into other sector resources. An anti-statesman can use support in the same way to obtain resources from sectors. As far as he is concerned, support is a store of value and a standard of deferred payment for legitimacy. Where an electoral system operates, support for the anti-statesman may be expressed in terms of votes. Where there is no electoral system, support may be used to secure economic resources, information, or violence.

The value of support given to the statesman or anti-statesman can be assessed only in terms of the quantity of various resources the sector will provide when he later tries to redeem the pledge. Support that cannot be converted into money or goods and services, status or prestige, information, violence or no violence, or legitimacy is worth nothing at all. Neither is support valuable to a regime or opposition if it cannot be exchanged for the resource or currency desired or needed. When an anti-statesman wants to employ violence against the regime, the support a sector gives him is worth little if it will not indeed provide him with violence.

Votes may demonstrate either allegiance or support. In plebiscites or elections to ratify a constitution, an "aye" vote indicates allegiance to the regime and its authority roles, while a "nay" vote denies legitimacy status to them. In elections where persons are chosen for office, votes manifest support for one leader or another. We know, of course, that votes may be secured by money or by force and thus may not be voluntary confirmations of legitimacy. Yet the consequences of votes secured in this way differ in degree rather than in kind from those of free elections, as the "success" of so many rigged elections attests. By and large, people will give some sup-

[49] Allegiance is accorded to what Easton would term a "regime." See Easton (1965: esp. 191–193).

port and accord some legitimacy to political leaders who have received a majority of votes by whatever means.[50]

Payment of money by a sector to the statesman or his opponents may indicate allegiance or support. As W. Arthur Lewis has said of taxation, a government will be concerned not only with equity and adequacy, but also with "the political desirability of making everybody pay some amount, however small, in direct taxes." He observes that paying a tax has in the past been a symbol of allegiance, and that "this is important in new states where the legitimacy of the Government is not always accepted." [51] He notes that taxation is also a symbol of full-fledged citizenship. Citizenship status carries with it certain rights, or established claims on resources, and is conferred in return for legitimacy granted by the individual to the state. When support is given to an anti-statesman and legitimacy is denied to the regime in authority, one indication may be the transfer of money flows from the regime to its opposition. An apt illustration is found in Young's account of Congolese politics during the period just prior to the transfer of authority from the Belgian colonial regime to an African republic:

During the terminal colonial period, when the legitimacy of the colonial state was challenged by nearly the entire population, the "people" were in a sense outside the state. . . . this withdrawal from the colonial state was consummated in the Congo when, during the last months before independence, the population in many areas ceased paying the head tax due the state and instead bought, for a roughly equivalent price, party membership cards.[52]

How support may be given to or withheld from a regime and what the regime may do to acquire it are illustrated by the relations between Nkrumah's regime and the Ashanti region in Ghana during the 1950's. In 1954, Nkrumah's party won a majority of votes in the election on the basis of its pro-independence policy. Yet after the election, Nkrumah lowered the price to be paid to producers of cocoa, the main product of Ashanti. At first the Ashanti protested. They then withdrew their support from the Convention People's Party, and helped to form an opposition party, the National Liberation Movement. The NLM received support, and thus votes and money, from the Ashanti. NLM supporters increasingly disobeyed government directives, and during the height of the conflict be-

[50] It should be noted that freely-given consent may be freely withdrawn, so that such support may be less stable than that coerced or "bought."

[51] Lewis (1966:126).

[52] Young (1964:273).

tween the CPP and NLM, violence was used against CPP supporters. Through the use of economic inducements (selective loans to cocoa farmers), ideological appeals to the young Ashanti (promises of preferable resource allocations in the future), and the application of coercion where it appeared necessary, Nkrumah won back some support and was eventually able to reintegrate Ashanti into the political life of Ghana.[53] Throughout his political career, however, one of Nkrumah's strongest claims to legitimacy was his militancy and success against colonial rule. As economic progress became more and more the criterion for legitimacy status, and the regime delivered fewer and fewer promised goods and services, Nkrumah's support fell, and finally, so did he.

To understand why sectors do not cease their compliance pending new agreements whenever a new regime takes over the authority roles, or why a sector closely allied with an ousted statesman nonetheless complies to some extent with the decisions of his hostile successor, we need to consider the importance of authority roles per se. These roles may and usually do receive some legitimacy from sectors quite apart from their particular occupants at the moment. To the extent that the roles are considered legitimate in themselves, certain resources will accrue to them, and thus to any persons occupying them. At least initially, successors may receive more or less the same legitimacy as their predecessors did, and may therefore receive similar flows of resources from the sectors; this is what happens in the "routinization of charisma." A particular division of political labor is legitimated through continuous exchanges with the sectors. Political prestige is transformed into political status for certain roles, which in turn confer political prestige on whoever occupy them. Seldom have political leaders in developing countries sought to destroy existing authority roles. Rather they have aimed at occupying the roles themselves. Many, in order to enjoy the legitimacy previously accorded to these roles as well as the other resources the roles have commanded, have continued to invoke the symbols of colonial or *ancien régime* authority.[54]

[53] See Apter (1963a:68n) and Lewis (1965:53). See also Nkrumah (1968:57).

[54] In an effort to capitalize on the power of colonial authority roles, each of the post-independence Presidents in Ghana, Guinea, Mali, and Senegal took up residence in the former governor's palace. In the Ivory Coast, President Houphouet-Boigny chose to raze the governor's palace, which had recently been modernized at great expense. He had erected on the same spot "a glass, steel and marble marvel which leaves no doubt as to where the power lies." Zolberg (1966:110–111).

AUTHORITY.

To treat authority as a resource, we must clearly distinguish it from power. Power is often considered to be synonymous with authority because those in authority possess resources as means to power. It must be remembered, however, that there are some persons who have authority, but little or no power. The difference between power and authority is a critical one for political science. Authority is the right to speak in the name of the state and to declare public policies. It derives from the occupancy of authority roles. Power, the ability to secure compliance, derives from the net resource advantage of a regime or sector. To the extent that a person occupying an authority role has resources at his disposal, he has potential power. Furthermore, to the extent that he is accorded legitimacy, he can secure more compliance with a given amount of other resources than he could if he were a private individual having only non-legitimate power means. Having only non-legitimate sources of power does not necessarily make the private individual less powerful than the man in authority. With sufficient money, status, information, or violence a private individual may be able to get his preferences implemented by others. Still, other resources being equal, the addition of legitimacy gives a person more power.

Easton suggests that "every system has roles through which authority is wielded, and some rules governing the use and exercise of political power. The fact of occupying these roles and of abiding by the rules applying to them will normally in and of itself place the seal of moral approval on the authorities." [55] Conferral of legitimacy on the possessors of authority is not, however, an all-or-nothing proposition. Even if authorities follow the "rules," some sectors may not regard certain areas as legitimate for government action. Thus we need to distinguish amounts of legitimacy accorded by different sectors to authoritative decisions in different areas. The effectiveness of authority may be augmented by the political prestige of an individual leader, by shrewd "payoffs" to certain sectors, or by the use of coercion. Legitimacy and authority, therefore, should not be equated. It is possible, at least in theory, that occupants of authority roles could have no legitimacy whatsoever. With enough other resources, compliance with public policies might still be secured.

Authority is likely to be valued by any individual or sector. Through the exercise of authority, some sectors can obtain advantageous allocations of resources more "cheaply" than they otherwise could. For this reason then,

[55] Easton (1965:299).

it is worthwhile for a sector to relinquish certain resources to the statesman in return for the right to make or influence authoritative decisions in certain areas of interest. (Of course, it is unlikely that a sector would pay more for a share of authority than it would to secure the same benefits through private channels.) To secure other resources in exchange, therefore, the statesman may delegate his authority, permitting sectors to speak in the name of the state on certain issues or allowing them to influence certain of his policy decisions.

Because authority presumes maintenance of a superior-subordinate relationship, it is by definition a scarce resource. If all have equal authority, none can secure compliance with decisions or preferences. The more persons who are able to speak in the name of the state, the more conflict there will be over what authoritative allocations should be made. The greater the conflict, the less effective authority will be in achieving any particular objective. Thus authority derives its value from the fact that its possessor has a monopoly. The less widely authority is shared, the more a sector will usually be willing to pay for a share in it. The regime may ask a higher price for authority than a sector is willing to pay—i.e., the benefits a sector expects to get may not be commensurate with the cost of securing them—but participation in authoritative decision-making is desired by sectors as long as the price does not exceed the benefits they expect to receive.[56]

It may be difficult to see how authority is allocated. Appointments to government posts allocate certain measures of authority. The statesman may wish to have final authority on all public decisions, but in practice, especially for less than major issues, authority is delegated to subordinates. Thus to appoint as Minister of Agriculture a university professor of agricultural economics rather than a large landholder or the secretary-general of a peasant's organization is to give the intellectual or professional sector some

---

[56] It is understandable that sectors would want to participate in authoritative decision-making. In discussing politics in West Africa, Lewis argues in favor of regimes that give all sectors, and especially minority groups, an opportunity to participate in decisions. Such political arrangements will, he says, make members of minorities full members of the nation, respected by their more numerous brethren, and owing equal respect to the national bond that holds them together. See Lewis (1965:57, 65, 72). In our terms, granting a share in authority to minority sectors also confers some status on them, and these otherwise dissident groups will give legitimacy to the government and accept its authority. If not given some authority or influence, minorities might not comply with regime policies unless the regime expended some coercion or threats of coercion.

authority that the other sectors do not enjoy. Appointments usually involve fairly specific allocations of authority. For example, the Minister of Agriculture will probably not be able to determine which trunk roads will be improved during the coming fiscal year. Authority to make this choice will probably belong, if only temporarily, to a person representing the interests of another sector or group of sectors.

Through the appointment of supervisory bodies to control the operations of certain government activities, authority can be allocated quite specifically. Certain sectors will be represented, others not. Those sectors without representation are denied authority in the particular area in question. The larger the supervisory committee and/or the more numerous and diverse the sectors represented, the less value will be attributed to the share of authority granted to any participating sector. Although the authority of Members of Parliament varies from country to country and over time, and is often not very great, still, a regime which controls party nominations to Parliament can allocate some limited share of authority to sector representatives in this way.

The point we would emphasize is that while authority is allocated to individuals, not to sectors, individuals must be seen as representatives of sector interests. We make no assumption that every person is narrowly attached to the interests of one or a few sectors, but we take it as evident that no person in any important position of authority can satisfy all demands, and thus must favor some sectors over others. To impose egalitarian and presumably impartial allocations is to abet the interests of the previously less favored; to perpetuate the status quo favors the privileged. Appointments and nominations confer authority or influence of value; otherwise sectors would make no special effort to get these for their members.

If the statesman can avoid doing so, he will not grant authority outright to a sector, except in some matters of self-regulation, such as, for example, when coffee planters are permitted to set acreage allotments or doctors are permitted to issue medical licenses without any appeal to the regime. Persons who do not occupy acknowledged authority roles usually derive little benefit from grants of authority per se. It is unlikely a tax levied by industrialists for their own benefit would be paid by other sectors. If, however, the tax were levied by the regime or a legitimate legislative institution, the situation would be different. Sectors would probably pay an excise tax on consumer goods, the revenues from which would subsidize industrial investment by private persons. Thus getting the statesman to promulgate desired decisions authoritatively is usually acceptable to sectors in lieu of direct authority. The statesman is usually reluctant to grant authority to a sector because that authority may be used contrary to his wishes and may not be readily reclaimed once it is delegated. If, for example, he gives a farmers association authority over marketing, and this association discriminates against small peasants, he may have to invest considerable resources to get that authority back. This will be true especially if by using the resources accruing to the authority it was granted, the association has developed some amount of legitimacy for its operations.

Rather than delegating authority outright, the statesman usually prefers to give sectors *influence* on policies in certain areas. Influence serves as a currency for authority in that it is a store and measure of value, a medium of exchange, and in particular a standard for deferred payment. If too many sectors are given an opportunity to influence policy in a certain area, the influence given will be inflated and depreciated in value. The different demands of the sectors will nullify each other, and influence will yield to none the desired policy.

Influence may be granted over as narrow an area as soybean price supports or over as wide an area as agricultural policy as a whole. The distribution of influence, like that of authority, is reasonably tangible, though not always easily discernible. For example, a regime may give landowners a large measure of influence over agricultural policy in order to secure their support on other issues. Business interests and labor unions may vie for influence over wage policy and over decisions limiting or sanctioning collective bargaining. The amount a policy diverges from the statesman's own preferences indicates the amount of influence he has granted one sector or another, probably in return for needed resources or currencies. The most influential sectors will be able to affect authoritative decisions on many issues. The statesman will know reasonably well which sectors have how much influence in what areas and what this influence will cost him in terms of achieving his own goals. Except where a regime accords some influence to sectors within its core combination and ideological bias, it requires some *quid pro quo* for influence, whether it be support, economic contributions, or whatever. The amount and distribution of influence in circulation change over time. It should be possible, however, to assess and perhaps to measure influence on authoritative decisions at any one time.[57]

[57] Much of the writing on influence in American political science equates influence with power. As such, influence becomes a proxy for the sum of diverse political resources. See Dahl (1957) and (1963: Chap. V). While "social standing" or money contributions may influence authoritative decisions, they do so only if the person in authority chooses to accept these positive inducements.

Faced with a sector's demands for certain authoritative decisions, a regime may defer meeting them by promising that sector influence over certain future decisions. By issuing this political currency, the statesman may reduce immediate claims on the polity's scarce resources. Another reason the statesman prefers granting influence rather than authority is that he can control when, how, or if the former is converted into authoritative decisions favorable to the sector. He may even invalidate influence if he so chooses, although to do this of course involves costs. The sector may retaliate by voiding currency it has given to the regime or by withdrawing its resources.[58] Whenever possible, the statesman will probably prefer to keep the right to speak in the name of the state for himself and his regime.

When given, authority is usually only delegated, e.g., lent, in which case it may be reclaimed. In such circumstances the authority wielded by the sector is not final, and sector decisions may be appealed to the regime for a definitive ruling. We can see how authority might also be invested, that is, spent or lent to augment its future value and that of other resources.[59] A statesman might well decide to invest some authority in an extended local government structure, granting to that structure the right to levy taxes and conscript labor for local development projects. If all authoritative pronouncements were complied with, greater resources would probably be received from the sectors, and the delegated authority would have the same or greater value. On the other hand, if compliance were negligible, speaking in the name of the state in this particular area would yield nil resources, and the authority itself would depreciate in value.

Thus we think it important to treat influence as separate from the various political resources used to affect the exercise of authority. Status or money do not automatically influence decisions, nor does violence, for that matter. The statesman—or mayor—still has some discretion, though he must face the consequences of his choice. Various studies of political influence, authority, and power are Banfield (1961); Dahl (1961); Bachrach and Baratz (1962:947–952); Hunter (1953); Mills (1956); March (1965:431–451) and (1966:68–70); and Parsons (1966).

[58] The Ashanti supported Nkrumah in 1954 in part because they believed that they would have more influence over cocoa prices if Africans rather than British occupied positions of authority. Whether Nkrumah actually promised the Ashanti such influence is not clear. Once he was re-elected as Prime Minister, they certainly pressed for influence over this price policy. When it was clear they could not influence his decision, they withdrew their support and other resources.

[59] As we noted in Chapter II, investment transactions differ from expenditures only in degree, in that they involve a longer time horizon and greater uncertainty of return or benefit.

To return to the relationship between authority and power, we may say of authority that to the extent its supply is monopolistically controlled, its price will depend on the sector demand for it. This demand, in turn, is a function of the effectiveness of authority in securing compliance, in other words, a function of power. As a regime's resources increase, its power is likely to increase, and hence the demand for and value of authority would increase. Of particular importance is legitimacy, which can increase compliance without direct reciprocal expenditure of regime resources, though indirect expenditure is usually involved. As the regime's authority is increasingly accepted as legitimate, its power increases, as does its ability to command resources from sectors in exchange for granting sectors influence or participation in authoritative decisions.

Since a regime's control over resources is also a function of its power, it is easy to see how a "vicious circle" of weak authority could persist.[60] One of the principal problems for regimes in developing countries is the small degree of control they can exercise over economic and social resources. Until the process of nationalization has reduced the autonomy of subsistence economies, social stratifications, and polities, demand for participation in the central authority will be low, and the statesman will be less able to secure resources with his prime resource.[61] One thing is clear. The more skillfully the statesman uses the authority he has, the greater sector demand will be for influence and a share in authority.

Compliance

From the statesman's point of view, the acquisition and use of resources are meant to secure compliance with his policy choices. His goal is not the simple maximization of resources. It profits him little if he has great coercive power at his disposal but cannot convert members of sectors to his preferred ideological persuasion. Even if he has some measure of political status, it is possible that all his power cannot secure the social esteem and deference he desires. His resources may be quite sufficient to keep him in

[60] In Chapter IV we discuss how a regime may avoid a "low legitimacy" trap that might be thought of as similar to the "low productivity" trap postulated in the literature on economic development.

[61] Zolberg points out that in West Africa half to two-thirds of economic production is in the subsistence sector and is "practically speaking, outside the domain of the party-state's allocative authority, even when it claims the legal right to make decisions that affect it. Yet there can be no doubt that in this residual sector rules and regulations exist, together with authoritative agencies to settle disputes, change rules, enforce obligations, etc." Zolberg (1966:132–133).

authority but may not be sufficient or appropriate for making long-range investments to centralize and socialize the economy. Though it is usually preferable to have more rather than less of any and all positive resources, the statesman will measure his success in qualitative rather than quantitative terms.

The resources that a statesman wants or needs are those that will secure compliance from the sectors for his policy choices. Depending on the positive and negative inducements, sectors can provide economic resources, status, information, violence or no violence, and legitimacy. To get these the statesman can give or threaten to reduce economic resources, status, information, coercion or no coercion, and authority. These are his factors of political production. Sectors in most cases will prefer authority to other resources because it can secure any or most of the others. So, too, the statesman desires legitimacy status, which reduces the cost of securing other resources. If he had his choice, he would usually prefer to secure compliance with his policies entirely on the basis of legitimacy, because this course would involve the least direct cost to his regime. But because according legitimacy status to the regime has real costs to the sectors, sectors are unlikely to accept such a compliance relationship indefinitely or to make it unconditional.

It is possible, though unusual, for a regime to rule entirely by coercion. Though no legitimacy might be accorded to the self-appointed authorities who had conquered a community by force, compliance might initially be secured without any positive inducements to the sectors.[62] The resulting political division of labor might begin to receive minimal acceptance as the new rulers provided some benefits, perhaps a reduction in coercion and the distribution of some goods and services.[63] Generally, compliance based strictly on coercion or legitimacy, whether for a single policy or for the aggregate of regime policies, is unstable. As we will discuss in the next chapter, the marginal utility of any one resource to the sectors, and therefore the marginal productivity of any resource to the regime, is unlikely to re-

[62] Under a conquest regime there may be a quisling sector that accords legitimacy to the rulers and receives economic and other benefits. Other sectors might accord this sector negative esteem because of its collaboration, but if the regime were willing to spend enough coercion, it might force the sectors to give the quislings ostensible deference.

[63] Such a situation was found in Arab areas occupied by Israel in June, 1967. At first, compliance with Israeli commanders was secured only through force or threats of force. But as food and relief were given, some minimal legitimacy, even if deemed "temporary," was accorded. Compliance then could be obtained with less expenditure of force or threats. How much legitimacy will be accorded or for how long remains uncertain.

main steady over time. Therefore, the regime will usually use some combination of resources in trying to secure compliance. This is especially true because sectors generally value positive inducements—economic resources, status, information, and authority—most highly. The mixture of resources offered to the sectors will vary over time, either from policy to policy, or in the aggregate. The particular combination of resources used to achieve certain policy objectives is determined through the process of political exchange.

The points we are making about compliance can best be understood diagrammatically. In Figure 3, the vertical bars represent alternative combinations of resources which may be used as inducements to secure compliance with a single policy or with the sum of regime policies. At one extreme would be only coercion (A), while at the other would be legitimacy (I). Intermediate would be combinations that included some of each plus larger or smaller amounts of positive inducements. The heavy lines within the margin represent parameters of securing compliance. These parameters are determined by the interaction of sectoral propensities and the regime's resource position. The parameters suggested in Figure 3 are ideal-typical; they would differ for each regime and probably would differ for particular policies. The rectangular margins of the diagram are also ideal-typical and could be practically any polygon, the shape and dimensions of which would be affected by the aggregate supply and demand of resources.

INDUCEMENTS

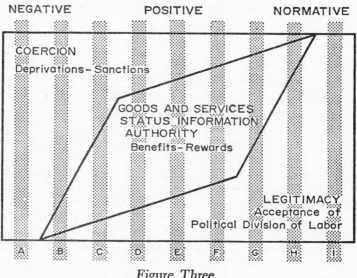

Figure Three.

The diagram may also be used to suggest the differential relationship of sectors to the regime. Sectors in the extra-stability group would comply only with Combination A because they accorded the regime no legitimacy and it would offer them no positive inducements. Core combination sectors would enjoy whatever combination of resources they regarded as most favorable, perhaps Combination F, while those sectors in the stability group would most likely receive Combination C or D. By varying the construction of such a diagram, we could depict alternative combinations of resources used to secure compliance in different political communities, from different sectors, or with different policies. However, use of this simple diagram requires an understanding of political exchange, which is the subject of our next chapter.

Ambiguous Factors

Several factors of relevance to politics have not been treated in our scheme. These may or may not be thought of as resources. Let us take *obedience* as an example. To simplify our presentation of political resources and to reduce ambiguity, we have not included obedience with other resources, though it might be regarded as a resource that the statesman needs and the sectors either give or withhold. The principal difficulty in discussing obedience as a resource is that obedience is virtually synonymous with compliance. Moreover, almost all kinds of obedience can be seen in terms of the resources we have already described. Payment of taxes is giving money or goods and services; military conscription is rendering of a service to the regime; responding to a census is giving information; halting brigandage is refraining from violence; and so forth. Obedience may also be treated generically as a function of legitimacy status accorded to the authorities, that is, as political deference. Obedience as a function of legitimacy may thus be manifested as giving up or withholding other resources as directed by the authorities.

Still, there are some areas of behavior that have political consequences and affect the exercise of authority but do not involve one of the more tangible resources. Obeying traffic laws upholds authority and disobeying them undermines it. A regime employs coercion or economic penalties when traffic laws are broken. Some form of political exchange is involved here, but it stretches the imagination to regard driving legally as a service. Possibly obedience should be regarded as a factor of political production not fully accounted for by our scheme of resources. Almond and Powell include sector obedience and regime regulations of behavior in their exchange model. At this stage in the development of our model, we prefer to try to analyze political interaction without adding obedience as a distinct resource. Those activities and attitudes that have political consequences but are not covered by the other resources appear to be relatively unimportant.

Time is clearly relevant to political analysis and has been considered by some as having resource characteristics (witness the adage "time is money"). We do not include time as a resource in our model for various reasons, but it deserves some consideration because of its productivity and its frequent scarcity in politics.[64] Only in an abstract sense is time a "free good" like air. Whereas time itself is infinite, the length of time in which a certain action may or must be accomplished is not. As in economics, the value of a resource is some function of how long it is possessed. The longer a resource is held, the greater opportunity there is for continuing use or possibility of putting it to more productive use if such an opportunity presents itself. Still, time by itself produces nothing. Rather it represents one aspect of a resource's value.

The language of politics takes note of the productive characteristics of time when it refers to "bargaining for time." As a rule, the more quickly a regime seeks compliance with a given policy, the greater the expenditure of resources that will be required to secure compliance. It generally costs a regime dearly to achieve a goal if it has little time in which to do so. On the other hand, being able to wait for a result can save resources. If time were treated analytically in resource terms, its currency would probably be *deadlines*. These fix time limits within which processes or actions are to be completed. They can be exchanged and are subject to inflation and depreciation. In our analysis we treat the temporal element of political bargaining and valuation only implicitly. A more complete analysis of the political process would have to consider time more specifically in all its calculations.

Let us also consider *symbols*. Though symbols clearly play an important role in the political process, we do not regard them as a political resource or currency. In our model they *represent* currencies and resources.[65] Since

[64] For an extended discussion of the relationship between time and resources, see Uphoff and Ilchman (1968).

[65] Deutsch says of his cybernetic model of politics that extending it would involve "the exploration of such matters as legitimacy and its symbols, which may turn out to be a currency in some of the interchanges between politics and culture." Deutsch (1963:127).

their value will depreciate if they are not used sparingly and skillfully, and since the resources they stand for are themselves limited, symbols cannot be regarded as "free goods." Extraction of resources from sectors by means of manipulation of symbols involves real costs to the sectors, which may not accept losses without some compensation in return. (Although they may be prevented by symbols from perceiving the loss, this may not and need not continue indefinitely.) Furthermore, the effectiveness of symbols may depend on political investments in infrastructure such as ideology, or behavioral parameters such as patriotism.

Symbols are ubiquitous in politics, as Edelman illustrates in his book, *The Symbolic Uses of Politics*. We feel that a better title for the book might have been *The Political Uses of Symbols*. There are symbols representing the full range of political resources. Status symbols are signs of individual prestige. What are called symbols of authority are more often than not symbols of legitimacy status signifying the propriety of the office and its incumbent. A "show of force" is a symbolic threat of coercion or violence. All information is communicated through symbols. The productive as well as the distributive aspects of political symbols have been recognized, though they have seldom been systematically examined.[66] Symbols may often be used, as Almond and Powell point out, with relatively little cost to the regime. Edelman suggests how symbols may be used to reduce a regime's expenditure of resources.[67] Political symbols always stand for resources or currencies such as status or support. Even if they themselves are intangible, they represent quite tangible activities and attitudes. The effects of symbols must be tangible or the symbols have no import for political analysis.

All resources and currencies, ambiguous or obvious, are characterized by their value to persons. We agree with W. D. Lamont that there is a distinction between "value-in-use" and "value-in-exchange." [68] Our analysis is in terms of the latter. We do not consider values per se; value for our resources is designated by the price they command in exchange. Thus our discussion of resources remains abstract until we relate it to political exchange. To that task we now turn.

[66] For short but useful statements on this matter, see Edelman (1964:13–14); Easton (1965:356, 465); and Almond and Powell (1966:199–201).
[67] Edelman (1964:24–28).
[68] Lamont (1955:23–29, 59–73).

IV

POLITICAL EXCHANGE

> The success of the Indonesian Revolution . . . meant an opportunity [for indigenous businessmen] to legislate a new and commanding business position into existence, to stabilize themselves by means of their political influence, and to start reaping handsome profits, again not because their business and managerial skills could not be fully utilized or deployed, but because they could capitalize on their political position and connections.
>
> Justin van de Kroef [1]

By giving support to Sukarno and other nationalist leaders immediately after World War II, Indonesian businessmen, however much they may have sympathized ideologically with the independence movement, saw an opportunity to improve their resource position. If an Indonesian regime could come to occupy the national authority roles, members of the business sector could expect political influence and a higher place in the country's political stratification. Though the support pledged by businessmen may have appeared to be a simple gift, more intricate exchange relationships were involved. The amount of support businessmen gave to the independence movement varied according to their expectations that the Dutch could and would be ousted, and that they themselves would be given influence over economic policy under nationalist rule. They sought this influence in order to affect government decisions on licensing, imports of raw materials, currency exchange rates, subsidization of enterprises, and taxation. While the exact amount of economic resources to be gained through influence could not be determined, businessmen expected that it would be substantial.

To what uses could the nationalists have put the support of businessmen? Since support is the most generalized political currency, it might in

[1] van de Kroef (1955:125).

principle have been converted into any of the other resources, but the independence movement needed certain specific resources, and businessmen had only certain resources to give. The violence they could contribute against the colonial regime was minimal. Their esteem and deference were not particularly prized. They possessed little information of political utility. However, their support could yield economic contributions, and these in turn could finance the movement's activities and equip and maintain its armed forces. While other sectors supplied violence, information, and services, and withdrew their general support from the Dutch incumbents, businessmen helped finance the campaign for independence.

Thus when the nationalist regime did oust the Dutch authorities, it did not begin its rule with a free hand on economic matters. Its commercial and industrial policies were "mortgaged" to some extent. If its policies were not necessarily the most productive for development of the economy as a whole, they still benefited those sectors that had helped make the achievement of independence possible. We cannot say whether Sukarno's regime could have afforded politically to default in its obligations to the business sector. We do not know how valuable continued support from this sector was to the regime, or what would have been the cost of sanctions the business sector could impose if the influence promised it were not accorded. Nor do we know the cost of obtaining equally valuable support from other sectors, or whether the support of the business sector was indeed replaceable. Perhaps the cost of reducing this sector's privileges would have been in terms of ideological values, inasmuch as the regime favored development of indigenous enterprise. While Indonesian businessmen were not in the regime's core combination, they seemed to be within its ideological bias.[2]

Eventually the pursuit of policies benefiting the business sector led to a loss of support from other, more powerful sectors as inflation spiraled, standards of living fell (except for businessmen), and the economy stagnated. Achievement of economic development, it turned out, was inconsistent with other economic policies and sectoral preferences. However, to understand the political consequences of the different policy alternatives open to Sukarno, we must first understand the workings of political exchange. The statesman has to estimate the costs and benefits of different exchanges with various sectors and choose which exchanges to make or maintain and which to avoid or terminate. Political economy should help to clarify the ramifications of such political decisions.

[2] For a useful debate on the economic consequences of Sukarno's political commitments, see Schmidt (1962); and Glassburner (1962) and (1963).

Most goods and services, status, and information are exchanged directly between members of sectors without regime interference or involvement. These exchanges are not political. However, many exchanges involve authority or other resources held by the regime. Whenever sectors use resources to affect public policy or the statesman combines his resources into policies affecting resource allocation and aiming at compliance, these exchanges are political. According to the situation, exchanges may be on a large or small scale, continuous or intermittent, explicit or implicit. They are often characterized by what Carl J. Friedrich calls "anticipated reactions." [3] In exchanges, offers and actions are commonly premised on calculations of what a regime or sector thinks the other will accept.

Although we tend to speak of exchanges as separate transactions, we do so for the purposes of analysis and exposition. In practice exchanges seldom occur in isolated, explicit, or barter situations. Rather resources are usually exchanged as flows, with changes made at one time affecting subsequent flows. As in economics, calculations are made essentially by comparing the marginal value of particular resources with that of other resources.[4] As a rule, prevailing values or exchange rates established by past patterns of supply and demand determine the amounts and directions of resources exchanged. Valuations are usually determined according to the respective and relative supply and demand for each resource. When there are changes in supply or demand in the political market, more explicit bargaining between possessors of resources may occur. To the extent that authority is more effective or economical than other resources in obtaining more favorable allocations, less exchange within a society will be outside the political market.[5]

[3] Friedrich (1950:49) and (1963: Chap. XI).

[4] While we draw on a number of the basic concepts of economic exchange, we are not attempting to incorporate into our model the whole conceptual apparatus of economics. Boulding (1962) has gently criticized Homans' work (1961) for not utilizing more fully the economic theory of exchange. We think that it would be pretentious and premature for us to attempt at this stage of the model's development any calculation of indifference curves, bargaining paths, Pareto optima, or the like. The conceptualization and measurement of political resources has not yet progressed far enough. Indeed, political economy may not get much beyond hypothetical and illustrative representations of such relationships, but then neither has the discipline of economics moved much beyond the theoretical calculation of such elements of exchange.

[5] Although Homans does not suggest the kind of distinction between economic, social, and political markets that we find useful, he feels that the notion of exchange is a valuable integrating concept. We would agree. The principles of exchange can illuminate interaction, whether the interaction is that of small

Markets

The scope of economic, social, and political interaction and exchange varies over time and between countries. As we suggested in Chapter II, we find it useful to think in terms of three markets within which the exchange of economic, social, and political resources takes place. It is possible, however, for exchanges to take place between as well as within markets, so that economic resources, for example, might be exchanged for authority, or authority for status.[6] When we examine exchange in developing countries, it may also be helpful to think in terms of dual sets of markets with exchange going on more or less at two levels. Central markets for goods and services, status, and authority have prices, criteria, or standards that apply more or less nationwide, though participants in these markets may only constitute a small proportion of the population.[7] On the other hand, exchange of economic, social, and political resources may occur within a plurality of smaller peripheral markets that are limited in scope and function and operate more or less on a subsistence basis. These markets have been conventionally regarded as "traditional" to distinguish them from the more "modern" central markets. In using this rough distinction, we attribute no particular set of values or behavior patterns to one type of market or the other, but rather define each in terms of the scope of its interaction and exchange.[8]

groups or that of massive structures such as classes, firms, communities, and societies. See Homans (1957) for the initial presentation of his approach, and Homans (1961) for an expansion and elaboration of it.

[6] While our terminology differs in some respects from that of Aaron Wildavsky, his conception of political markets (he calls them "public arenas") is similar to ours. For an interesting article in what may be thought of as the emerging tradition of political economy, see Wildavsky (1965). For a theoretical discussion of politics as exchange of values, building critically on Dahl's consideration of power and resources, see Harsanyi (1962).

[7] We do not mean to imply that all sectors receive equal treatment within central or national markets. Sectors in the core combination may have an advantageous position vis-à-vis the regime, while other sectors may be only marginal customers to which different rates of exchange apply. A central market is not necessarily egalitarian, but it is characterized by its extensive scope. The implications of egalitarianism for exchange relationships in the political market will be considered in Chapter VI.

[8] We would like to call attention to Cyril E. Black's discussion of modernization (1966). Black regards modernization as a process of adapting historically

NATIONALIZATION.

The central or national institutions that govern the exchange of economic, social, and political resources usually affect only a part of all the resources exchanged within a country. Yet as development proceeds, these national institutions become increasingly important in people's lives. Very few villages remain untouched by the national economy or by the use of money as a medium of exchange. As goods and services are exchanged between the national economic market and various local markets, there is a degree of nationalization or centralization. The same is true for status and authority in the social and political markets.

Neither "nationalization" nor "centralization" is a very satisfactory term. Nationalization has political connotations implying expropriation, and the term is now associated with the notion of "nation-building." What we mean by nationalization is akin to nation-building, but we make no assumptions about "requisites" or "prerequisites" in our analysis. Rather we feel that it should be possible to describe a particular situation and calculate how it might be improved to the statesman's advantage. Centralization has been interpreted to mean that the center has total control, whereas what is involved in our analysis is a reorientation of activity toward a central set of institutions and values by means of which interaction and activity take place. The process we are describing is one in which central institutions of national scope assume increased importance in the lives of persons, whether these persons participate directly or not. It is not our intention to analyze the process of nationalization or to discuss measurement of change. Rather we wish to introduce a way of thinking about the process in order better to understand the political economy of change. The fact that local and central markets are not integrated and much exchange takes place outside the control and even the knowledge of central authorities affects the choices a statesman must make and conditions the effectiveness of his policy instruments.[9]

evolved institutions to rapidly changing requirements. His emphasis on adaptation underscores the probability that many features of traditional institutions will survive. While he notes a growing similarity of functions in Japan and France, the U.S. and the U.S.S.R., and Mexico and Poland, he sees no comparable convergence of institutions. Like Black, we believe there is no true dichotomy between what is "traditional" and what is "modern." Yet for the sake of discussion and analysis, we speak of institutions or structures as being one or the other, and thus make gross commonsense distinctions. See also Rudolph (1965) and Whitaker (1967).

[9] See Kunkel (1961:51) and Zolberg (1966:128–134).

The process of monetization—through which economic exchange is generalized and economic relations become national in scope—is well recognized. Certainly the extent of monetization affects the power of any statesman in a developing country: the greater the extent of monetization, the greater access he has to resources. Similarly, in countries where there is still a plurality of status criteria and little generalized social exchange among traditional communities, a regime is hindered in any efforts to reallocate status on a national basis. If diverse or traditional criteria dominate, a statesman cannot readily, for example, upgrade an untouchable caste or raise the status of women. Developing a national status market with common standards for according status may therefore be of great importance to the statesman. Otherwise he cannot use status effectively as a political resource. Nationalization of the economic, social, and political markets need not proceed at the same pace though the three markets are not really autonomous. Nationalization of one will usually affect nationalization of the others.[10] Thus monetization may hasten the reorientation of local social and political markets toward exchanges of status and authority on a national scale. Indeed, some of the problems and demands a statesman faces may originate from disparities in the nationalization of the various markets.

In the sphere of social relations, the nationalization process may be described as "social mobilization." [11] Changes in literacy, urbanization, and occupational mobility certainly contribute to development of a national status market and have consequences for the economic and political markets as well. Rates of social mobilization may be measured and correlated, as Deutsch has done; the process is quite real. We would prefer, however, to deal with social mobilization in terms of the three markets. In this way it is seen and described as less monolithic than the certitude of aggregate statistics would suggest. Our approach provides members of sectors and statesmen more latitude for making choices.[12]

[10] In this regard, Fallers maintains that roles are essentially determined by the supply of goods and services that serve as facilities for performance of roles or as symbols expressive of them. Thus changes in the supply and control of goods and services exert an influence on social stratification. He notes also that the distribution of authority and influence is itself influenced by stratification systems, much in the way that economic systems are. See Fallers (1963).

[11] Deutsch (1963).

[12] For an interesting study bearing out the "selectivity" of acceptance of integration into national markets, see Kunkel (1961).

POLITICIZATION.

The politicization of a country is comparable to the monetization of a national economy. As the politicization process advances, an increasing share of the efforts to alter or preserve allocations of resources is channeled through national political institutions. Monetization and social mobilization may contribute to these efforts, but they are separate and often independent processes. What Zolberg describes in West Africa as "an increased awareness of the central authorities, [with] . . . more demands . . . directed at them," is politicization.[13]

In so-called traditional societies, allocations of resources and rates of exchange are more or less stable. However, contact with more industrialized nations has introduced new values and patterns of exchange which have given rise to conflicting demands for change or protection of allocations. While many of these demands may be resolved by accommodating exchanges between sectors many more are now presented to the regime. The regime is expected to use its resources, especially its authority, to make or prevent changes in allocation. The regime's ability to deal with rising demands is circumscribed by the relatively narrow bounds within which the exercise of authority is acknowledged as legitimate. The proportion of issues and persons considered legitimately subject to central authority is much smaller in the developing than in the more developed countries. As a consequence, regimes have less legitimacy status to draw on in seeking compliance with their decisions and must employ a proportionately larger amount of other resources as positive or negative inducements for compliance. Thus a paucity of legitimacy status increases the statesman's need for other resources, which are, of course, also scarce.

Demands for change mount as a result of what has been termed "rising expectations," but all these demands are not compatible.[14] Demands for more progressive or for more conservative policies place greater strain on the statesman's resource position, but they also enable the statesman to bargain for increased legitimacy from the sectors. As the process of politicization extends the legitimate boundaries of authority and brings about acceptance of a more broadly based political division of labor within the

[13] Zolberg (1966:41). An interesting discussion of politicization which treats it in part as a function of nationalization and social mobilization can be found in Rokkan (1966:250–252).

[14] See Deutsch (1961:497–498). Unfortunately, Deutsch pays little attention to the demands and pressures from more conservative sectors which have vested interests in the status quo. These sectors often possess more political power than the more numerous disadvantaged groups. See also Lerner (1963).

community, the regime should be better able to secure compliance from the sectors. Of course, the statesman bargains for other resources besides legitimacy. If he does not, he will face serious political inflation as demands drastically outstrip supply. To deal with such a situation, we must analyze supply and demand according to the terms of political economy.

Supply and Demand

EXCHANGE RATES OR PRICE.

The value of political resources is determined by the interaction of supply and demand in much the same way that money prices are set for goods and services. In political economy, because of the diversity of resources and the absence of a common denominator of value such as money, the *price* or value of a resource amounts to an *exchange rate*: how much of one resource would be given up to gain a given amount of another resource. Although, as we have noted, we speak of exchanges in simple, even barter terms, what is involved is a process of adjusting supply and demand. This process takes place over time through marginal changes in the flow of resources between sectors and regime. Thus the satisfactions and sanctions of one period have consequences for supply and demand during the next period.

Resources produced and consumed within a sector provide satisfactions and have value, but as they remain outside the public domain we do not consider them here. In political economy values can only be determined for resources used in exchanges with a regime or other sectors. Each regime and sector places a different value on a particular status or piece of information. Thus there is no way to ascertain the value of a resource except through its ratio to other resources—i.e., how much of another resource would be given up to gain that particular status or piece of information. In other words, the value of a resource possessed by a regime or sector should be considered equal to the value of those resources its possessors can secure for it through exchange. We recognize that there are philosophical as well as practical problems in arriving at valuation when no absolute fixed standard exists and valuations vary intersubjectively. However, when concrete alternatives are posed—is *x* increase in status worth *y* amount of money?—relative valuations, if only intuitive, become much easier to make and are more tangible.[15]

In arriving at a value for a resource, a regime or sector must take into

[15] Lamont (1955). See also Curry and Wade (1968:9–26).

account the opportunity costs of alternative uses to which the resource may be put. If the resource is consumed, it cannot be exchanged. If given to one sector, it cannot be granted to another. This fact of opportunity costs clearly applies to economic resources, but some qualifications must be made for other resources. Status is valued not only in absolute, but also in relative terms. Sectors usually want not just more esteem and deference, but more than others have, especially more than those sectors with which they are in competition. Thus if a regime granted more status to the trade unions, it might receive a larger flow of resources from them, but other sectors such as the business sector might reduce their contributions to the regime. The net gain or loss resulting from according more status to the unions may be greater or less than that which would result from giving the same increase in status to businessmen. A regime needs to weigh both alternatives and others as well when it seeks to use status as an inducement. The opportunity costs are varied but real. To increase the status of both sectors equally would perhaps result in no resource gain to the regime because each sector would perceive no improvement in its well-being unless accorded more status than the other.

Information differs from status in that it can be shared as widely as its possessors choose, but its value falls as dissemination increases. Knowledge possessed by one sector may be desired by both the regime and another sector. For the sector possessing the information, the opportunity cost of divulging what it knows to the regime is equal to those resources another sector would give up to have the information if the regime were not informed, or may be equal to the resources lost if the regime were informed. Giving the information to both might yield more resources than communicating it just to one, in which case the opportunity cost would be the resources foregone by giving it only to the regime or to another sector.

For a sector to give effective support to an anti-statesman, it must reduce the legitimacy status it accords to the regime. This course of action will probably result in decreased benefits from the regime. If it is receiving relatively few benefits, the sector has relatively little to lose by supporting the regime's opponents. We would say that its opportunity costs of supporting the opposition are low. The anti-statesman probably need not promise such a sector as much for its support as he would a sector benefiting more from the regime in authority. For a regime to grant influence over agricultural price policy to the middle peasantry rather than to small peasantry has certain opportunity costs—the resources foregone from one by granting influence to its competitor. On the basis of his ideological preferences, a statesman may grant influence to the sector that can give him less than the other. This he is free to do, but at the same time he has to consider the opportunity costs of pursuing his value preferences. Similarly, a statesman must also calculate the opportunity costs of using force. The likelihood of retaliation makes it especially important for the statesman to consider what *net* gains may be achieved when coercion or violence is employed.

In choosing among alternative uses, a regime or sector seeks to maximize the value of benefits gained and deprivations averted while minimizing that of benefits foregone and deprivations incurred. We thus assess a resource's value in terms of the net gains or losses of other resources. No resurrection of hedonistic pleasure pain principles is intended by this formulation. Resources may be sought and used for quite altruistic ends if statesmen or sectors are so inclined. The point is that both will seek, according to their valuations, to increase benefits net of losses rather than the reverse.

The amount of resources produced and offered for exchange by sectors and regime is not fixed. Rather it depends on the inducements offered by others. Legitimacy, authority, status, information, coercion, and economic resources all entail some costs to the regime or sector producing and exchanging them. Positive and/or negative inducements must exceed the cost of production or the product will not be made available for political exchange. Thus the supply of a particular resource is influenced by the exchange rate offered. The reverse is also true. Unless inducements make it advantageous to interact outside the private sphere, resources in general, not just political resources, will be withheld.

Rates of exchange depend to a large extent on the demand for resources, though they also influence the level of demand. Both regime and sectors will, of course, seek rates of exchange favorable to themselves so that they need give up relatively fewer of their own resources to obtain those held by others. When a regime or sector wants to improve its position vis-à-vis the other, it may withhold certain resources from the flow or reduce its contribution of resources. By decreasing the supply of a resource, it can raise that resource's value and obtain more of other resources in return as long as the shift in exchange rates lasts. If, however, after a resource's price has been raised by this means the supply returns to its previous level, the price will also return to its former level, providing the level of demand has not changed. Only a temporary advantage is gained unless the shift in supply or demand is lasting.

An exchange rate is greatly influenced by the relative dependence of the regime or sectors on a particular resource at a certain point in time. A regime faced with fiscal bankruptcy will offer more positive inducements or will use more coercion to acquire economic resources than will one that is more solvent financially. Availability of alternative sources of supply and the satisfaction of demands with substitute resources also affect the exchange rate, as these alter dependence on certain resources. As long as supply and demand conditions do not change, or as long as they fluctuate within a relatively narrow range, exchange rates will be relatively stable. Often there will be *prevailing rates of exchange* between resources—e.g., this kind of information will bring that much status, or a certain amount of influence will yield an advantage in the allocation of economic resources. These rates facilitate regime and sector calculations of what each must offer the other to obtain desired resources. We are not saying, however, that a regime will have the same exchange rate with all sectors for a given resource. The political market, unlike the theoretical market in economic analysis, is not egalitarian.

The only useful standard for comparison of resource values is a marginal standard. For example, the amount of support a sector must promise the regime in order to receive some measure of influence over employment security policy will depend on the marginal value of that sector's support to the regime and the marginal value of resources committed to the regime in pledging support. The amount also depends on the marginal cost to the regime of giving up influence over this policy area and on the marginal benefit a sector receives from gaining such influence. If a regime has plentiful support and does not need more support from this particular sector, or has little need for the additional resources that could be gained by having more support from the sector, its statesman will probably require support from the sector on a broader range of issues before he will give up his monopoly over decisions on employment security. He might even refuse to make any exchange, especially if he believed that the sector would use the influence granted it contrary to regime objectives. If, however, he needed support for reserves or to accomplish other objectives, he might be less demanding in the exchange he would make with the sector.

The sector, for its part, might consider influence in this area so important, i.e., productive, that it would offer economic resources to the regime as well as pledges of support. It might threaten violence or non-compliance with regime policies in other areas, thereby requiring the regime to expend coercion or other resources to further compliance with these policies. If, under the circumstances, the regime attached high marginal value to the resources it would have to expend to secure compliance from this sector in these other policy areas, it might more readily relinquish the desired influence. If it cared less about avoiding violence or coercion, it would resist the sector's demand more firmly. The final balance of exchange, then, depends on the regime's and sectors' marginal valuations of the resources involved. The less dependent either is on the resources of the other, the better its bargaining position will be, and the more favorable exchange rate it can usually obtain. For example, a sector that has not become involved in monetized exchange or one that has no generalized criteria of status is diffi-cult to retaliate against if it defies regime authority. Perhaps only coercion can secure obedience to the regime, and then probably at a high cost in terms of present and future support foregone.

The interaction of supply and demand also affects the value of currency through the relation of currencies to the resources for which they stand. Currency may be bargained for or bargained with instead of, or in addition to, a resource itself. The value of currencies as future claims on goods and services, status, force, legitimacy, and participation in authoritative decision-making will vary, depending on present and anticipated future needs. The conversion of currency into resources is not necessarily automatic. Not all currencies relate to their resources as precisely and predictably as money does to goods and services. Usually, however, an implicit rate of exchange will prevail. A given commitment of support to the regime from a sector can thus usually be converted into resources that assure compliance with specific kinds or numbers of decisions. Allegiance may likewise be con-verted into legitimacy on the grounds that the conversion is in accordance with the political division of labor. A threat of coercion may be converted into coercion if the threat is not sufficient to secure compliance. The sig-nificant factor in the conversion of currency into resources is whether or not the amount of currency in circulation is in line with the amount of resources available to back it up.

PERFORMANCE AND SANCTION.

With a little modification we have adopted the economic variables of sup-ply and demand into our analysis. Supply and demand are usually seen as functional relations between quantity and price. The theoretical supply curve slopes upward; the greater the amount supplied, the higher the price. In contrast, the demand curve slopes downward; the greater the amount demanded, the lower the price offered. We must ask at this point what justification there is for treating such heterogeneous factors so uniformly. Is the similarity between economic and political variables only metaphori-cal, or can we point out basic underlying relationships between economic, social, and political interaction? These questions are hardly susceptible to proof, but the work of Parsons and Smelser suggests a common conceptual bond between the various types of interaction we have been discussing.

When tracing similarities between those phenomena economic theory treats and those treated by more general social theory, Parsons and Smelser distinguish between the performance and sanction aspects of any social act:

> In the process of interaction, an act analyzed in terms of its direct meaning for the functioning of the system, as a 'contribution' to its maintenance or task performance, is called a *performance*. On the other hand, an act analyzed in terms of its effect on the state of an actor toward whom it is oriented (and thus only indirectly, through his probable future action, on the state of the system) is called a *sanction*. This is an analytical distinction. Every *concrete* act has both a performance aspect and a sanction aspect. But in the analysis of any particular process in a system, the distinction— in terms of the relative primacy of one of these two aspects—is of the first importance.[16]

Parsons and Smelser found that distinguishing these aspects is especially pertinent to making analytical distinctions between short-term supply and demand. The production of utility or economic value is called supply, and is considered in terms of its contribution to the functioning of the economy. Demand is the disposition to "pay" for the availability of goods and services:

> The economist interprets the *significance* of any given state of demand in terms of its bearing on the disposition of the relevant supplying agencies to produce in the future. Thus only indirectly does the state of demand bear on the performance of function in the economy.[17]

Parsons and Smelser suggest that the same performance-sanction relationship holds for all social interaction.[18]

This very perceptive distinction between the two aspects of social interaction helps to account not only for the fact of political exchange (in

[16] Parsons and Smelser (1956:9).

[17] Parsons and Smelser (1956:9–10).

[18] When we consider elasticity of supply and demand in the next section, we will treat price as a function of supply and demand relations. Here we treat supply and demand as a function of price.

which some actions are primarily performance and others primarily sanction), but also for the fact that such exchange is not necessarily on a barter basis. Since resources flow from activities and attitudes, the various sanctions, deprivations, rewards, benefits, and satisfactions affect the subsequent allocation of political production. But production need not and usually does not wait for agreement on allocation. It is continuous. Changes in allocation, mostly marginal, occur in response to changes in sanctions, which are themselves performances in their other aspect. A regime's threat of coercion (sanction) keeps a sector from resorting to violence to achieve its aims, but this same threat of coercion also contributes to the maintenance of the political community. A sector may accord the regime legitimacy status (performance) because of the implicit sanctions that would result from failing to keep law and order. On the other hand, the regime must regulate behavior to maintain law and order (performance) or risk a decline in its legitimacy status from the sectors (sanction). However, the generalized application of the principles of supply and demand raises the question of elasticity of supply and demand, and the questions of marginal utility and productivity.

ELASTICITY OF SUPPLY AND DEMAND.

The shape of supply and demand curves and their slope, or elasticity, are derived from two of the most basic laws of economic analysis—the law of diminishing returns and the law of diminishing marginal utility. By inverting the usual statement of functional relationships between the curves and stating that price is a function of supply and demand, Parsons and Smelser describe the curves in a way that makes the connection between them quite clear. The influence of diminishing returns and diminishing utility on the level of supply and demand hence becomes more evident. Parsons and Smelser's formulation is especially useful because it demonstrates why political and other resources, subject to the constraint of scarcity but having the production and utility characteristics of goods and services, should have their value determined by supply and demand interaction in a way similar to that of economic analysis.

DIMINISHING RETURNS. Without significant exception, for a given state of technology or a given production function combining different factors in certain proportions, diminishing marginal productivity of any particular input will sooner or later be encountered as production is expanded. This condition is similar to the phenomenon of decreasing returns to scale.[19] As inputs of factors of production are increased, they will at some point yield proportionally smaller increases in output. This condition may be encountered from the beginning of production. The opportunity costs involved in expanding production are such that the greater the amount supplied, the higher the price.

DIMINISHING MARGINAL UTILITY. The law of diminishing utility determines the downward slope of the demand curve. Whether additional units of a resource are valued less than the previous units because of satiation or because of diminishing returns depends on whether the resource is used for consumption or production. It is not just that demand increases as price falls, but that price must fall in order for demand to increase. There are certain exceptions to this situation. Where there are indivisibilities or thresholds, a certain quantity of the particular resource must be possessed before any of it can be utilized. In most cases, however, additional units of a resource provide less satisfaction or production than did previous units.

THE CONCEPT OF ELASTICITY. In our discussion here, price elasticity is a statement of the proportional change in supply or demand resulting from a change in price, this change in turn being affected by changes in demand or supply. Demand for a resource is *elastic* if it increases or decreases more than proportionally in response to changes in price. Demand is *inelastic* when the quantity demanded changes less than proportionally as price varies. Unit elasticity is the condition in which demand varies directly in proportion to changes in price. Price elasticity and inelasticity of supply are similarly defined.[20] To analyze elasticity of supply and demand, we must treat the level of supply and demand as a function of price or the rate of exchange. Thus we invert our earlier statement of the relationship between price and supply or demand. Demand for a resource is elastic

[19] Despite whatever disagreements we may have with Karl Wittfogel's analysis of oriental despotism, we feel that Wittfogel suggests a very interesting "law of diminishing administrative returns." He discusses the forbidding cost of total social control and suggests that the benefits could not possibly be greater at this point than the expenditure of resources on control. In an effort to balance costs and benefits, he comes up with the objective of reaching a "managerial optimum" where the ruler receives maximum revenue with minimum effort. Linked to this conception is his suggestion of a consumptive optimum for rulers that would permit them to consume a maximum of resources while minimizing costs. See Wittfogel (1957:109–111, 129).

[20] Blau formulates his definition of elasticity differently, but his formulation has some usefulness as an alternative conception. According to Blau, if a change in supply (or demand) affects the volume of transactions more than it affects the price of the commodity, supply (or demand) is elastic. If price is more affected than volume, supply (or demand) is inelastic. See Blau (1964:195).

when marginal utility is declining relatively little. However, at the point where marginal utility declines more rapidly, demand will become more or less inelastic.

A sector with high status may have little demand for additional status because the marginal utility of status is low for that sector. At the same time, a low-status sector may have increasing or constant marginal utility for status increments. In the first case, demand is price-inelastic, but in the second it is price-elastic. Explained in terms of utility, units of status already possessed are valued more highly per unit than additional units of status, if in reality we can deal with status in terms of comparable units.

The law of diminishing marginal utility, expressed in terms of elasticity or inelasticity of demand, accounts for the generally observed political phenomenon that absolute reductions in the holdings of a resource will be resisted more vigorously than equivalent increases will be sought. A regime understanding the implications of elasticity of demand would try to avoid making *re*allocations of resources that would reduce in *absolute* terms the holdings of one or more sectors. Instead it would try through marginal changes in the flow of resources to accomplish relative changes in the pattern of allocations. As a general rule, a unit of resources foregone is valued less than one taken away.[21] A regime that could make judgments about the elasticity or inelasticity of a sector's demand for particular resources would be better able to maximize its own margin of benefit from the exchange.

Elasticity of demand may be empirically verified, if only in a crude way. It might be established, for instance, that sectors and regime have a relatively inelastic demand for no coercion or no violence. This means that both will refrain from using force for relatively small inducements, positive or negative. Perhaps just the threat of sanctions will deter the use of coercion or violence. A strong regime, able to contain violence by greater use of coercion, will usually have a less inelastic demand for no violence because the net damage inflicted on it will be relatively less than that which would be inflicted on a weaker regime. Such a regime is thus likely to be freer to threaten coercion than the sectors are to threaten it with violence. If a sector whose demand for coercion is inelastic seeks to avoid coercion, it will have to give up greater amounts of resources as more coercion is threatened or used. To be sure, at some point violence may become its most (or only) effective resource for reducing regime coercion.

Elasticity of supply is related to the costs of production or the rate at

[21] See Hirschman (1958:61) and (1963:353) for a discussion of this phenomenon.

which returns from the use of a resource decline. A sector is unlikely to provide an elastic supply of legitimacy to the regime because its other resources will be reduced as political deference is called for by the regime. In most cases a sector has little to gain from providing an elastic supply of resources; thus the supply of a resource will more often be inelastic than elastic. We think it evident that the concept of elasticity is appropriate for analyzing the exchange of political resources. Less apparent are the means of applying the concept in predictive as contrasted to descriptive analyses. It should be possible to extrapolate predictions about elasticity from *post hoc* descriptions of exchange relationships, but any serious use of the concept must wait for development of means for measuring the volume of political resources. Therefore we do not expand upon the idea in our initial presentation of the model.

COMPARISON OF VALUE. While measurement of political resources cannot be made in cardinal terms, comparisons of value can be made in ordinal terms once the marginal utility or productivity of a resource is assessed and the elasticity of supply estimated.[22] Let us explore a hypothetical situation in which such comparisons might be made. How might a statesman assess the effectiveness and consequences of using coercion to enforce anti-smuggling laws that would increase his regime's tax revenues? First, the statesman must determine the marginal utility to the smugglers of increased goods and services from continuing illicit activity. If returns are high, the disutility of compliance is great. Other things being equal, the higher the profitability of smuggling, the more coercion the regime must use to secure a given level of compliance or the less compliance there will be for a given expenditure of coercion. Also, the more inelastic the smugglers' demand for money, the more coercion the regime must use to stop smugglers' violations.

The use of coercion might well halt any flow of support from the sector affected. If this support is considerable or valuable, perhaps because of the sector's size or the regime's current need for support, the cost of using coercion will be quite high. The use of coercion may, however, generate more or less support from other sectors. If the smugglers are an unpopular minority, the regime might gain considerable support by suppressing them; such support might more than offset that lost from the smugglers. On the

---

[22] To some extent, the value of a resource will be affected by its general convertibility of that resource into other resources. Although we recognize the importance of this feature, we cannot yet describe it adequately in theoretical or empirical terms. A promising attempt, using a wider but less rigorous definition of resources, is Clark (1968:60–65).

other hand, if smugglers are in or related to the core combination, loss of their support and the support of sympathetic sectors will be more important to the regime than it would be if smugglers were positioned more toward the periphery of the political community.

Whatever the situation, the statesman will need to consider whether the flow of legitimacy status to the regime would be more adversely affected by the use of coercion to end smuggling or by the toleration of smuggling. He will want to know what it is likely to cost the regime in terms of other resources if the use of coercion fails to halt the illicit traffic. If the regime did fail, it could lose considerable legitimacy and support as well as economic resources. He will also want to determine how much marginal utility (or productivity) the amount of taxes lost from smuggling has for the regime. Clearly, if the regime is hard-pressed to satisfy its financial needs, this leak is much more important than it would be if the regime were in a more solvent position.

If coercion seems too costly a means of coping with smuggling, the statesman might see whether or not other resources could be used. Perhaps information that would facilitate enforcement could be procured from other sectors. Or perhaps the regime could undertake a campaign against smugglers to lower their status and prestige and stigmatize them socially. In this case the statesman would need to find out how elastic or inelastic the smugglers' demand for status is. If their status is low, they have little to lose and may ignore this particular sanction. If, however, their demand is relatively inelastic, threats of lowered status may be an effective inducement for compliance. A higher-status group will usually be more affected by the sanction of reduction of status, though the effectiveness of this sanction is still conditioned by the relative utility of economic gains made from disobedience of the law. Conceivably, manipulation of status might end the smugglers' activity with little cost to the regime. Thus even though we cannot attach numerical values to the different resources and currencies, we can by using the political economy approach evaluate alternative courses of action in such a way that relative costs and benefits can be compared.

Regime Exchanges with Sectors

A discussion of some exchanges between regime and sectors will illustrate the statesman's consideration of supply and demand, marginal productivity, marginal utility, and elasticity.

STATUS, WEALTH, AND AUTHORITY.

In *The Political Basis of Economic Development*, Robert Holt and John Turner try to account for the relatively greater development of England and Japan as compared to that of France and China. Comparing factors in the seventeenth and eighteenth centuries that seemed to facilitate or detract from rapid economic growth, they find that "one of the most striking differences between the two sets of cases [lay] in the governmental activities relating to the stratification system of the society." [23] In France and China opportunities were provided for upwardly-mobile commercial and manufacturing groups to join the most prestigious classes. In France titles and offices could be bought—in China academic degrees. In both countries merchants and manufacturers were permitted to purchase land, the most prestigious form of wealth, with the capital they accumulated from business activities. Holt and Turner report that in contrast, England and Japan had effective restrictions that prevented admission to aristocratic status.

It is Holt and Turner's hypothesis that in England and Japan government limitations on the acquisition of higher status facilitated economic development because the aristocratic classes had a higher marginal propensity to consume, while commercial and manufacturing groups were more likely to save and invest their income. It is doubtful whether the governments of these countries understood the situation they created or intended its consequences, but that they restricted the exchange of wealth for status is evident. The result was increased economic production on the part of those sectors excluded from higher status positions.

Considering exchanges of status, wealth, and authority in more general terms, Holt and Turner propose that "if a government is to tax heavily and to control the economy in minute detail, it must distribute prestige to those who are tightly squeezed [and] in a position to be potentially an effective opposition." According to their argument, the government must sell prestige in return for the economic resources it extracts, but must not sell power (authority in terms of our model). An inheritance system that splits up estates would help, they suggest, to limit the build-up of groups or sectors capable of competing for authority: "The family whose aspirations to *purchase prestige* are satisfied in one generation may, if its wealth continues to accumulate, try to buy *power* [authority] in the next generation." If

[23] Holt and Turner (1966:318).

the ascendant sectors cannot buy or are not satisfied with status and prestige they may choose to seek authority by violent means.[24]

LEGITIMACY AND AUTHORITY.

A more hypothetical discussion of exchange of legitimacy and authority between regime and sectors will illustrate further the interaction of supply and demand. It will also point out a dilemma many regimes in developing countries face as they seek to achieve political goals while maintaining political stability. In countries that are relatively stable politically, the sectors accord considerable legitimacy status to the central authorities. This flow of legitimacy is relatively inelastic and is not very responsive to changes in regime performance. Unless the regime is quite ineffective in providing basic order and security or is malevolent in its dealings with sectors, sectors will not withhold legitimacy as a sanction. The regime possessing greater legitimacy status can thus secure compliance more effectively and efficiently.

To the extent that regime authority is effective, sectors will want to participate in making authoritative decisions concerning allocations, or will at least want to influence these decisions. In other words, when regime authority is effective, the demand for authority is great. However, the regime can keep the amount of authority it shares with sectors relatively scarce because it has a monopoly on the supply and distribution of authority. The statesman in a stable polity is not challenged by contenders for authority except through legitimate, legal channels of competition. Thus the supply of authority is limited, while the demand is great. When a country's political institutions are established and authority can effectively allocate other resources, the marginal productivity of authority is high and not diminishing. Demand for authority is likely to remain high and inelastic, relatively unresponsive to changes in price. Under such conditions a regime might secure considerable other resources from the sectors in exchange for authority and influence. Where speaking in the name of the state is highly valued and the regime monopolizes authority, regime stability will be considerably greater than it is in less politically integrated countries.[25]

[24] John A. Ballard's account of the career of Bartolemy Boganda, nationalist leader of Oubangui-Chari (now the Central African Republic) during the fifties, provides a more recent example of how an anti-statesman may manage the exchange of status, wealth, and authority. See Ballard (1966:264–265).

[25] Lipset (1960) counterposes legitimacy and effectiveness. Naturally enough, if both are present, there will be greater political stability. He says,

In most developing countries, however, the legitimacy status of regimes is relatively low.[26] The productivity of authority for securing desired allocations is also low, lessened in part by the meager legitimacy statesmen are accorded. Under these circumstances authority is not very effective in obtaining control over other resources. It is often expended unwisely to boot. If the marginal productivity of authority is low and diminishing, there is little demand for authority or for influence in the decision-making process. Consequently the regime has little bargaining power with the one resource that is its special factor of production.[27]

If a regime has little legitimacy, it is seriously short of political capital. In situations where little legitimacy is accorded, authority is devalued and the demand for it reduced. However, the statesman can attempt to make the most efficient use of the regime's resources in the same way that economic planners might utilize plentiful labor if they lacked financial capital. Factors of production are to some extent substitutable in securing compliance. By using what goods and services, status, information, and coercion it has, a regime may still enforce its decisions. It may, for instance, have considerable economic resources to exploit as a consequence of revenue from petroleum. It may trade on the status accorded it from abroad in the form of diplomatic recognition or use foreign economic aid or coercive force lent to it by foreign powers. Since authority—granted in the form of participation in decisions—is only one of the resources a regime may use to secure compliance, a regime need not be permanently condemned to a "legitimacy trap" from which it cannot escape.

however, that one can compensate for lack of the other. We would agree, as our compliance model at the end of Chapter III suggests, but we feel that Lipset fails to develop a satisfactory link between legitimacy and effectiveness. See Chapter III, pp. 87–88.

[26] The elasticity of supply with respect to price varies from country to country, to be sure. In some countries the supply of legitimacy from the sectors is quite responsive to changes in the inducements offered by the regime. In others, where many or most sectors feel threatened by change and are unwilling to accept it, sectors may rigidly withhold legitimacy from the regime. In these cases the supply will be relatively inelastic, unresponsive to changes in price.

[27] This predicament might be compared with the "low productivity trap" confronted by economies of underdeveloped countries. An economy with little accumulation of capital will have low productivity and thus low output and income. This means that there will be low effective demand and low savings, which will in turn result in low capital formation and low incentive for investment. A "vicious circle" results. One analysis of this problem for unproductive polities is offered by Daniel Lerner (1963:346–349). While his model is based on different assumptions than ours, he comes to some of the same conclusions about the consequences of low demand for authority.

A resourceful statesman will seek to maximize the effectiveness of his decisions by using whatever inducements he has in accordance with the elasticities of demand of the different sectors. In particular, he will probably try to avoid making unenforceable decisions that would call attention to the impunity with which regime authority could be flouted.[28] As sectors come to see and experience the increasing productivity of speaking in the name of the state, they will more and more desire and demand a share in authority. Thus the price a regime can command for permitting sectors to make or influence authoritative decisions will go up, and the other resources possessed by the regime will increase. Of course, if the statesman is too generous in parceling out authority, and the supply he makes available to the sectors keeps pace with their demand, he will augment his resource position relatively little. It is to his advantage to keep the supply of authority relatively scarce.[29]

The method of development we have just described may not be effective or possible if there are strong competitors for occupancy for the authority roles or if there are proponents for creating an entirely new regime with new roles and new political relationships. The regime in authority cannot under these circumstances afford to be parsimonious in sharing its authority. If the statesman asks too high a price for authority, his opponents may offer to share authority with certain sectors at a lower price. In particular, an anti-statesman may seek to divert support and allegiance from the regime in order to secure the various resources to which these currencies give him a claim. If support, allegiance, and various resources are withdrawn from the regime, the regime is likely to become politically insolvent and bankrupt.

A weak resource position often forces a statesman to make unfavorable exchanges. A regime that has little legitimacy is as a rule more vulnerable and unstable than one that has more of this resource. The regime's high and inelastic demand for legitimacy forces such a regime to pay a high price for sector resources or to accept a lower price for its own. Economic payoffs, which may be considered "corruption" by Western observers, may be one means whereby authorities lacking legitimacy may establish at least a simple self-interested basis for gaining it, support, and various other re-

[28] We are not saying that a statesman must avoid taking any risks. To raise the value of authority, he will probably have to take some gambles. If he can enforce a decision thought unenforceable, he will be better able to secure compliance with successive decisions.

[29] Nasser's regime in the United Arab Republic is a good example of a regime that has kept the supply of shared authority very scarce. See Binder (1966:220–221, 237–240) and (1965:400–402, 406–407, 419–423).

sources from the sectors. When a statesman has only limited resources and alternatives, we must thus consider the impact of *political necessity* on his decisions. He may have no choice but to give in to the demands of certain sectors because he may desperately need the particular resources these sectors can provide. However, in making judgments about the statesman's options, we need to know more than his resource position and that of the various sectors. We must also know what behavioral patterns affect how sectors make demands, how sectors bargain for resources, and what preferences they have.

Political Behavior

Obviously the different behavioral patterns of various sectors have important consequences for the political process and particularly for the productivity of the statesman's choices. Those patterns that apply generally to most sectors we call *parameters* of behavior, while those peculiar to certain sectors we call *propensities*.[30]

PROPENSITIES.

As we noted in Chapter I, propensities correspond to the sociological concept of orientations to action. Both concepts describe reasonably regular patterns of behavior derived from certain values or beliefs held by individuals or groups. In our analysis we are concerned only with group characteristics and not with individual psychology. By considering aggregate sectoral behavior, it should be possible for us to make predictive statements with greater certainty as we try to ascertain the productive implications of different sectoral propensities for the statesman. Below we discuss a number of sectoral propensities. They have not been empirically verified or measured, nor are they exhaustive. We suggest them to illustrate the kinds of considerations a statesman needs to weigh—and probably does weigh in-

[30] Almond and Powell state that "in studying any political system, . . . we need to know its underlying propensities as well as its actual performance over a given period of time." They refer to the propensities that constitute the psychological dimension of the political system as the political culture. See Almond and Powell (1966:23). We prefer to make a distinction between parameters and propensities in order to distinguish general behavioral characteristics from those of particular sectors.

tuitively—in making exchanges with sectors. If a statesman knows the propensities of the sectors with which he is dealing, he can bargain more effectively and probably improve his resource position.

(1) To what extent does the sector prefer *material gains* to *psychic gains*? A propensity to favor material gains would make the sector's demand for status low and inelastic, and its demand for goods and services quite elastic. Thus offers of goods and services would be more effective inducements to such a sector than offers of status.

(2) A sector may value *self-interested goals* more highly than *altruistic goals* of community interest, or the opposite may be true. A sector that demanded a reduction in taxes but valued altruistic goals more highly than it did self-interested goals might, if an appeal were made to its nationalistic values, be persuaded to give up its demand even though it favored material over psychic gains. Any sector that is quite self-interested will as a rule accord less legitimacy to the regime and will not obey authoritative decisions unless there are other inducements for compliance, such as money or threats of coercion.

(3) Some sectors value *immediate gratification* of demands more highly than do others, which will probably accept *deferred gratification*. A sector that prefers immediate gratification will, for example, value influence as a claim on authoritative decisions in the future less than it will some measure of participation in making specific authoritative decisions in the present.[31]

(4) Sectors react differently when their demands are not met by the regime. Some tend to *withdraw* and others to *act more aggressively* in pressing their demands. A statesman who knows that a sector tends to withdraw when its demands are frustrated will make less effort to meet these demands since they may well be dropped anyway. He must, however, also consider whether this reaction of withdrawal also involves withdrawal of support, a propensity of some sectors that are frustrated in their demands.

(5) When a sector has a demand and is faced with a demand from the regime in return, it may tend to engage seriously in *negotiation*, or it may tend to resort to *violence* or threats of violence. A statesman needs to know which course the sector will follow. If the sector's propensity for the latter

---

[31] As is apparent, regimes may have such propensities as well. For example, a statesman may favor immediate over deferred gratification. However, if he has a low level of resources available, he will prefer resources to currency, goods and services to money, legitimacy to allegiance, not just because of a particular propensity, but because of the situations he faces.

is strong, he must usually be prepared to meet violence with coercion when trying to get such a sector to agree on the exchange of resources.[32]

(6) Some sectors prefer to make their demands through *direct confrontation* with the regime, while others prefer to *act through intermediaries*. Moreover, some may tend to use *non-legitimate methods* rather than *regular public channels* to affect exchange.

Propensities affect the elasticity of both supply and demand, and hence the exchange rates with which the regime must reckon. Although subject to change, the regularity of propensities provides an element of stability in exchange relationships. In certain cases the statesman may try to alter the propensities of sectors, but some propensities may be relatively impervious to change.

PARAMETERS.

As statements about patterns of aggregate behavior, parameters are necessarily described in average or modal terms. There are, of course, variations among sectors with respect to any particular kind of behavior. Yet whenever similarities in behavioral patterns are meaningful and predictable enough to have productive consequences for the polity as a whole, we may speak of parameters. One of the most important parameters affecting the political process is analogous to the economic "commitments" discussed by Parsons and Smelser. Parsons and Smelser write of these as institutionalized value patterns that commit a flow of resources to economic production.[33] These commitments specify the relative importance of economic production to members of the society. In effect, a certain amount of any society's resources are segregated from other uses in order to be contributed to economic production.

The same phenomenon is to be found in political production. In order

[32] Almond and Powell discuss the propensity to use violence to make demands, suggesting that it has serious liabilities as a form of access, in particular the real danger to life and property involved for those who use it: "Characteristically, violence has been employed by those groups in the political system which feel that they have the least to lose from chaotic upheaval, and which face an enormous gap between possessions and expectations." In addition, they say that violence is less frequently used when other channels for articulating and pressing demands are available. See Almond and Powell (1966:82). This view overlooks the different propensities for more or less violent political action that are independent of objective opportunities for non-violent claim-making. See Stinchcombe (1965).

[33] Parsons and Smelser (1956:41–42).

to maintain basic operations of government such as preservation of law and order, protection against aggression, and provision of essential services, sectors may be willing to accord at least a minimal amount of legitimacy and other resources to the regime. These resources are available for regime use without bargaining. The favorable position of a regime vis-à-vis the sectors originates in this relatively free flow of some resources to the regime. If the regime uses these resources wisely, it may maintain the confidence and good will of the sectors and continue to take advantage of their propensity or disposition to be generous in exchanges with it. From these exchanges a larger stock of resources may be built up for saving or investment in achieving regime goals. This parameter has been given various names. It may be called *political solidarity* and represents the positive valuation of the political division of labor and the existing political stratification. In more common terms, it is known as *patriotism* or *loyalty*.

Comparable to political solidarity is a parameter that may be termed *social solidarity*. This parameter represents individuals' ability to maintain trans-sectoral identifications or to transcend their particular interests for the sake of the community. If individuals lacked feelings of solidarity, their unrestrained pursuit of higher status would make stratification unacceptable and hopelessly mobile. Those persons with lower status would be especially unlikely to accept their roles and the requirements thereof—an inequality of obligations and esteem and deference. Our interest in solidarity as a parameter in political economy lies in its contribution to the defense of, or assault on, the status quo. In a community with low social solidarity, we would expect ideologies favoring the status quo to have little power and revolutionary ideologies to have great impact. Where solidarity is high, we would expect the opposite to be true. Thus a statesman would usually wish to increase solidarity, and an anti-statesman would try to lower it.[34] Parameters are not easy to alter, but a statesman would probably try to increase feelings of social solidarity just as he would try to instill greater patriotism and loyalty in members of the political community. If he were successful, he would reduce demands for status reallocation as the existing stratification won greater acceptance.[35]

[34] Solidarity generally derives from the satisfaction a person gets from performing his role and from his notion that his role is right and proper for him. Lowered solidarity usually increases the incidence of anomic behavior and makes persons more open to radical ideological appeals, thus aiding an anti-statesman.

[35] In our discussion of political investments in Chapter VII, we will consider *solidarity investments* along with *legitimacy and stability investments*. See also Ilchman and Bhargava (1966) for a discussion of these kinds of investment.

Two behavioral parameters affecting progress toward economic development are *reverence for tradition* and *valuation of time*. Where the first is high and the second low, the statesman will probably find it difficult to induce changes in work and patterns of behavior. Yet if he desires to slow the pace of change, perhaps to maintain institutional coherence or contain inflationary pressures, he will find these parameters quite supportive. The statesman needs to consider these and other parameters that affect the behavior of his countrymen; where possible he may attempt to alter them in desired, more productive directions.[36]

Bargaining

The conventional language of politics, which uses terms such as trading favors, making deals, cashing in political debts, using up assets, spending freely, pledging allegiance, and withholding support, bears witness to the ubiquity of bargaining. Although often deprecated formally and sometimes disguised by formalism in social relations, bargaining is an essential part of the political process in developing countries.[37] In these countries old ex-

---

[36] One parameter often discussed—though not always convincingly—is the aggregate propensity to use violence. Political communities may differ in terms of their normative attitudes toward the use of violence. Easton (1965:259) has commented on this difference, but suggests that it involves matters of substance as well as political style. A discussion of a "nearly endemic resort to violence" in Mexico's political culture is offered by Robert E. Scott (1965:344–345). Whether his particular observation is correct or not, such considerations are important for political analysis. A statesman having to deal with sectors that manifest violence as a behavioral parameter might invest some coercion to alter this inclination to use violence or might use other resources to develop strictures on it.

[37] Robert E. Ward says that "bargaining and compromise within the circles of the elect has steadily been the style and preference of Japan's political elite." See Ward (1965:55). According to Yoshio Sakata and J. W. Hall, this has not always been the case. They say that following the Meiji restoration, the equilibrium among various political institutions broke down. As established *quid pro quo's* fluctuated, an implicit bargaining process developed. Various imbalances emerged during the period of development, bringing about certain changes in response. See Sakata and Hall (1956:31–50).

India is one country where explicit bargaining is conventionally disapproved of. Myron Weiner tells how in industrial relations, conciliation and arbitration are preferred to collective bargaining. Within the Congress Party as well, conflicts are more commonly decided by arbitration than by bargaining and com-

pectations have been undermined, and growing demands make the scarcity of supply of valued resources even more acute. Less exchange can take place at prevailing rates, and there are often many different prevailing rates because the various markets are not integrated. A politician may get as many votes from an outlying community as from a suburb of the capital, but he will obtain them with many fewer benefits promised, owing to the villagers' unawareness of the returns their support might bring from other politicians.

The resources held or generated by regime and sectors are exchanged or withheld as best suits the purposes of each. *Policies* consisting of certain combinations of resources are offered by the statesman to the sectors to obtain sector compliance or to redistribute resources in a preferred way. Implementing policies involves securing from the sectors goods and services, status, information, violence (or no violence), and legitimacy, as well as their respective currencies, so that the statesman's political objectives may be satisfied. To achieve these objectives, the statesman may need a large holding of resources, or perhaps a small stock may be sufficient. Both the amount and kind of resources needed vary according to how much of what resources are desired by the sectors and at what exchange rates. As long as there are no major shifts in supply or demand, exchange may take place at prevailing rates with little or no bargaining. When rates do change, the extent of supply and demand will be ascertained by bargaining. Bargaining will establish resource price elasticities, themselves functions of marginal utility and productivity.

A regime will usually want to have some reserve of resources beyond those needed to fulfill its definite requirements. This reserve not only serves as a hedge or buffer against changes in demand or exchange rates, but also permits pursuit of autonomous regime goals. The sectors, on the other hand, generally prefer to have resources in their own possession rather than to commit them to the regime for its future but indefinite use. For example, sectors might agree that the regime should have some reserve of secret political information for purposes of national security. However, if the regime possessed a great deal of such information, it would be possi-

promise. Weiner notes, however, that it is "the strategy of weaker factions to press for external intervention in the hope that they can get better results than they might otherwise obtain through their own bargaining power." Thus appeals to authority may reduce bargaining at the local level, but the process is not absent. While noting that bargaining is not ordinarily a part of the political culture, Weiner does observe that bargaining in India is increasing. See Weiner (1965:214–215).

ble for the statesman to use some to extort resources from certain sectors. Therefore, the size of reserves of information and other resources is also a subject for bargaining between sectors and regime.

RESOURCE POSITIONS.

In Chapters II and III we discussed the resources and currencies the regime and sectors produce and those they must secure from each other in order to achieve their respective objectives. At any one time, depending on past exchanges and production, the regime and each of the various sectors will have a particular holding consisting of certain types and amounts of resources and currencies. The level of various resources and currencies held by the regime is to some extent a function of the regime's having satisfied the demands of various sectors, but it also results from the efficient use and effective management of resources. In political economy, political bargaining is not simply a matter of the regime's processing demands from the sectors. To maintain and improve its resource position, a regime must take initiatives and advance new programs, in short, provide leadership.[38] What the sectors demand from the regime depends on their own particular resource positions as well as on their particular preferences and propensities. The differential distribution of resources among the sectors invariably means that the welfare of all sectors is not equally enhanced by the political process. As a rule, those sectors with more resources or more valued resources are able to secure more of the resources they value from the regime. Striking too hard a bargain with the regime, however, may lead the regime to use coercion to secure a desired scarce resource.[39]

[38] Though his model assigns secondary importance to regime goals, Easton does recognize that these goals are intrinsic to politics: "In voicing their own demands or ideas of what ought to be done, authorities may seek to direct or redirect the energies of the members in the system, as in the case of the developing nations today, or to lay hold of resources available in the environment." Easton (1965:346).

[39] A dramatic example is Sir Thomas More's refusal to grant legitimacy to King Henry VIII's break with the Roman Catholic Church and establishment of a Church of England, the purpose of which was to legitimate his marriage to Anne Boleyn. More's esteem was so great in England at the time—he was regarded by commoners as perhaps the only honest man in public life—that Henry insisted on More's assent. Unless More accorded legitimacy status to the new Church and the marriage, Henry feared that others would also withhold

Those resources of particular sectors needed by the regime for use in specific policy areas weigh differentially in the political calculations of the statesman. For example, in an attempt to implement a program for modernized growing of cotton, securing legitimacy status from the affected sectors—peasants, landlords, laborers, even merchants—will be crucial. If these sectors do not regard the program as legitimate, they will require additional inducements for compliance. Coercion or threats of coercion may be effective in securing compliance from some sectors; sharing influence in shaping the program may bring about the cooperation of others. Monetary incentives may be necessary for compliance from many of the affected sectors, and perhaps manipulation of status will have an effect if modern farming can be made to seem prestigious. If the statesman knows a sector's general resource position, as well as its demand for each resource and its propensities, he can develop bargaining tactics and strategies more intelligently.

TACTICS.

The tactics of bargaining are familiar to students of practical politics. While political economy may refine the calculations of political tactics, it does not supersede the insights of experienced observers of or participants in the political process who know well that a statesman's ability to secure compliance rests not just on his resource position, but on his tactical skill in bargaining as well.

A familiar regime tactic is to offer sectors *concessions* from time to time, thereby reducing the strength of their demands or their determination to employ sanctions. This practice need not be deprecated as Machiavellian if we understand that the statesman's resources are limited and that he cannot satisfy all demands at one time. Resorting to the tactic of granting concessions is frequently necessary if the regime is to maintain itself in authority. Another regime tactic is maintaining a certain ambiguity about the amount and kind of government services rendered. Sector leaders may indeed collaborate with the regime in acknowledging benefits not really con-

legitimacy, thus undermining his authority. More's refusal to compromise finally led Henry to execute him on trumped up charges of corruption (an attempt to reduce his prestige). Robert Bolt's stage play, A *Man for All Seasons*, dramatically portrays the interplay of status, legitimacy, authority, and coercion.

ferred because this practice improves both their standing with members of their sector and their ability to appropriate resources from sector members for collective sector aims. Of course, sectors and their leaders as well may be misled by a statesman's skillful manipulation of symbols.[40]

Sectors also employ bargaining tactics. One of their most effective tactics is to form *coalitions* on particular issues. Many regime decisions need not result in zero-sum distributions of rewards among competing sectors. Sectors may gain if each compromises its demands somewhat in order to put greater total resources behind the combined demand of all the sectors in the coalition. To some extent this tactic can offset the advantages of the regime's monopoly position. According to Easton, "where demands are genuinely negotiable among members of the system, it may involve more than just agreeing that each gets some of the available values. The attainment of compromises suggests that members have learned to formulate their demands in such a way that others perceive that they too may benefit from them." [41]

Both regime and sectors may use the tactic of trying to exploit the other's "weak suit." Neither knows for sure how effective some resource may be in securing compliance or bringing about favorable changes in the allocation of resources. Consequently each will try to avoid demands on a resource the effectiveness of which is uncertain. Instead each will try to shift the other's demands to more plentiful resources that have already proven effective. Each will, however, make demands on those resources that the other is trying to shield from demands. For example, a sector may not know how effective its voting power will be in bargaining with the regime. If it wants to avoid testing out this "suit," it will have to compensate by giving up more of other resources when demands are made on the resource that is still uncertain in effectiveness. In order to avoid showing the regime its inability to exert pressure by using violence, a sector may give in to regime demands and in this way avert a showdown over use of the questionable resource. A regime that knows the weak points of a sector's resource position can use its advantage when bargaining and will try to minimize the effects of similar sectoral tactics.

STRATEGY.

Political strategies are more substantive than procedural. At their grandest level they represent significant commitments of resources by the regime to

[40] Edelman (1964:24–28).
[41] Easton (1965:236–237).

achieve certain objectives, such as changing the stratification or orientation of the political community. At other levels they may deal with problems such as increasing regime revenues or implementing educational reform. The statesman's time horizon is longer when formulating strategies than when employing tactics. Various tactics may be used successively or simultaneously, but because strategies require a greater commitment of resources than tactics do, strategies are more often mutually exclusive. Consequently strategies are more fundamental to a statesman's success or failure. Using the framework of political economy, the statesman and the political scientist should be better able to evaluate alternative courses of action in terms of how to achieve policy objectives with a minimum expenditure or the greatest return of valued resources.

It may be objected that we are advocating what Lindblom has called the "root" strategy of decision-making. This "rational-comprehensive method" would require clarification of values and objectives as the first step in making decisions, followed by exhaustive examination and comparison of all possible alternative means. Lindblom would argue that statesmen have no choice but to follow the "branch" strategy of "successive, limited comparisons." They would select certain goals or objectives to begin with, recognizing that ends and means are intertwined. To Lindblom the test of a good policy is not proof that the most appropriate means to the most valued end have been chosen, but that there is agreement among policy-makers that the best available course has been chosen. He suggests that "muddling through," successively making comparisons of incremental changes to determine whether changes are in the desired direction, reduces reliance on theory.[42]

Political economy aims at decisions more optimal than those arrived at by "muddling through." With an integrated scheme of analysis that does not confine itself to economic, social, or political considerations, analysis of alternatives need not be as drastically limited as Lindblom suggests. Lind-

---

[42] Lindblom (1959:79–88). A less colloquial designation—"satisficing"—was given to this approach to decision-making by March and Simon (1958: 169). Yehezkel Dror (1964) objects to "muddling through," stating that it is inappropriate for use in cases where new and unfamiliar problems arise, where the present means may be unavailable for future or expanded use, and where new ends may be sought. We concur with Dror, but would go beyond this criticism. We see no need, even in the face of complex problems to solve or ends to achieve, to make such a virtue of necessity. "Muddling through" may be preferable to abortive "comprehensive" decision-making, but it is not a virtue in itself. Moreover, we would ask the question: whose values are served by this piecemeal method of decision-making? See also Etzioni (1966).

blom acknowledges that important possible outcomes, policies, and values are neglected as a result of "muddling through." The incremental approach to decision-making, which recognizes the interaction of means and ends as well as the need to accept certain objectives or values as "given," need not neglect "important" outcomes, alternatives, or values. Means for making more reliable calculations should increase a statesman's ability to include more considerations in his decisions. One of the first tasks of the new political economy will be to analyze the successes and failures of various strategies employed by statesmen in developing countries.[43] At this point we can only provide several historical and hypothetical examples that will illustrate the use of political strategies.

ALTERING THE CORE COMBINATION. A statesman may make the judgment that he can improve his political resource position by shifting the core combination, either expanding it or substituting some sectors for others. This strategy may alter the grouping on which the regime relies for the bulk of its support and contributions. In recent years the Shah of Iran has attempted to change the core combination on which he depended in the past. Richard Pfaff describes the Shah's strategy, and its risks, in this way:

> The Shah has seriously weakened the political strength of the landlord class through the land reform program—a class that has been the traditional source of support for the monarchial system in Iran for years. While the peasantry too are deeply loyal to the Shah, their loyalty is more a matter of religious awe than shared interest. More significantly, the Shah's acceptance of the peasantry as his chief source of political strength is a gamble which runs counter to two basic trends in the politics of developing areas.

[43] Foltz has observed (1963:128–129) that the leaders of the new states will have difficulty steering a policy course between the extreme of exacerbated pluralism, with its possibilities for internal strife and disintegration, and a program of restrained social and economic change at "a level that can be handled by the existing political structures." He contrasts the strategy of transforming the regime completely to the profit of the new post-nationalist elites, "with the attendant danger of losing political attentiveness to popular demands and what remains of the prestige . . . of the nationalist government" with that of constricting access to the political elite, "with the possibilities of political stagnation and turning the younger generation of elites against the regime." Unfortunately, having posed the problem of choosing an optimum strategy, Foltz offers no means of discerning how best to strike a balance between these alternative courses or of altering the existing political structures in some productive fashion.

First, the Shah is challenging the proposition, long considered a truism in Iran, that it is Tehran that counts, politically, and, in general, the provinces may be ignored. Second, he is assuming, again contrary to all previous evidence in Iran, that the peasant will be as reform-minded as his brethren in the city.[44]

Since landownership is a criterion of social status in Iran, land reform not only reallocated economic resources, but gave greater status to the peasantry as well. The Shah may have decided to base his strategy for development on the peasantry rather than on the urban proletariat because the former are much more numerous. It is more likely that he chose to favor the peasants because they are less apt than their urban brethren to demand a share in authority.

There is some question as to whether U.S. occupation forces in Japan after World War II really intended to alter the core combination that had ruled Japanese politics through the first half of the twentieth century. Certainly there was a deliberate attempt to alter political values and power alignments. Robert E. Ward describes how General MacArthur's headquarters went about trying to reconstitute Japanese society along democratic lines:

In general, this [reconstitution] was to be achieved by vesting major segments of the population with new and valuable political, economic and social rights with the expectation that they would subsequently support the over-all structure of democratic reform in their desire to preserve intact their own particular gains. Thus women were enfranchised, and given new legal and social status; labor was encouraged to form unions and to bargain collectively; tenant farmers were converted into freeholders; youth was given expanded educational opportunities and the voting age was reduced to twenty; and localities were given new rights of autonomy and home rule vis-à-vis the national government and its previously omnipotent ministries.[45]

Rights here represent accepted or established claims on the polity's resources. According to Ward, this granting of rights by the allies drastically altered Japan's elite structure and thrust "entire new socio-political strata of the population upon the political stage." The consequences of this policy of democratization have, however, been ambiguous, as Ward himself recognizes.

[44] Pfaff (1963:98).
[45] Ward (1965:52).

Perhaps the most significant change in the Japanese political community was the destruction of the military's political power. This loss of power was probably more a result of defeat in war than of Allied reforms, though constitutional prohibition of rearmament presumably assured the eclipse of military influence in Japanese politics. If we examine the present core combination in Japan, we see that authority and power are held by the same sectors that held them before the war, though there has been some change in the political values espoused by these sectors. The same political elite dominates the political market in cooperation with the industrial and commercial sectors, which dominate the economic market. Those sectors in which General MacArthur's regime invested—women, workers, farmers, youth—are not a part of the core combination at all. Women and small farmers are perhaps within the present regime's ideological bias, while workers and students together with intellectuals form the political opposition.

What did result from the Allied reforms was a more competitive political market for Japan. In particular, the unions and student associations now have resources and the will to use them politically, both of which they lacked before the war. With the exception of the military—which was downgraded in political status but still seems to be within the regime's ideological bias—there were no reversals in the political stratification. There was, however, some equalization of political power. While this is certainly a significant achievement, the core combination remains basically unchanged, having adapted itself to the exigencies of garnering support through an electoral process.

RAISING REVENUE. Increasing a regime's revenues is a perennial problem in most developing countries. The sectors present myriad demands for economic allocations, and the statesman himself may have many policy goals that require money expenditures. How might a statesman go about trying to raise his revenues by levying a new excise tax on luxury items—autos, television, jewelry, and so forth? One approach would be to decide how much additional money would be needed from the sectors and then to establish a level and incidence of taxation that would yield this amount. If he adopted this approach, the statesman would be committed to using whatever coercion was necessary to secure compliance. If tax-evasion occurred and were countenanced, he would probably soon find his other revenues decreasing as sectors tried to evade other taxes as well.

This is the approach most scholars, including economists, would follow. It is, however, essentially an apolitical approach. A statesman adept at using his political resources might consult various sectors about how best to raise this additional revenue. By permitting sectors to have some influence on his tax decision, he might well reduce the costs of coercion that would otherwise be required. As a result of receiving some influence, which they in effect expend to get a more favorable tax, sectors might comply more readily with the regime. It should be clear that in this situation the statesman is not getting something for nothing. The influence he grants has very real costs. Once influence is granted, the sectors are likely to insist, as the price for compliance, on a different level and distribution of taxation than that preferred by the statesman. Indeed, sectors will only value influence if it enables them to achieve more favorable allocations of resources. They may really have wanted no additional taxes, but if persuaded by the statesman of his intention of obtaining some increase in taxation even at the cost of coercion, they will probably settle for a tax that is more to their liking than his original proposal.

If the statesman considers both alternatives, his preferred tax scheme and the scheme that involves expenditure of influence, he must evaluate the costs of the former as well. The scheme he prefers may lead to decreases in support, information, and/or legitimacy from the sectors. The use of coercion to enforce his decision may in itself be as important a factor in causing these decreases as the increase in money taken from the sectors. Against the marginal costs of the initial tax plan, the statesman weights the marginal benefit to his regime of securing the full increase in taxes desired and determines the difference in revenue brought in by the two tax plans. The coercion or support he would save as a result of implementing the tax plan acceptable to the sectors may be greater in value than the revenue he will fail to acquire if he gives up his original plan—or they may not.

The choice of plans depends on such estimates of total net benefits to the regime. Given the statesman's various objectives, insistence on his original plan might result in losses for the regime that would be proportionately greater than the benefits he would receive from achieving the particular additional fiscal revenue. True, he might have more money as a result of adopting his original plan, but if we figure political costs and benefits as well, he may have reduced his ability to achieve other, more valued objectives. Only an unwise statesman would persist in opting for such a tax plan. Calculations and comparisons of the costs and benefits of alternative tax policies in other than strictly economic terms may be rough and approximate, but they must be made if such policies are to be rational from a political point of view.

When a statesman is working out the details of a strategy, the difference between strategy and tactics may become ambiguous and unimportant. For example, if the statesman felt that he needed the entire increase in revenue projected in his tax plan but was not willing or able to pay the necessary price in coercion and various losses from the sectors, he might offer to accord some degree of influence to potentially compliant sectors on other matters of policy. Merchants might accept the tax if they could have some influence on tariff policies. Consumers might go along with it if they could receive some assurance that the regime would make greater efforts to curb inflation. Influence is, of course, usually quite expensive for the statesman to grant as an inducement; sectors may attempt to cash in their accumulated influence to alter policies very important to the regime. Another way of securing compliance with a tax increase might be for the statesman to procure commitments of support from the sectors affected by the tax. He might do so by according sectors greater status as "contributors to the nation's progress." He might then cash in the support he received to secure compliance with the tax. To be sure, the compliance will still have cost him something—whatever he had to give to get the promises of support— but what he expended to get this support should have been of less value to him than the increased revenue. Otherwise he would have acted uneconomically.

Once a regime has granted some measure of influence to a sector over a particular policy area or over policy more generally, there are good reasons for not reneging on this pledge. To do so would depreciate the value of influence given to other sectors—and would be equivalent to a loss of confidence in the currency, so to speak. Any depreciation of the value of influence accorded to sectors to obtain a favorable flow of resources from them will probably reduce the support, allegiance, legitimacy, or information sectors accord to the regime. When the regime is faced with a situation in which it is obliged to cash in a sector's claim to influence, it may be able to get the sector to postpone the claim. Or it may persuade the sector to accept some substitute policy area in which to use its claim to influence authoritative decisions. This substitute area might be an area less important to the regime at the time but equally important to the sector. Or the regime might get the sector to accept a resource other than authority if in return the sector would relinquish its claim to influence authority in this particular situation. This practice amounts to buying off the claim given at some earlier time.

EDUCATIONAL REFORM. Suppose a statesman wanted to alter the basically classical and formalistic bias of the primary school curriculum in favor of a more practical, technical orientation. What alternatives might he consider in combining resources to effect this particular policy? His cal-culations would be complicated by the fact that this reform is only a part of a broader plan he has for making the educational system contribute more effectively to his country's development effort. Ideally he would like to be able to make the change without reducing the flow of resources to his regime in the short run. Still, he may be willing to accept a short-term de-cline in resources flowing to the regime if in the long run he expects a sig-nificant gain in resources to result. Perhaps he can cope with short-run de-creases by making them up with other policies. We are, however, assuming that the statesman has little political surplus to go on and must figure his gains and losses carefully. We might anticipate that when first proposed, the reform would encounter stiff opposition from several sectors. These sectors might threaten to withdraw support from the regime and/or stop paying school fees if the reform were made. If the statesman accedes to the dissident sectors' demands that no change in curriculum be made, he must give up or drastically modify his ambitions for educational reform. What considerations, then, must go into formulation of an optimal policy, not just an acceptable one?

How important are the support and revenue that may be lost if the statesman perseveres in his plan? He can determine their importance by considering the policies in other areas that might have to be sacrificed if support and revenue were to decline. He must calculate whether the gains in the area of education are worth more to him than the concomitant losses elsewhere. His calculations give him some estimate of the marginal utility or productivity of support and revenue. He may be able to reduce the costs of educational reform, but first he must establish whether his in-itial preference yields net benefits or losses.

Since support is such a versatile and valuable currency, the statesman may consider how to minimize its loss. The support of various sectors varies in value for the statesman, just as the monetary currency of different governments is more or less valuable to him according to the real resources that may be purchased at certain exchange rates. If the sectors threatening to withdraw support are important contributors to his regime, the states-man may have little choice, at least for the present, but to give up his plan for curriculum reform. The marginal utility of support from core combi-nation sectors is quite great. Bureaucrats may oppose reform because they fear that it will result in inferior education that might fail to qualify their children for bureaucratic posts. The support of bureaucrats could be re-placed by support from other sectors, but this would involve shifting the political stratification, always a risky move.

If, on the other hand, the dissenting sectors are more peripheral, the statesman might decide to proceed with his reform and threaten coercion against those sectors that interfered with it. He should, however, consider more than the value of the support of the sectors in question. Their propensities for political action—their likelihood of using violence in response or their willingness to bargain—may make enforcement of his decision either quite costly or relatively inexpensive. The statesman also needs to consider the elasticity of the sectors' demand for no coercion and the value of other contributions they may withdraw from his regime. In addition, he will have to estimate the likely net gain or reduction in contributions from other sectors if he uses whatever coercion is necessary to gain compliance.

One way of increasing compliance and reducing costs would be to offer the sectors some share in authority over curriculum reform. The statesman could consult sector leaders on the proposed changes. Perhaps he might make them members of a commission to draft guidelines for reform. Unfortunately, the resulting recommendations would probably satisfy the statesman's plan only in part, but this strategy might prove relatively inexpensive for securing compliance with at least some of his reforms, especially if the sectors that objected were important and powerful enough to block his original plan.[46]

Let us assume, however, that the reforms in their entirety are valuable enough to the statesman that he wants them implemented practically *in toto*. There may be ways for him to reduce the costs imposed by dissident sectors at relatively little expense to his plan. He may, for instance, give dissident sectors some small influence over the implementation of the policy by consulting them on the appointment of educational administrators. This influence would give sectors only minimal power to affect the curriculum, yet it might mollify them somewhat and reduce their withdrawals of contributions. It may be important to these sectors that the regime at least show some respect for their interest or gloss over their inability to block the policy itself.

Whether a sector will value and accept currency as a substitute for a resource depends in part on its propensity for immediate as opposed to deferred gratification. In this particular case, the statesman must consider the strength of the sector's demand for no change in the curriculum as a function of how that sector values the resources it fears to lose from the reform, perhaps status and money. If its demand for these resources is quite inelastic because the marginal productivity or utility of these resources is not

---

[46] To "block" a policy means to make the cost of its implementation prohibitive or exorbitant to the regime.

diminishing, the sector may be difficult to satisfy. Much will depend on the value it places on the authority or influence offered it. It is possible that if the sector has a propensity for compromise and does not insist on total satisfaction, the regime might even increase the level of the support it receives from this sector by reaching a generous compromise.

In deciding how far to compromise with dissident sectors on the issue of curriculum reform, the statesman must also consider what losses of support he may incur from other sectors if he grants some authority or influence to the dissidents. Possibly he could lose more support by acceding to the dissidents' demands than he could by denying them. Before reaching a decision, he would have to compare the marginal disutility of losses of support resulting from either course of action, or the costs of offsetting actions in either case.

Support, however, is not the only cost with which the statesman must reckon. If he decides to ignore the demands of the dissident sectors, he must consider their threats to stop payment of school fees, which if carried out would cause a reduction in his money income. By threatening to expel students not paying fees, he might nullify the sectors' challenge. In this case he would be depriving these sectors of a service, using coercion if necessary to carry out his threat. Such a threat might be especially effective if the dissident sectors placed a high value on continued school attendance. The future status and money education represented would be lost to them if expulsions took place, and they might consider this loss greater than the value of averting certain curriculum changes by sticking to their demands and winning some authority or influence over curriculum.[47]

The effectiveness of the regime's counterthreat could thus be seen in terms of the elasticity of demand for schooling. If the threat to stop payment of fees were made by a religious sect that was anxious to avoid attending secular schools in the first place, members of this sect might gladly have their children expelled. The use of coercion to keep them in school would serve little educational purpose. What is more, permitting these children to stop attending school would undermine the effectiveness of the regime's compulsory school attendance law, which as political infrastructure is intended to secure compliance at less expense to the regime. In such

---

[47] If the regime's threat were made shortly before the annual examination for advancing students to the next year of study, it would probably be more effective than if it were made at the beginning of the school year. The regime could set the children of dissident parents back a year in school by expelling them at this critical time of the school year. This action would make the cost of dissidence clear to the sectors.

a situation, the statesman would presumably prefer to use coercion to compel attendance and fee-payment. However, this choice might prove very expensive indeed!

Under some circumstances the statesman might be reluctant to order pupils expelled for not paying fees. If his order were not carried out, his authority would be undermined and depreciated. By ordering expulsion of those delinquent in paying their fees, he would be delegating authority to the schools to carry out the decision. If no compliance resulted, the authority spent in this way would have been wasted. In the future, authoritative decisions in this area would be less likely to be obeyed, and the value of authority in this area would be depreciated. Since the costs of using authority or coercion to implement his reforms might be considerable, the statesman would be anxious to find other ways of securing compliance.

In this case the statesman might consider the marginal utility of money collected from school fees. Perhaps he could afford to overlook the non-payment of fees by some. However, this course of action would probably not provide a good solution to his dilemma. Since the marginal utility of money to the sectors is usually quite high, permitting non-payment by some might touch off wholesale refusal to pay the fees. If the regime's fiscal position were affluent, the marginal utility of money to the regime would be relatively low. In such a situation, the opportunity costs of giving up all revenue from school fees would not be too great. Therefore, the statesman might decide to abolish school fees altogether when making his curriculum reforms.[48] A reduction in money obtained from the sectors would probably increase the support and even the legitimacy accorded to the regime. With this new fund of currency and resources, the statesman could afford to dismiss the dissident sectors' threat to withdraw their support. The marginal utility of these sectors' resources to the regime would have declined as a result of the increase in total support available. Indeed, with this increase, the regime could probably afford to use coercion to compel school attendance and could possibly even undertake more extensive curriculum reform, to be financed by this new backing.

We must, however, remember that the statesman's choices are made under the limitations of resource scarcity. It is very helpful for a regime to have a surplus of money that can be used in place of authority or coercion to secure compliance, but because the regime probably has many uses for the money foregone by abolishing school fees, fees could probably not be

[48] For one thing, abolition of school fees would nullify the threat of dissident sectors to stop paying fees, and the statesman would neither have to risk wasting his authority nor losing support by using coercion.

eliminated without great cost to other policy goals. The statesman must consider in political terms the marginal utility and productivity of money spent for a variety of different purposes. His aim is to spend the money he has in whatever way will yield the greatest net political benefits, not just in the present, but over a certain period of time.

A statesman who is not financially solvent might nevertheless feel compelled to abolish fees and run a budget deficit. While he might want very much to carry out curriculum reforms that he judges to be vitally important to his country's future, he perhaps cannot afford to spend any authority or coercion or risk any loss of support. Thus a fiscal budget deficit, even if it will contribute to monetary inflation, appears to be his best solution. The resulting depreciation will make money a less effective currency in the future for obtaining resources needed by the regime. Still, necessity may dictate this policy course when other resources and currencies are even scarcer or less productive. A statesman may be willing to gamble that there will be in the not too distant future an increase in the output of resources sufficient to reduce the inflationary gap and restore integrity to the regime's currencies.

When hardest pressed, the statesman may have to share some of his authority. Yet if he gives one sector a share in authority over curriculum, others may demand an equal voice in making policy and may threaten to reduce their support and other contributions if denied. If the statesman grants equal authority to each of these others, he reduces the value of authority, which depends on scarcity. If only one sector has some authority over curriculum, it gets the curriculum it desires and the others probably do not. But if many competing sectors have some control over the state's decision, none will get the kind of curriculum it desires.[49]

When several competing sectors seek to participate in or influence the statesman's authoritative decisions, the increased demand raises the price of authority. This situation normally works to the statesman's advantage. However, these same sectors may not offer only positive inducements to the regime. If the question of curriculum reform becomes a matter of controversy, there may be many demands for a share in authority (performance) accompanied by threats of withdrawal of support or other sanctions. The statesman may find that he cannot make a decision or share authority with any sector without incurring large losses. In some controversies a statesman cannot win for losing. One way for the statesman to limit his losses would be to delegate authority over curriculum to a publicly-elected school board. Here the sectors' representatives could thrash out

[49] The same relationship holds for the currency of influence.

their competing preferences and arrive at some compromise curriculum. This plan would cost the statesman some amount of authority. The more he valued his curriculum reform, the higher the price he would be paying, since the resulting changes in curriculum would probably be considerably different from those he intended. Yet dissatisfaction felt by sectors would be directed at other sectors or at the autonomous school board that thwarted their desires, rather than at the regime. Therefore, creation of this board could minimize widespread loss of support from the sectors and would lessen the regime's vulnerability, but only at the cost of reducing the scope of regime authority by some measure.[50]

Our discussion of education reform suggests the kind of considerations involved in formulating strategies for reaching policy goals. We cannot give an answer to the question, "Should the statesman undertake curriculum reform or not?" Indeed, we cannot do so without knowing the relevant factors and variables in the particular situation.[51] Actually, the aim of political economy is not to make such decisions. Rather political economy aims at aiding in calculating *how best* to achieve given policy objectives. It provides a framework of analysis for relating a wide range of factors and considerations in terms of one another so that the decision that is reached will have taken into account the interrelation of the most salient elements affecting political exchange and the achievement of goals. The framework of political economy will suggest alternative courses of action or potential difficulties that would not necessarily be evident from a cursory examination of a policy problem. For instance, the possibility of altering status relations is often overlooked in political analysis. So too is the effect of threats, however implicit, of violence or coercion. To the extent that our analytical framework is comprehensive and efficient, it should assist in calculations of strategy and resource management.

The model should also indicate to a statesman or political scientist what

[50] An alternative would be for the stateman to create an appointed school board over which he would have more control. This board would probably support reforms more to his liking, but it would not be as effective in limiting his losses from the sectors. Because he maintained more control over the substantive decisions in this policy area, the desires of the sectors would be less satisfactorily met, and sectors might be inclined to respond accordingly in their exchanges with the regime.

[51] Similarly, an economist cannot advise whether to invest in AT&T stock without knowing the supply and demand for the stock, as well as the investor's resource position, his marginal utility for different uses of money (vacation in the Bahamas, college education for his children, etc.) and his particular propensities. The analytical framework of economics does assist in making choices that increase the welfare of the individual.

he needs to know to make successful calculations. It should help him to ascertain the important sectors, resources, supplies, demands, propensities, tactics, and strategies relevant to a particular policy decision. If full information cannot be secured, the model should still enable him to make more efficient use of his resources for achieving policy objectives on the basis of what information he has. Effective management of political resources should be greatly facilitated by a comprehensive analytical scheme. A developed discipline of political economy should provide such a policy tool.

V

POLITICAL INFLATION
AND DEFLATION

> . . . the interaction between ruling groups and their opponents
> has produced a distinctive shift from one form of political conflict,
> which consisted mainly of electoral competition, social pressure to
> conform, and attempts by the dominant party to co-opt oppo-
> nents, to another form of political conflict marked on the govern-
> ment side by more ruthless attempts to eliminate opponents by
> means of legal and extra-legal coercion, and on the other side by an
> increasing resort to violence, including civil disobedience and even
> political terrorism and assassination.
>
> Aristide Zolberg [1]

In describing what he calls the "inflationary spiral of coercion and violence" in West Africa, Zolberg illustrates both the full range of political
resources and the use of such resources in exchange. The political institutions and infrastructure left by the West African colonial regimes provided
for competition and the adjustment of conflicting interests through electoral processes, with votes manifesting legitimacy and the currency of support. The statesmen who first occupied the top authority roles in the new
regimes sought to maintain their positions and their power by various
means: they employed social pressure as a means of manipulating social
status and co-optation as a means of judiciously sharing authority. However, as the means employed did not effectively contain the growing demand for authority, these statesmen turned increasingly to the use of their
most effective remaining resource, coercion. Once electoral means of obtaining authority were blocked by the regime, anti-statesmen turned in-

[1] Zolberg (1966:87). See also Chapters III and IV.

creasingly to violence, which rapidly became their main political resource. Civil disobedience represented a denial of legitimacy. While Zolberg's depiction of political activity in West Africa may be overdrawn, it raises dramatically the issues of political inflation and deflation for our analysis of regime choices and policies.

Price Stability and Regime Stability

Maintaining the desired balance between supply of and demand for political resources is a critical problem for any regime. There is no necessary virtue in an enduring balance. An equilibrium condition for supply and demand may indicate political stagnation, with no increase in welfare for anyone through the political process. The ideal condition in economics is a dynamic equilibrium in which increases in demand are matched by equal increases in supply, or vice versa. Dynamic equilibrium is the utopian ideal for the polity as well, but as long as involuntary exchanges may be forced by coercion or violence, or the constraint of scarcity prevents the satisfaction of all demands, such equilibrium remains utopian in conception. Equilibrium—if such a condition can be said to exist in politics—serves particular interests and not necessarily any general interest.

The statesman may favor the existing allocation of resources, with its concomitant levels of supply and demand in the political market, or he may desire shifts that seem to him more equitable or profitable. Stable exchange rates for political resources indicate that there are no unbalancing shifts in supply or demand, since significant shifts in either will raise or lower the price of a resource. As we will see, price changes, especially those affecting authority, have important consequences for regime stability. It may be possible for price stability and increasing productivity in the political market to go hand in hand in the more developed countries. In these countries the allocations of resources have been altered to approach some optimum pattern. In developing countries, however, this marriage of stability and productivity is uncommon, if only because the process of nationalization of market causes frequent shifts in supply or demand. In particular, the advance of politicization leads to changes in the demand for authority that are not always matched by changes in the scope, effectiveness, and allocation of that resource.[2]

[2] In developing countries it becomes important to consider the respective price-elasticities of supply and demand for different resources. If both supply and demands are relatively elastic, shifts in price level will not be as great as

A statesman may have some a priori preference for maintaining stable prices for political and other resources. Stable prices stabilize expectations, encourage production and exchange, avoid unearned transfers of purchasing power, and may ease pressures on the government to redress imbalances or inequities in resource holdings. However, they primarily serve the interests of those who benefit from the status quo, among whom are the occupants of authority roles. Whenever a statesman is not satisfied with prevailing allocations and tries to alter them for the benefit of third parties or his regime, he upsets the balance between supply and demand and affects political price levels.[3] If a statesman's own resource position is weak, he is more likely to prefer relative price stability. Considerable shifts in supply or demand usually produce conflicts over exchange and allocation and thus demands for the intervention of authority. If the statesman is unable to control or offset the changes that such shifts bring about, political inflation or deflation may reach extremes and decisively undermine his ability to remain in authority.

Changes in supply or demand do not necessarily lead to a different equilibrium position. Some sectors are likely to be disadvantaged by any change (the optimality rule of Pareto is almost never satisfied) and will seek to restore or improve their own positions. Through some expenditure of regime resources, perhaps of coercion, what appears to be an equilibrium may be established, but as long as conflicts of interest remain there is no they are when either or both are relatively inelastic, as the diagrams below illustrate:

PRICE ELASTICITY   PRICE INELASTICITY

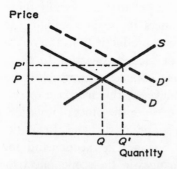

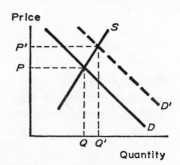

[3] The price level resulting from changes in supply or demand depends on the respective elasticity or inelasticity of supply or demand. The shape and level of demand curves probably vary more than those of supply curves. We are only speculating on the shape of supply curves for political resources, but it would seem that the curves would be price-inelastic with respect to rising demand and

inherently stable equilibrium in politics. Thus in political analysis the term lacks the precision it seems to have in economics and the natural sciences. It should be clear that across-the-board judgments about price stability or equilibrium in the political market are of little use or value. In economics price stability is desirable only if the distribution of resources is more or less acceptable to all and is thus productive; then the level of resources produced, exchanged, and consumed may increase with relatively little change in price. If these conditions and consequences are lacking, stability may mean stagnation, the only virtue of which is prevention of descent to a still lower level. When the interests of all parties are not identical, as in, for example, a debtor-creditor situation, price instability is desired by some and resisted by others. The preference of whichever group is politically more powerful is likely to prevail.

The nature of the political market makes a priori preferences for price stability less pertinent than they are in the economic market. The interests of the regime, while similar or synonymous with those of some sectors, are not those of all sectors. If the value of resources held by the regime appreciates, sectors must give up more of their resources to gain a given amount

price-elastic with respect to falling demand. In a simplified (linear) representation, rising costs of production due to mounting opportunity costs would mean that as demand increased from D_1 to D_2, the increased output from Q_1 to Q_2 would be at a proportionally higher cost $(P_2 \text{-} P_1)$. Conversely, a drop in demand to D_3 would result in a considerable decrease in output even though the price decline were proportionally less—Q_3 and P_3.

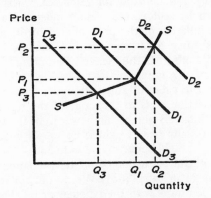

Our representation is, of course, highly idealized. The supply curve would seldom be "kinked," but would change from price-elastic to price-inelastic as the costs of production increased. Moreover, the demand curves would seldom be linear. They would change from price-inelastic to price-elastic as the marginal productivity or utility of the resource declined.

of regime resources. Those sectors seeking regime resources are thus less well off than they were before, although it must be borne in mind that the regime does not necessarily require the same price from all sectors for a certain resource. Preferential exchange rates are common in politics. Just as changes in the price level have opposite effects on debtors and creditors, inflation of the regime's resources means deflation of the resources held by the sectors, and vice versa. In the analysis that follows we will deal with price changes from the viewpoint of the statesman, though we reiterate that his gains and losses may be those of certain sectors as well. The consequences of inflation and deflation affecting sector resources will be considered in less detail.[4]

Political Inflation and Hyper-Inflation

When effective demand for a resource exceeds supply, the price of that resource will be bid up. As we are considering political economy from the statesman's point of view, we are applying the term *political inflation* to cases in which effective demand for authority and other regime resources exceeds the available supply. Authority (or its currency, influence) is valued according to its effectiveness in obtaining or compelling compliance. Demand from sectors for authority thus depends on this effectiveness, but the supply of authority depends primarily on how widely the statesman is willing to share his right to speak in the name of the state.[5]

[4] Changes in supply and demand for resources, whether the resources are held by the regime or by sectors, are seldom independent of one another. A regime benefits from inflation of the price offered for its authority or from deflation of the sectors' price for legitimacy. But changes in supply or demand may be relatively easily offset. If the demand for authority rises without a concomitant tightening of the supply of resources that sectors are willing to exchange for authority, the value of authority appreciates vis-à-vis that of other resources. This appreciation adds to the value of the regime's general resource position and in effect transfers purchasing power from the sectors to the regime. Sectors, however, are usually free to tighten up supply or reduce their demands if exchange rates become highly unfavorable to them.

[5] A novel and thoughtful discussion of political inflation is offered by Bredemeier and Stephenson (1962:387–392). We do not follow their approach because they are concerned more with the typology of inflation than with measuring degrees or proposing policy remedies, and because they emphasize and value equilibrium to a greater extent than we do. In addition, we find the procurement-disposal conceptualization they use less valuable than the economic concepts of supply and demand (upon which their concepts are obviously modelled), because we are interested in how much as well as what kind of interaction occurs.

From the statesman's point of view, it is usually true in politics that where authority is concerned, some excess of demand over supply is preferable to an equivalent excess of supply over demand. These conditions hold despite moderate price inflation. The higher the price that sectors are willing to pay for authority, the more resources the regime will possess and be able to use in securing compliance. Increased compliance as a rule further raises the value of and demand for authority. When demand for authority is less than the supply the statesman is willing to make available, whether because he asks too high a price or because the authority is not effective for sector purposes, the regime's resource position will deteriorate. In politics, unlike economics, it would seldom be advisable for a statesman simply to meet demand by varying the supply of authority available to the sectors. There is little to be gained from maintaining price stability per se or from maintaining a price level that "clears the market." To do either would be to surrender all control over public decisions to the sectors and would result in more chaos and anarchy than democracy. If everyone's preference cannot prevail, the preferences of those whose political resources are most effective will take precedence.

An increase in demand for authority reflects an increase in power on the part of those occupying authority roles, i.e., a greater ability to secure compliance. Increased ability to secure compliance may also result from an increase in the areas in which the authorities are accorded legitimacy status for making allocations or from an increase in other of the regime's resources—goods and services, status, coercion, and information. Both increases in authority and increases in the number of areas in which government was considered legitimate were notable in West Africa during the 1950's, as Zolberg describes:

. . . the authority of representative councils and of African executives was widened until, immediately before independence, it extended over most aspects of public life. . . . In order to be successful, organizations had to mobilize support from much larger bodies of people and compete with an increasing number of political entrepreneurs drawn into the game once the risks of punishment had practically disappeared and the rewards had become more tangible.[6]

As long as the supply of and the demand for authority do not get too far out of line with one another, inflation may contribute to the establishment and legitimation of the authority roles themselves. Legitimation of authority roles strengthens the position of the incumbents and better enables

[6] Zolberg (1966:19).

them to cope with the demands for authority and other resources coming from the sectors and the regime's opponents. Some statesmen may be more successful than others in containing and channeling the demand for authority.

If we compare the regimes in the Ivory Coast and Ghana, we can see how a statesman in each tried to cope with rising political inflation. President Houphouet-Boigny of the Ivory Coast literally bought off his opposition with positive and negative inducements. On one hand he judiciously co-opted some of the ablest radical student leaders by giving them important government posts, while on the other hand he used coercion extralegally and forcefully against those opponents whom he apparently judged could not be bought off or whose price would be too high. If we take death sentences as an indicator of the use of coercion, Houphouet-Boigny's regime has been the harshest in West Africa. Yet he himself has remained firmly in authority by using his resources adeptly and consolidating his resource position.[7]

In Ghana President Nkrumah did not manage so well. He felt that if he did not possess a monopoly of authority he would have to give up his goals for rapid economic, social, and political changes in Ghana and on the African continent. By means of coercion and threats as well as manipulation of status and economic resources, he was able to eliminate overt opposition and thus maintain for himself the sole right to speak in the name of the state.[8] However, monetization of the economy, social mobilization, and politicization were all more advanced in Ghana than in the Ivory Coast, making the demands on Nkrumah's regime and the challenges to his authority stronger. While he correctly judged the strength of his opponents' demands for authority and different policies, Nkrumah misjudged the substitutibility of coercion and other resources for more widely shared authority and the benefits thereof. Despite his continuous efforts to demonstrate "support" through the party-controlled press, constitutional plebicites, and trade unions and other organizations, actual support declined. Although it is not clear whether a popular uprising could have ousted Nkrumah while he maintained control of the police, support decreased to

[7] Zolberg (1966:36). Zolberg notes that it is not clear whether the nineteen or more capital sentences for "plots" against the President have been carried out. For a fuller account of Houphouet-Boigny's political strategies, see Zolberg (1964a) and (1964b).

[8] In his study of Nkrumah's rule, Bretton (1966) argues that authority had become more centralized and concentrated in Ghana under Nkrumah than in any other African country. Bretton's emphasis on Nkrumah's "personal rule" ignores, however, the various other power relationships inside and outside Ghana that influenced policy choices.

such an extent that there was virtually no popular resistance to the military and police coup that occurred in February of 1966. Indeed, the Trade Union Congress and Young Pioneers, previously the most vociferous supporters of the Nkrumah regime, pledged their full support to the new regime almost immediately.

Because in the years after independence popular support for Nkrumah had in large part been generated by promises and modest achievements of economic progress, some would ascribe the ouster of Nkrumah to the failure of his economic policies and to the fact that by 1965 serious inflation had set in and standards of living had actually declined.[9] We, however, feel that political inflation was more decisive than economic inflation in Nkrumah's ouster. If Nkrumah had not alienated the Ghanaian army, he could probably have maintained himself in authority for at least several more years. Although the grievances of the army as a sector were many, probably its most basic dissatisfaction with Nkrumah resulted from his intervention in what it considered to be its internal affairs. Army leaders were forced to give up their authority to make decisions concerning promotion, retirement, and overseas training of officers as well as their influence over how and where their troops were to be used.[10] This loss of authority and influence made army leaders more sympathetic with the efforts of regime opponents to remove Nkrumah from authority. Nkrumah fell, not necessarily because he was somehow less virtuous than Houphouet-Boigny, but because he was less successful in satisfying or nullifying the effective demands of powerful sectors. When regime allocations of authority and other resources become unsatisfactory to sectors that possess more effective resources than the regime can muster, the opportunity for a new regime arises.

In politics, as in economics, it is a matter of judgment when inflation becomes *hyper-inflation*. In Ghana the extreme scarcity of authority seems to have brought about the latter, more extreme condition. Yet Houphouet-Boigny's success thus far has shown that an inflationary spiral need not turn into hyper-inflation. His regime has curbed the demands for authority, in part by accommodating them, in part by reducing them through coercion, yet he as President has retained ultimate control. Though at the

[9] According to current market prices, national product grew in 1965 by almost 17 per cent, but in real terms it fell by 0.2 per cent. When population growth of 2.5 per cent or more is allowed for, per capita income and living standards declined on the average by as much as 3 per cent during that year. See Ghana, *Economic Survey* (1966:13–14).

[10] For a discussion of the views of the army leadership, see Alexander (1965) and Afrifa (1966); for Nkrumah's views and calculations about the army as a sector, see his recent book (1968: esp. 36–39).

time of independence Nigeria appeared to be one of the most stable countries in West Africa, Bretton foresaw there what amounted to political inflation tending toward political hyper-inflation:

> In fact, as soon as such positions [of authority and influence have] increased in value as a result of accrual of power, the struggle will become intensified. Then drastic political change will become more worthwhile because the stakes will be higher; and the political system will be subjected to increased pressures toward the creation of conditions that will facilitate a new transfer of power.[11]

His prediction of more radical and even revolutionary politics in Nigeria during the 1960's has thus far not been borne out. However, the increasingly radical orientation of the Action Group Party under Chief Awolowo once that group was excluded from authority might have led to revolution had the Federal Government not intervened to jail Awolowo and his main associates. Certainly it was the denial of authority in the national government that prompted the Action Group to take a more aggressive attitude toward the political process and perhaps even to attempt unconstitutional means of seizing authority by force.

In a situation of hyper-inflation, would-be possessors of authority bid up the price of authority with escalating offers or threats. If the supply is not expanded and authority is not shared, sectors that are denied authority may withdraw resources as a sanction against the regime. The disengagement of the Western Region of Nigeria following the fraudulent 1964 elections is an example of such withdrawal. Of concern to the statesman in authority is the likelihood that dissatisfied sectors will give resources to an anti-statesman who offers to share authority with sectors at a lower price if he is able to displace the statesman. We emphasize that a statesman will not give authority to just any sector that makes offers or threats. If he delegates authority judiciously, he will assure that the power of authority will most often be used for political ends of which he approves. When faced with demands for authority from powerful sectors, some statesmen prefer to remain in authority and to compromise certain objectives. Other statesmen would "rather be right than be President."

Political Deflation and Depression

From the statesman's point of view, a supply of political resources that exceeds demand causes a situation of *political deflation* or the more extreme

[11] Bretton (1962:5); see also Sklar (1965:201–213).

political depression. Say's law has limited validity in economics; in politics as well, supply does not necessarily create its own demand.[12] A statesman may have authority that he is willing to share for a price, but there may be no takers at the price he asks. This will be the case whenever the price required by the statesman is greater than the benefit sectors can derive from using the authority made available. When the demand for a statesman's resources falls or remains low, the relative size of the public sphere is contracting or is small. Perhaps sectors could obtain greater satisfactions through the auspices of the state, but under the prevailing conditions of the political market sectors prefer to seek their objectives through private intersectoral exchanges. Authority is judged to be either too ineffective or too expensive relative to the cost of securing it and the benefits sought from it. It is possible that the welfare of sectors may be greater with little or no resort to the state, yet from the statesman's point of view, political deflation and depression reduce the purchasing power of his regime and his ability to pursue and satisfy his goals for the community.

If the demand for regime resources, and for authority in particular, falls, but not to a seriously low level, we speak of this decrease as deflation. Deflation indicates a loss of confidence in the government. Under such circumstances sectors may make their resources available to the regime's opponents, who offer or promise a more advantageous relationship to the exercise of state authority. As a rule, a statesman will try to maintain a high level of demand for his authority. To stimulate demand he may operate with a deficit political budget, or in effect make loans of authority or influence to sectors. By expending more resources and currencies than he receives, he thereby gives sectors more purchasing power and a taste of what benefits may come from using the resources of the regime. He thus may be able to raise the level of demand and reverse deflation before it becomes depression. It should be noted that a statesman may not always seek to counteract deflation. Indeed, he would probably desire it if inflationary

[12] One explanation for the lesser validity of Say's law in politics is that production of political resources seldom involves any intersectoral payments to factors of production. A sector produces and exchanges as much of a political resource as it feels it is adequately compensated for, considering opportunity costs. The production of economic resources, on the other hand, usually requires payments to other sectors for land, labor, and capital. If an excess supply is produced, the income of these other sectors will have been increased in the process so that there is at least potentially increased demand as well. In politics the needs, wants, and intentions of sectors and regimes determine the price they are willing to pay for a resource, and the price in turn determines how much will be produced and offered for exchange. Demand is a greater driving force and determinant in the political process than supply.

pressures had built up and threatened his regime with hyper-inflation.

The drop in demand for a regime's resources and the corresponding decrease in the regime's ability to secure adequate resources from the sectors may be due to foolish actions on the part of the statesman. A statesman who is apolitical and does not know how to evaluate or utilize his resources may lower their value by being too generous with the supply he gives to the sectors. He may, for example, broadcast his intentions widely, keeping no regime secrets. By doing so he undermines his ability to bargain with sectors, since they already know what he intends to do. A more astute statesman would leak certain information to raise competition for his resources but would maintain uncertainty about what his final decision would be. Some statesmen may not know how to exercise authority effectively. In seeking compliance they may use the resources at their disposal inefficiently, giving too much for what they get. Or they may have little understanding of how to alter resource distributions to make them more productive. At the same time, a statesman with more political wisdom may nonetheless find his resource position jeopardized. If he refuses to share authority with sectors that have important resources to contribute, and uses that authority in ways they do not approve of, political depression may result. The productivity of the polity could probably not be raised until authority roles were occupied by leaders who represented to a greater degree the ideologies and desires of the more powerful sectors.

If political inflation confronted the regimes of Houphouet-Boigny and Nkrumah in West Africa, political depression threatened to destroy the regime of Joaquin Balaguer in the Dominican Republic following his election as President in 1966. Many sectors wanted to speak in the name of the state, but not within or through his regime. Consequently the resources Balaguer could get from the sectors declined, and it appeared for some time that he could not enforce his authority or maintain it. We feel that a consideration of the difficulties Balaguer encountered will illustrate some of the problems causing or accompanying political depression.[13]

In April, 1965, supporters of reformist Juan Bosch tried to restore his regime, which had been ousted two years before by military force. Since the Boschist regime could not be restored through electoral channels, worker and student sectors resorted to insurrectionary violence. They were halted by military force, but only after the United States had interjected its own

[13] An analysis of the Dominican political situation by Sidney Lens (1966: 3–4) comes very close to that of political economy. We draw here on his descriptions of contending sectors, demands, resources, anti-statesmen, and propensities.

military force to "keep peace." [14] Even after the fighting had ceased, the
military and its allies continued to use violence, beatings, and assassinations
to quell their political foes. As a countermeasure the Boschist and Fidelist
oppositions engaged in work stoppages, strikes, and demonstrations. Representatives of the Organization of American States, trying to restore political peace, arranged for elections by June, 1966.

Even though the 1966 elections were supposed to have been free and fair,
there is little doubt that the use of force by right-wing sectors made a considerable difference in the outcome.[15] In the climate of coercion, many
voters were convinced, not without reason, that a vote for Bosch was
wasted because the military would use force to prevent him from taking
office. Balaguer's campaign was well financed by the oligarchy, and he was
able to accumulate a commanding majority in the more conservative rural
areas. It seemed to the inhabitants of these areas that the election of Balaguer was more likely to restore peace to the strife-weary community than
was the election of Bosch. By whatever means support was gained, votes
registered a two-to-one preference for Balaguer. Before long, however, the
military was reportedly plotting Balaguer's ouster. It disapproved of Balaguer's reallocation of economic resources and objected to the exile status
given its leader Wessin while Communist leaders still enjoyed full political
status and an opportunity for influence.

The military was not the only part of Balaguer's core combination to reduce its support and other resources. According to Lens, the Dominican
oligarchy had expected a bonanza—price supports for tobacco, continued
luxury imports, greater curbing of the unions, and similar measures. Instead Balaguer, though he had frozen wages and abolished the right to
strike, decided as well to collect income taxes with greater vigor. While he
improved the economic position of the most populous sectors by slightly
reducing the price of meat, rice, and edible oil, he made luxury imports far
more difficult to obtain. The gentry, therefore, were unhappy and were not
averse to discussing military measures to oust Balaguer.

When Balaguer's rightist support disappeared, his government was kept
in office largely by the opposition party, the PRD. Although Bosch dis-
agreed with Balaguer's policies, he preferred that Balaguer serve out his

[14] For a detailed account of the U.S. role in the Dominican crisis, see
Draper (1965:33–68).

[15] Lens (1966) says that Bosch could not campaign in the interior of the
country without a three-to-one chance of being killed: "The army terrorized
thousands of people and then stole scores of ballot boxes which it had duly
stuffed with the 'right' ballots." He adds, however, that Bosch probably could
not have won even if the ballot boxes had been sacrosanct.

four-year term. By accepting the position of responsible opposition, Bosch and his PRD party were making a legitimacy investment. While Balaguer lacked support from sectors in his core combination, Bosch and his followers gave the regime allegiance and legitimacy status, though they did not necessarily support Balaguer and his policies.

Through the allegiance and legitimacy accorded by Bosch and the PRD, Balaguer was by and large able to secure compliance. He could not have done so had he had to rely entirely on his erstwhile "supporters" for the resources necessary to enforce decisions. Nor could he have done so had he had to secure resources for his regime by sharing his precarious authority. The allegiance and legitimacy invested by the PRD aimed at building up the role of President, which Bosch hoped to occupy after the next election. To the extent that the role itself was legitimated it would receive resources from sectors no matter who occupied it. If the role lacked legitimacy, its authority might be worthless and its occupant might again be displaced by the military. Bosch's investment decision and strategy saved Balaguer's regime from political bankruptcy, since the regime could not even rely on the coercion of the army and police to back up its decisions.

Balaguer's even-handed economic deprivations, made in an attempt to restore economic prosperity and development, cost him the support of the socially important sectors. The unions, however, though similarly deprived, were willing to accept his measures, preferring long-run economic and political development to short-run economic gains. Balaguer's economic policies even earned him some legitimacy from the unions. The fairness with which he used government power against the oligarchy, perhaps for the first time in Dominican history, certainly pleased the unions and gained good will for the regime.

If Balaguer's measures for economic recovery are successful and unemployment can be reduced, his political strength will increase. His authority will come to be valued more highly because his allocation of economic and social resources will be more substantial. Whether his "tough" policies pay off will depend in large part on whether the Boschists are willing to collaborate or at least to accept the decisions of the regime. As long as Balaguer can count on the compliance of the large bulk of workers and peasants, a rightist coup against his regime will be less profitable and more unlikely.[16] At present there are few sectors within his core combination,

---

[16] This relationship between support and military non-intervention is traced by Ali Mazrui and Donald Rothchild in their analysis of military intervention in East Africa. They say that less military force will have to be expended to oust a dictator than to overthrow a government with popular support. See Mazrui and Rothchild (1967:86).

though some powerful ones are within what we would call the stability group.

The fact that Balaguer has remained in authority has surprised many observers. His tenure of office can be attributed not just to the alignment of sectors in the Dominican Republic, the policies he has pursued and the foreign aid he has received, but also to his having followed one particular canon of political economy. When the demand for authority is low, the supply of authority must be reduced to maintain the prevailing price. This Balaguer has done. He has centralized authority to a high degree, even to the point of granting and signing all visas himself. This practice is time-consuming, but by directing all sector claims and benefits through his office, Balaguer has given himself the opportunity to secure maximum support and other contributions in return for benefits conferred by the state.

Balaguer's future is still not completely secure, but the results of the May 1968 municipal elections indicate that he may have led his regime from political depression to relative prosperity. His *Reformista* party gained about 90 per cent of the mayoralties and city council posts at stake.[17] While less than even-handed economic policies, economic recession, or a reduction in external aid could reduce his current level of support, because the value of authority has been raised, Balaguer should be able to build a stronger base of support by sharing some authority with a number of sectors making up a working political majority of the community. It is possible that he will choose not to share authority, being a believer in *personalismo*. If he continues to have this approach to government, political inflation, with the attendant dangers of hyper-inflation, is likely to set in.

Sector Inflation and Deflation

In the political market the position of sectors is opposite to that of the regime. Excessive demands made by the regime on sector resources inflate the value of these resources and deflate the value of regime resources. Thus sector inflation is the other side of the coin of political (regime) deflation.

[17] Voter participation in the election was considered high, despite pleas by Wessin and Bosch for heavy abstention. Bosch in particular had been banking on his ability to maintain his power base of political support and not lose it to Balaguer. Apparently this base has diminished and now mainly consists of certain trade unions and intellectual groups. The labor and intellectual sectors on the far left no longer support Bosch, but neither has Wessin maintained his base of support. The island's upper classes are benefiting from the upsurgence of economy and appear to be satisfied with the incumbent regime, at least for the present.

The effects of both are the same, though the causes differ somewhat. In the former case, regime demand is too high vis-à-vis the supply of resources available from the sectors; in the latter, sector demand is too low in relation to the supply of resources available from the regime. Sector inflation can be readily dealt with by the regime, by merely reducing its demands on the sectors. To be sure, this course of action has costs for the statesman; he must forego those policies dependent on a greater amount of sector resources. But he would have to forego many of these policies anyway if he allowed the value of sector resources to inflate and that of his own to deflate.

We would expect a statesman to find some comfort in sector deflation. In such a situation, sectors have available a greater supply of their resources than the regime demands. Consequently the value of sector resources is deflated and that of the regime's resources inflated. This is an advantageous situation for the regime, at least in the short run. If it persists, however, sectors may disengage themselves from the rest of the political community.[18] They may either aim at greater self-sufficiency outside the political market or they may offer their resources to an opponent of the regime who may use them to gain authority.

Political Stagnation

It is quite possible that a political market may be in an equilibrium position: no new demands are made and no new supplies are forthcoming. Whether demands are stable because they are satiated or because they are stalemated makes little difference for the workings of the market. In such a situation, the political process is moribund and contributes little to improvements in welfare. The productive potential of authority may not be recognized or appreciated. The condition of political stagnation usually appears more serious when the equilibrium of supply and demand is reached at a low level of production and exchange. In this case the contribution that politics could make to mobilizing resources and raising welfare is clear. But political stagnation is possible at a high level as well. Just as

[18] Disengagement from the political process is likely to result if sectors judge the rewards from political interaction to be unsatisfactory, that is, if benefits are less than costs. However, sectors, even if dissatisfied may nonetheless be forced to contribute resources to the regime. This is the history of most past relations between central governments and the peripheral, usually rural sectors. Such disengagement is of interest because it raises the costs of compliance for a statesman.

economic stagnation might appear less serious in Belgium than Liberia, it might be argued that political stagnation at a high level is less unsatisfactory. A country like Sweden apparently has a dynamic political equilibrium, with moderate increments in demand matched by increases of supply. Traditional monarchies probably provide the best examples of political stagnation. In Kuwait, for example, tremendous economic resources have been received from outside but have been channeled into the royal family. They have thus been kept from the political market except for tactical expenditures to contain demand. It now appears that even in Kuwait, demands from various sectors such as the students and educated elite are being made and felt. Perhaps Kuwait is about to enter a period of rising political inflation.

Anti-Inflationary and Anti-Deflationary Measures

We can summarize the different conditions of the political market as follows; the notations refer to the demand for resources (D), or supply of resources (S), emanating from sectors ($_s$) or regimes ($_r$):

POLITICAL
HYPER-
INFLATION
$(D_s >> S_r)$ POLITICAL   SECTOR
                   INFLATION   DEFLATION
                   $(D_s > S_r)$ POLITICAL $(S_s > D_r)$
                                     EQUILIBRIUM
                                     or STAGNATION
                   POLITICAL $(D_s = S_r, D_r = S_s)$ SECTOR
                   DEFLATION   INFLATION
POLITICAL $(S_r > D_s)$ $(D_r > S_s)$
DEPRESSION
$(S_r >> D_s)$

Much empirical study could and should be devoted to these different political conditions. It might be established, for example, that coups d'etat were more likely to occur when political hyper-inflation had developed, while social revolutions resulted from severe political depression. Or it might be found that the political situation of regimes experiencing coups would differ according to the prior condition of the political market, depending on whether the market was experiencing inflation, deflation, or stagnation. Here we can only suggest what measures might be undertaken by a statesman trying to achieve his objectives subject to the constraints of the political market.

Political inflation will usually be welcomed by a statesman. His concern will not be to end it, but to keep it in check. Handled skillfully, the demands accompanying political inflation may be used to expand the scope of the public sphere. This expansion itself acts to absorb demands for authority. As the state effectively allocates resources in more areas, there are additional ways in which a statesman can share authority without diminishing his own. The simplest means of reducing excess demand for resources is, of course, to meet the demand. Policy responsiveness is viewed by some social scientists in a somewhat schizophrenic fashion. It is seen as being democratic on the one hand, and Machiavellian or opportunistic on the other. Appearances and motivations, however, are commonly misleading. It is far better to examine what resource allocations are involved, how changes conflict with or further the statesman's valued objectives, and how widely shared these objectives are within the political community. Decentralization is a special form of policy responsiveness because it entails the delegation or sharing of the statesman's most valued resource, his authority. We have already suggested why decentralization is an expensive action for any regime: delegated authority may be used to make claims on other resources and perhaps may be used to counter the statesman's own valued goals. If authority is granted to a sector possessed of a government structure, this amounts to decentralization of authority. However, influence given to non-governmental sectors may have the same effect on allocations. Where authority is given to individuals, this amounts to co-optation.[19]

In addition to employing policy responsiveness to reduce excess demand from the sectors, a statesman may employ measures that aim at decreasing sector demand. Increasing political taxation is one such measure. The increased use of coercion may also curb demands made on the regime. There are very few countries in which increases in the supply of resources can generally keep pace with demand unless measures are taken by the regime to reduce or constrain sectoral demand. Indeed, usually the more demands

[19] There has been surprisingly little study of co-optation in the political process. The inference is that persons representing potential or real threats to the government (i.e., persons who might dispossess the incumbents of their authority roles) are somehow bought off and are presumably satisfied with economic and social rewards. But in practice co-optation often means a sharing of authority as well, so that the new members of government are able to advance their policy preferences at least in part. See Selznick (1949: esp. 259–264) for one of the better discussions of co-optation.

are satisfied, the more rapidly they grow. A statesman who understands
the dynamics of this situation will try through political taxation of various
sorts or through stringent bargaining to reduce sector holdings of resources.[20] In this way he can reduce the sectors' effective demand for authority and other resources or at least hold it to a moderately rising level.
Probably the most effective strategy for containing inflationary pressures
would be some combination of the two approaches. The demand for authority is commonly related to the extent of politicization i.e., the size of
the public domain in relation to the size of the private domain. Inflation
is more likely to occur if politicization is more advanced than the nationalization of the economic and social markets. If the three markets have not
expanded more or less evenly, a statesman may lack the control over economic and social resources that could help him satisfy political demands.[21]

If a statesman is confronted with political deflation, he may increase demand for his regime's resources by reducing taxation, being more generous
in his exchanges with the sectors, and using less coercion. These measures
are the equivalent of deficit fiscal budgets to stimulate demand, or "pump-
priming," to use a more graphic expression. He cannot, however, simply
follow courses of action opposite to those he follows when dealing with
political inflation. He may only worsen his situation if he tries to reduce
the supply of regime resources available to the sectors by policy unrespon-
siveness or by centralization of authority. The imbalance between supply
and demand may be more a matter of excess regime demand for sector resources (or sector inflation) than of deficient sector demand for regime resources vis-à-vis supply. For a regime to contract the supply of available
authority when demand drops may only compound the disengagement of
sectors from the regime or from the political community itself. If the pub-

[20] For an excellent treatment of regime responses to political inflation, and
especially of the consequences of using coercion, see Zolberg (1968:76–77).
See also Parsons (1964:64).

[21] In his consideration of political development and institutionalization,
Huntington suggests what amount to anti-inflationary measures, though he does
not call them by that name. He fears that mushrooming demands made on the
state will lead to political degeneration. These demands he sees, much as we do,
as stemming from politicization or socialization. Among his suggestions for
ameliorative government actions are: increasing the complexity of the social
structure; limiting or reducing the volume and scope of communications; minimizing competition among segments of the elite; and channeling political interests away from national interests—"localization" of politics. While his first
suggestion is somewhat abstract, the others have practical value even if they are
not easily implemented. See Huntington (1965).

lic sphere shrinks due to reciprocal reductions in the political resources made available and in the demand for them, we may expect deflation to become political depression.

Thus the problem for a statesman who finds demand for his resources declining is not to reduce supply to balance demand but rather to stimulate demand so that it may return to—or surpass—its previous level. Stimulating demand will usually require some measure of policy responsiveness, the same prescription for containing inflation, though used for a different purpose. As an anti-inflationary measure, responsiveness primarily involves political resources and has secondary consequences for the allocation of other resources. As an anti-deflationary measure, it may well require the distribution of economic and social resources through the political process. In the latter case, the aim of policy responsiveness would be to tie sectors to the regime and the community by demonstrating to them the benefits of political participation and commitment.

Sector deflation, occurring when the supply of sector resources available is greater than the regime's demand for them, is even more advantageous for a statesman than political inflation. It is most common in times of national emergency such as war or disaster. Sector deflation provides the statesman with an unusual opportunity to improve his resource position; he may, for example, be accorded legitimacy for government allocations in areas previously reserved for private decision. No statesman would take measures against sector deflation as long as it continued within limits. He might enjoy his affluence, like the grasshopper, or use this opportunity to strengthen his position through saving and investment, like the ant. But the limits of sector deflation are not always easily discernible. If it becomes relatively disadvantageous for a sector to continue its intercourse with the regime, that sector may disengage itself from the regime or even from the political community, an undesirable situation to be sure for the statesman who has been enjoying a net benefit from exchange with the sector due to favorable terms of trade. There is no rule to follow for keeping sector deflation within limits. A statesman would have to know the propensities and ideology of the sector involved in order to decide how far to exploit his advantage.

If the opposite situation, sector inflation, occurs, no statesman can acquiesce to the sectors without concern. Because the regime is then usually more dependent on the sectors than the sectors are upon it, the terms of trade are unfavorable to the statesman. He may try to reduce this dependence by finding other sources of supply, perhaps by mobilizing hitherto unmobilized sectors. Or he may have to reduce his ambitions, expectations, and demands. His choice is not an easy one, but if he lets the inflationary level of demand continue, he will only reduce the purchasing power of his resources without yielding proportionate benefits to his regime.

If he has not tried anti-inflationary or anti-deflationary measures in the past, or if he has found such measures unsuccessful, the statesman who finds himself in the midst of political hyper-inflation or political depression may have few acceptable courses of action open to him. His tenure is tenuous, to say the least. His general strategy should be to try to reduce sector demand for political resources, in the first instance, to stimulate it in the second. Whether he can or will be successful may depend on circumstances peculiar to his situation. President Balaguer was fortunate to have compliance from the sectors supporting Juan Bosch. Other statesmen have not been so lucky. Still, under whatever circumstances, political economy clarifies the issues and the directions in which policy should aim if the statesman desires regime stability. Political price stability, if not a virtue in itself, is at times a very important proximate goal.

There are few statesmen who find themselves in a situation of political stagnation. Presumably they enjoy maintenance of the status quo and have made little effort to stimulate the demand for or to increase the supply of authority. What holds the political community at dead center is probably the particular distribution of political resources. Effective demand is at the level of available supply. Perhaps the majority of the sectors lack the wealth, status, infomation, or authority to make claims on the polity. Or because of particular values or ideologies, sectors may accept the status quo or eschew violence as a means of making claims. However, we have seen again and again that as the exchange of resources in other markets increases, exchange in the political market increases. Sectors have more money, status, and information that they can use in gaining some share of authority. Acquisition of some authority in turn leads to other changes in allocation, so that the structure and stratification of the political community may be changed. Political inflation is probably the first consequence of moving off dead center, but once a dynamic political market is established, any of many different conditions may prevail.

Depreciation and Appreciation

We have discussed political inflation and deflation in terms of excess or deficiency of demand for a resource relative to supply. When we deal with political currencies, we usually speak of *political depreciation* or *apprecia-*

tion. If a balance is not maintained between the amount of a political currency held by sectors or regime and the amount of resources available to be claimed with that currency, the value of the currency will depreciate or appreciate as the case may be. Raising or lowering the price of a resource in terms of its currency contributes to political inflation or deflation.

Just as inflation may be more common in developing than in developed countries, so too may depreciation. Influence may be given more widely than there is authority to be wielded. More symbols of status or prestige may be in circulation than there is equivalent esteem and deference to be accorded them. More threats of violence or coercion may be issued than there is effective force to back them up. At the same time, promises of support and pledges of allegiance may exceed the resources on which these currencies can draw. If a regime can restrict the issuance of currency claims on its resources while its store of resources increases, the value of its currency will appreciate. Thus it may develop greater capability to use coercion without having made more threats, or its authority in a certain area may become more effective without more sectors being entitled to influence the allocations affecting that area. Sector currencies, of course, may also appreciate or depreciate. The effect of sector currency appreciation or depreciation on a regime's resource position depends on which currency is involved and on which sectors hold it.

When a regime is scarce on resources, it may try to get sectors to accept currency instead. It may offer influence instead of authority, prestige for individuals rather than status for the sector, or money in lieu of physical goods and services. For a regime to issue currency without a concomitant increase in resources of course depreciates that currency. In such a situation, the value of currency is depreciated because the currency can secure fewer resources per unit. Indeed, if there are already inflationary pressures, a sector, like the regime, will prefer to receive resources rather than currency. Clearly the statesman must determine whether to issue currency in lieu of transferring resources themselves. He may, however, have little control over the activities and attitudes of the sectors. For instance, the balance between prestige and status may get seriously out of line, affecting his resource position without his being able to correct the imbalance. There are no assured methods of controlling depreciation and appreciation. When depreciation is occurring, the statesman should of course insist on securing resources from the sectors instead of currency "IOU's." But the sectors may not be willing or able to provide the resources themselves. When he cannot control supply, a statesman can only try to affect the level of demand and in this way restore some correspondence between the levels of currency in circulation and the resources available.[22]

Monopoly and Monopsony

The statesman's ability to maintain stable and favorable exchange rates depends to some extent on the degree and kind of monopolistic control the regime or sectors exercise over the supply and demand of resources. If the regime enjoys a monopoly as the only seller or a monopsony as the only buyer, sector deflation may result. The inflation of the value of sector resources vis-à-vis that of regime resources is bound to occur when a sector or group of sectors can exercise monopolistic or monopsonistic pressures. For example, if the army and police together have a monopoly on the coercion available to the regime, they may be able to command a very high price from the statesman. Monopoly or monopsony permits a sector to make either supply or demand inelastic and thus make volume relatively unresponsive to price. Clearly regime stability as well as price stability is at stake when sector monopoly or monopsony becomes extreme. A statesman may formulate and carry through an anti-trust policy in some form or other, though permitting, to be sure, greater degrees of monopoly and monopsony to exist for sectors higher in the political stratification. Usually governments would like to have some degree of monopoly power over resources in order to facilitate carrying out certain policies. But there are limits to the practicability or desirability of monopoly even for a regime.[23]

[22] In the process of nationalization, be it political, economic, or social, more resources are generated. If the value of currency is to be kept constant, more must be issued in proportion to the increase in resources. If there is no proportionate increase in currency held by sectors or regime, the value of currency will appreciate and command more resources for its possessor.

[23] Eisenstadt (1961:28–31) sees a tendency on the part of political elites and bureaucrats in developing countries to monopolize authority and prestige. Business groups and middle and working classes, he says, are prevented from becoming centers of social power because they are viewed by the elite as interfering with stabilization of the new basic institutional framework and with the development of universal allegiance to the new common symbols of the regime. The potential or actual lack of stability in the development of modern political institutions he attributes to "the strong emphasis on acquisition of power and the tendency of the elite to monopolize as many activities and values as possible." We would suggest that his generalization, however suggestive, cannot be applied universally, since in some countries political stability would be enhanced by more rather than less regime monopoly over resources.

In this study we do not pass a blanket judgment on monopoly concentrations, but rather try to provide an analytical basis for evaluating their consequences for achieving political ends.

A regime cannot permit any sector to have an uncontrolled monopoly on any resource. A common conflict over monopoly powers arises from the virtual monopoly on coercion that the army and/or the police enjoy. If an army has such a monopoly and is able to withhold coercion, or is able to use coercion outside the control of the regime, the regime's resource position is significantly, perhaps fatally weakened. There may be situations where a caste has a virtual monopoly on social status; it is accorded the greatest esteem and deference by other sectors, and the greater esteem it accords to some of the "lower" sectors rather than to others determines the respective status rankings of these sectors in the stratification system. It is also possible for a class to have practically a monopoly on economic goods and services through landownership or control of capital. A sector with a monopoly on coercion, status, or economic resources is likely to be part of the core combination, since any statesman in such a community would either be greatly dependent on it or could not buck its power. If the sector is not included in the core combination, the statesman will probably spare no effort to destroy its monopoly. Indeed, even if it were included, he might try to undermine its monopoly if that monopoly hindered his achievement of important political goals for the community.

When faced with a monopoly situation, the statesman should keep two economic alternatives in mind. If the supply of a resource is inelastic because of monopoly power, the regime can make the situation more competitive by finding or establishing alternative suppliers. The recent creation of the Red Guards in China may have been a way for Mao Tse-Tung to ensure himself an alternative supply of force. Perhaps he thought that by making supply more elastic he could reduce his dependence on the army, that is, lower the effective price the army could command for its force. With the creation of the Red Guard, the People's Liberation Army would be less able to extract political or economic concessions from his regime. When a statesman considers the price demanded for a resource too high, for whatever reasons, he may seek substitutes for the scarce resource. Perhaps Mao created the Red Guards to provide a substitute or supplementary means of securing compliance. If enemies of the regime in authority were not to be forced to comply through coercion, the Red Guards could enforce compliance by the threat of status deprivations. "Bourgeois" sectors were humiliated and denigrated by the vociferous and crude tactics of the Red Guard. Certainly creation of the Red Guard made Chairman Mao less dependent on the PLA and gave him a more flexible instrument to use against Party officials and even against workers and peasants. Possibly the army would not have agreed to use its coercion against these sectors.

The regime usually has a monopoly on the supply of authority. To be sure, if a regime has little legitimacy or if there are strong challengers bidding for positions of authority, this monopoly may be of little value; however, insofar as the regime's authority is valued by the sectors and its monopoly position is secure, it can secure other resources on favorable terms from those sectors that desire to share or influence authority. Sectors will frequently recognize the disadvantage they are at when bargaining individually with a monopolistic regime. Collective bargaining in politics is not a right but a fact, and sectors often combine to make their collective position stronger.[24] Even though each sector must usually give up some part of its demands in the interests of fashioning a collective position, the possibility of each's achieving at least part of its demands is improved by creating such countermonopolies.

Though we have presented our analysis in terms of monopolistic activities and counteractivities, we could offer similar analyses of monopsonistic relations. We neither endorse nor reject monopolistic or monopsonistic practices. It is up to the statesman to decide how he can best achieve his objectives; yet we feel that he can probably make more wise decisions if he understands the implications of the practices with which he is dealing. This, of course, is also our judgment about the statesman's decisions in regard to other general relationships between the supply of and demand for political resources. As our analysis now stands, however, the strategies available to the statesman are in too general a form. What is needed for political economy is a more specific range of policies to maintain advantageous relationships between supply and demand. It is to these policies that we now turn.

[24] Almond calls this kind of collective bargaining "interest aggregation." See Almond (1960). A different treatment of this phenomenon is found in Downs (1957). One of the best theoretical treatments of this phenomenon is Olson (1965). We would observe that as far as political participants are concerned, the "function" of interest aggregation is not to maintain the political system but to increase the power of those having interests.

VI

POLITICAL RESOURCE MANAGEMENT

> Kemal's political strategy over the next few years was to devise a
> phased sequence of issues, grouping and regrouping his followers
> at each turn: military defense of independence (1919–1922),
> establishment of a new state (1923–1928), legal and cultural re-
> forms (1926–1933), state-sponsored industrialization (1930ff.). If
> he had announced his total program at the start, he would have
> stood virtually alone against solid opposition. As it was, he used
> religious-conservative support to win the War of Independence,
> the support of liberal modernizers to found the Republic against
> conservative opposition, and the support of a younger group of
> professionals and bureaucrats to consolidate his dictatorship over
> the strenuous objections of the liberals.
>
> Dankwart A. Rustow [1]

Kemal Ataturk's success as a political entrepreneur in Turkey has become
almost legendary. His shrewd understanding of resource management enabled him to conserve, utilize, and exploit available resources to achieve his
political objectives. The essential tools he used to carry out his strategy
were the political equivalents of monetary policy, fiscal policy, taxation,
budgeting, and planning. Effective use of these political tools also required
an appreciation of the productivity implications of alternative distributions
of resources. It was Ataturk's appreciation of these implications that
helped him reshape the Turkish economy, society, and polity, and make
them more productive. By gaining and manipulating support, he was able
to reallocate status, wealth, and authority. For every Ataturk, however,
there are many statesmen in developing countries who are conspicuously
less successful in the management of their political resources.

Unless he is astute at exchange, saving, and investment, the statesman in

[1] Rustow (1966:121).

a developing country is likely to be inundated by conflicting and potentially debilitating demands for state activity and benefits. Opponents who have a commonsense understanding of the principles of political economy may succeed in occupying the country's authority roles or may create new ones through the process of political capital formation. A statesman (or anti-statesman) does not win conflicts over authority and policy solely on the basis of his resource position. His skill at resource management counts as well. We are well aware that our discussion of resource management uses terms more figurative than those terms we have previously used. To deal with problems of resource management, we must venture more frequently onto ground that has not been broken. Perhaps this area of analysis will not progress much beyond metaphor and analogy. Nevertheless, we hope that our analysis will explicate some of the realities underlying efforts to attain political goals.

Regime Policies

A statesman's success at resource management is surely related to his ability to control inflation or deflation (considered in Chapter V) and to his ability to make savings and investments (to be considered in Chapter VII). Here we consider the effects of the statesman's operating policies on resource conservation and expansion. We think that a political anti-monopoly policy such as that suggested in the previous chapter is important, but must be part of a broader approach to fulfilling the statesman's goals. An integrated approach will include the political equivalents of monetary and fiscal policy, taxation, budgeting, and planning.

MONETARY POLICY.

The statesman's political monetary policy aims at keeping the level of currency in circulation in line with the supply of resources available. As in economics, monetary policy is less effective than fiscal policy in the management of resources. It is a relatively passive instrument for affecting the level of demand or for stimulating supply. It may reward or penalize certain kinds of activity, but it does not necessarily change substantially the capacity of sectors to engage in those activities. The limited effectiveness of political monetary policy is due in part to the fact that there is no generalized political interest rate that can be readily manipulated for regime purposes. While there is such a thing in political exchange as an interest rate, it is implicit and otherwise difficult to determine or measure.[2] The regime is usually in a position to regulate some currencies. The supply of money is as a rule subject to government control; thus the regime may affect the price level of economic goods and services. The two specifically political currencies of the regime, influence and threats of coercion, may be increased or decreased as the statesman wishes. However, he may have little control over prestige or threats of violence issued by the sectors. Furthermore, it will be easier for him to reduce sector allegiance to or support for his regime through unpopular actions than it will be to increase them through popular ones. Increasing these two political currencies is desirable for the statesman, but usually costly.

When faced with an excess of effective demand for its resources, a regime may try to absorb some of the demand by issuing what might be thought of as *political bonds* in exchange for current sector resources. These bonds entitle certain sectors or persons to make claims on future resources. One of the most effective forms for such bonds is *plans*, which represent future promises or commitments of resources that can elicit tangible resources from sectors in the present. Bonds may also be issued in the form of promises of future influence and prestige. The promised currencies are substitutes for granting authority and status in the present. A policy of issuing bonds, however, involves the risk of inflation at some future time when sectors attempt to cash in the bonds for regime resources. To get sectors to accept deferred gratification of their demands, some implicit accrual of interest must usually be promised. Future satisfactions must be greater than present satisfactions foregone for sectors to accept the latter. If a regime grants currency, it must be able to increase its output of resources so that it can meet the larger future claims that will be presented at the time when conversion of bonds is proposed.

FISCAL POLICY.

Political fiscal policy is somewhat more tangible than political monetary policy. Instead of trying to alter the amount of currency in circulation through political monetary policies, a regime may use fiscal policies to try to lower or raise the level of effective demand by decreasing or increasing the sectors' holdings of resources in proportion to those of the regime. Control of demand will help the regime to control pressures making for political inflation or deflation. The regime has some control over its level of resources, its income, and its expenditures. It can vary its revenue—gotten

[2] See our discussion of political interest in Chapter VII.

through taxation, levies, transfers, exchanges, expropriation, confiscation, or however—or its spending. A balanced, a deficit, or a surplus political budget will have various consequences for the level of demand and corresponding supply. To cope with political inflation or deflation, a regime can through its policy decisions decrease or increase the purchasing power of the sectors. It can "cool off" or "pump-prime" demand for its resources. Most often the regime will have to reduce the level of demand. This reduction is in effect achieved by having a surplus in the political budget.

In his discussion of the financial problems of West African governments, W. Arthur Lewis considers the question of reducing demand. According to Lewis, most West African governments are overcentralized in that they have assumed responsibility for providing a wide range of services to local communities. A policy of overcentralization creates insoluble financial problems by eliciting heavy demand for services and risking disillusionment and loss of support if the demands are not met. Lewis suggests that if villages got, for example, only as much pumped water as they would pay for out of their taxes, demands would not exceed available funds to such a great degree. He points out that when services are on the central budget, the connection between demand and taxes is tenuous in the minds of villagers; the government is caught between unlimited demands for greater public services and very limited willingness to pay for what they cost.[3] He advises a greater decentralization of authority. Local committees would be vested with authority and responsibility for services, so that the connection between services and taxes would be quite clear. In Lewis' opinion, if villagers were granted the right to make authoritative decisions with regard to services, they would themselves increase financial contributions or reduce their demands. Whether the net effect of this measure is to provide a budget surplus or to reduce the deficit, the important point is to have increased for the sectors the costs of making demands.

A regime that is not attentive to inflationary pressures and does not increase its requirement of resources from the sectors whenever it is faced with too many demands will not be able to meet these demands with its available supply of resources. If a regime does not strike hard enough bargains with the sectors, it leaves them with resources to make further demands. These the regime then may not be able to meet because it expended its available resources to meet the earlier demands. If the regime strikes too hard bargains and extracts more resources from the sectors than it returns to them in terms of respective value, a deflationary situation may develop. We can conceive of such a situation developing in a totalitarian

[3] Lewis (1965:54–55).

state where the capacity for effective demand is so reduced that there is unemployment of resources. The sectors produce less than is possible or optimal because their incentives for or satisfactions from production are reduced. Deflation may also occur where there is little demand for the regime's authority. As we noted above, when demand for authority is reduced, the statesman could decide to run a political budget deficit, granting some authority to sectors without concomitant payment in order to stimulate their demand.

In shaping his regime's political fiscal and monetary policies, the statesman must give special consideration to the price level of economic resources and the value of money. This attention is needed partly because the range of satisfactions that can normally be secured with money is quite wide and partly because economic policies may or may not benefit the sectors favored by the statesman. As the marginal utility of money is quite high and not significantly diminishing, the loss of money or purchasing power is quite tangible to persons. Thus economic price level and the adequacy of goods and services available are of strategic importance in political economy. To the extent that a regime has the ability and expertise to pursue productive economic policies, its position will be considerably strengthened. The political dangers of monetary inflation arising from failure to control the supply of money or from a deficit economic budget are great for any regime. As we have seen, one of the factors contributing to Nkrumah's downfall was rapid monetary inflation. However, the statesman who uses the perspective of political economy should be able to weigh the consequences of economic policies in broader terms than will his economic advisors.

TAXATION.

Political taxation, of which economic taxation is a part, is the revenue aspect of fiscal policy.[4] Usually a regime is able to enjoy a minimal flow of resources from some or many of the sectors. To the extent that these sectors accept the political division of labor they accord the regime legitimacy status. The regime may in turn draw upon the legitimacy status accorded it to secure sector resources for performing certain governmental functions or

[4] We do not treat taxation in the way that Almond and Powell do (1966), in terms of an "extractive capability." We prefer to distinguish the bargaining elements of taxation from those based on agreement with regime activities.

carrying out certain policies.[5] Resources transferred to the regime as a con-sequence of the legitimacy accorded to it we call *transfers*.[6] Non-voluntary reallocations of sector resources we call *levies*. These are secured with the expenditure of other resources—goods and services, status, information, coer-cion, or authority. A sector may accept levies of certain economic resources on the condition that it may participate in the authoritative decisions allo-cating the resources levied. Often the difference between transfers and levies is a matter of degree. Sectors may perceive no diminution of welfare as a result of contributing some amount of resources to the regime for cer-tain basic services, but beyond a certain point—past which the marginal utility to sectors of the resources devoted to further government services is less than the marginal utility of alternative uses decided upon privately—the legitimacy of regime allocations is not unequivocally accepted by sec-tors. Taxation beyond this point is not accepted voluntarily and cannot take place without some compensation from the regime, though perhaps compensation may be in the form of coercion or threats of coercion.

The political problems associated with determining expenditure on na-tional defense will, we think, illustrate the distinction we are making be-tween transfers and levies. Most sectors will willingly provide the money and manpower necessary to maintain an army capable of resisting aggres-sion that is thought to be imminent. But they will be reluctant to maintain a level of armed force sufficient to deal with any possible aggression be-cause to do so would make greater and perhaps unnecessary demands on their economic resources and the personal freedom of their members. At the point where sectors begin to experience a diminishing in the marginal

[5] What are commonly thought of as basic functions of government are not without their distributive consequences and are thus not necessarily approved of or supported by all sectors. "Law and order" upholds the established order against changes by violence. It is not neutral, as recent events in our own coun-try have shown. Monetary stability benefits some sectors, while others stand to gain more from rapid inflation. Probably the most widely accepted activity of government is national defense. Yet disadvantaged sectors may feel indifferent about preserving the regime and the allocations it protects. Indeed, some sectors may favor the intervention of a foreign power in their community's affairs.

[6] Transfers may be seen in terms of the behavioral parameter of contributing resources to the maintenance of the regime, discussed in Chapter IV. They are similar to the "commitments" to economic production analyzed by Parsons and Smelser (1956:41). Or they may be seen in terms of allegiance to the govern-ment irrespective of its personnel and decisions. It is important to distinguish between those resources granted to a regime as transfers and those exchanged on a more explicit *quid pro quo* basis. See also Easton (1965:191, 217).

utility of increases in armed force, they will no longer simply accept the regime's attempt to transfer resources for the maintenance of a larger army. If the regime wants a larger army, for whatever reasons, it will have to bargain with the sectors, securing resources only through compensation, though again compensation may take the form of coercion or threats. If sectors consider the marginal utility of their money and manpower to be high, the statesman will find that the cost of expanding his army above the minimum level is also high. It may be that sectors will try to exact a particularly high price from the regime for using their men and money for military preparedness because of the disutility arising from possible future regime use of army coercion against them or from loss of life in the event of war. On the other hand, sectors may be relatively indifferent as to the particular use to which their resources will be put and will be more concerned about the general level of resources given up by them to the regime. In this case they may furnish the particular resources desired by the statesman if he reduces his demands for their resources equivalently in other areas.

Which resources or what share of them may be taken by the government as transfers is not static, but changes over time. For example, sectors may think it illegitimate for the regime to conscript men into military service before a wartime crisis, but may continue to accept postwar conscription as a necessary if onerous obligation. Certain kinds of information once thought of as "none of the government's business," for example, information on the practice of family planning, may come to be surrendered as a matter of course. In political taxation there may be what is known in economics as a "ratchet effect": raising supply or demand to establish a new equilibrium may make it unlikely that there will be a return to the old one. This phenomenon is perhaps most noticeable in fiscal taxation.[7]

Seen from the point of view of political economy, taxation involves more than money. Voluntary military service is a transfer, while military conscription is a levy. A census may involve either a transfer or levy of information. For example, individuals will freely communicate some information to an agent of the government. Other information, however, they may feel the government has no legitimate right to know. This information they will not divulge unless threatened with coercion or fines or unless offered economic or status incentives. A transfer of esteem and deference is involved when a person contributing valuable services to the state or nation is given an honor. People seldom expect recompense for the prestige they accord a national hero. However, as we suggested in our discussion of legit-

[7] See Peacock and Wiseman (1961:xxiv).

imacy, the levy of status for persons honored by the regime for "political" purposes will usually not be accepted without some *quid pro quo*.[8]

To augment the status, information, and restraint from violence received on the basis of legitimacy, the statesman engages in exchanges to levy a whole range of resources from the sectors. He needs to make careful calculations to ascertain what will or will not be accepted as transfers and what he must pay to secure those resources that will not be provided voluntarily. His analysis requires consideration of marginal utilities and elasticities of supply and demand in order to arrive at the most efficient policies of political taxation.

BUDGET AND PLAN.

The revenue and expenditure aspects of fiscal policy are operationally linked in the statesman's political budget and plan. For the sake of simplicity we have previously spoken of political exchange as though it were a matter of bargaining over particular policies. While policy considerations can be and are analyzed in specific marginal terms, a statesman also thinks of them in the aggregate as making up the political program of his regime. He deals with overall flows and marginal changes as well as with separate transactions. To secure needed resources, keep a manageable balance between income and spending, and provide for future needs the statesman must devote himself to budgeting and planning.

Like economic budgeting, political budgeting serves various purposes. A budget may be intended to coordinate diverse activities, to expand or limit certain activities, to discipline or reward certain sectors, or to mobilize the support of certain sectors that stand to benefit from the services provided.[9] The various policies a regime undertakes within a certain period of time represent the resources demanded from the sectors, in return for which sectors receive these same and/or other resources. A political budget estimates what expenditures of authority, influence, coercion, threats, status, prestige, goods and services, money, and information must be made to reach the desired level of revenue of legitimacy, support, allegiance, goods and services, money, status, prestige, violence or no violence, and information. Sectors will usually compete for preferred allocations in the statesman's budget, but the statesman obviously cannot satisfy all demands, es-

[8] See Chapter III, pp. 75–76.

[9] See Wildavsky (1964) for a thoughtful political analysis of economic budgeting.

pecially if he wishes to achieve his own goals for the polity. Political budgeting determines which sectors will be favored, which penalized, and which neutralized. It is an intricate and involved process. The statesman's success and fate rest upon his skills as political budgeteer and planner, yet he is seldom able to handle the tasks of budgeting and planning single-handedly. He relies upon his *political advisors* to collect requests, weigh the relative merits of each, try to accommodate conflicting demands, and get the most "mileage" out of the statesman's limited resources. Collectively such advisors may be thought of as the "Bureau of the Political Budget."

If political budgeting were simply a matter of balancing regime income and expenditures, the process would be simpler. However, the statesman is not merely concerned with bilateral exchanges between his regime and the sectors. To satisfy his particular values, his political budget—and his plan as well—will aim at affecting the distribution of resources among the sectors. The multilateral nature of political exchange, in which benefits or losses for third parties are desired by regime and sectors, is also reflected in a political budget and plan. A budget represents the statesman's immediate or short-term objectives, conditioned as these are by resource constraints; a plan represents his scheme of policies projected into the future. It would be a mistake to consider either one without reference to the other. Indeed, as Frederick Mosher says, a budget is a plan.[10]

Either a political budget or a political plan may be more a declaration of principle than a description of actuality. Neither may reflect any "planning," but may be simply a projection of the past into the future. If done well, both will prescribe the factors that condition and limit future action within their respective time periods. The two processes are theoretically linked and are really part and parcel of one another. Budgeting is the ingredient of planning that disciplines the entire process. Planning gives vision and purpose to the process of reconciling expenditures and income. Of central importance to both processes is the formulation of *programs*. The reduction of many possible courses of action into a small number of more concrete alternatives facilitates decision-making for the statesman. By weighing the estimated costs and benefits of each course of action, he can choose the one or several that should be included in his budget and/or plan. Consideration of budgets and plans usually begins with a certain number of existing or approved programs. These represent present commitments that while not immutable, cannot be ignored. Changes in these

[10] Mosher (1954:47). Many of the distinctions and relationships we draw between budgets and plans are taken from Mosher's analysis of budgeting as it relates to planning.

programs are suggested, and additions and subtractions of programs from the total budget or plan are made, often not so much on the basis of preference or desirability as of practicality.

Incremental calculations are necessary in part to keep the number of considerations from becoming overwhelming, but there are few possibilities for absolute valuation, even with money expenditures. Two programs costing the same amount are not likely to yield the same benefits from a statesman's point of view. A program costing more than another may nevertheless produce proportionally greater benefits for a regime. Thus with budgeting and planning, comparisons and judgments are made in terms of the marginal benefits and costs expected by the statesman. Intuitively or explicitly, the feasibility and desirability of undertaking each new program are assessed in terms of the program's relative political costs and benefits. Opportunity costs of the different uses to which a resource could be put are compared with the marginal utility of the new resources that might be obtained by exchanging or investing the resource at hand or using it in some other way.

The following are the kinds of questions that a political economist might raise for a statesman who is formulating his political budget (if the decision must be made imminently) or his political plan (if the decision remains to be made in the future): How much would it cost in support from other sectors to secure the additional money needed to initiate a generous civil service pension program? How does this support lost or spent compare with that to be gained from the civil service as a result of implementing such a program? Might more support be garnered by using this same amount of money to send an Olympic athletic team on tour? Since the amounts of support to be gained from these two uses of the money differ, how does the regime value the support to be gained in each case? Is the support of the civil servants more valuable even if it is quantitatively less?

In calculating a budget, the statesman estimates the level of political resources he can expect to get from certain sectors on the basis of the legitimacy accorded his regime. If revenue from certain sectors is insufficient to sustain certain basic services, the statesman will be in trouble. He may be successful in borrowing resources or issuing currency to maintain his regime's solvency; however, if he does not have enough legitimacy and support to ensure the performance of basic governmental functions, his prospects of achieving anything very ambitious are dim.[11] To finance regime

[11] Another question is how readily a currency such as support or money can in fact be converted into the desired resources from a particular sector. At times

activities beyond those supported by resources received as transfers, the statesman creates policies that combine transferred resources with levied resources to secure other and additional resources from the sectors. He may make levies on sector resources, assuming that the sectors will comply. If sectors feel that they are receiving essentially as much value from the regime as they are contributing to it, the anticipated flow of resources should be forthcoming. If not, bargaining, accompanied by greater positive and/or negative inducements, may secure the sought-after resources for the regime.[12]

As we have already mentioned, a regime's economic plan is part of its political plan.[13] A regime's *social policy* is also part of its political plan. Social policy aims at altering relative status as well as claims on goods, services, and authority. Granting equal rights to women and prohibiting child labor raise the status and well-being of these otherwise weak sectors. Unemployment compensation benefits lower socio-economic groups. Providing educational and employment opportunities to members of minority groups changes the position of these groups in the social stratification and in the economic and political stratifications as well. By affecting the allocation of status, social policy attempts to raise and reallocate the output of esteem and deference. It may also aim at increasing the share of resources going to the regime.

Just as a regime may set a target of growth for its economy and utilize its resources to achieve that rate, it may also have a target rate for political growth. Such a rate may be necessary in order to contain inflationary pressures by increasing the supply of political resources. Or it may be desired to generate sufficient new resources for the regime to achieve particular objectives. A statesman may also consider the pattern of growth: which

or in some cases, a currency may be quite versatile, and thus quite valuable to the statesman. In other circumstances its real purchasing power may be little or limited.

[12] James W. Wilkie has conducted an illuminating study of the politico-economic budgets and plans of Mexican statesmen. He points out that the federal budget has in practice exceeded the formal published budget by as much as 50 per cent annually since the 1930's. Thus since then, the President of Mexico has been free to make about half of federal expenditures at his discretion. In his study Wilkie examines the actual patterns of expenditure to determine political priorities and preferences. He relates changes in patterns of expenditure for economic, social, and administrative purposes to the ideologies of statesmen as these changed over time. See Wilkie (1967).

[13] Parts of an economic plan may be spurious and intended for "foreign consumption." They may be considered part of the statesman's international political plan but have no domestic relevance.

sectors receive a disproportionate share of the increased resources generated.

DISPOSABLE INCOME.

The rate and pattern of increase of political resources have an important effect on sectors' *disposable income,* their net income of economic, social, and political resources once some proportion of their output has been transferred to or levied by the regime. Inasmuch as coercion is negatively valued by sectors, reductions of coercion represent increases in sector income, and increments, decreases. There are no absolute limits to the rate at which resources can be diverted to the regime, but depending on the propensities and political power of sectors affected, reductions in sector income may have serious repercussions for the regime in authority.[14] Sectors that experience a decline in their income are likely to try to enlist regime assistance in raising that income to its former level. Or they may blame the regime and turn to its opponents for benefits. Relative changes in sector income are often as important as absolute changes. In its ideology a sector ranks itself vis-à-vis other sectors in the economic, social, and political stratifications. An "inferior" sector's achievement of greater relative gains is usually cause for concern to a "superior" sector, which considers such gains to be a threat to its own position.[15]

[14] The disposable political income of sectors is similar to disposable income in economics, that is, income net of taxes. In observing the problems of increasing the rate of capital formation in developing countries, W. Arthur Lewis has suggested that as a rule of thumb, the proportion of disposable income to national income should not be reduced by more than half of one per cent per year or political unrest will be likely. See Lewis (1966:163–164). We note that Nkrumah had been shifting this proportion in Ghana by as much as one per cent annually before he was ousted by a military coup. The decline in disposable *political* income in Ghana under Nkrumah would probably have been many times greater. Nkrumah had progressively consolidated authority in his own hands during the 1960's, and many sectors lost all political influence or authority. See also Bretton (1966).

[15] Mancur Olson, Jr. (1963) emphasizes the importance of considering disposable income as well as total output. Economic growth, he argues, leads to changes in political power and social prestige. There are losers as well as gainers from growth: the number of persons getting poorer will increase, and those unemployed by technological change will lose all income. Using the Harrod-Domar growth model, Olson shows how even the overall level of consumption can decline as the economy grows. Political observers since Tocqueville have noted that hunger and deprivation breed less discontent and disaffection than growth and improvement do. Few analysts of change in developing countries

Target rates of growth for economic, social, and political income become increasingly important to the statesman who is ambitious in his plans for the political community. Slow growth in the output of resources is a constraint on a regime's ability to increase its holdings. An increase in regime income reduces sectors' disposable income in relative terms. This reduction is likely to appear less disadvantageous, however, if the various markets are buoyant and sector incomes are rising in absolute terms. If this is the case, the regime can expand its resource position more easily with less resistance or objection from the sectors. If there is growth of output, sectors will think themselves better off even if the regime's share expands. Yet while changes in the disposable income of different sectors have consequences for the regime's resource position, the pattern of change is perhaps more significant than the absolute amount of change. Increases for sectors favorable to the regime and its objectives usually yield greater and more useful contributions to the statesman. Similar increases for opposition sectors may only strengthen the resource position of an anti-statesman. A statesman may thus try to reduce the disposable income of antagonistic sectors, though he must be prepared for the consequences of whatever resistance or retaliation they can mount. In general, giving due consideration to the pattern of political stratification, a statesman is likely to benefit more from increases in sectors' disposable income than from declines.

In order to cope with foreign aggression, natural disaster, economic depression, or some other national emergency, a regime may be able to reduce disposable incomes by a considerable margin without sectors objecting. It is, understandably enough, often in a regime's interest to maintain conditions that justify keeping disposable political income low. Under such conditions individuals are permitted less discretion over personal behavior; the regime receives higher commitments of support and allows sectors to keep fewer secrets. Apter's "mobilization" type of regime operates under such conditions.[16] In mobilization systems the crisis is usually more or less manufactured by the political leadership, but it may be a carry-over of commitment from a real crisis, a manifestation of the "ratchet effect" discussed above.

have dealt with the decline in social income. As traditional institutions and roles are undermined and denigrated, the esteem and deference received by the majority of persons may decrease.

[16] In such a regime, to use Apter's terms, coercion is used more than information, and ideological appeals to consummatory values are made to reduce demands on the regime for immediate gratification. These methods permit the regime to operate, at least for some time, with very low disposable income for the sectors. See Apter (1965: esp. Chap. X).

Productive Distributions of Resources

Participants in the political process aim at achieving or maintaining more productive allocations of economic, social, and political resources for themselves, for others, and/or for the community as a whole. How the outputs of different patterns of allocation are valued depends to be sure on the preferences of those receiving the resources. That they are valued is made clear by the competition to affect their distribution through public or private activity. When a particular distribution is altered, there may be a greater volume of resources accruing to a regime, to certain sectors, or to the community as a whole, not just as a result of reallocation, but as a result of changed incentives for production and exchange that make more resources available. Certain changes in allocation may increase the value of resources. Other changes may increase both volume and value. Changes in value depend on who is making the judgment. A resource a regime values highly may not be so valued by the rest of the community, and vice versa.

REDUCTION OF EXTREME DISPARITIES.

To manage his resources most effectively, a statesman must both appreciate and be able to estimate the productive consequences of different distributions of resources for his regime and for sectors. At this point we will take a closer look at these consequences by considering the case of Vicos, Peru, a local community in which dramatic and rapid economic, social, and political changes have been effected. Admittedly such a community lacks the scale and complexity of a nation-state, but the problems of Vicos and their ramifications seem to be sufficiently analogous to those of a nation-state to merit our analysis.[17]

Before the peaceful economic, social, and political revolution that transformed the *hacienda* at Vicos, all political, economic, and judicial power was concentrated in the hands of a single individual, the *patrón*. Indian *peones* supplied three days of free labor a week to the *hacienda* manage-

---

[17] If we were to study Peru as a whole, we would find that a small Spanish elite enjoys a relative monopoly on income, status, and authority. In contrast, the great majority of Indians conspicuously lack these resources and are at the bottom of all three stratifications. Relatively little change has taken place at the national level, so that productive consequences of change are not as readily apparent as they are in Vicos.

ment, as well as free services when demanded. In return they received a small plot of land for cultivation, to which, however, they had no rights. The disparities between the resources held by the ruling family and those held by the laborers were immense. Though not measured, the *patrón's* family income was perhaps fifty to a hundred times greater than that of the Indians. The *patrón* received most of the economic value produced, while the *peones* subsisted on their own meager output.

Because of the prevailing norms, great esteem and deference were paid to the *hacienda* owners, while they in turn regarded the Indians as inferior creatures. Though Indians accorded some esteem and deference to each other, they could under the circumstances have little self-respect. Thus there was relatively little exchange of status within the Indian community itself.[18] All authority was possessed by the *patrón*. Indeed, the only area in which the Indians had any right to govern their own affairs was that of religion. While Indians lived in relative ignorance, the landowner and his associates had practically a monopoly on information.[19] While it is true that legitimacy norms buttressed this gross inequality of resources, the *patrón's* authority was backed by the threat of coercion. If the Indians were to resist the landowner's decisions, the state police would come to his aid.

This grim and exploitative situation was to be altered by the Cornell project, an experiment in guided change.[20] The first step was the elimination of the abuses of the *hacienda* system. In particular the Indians desired an end to the *ad hoc* free services previously extracted at the whim of the *patrón*. Project personnel concentrated on improving nutrition and health, educational opportunities, and techniques of agricultural production. The project moved more slowly in stimulating social and political reorganization of the community. Gradually, however, indigenous leaders emerged who were able to determine what the community aspired to achieve. These aspirations were advanced as part of more general developmental goals so that their achievement would foster community growth. By 1957, the project turned over full authority to an elected body of proven leaders. Also, for the first time, Vicos residents were able to purchase the land they had

[18] This situation is not unique to Vicos. See Banfield (1958).

[19] It is clear that information may be a productive resource in the social and economic markets as well as in the political market. We have so far concentrated on information as a political resource, but in this discussion of Vicos, the significance of information as a non-political resource is quite evident.

[20] Our account of the Vicos experiment sponsored by Cornell University between 1952 and 1957 is taken from Holmberg (1960) and the March 1965 issue of the *American Behavioral Scientist*. Of interest are articles by Holmberg, Vasquez, Doughty, Dobyns, and Lasswell.

tilled. Since land was a measure of prestige, Indians acquired a new status as well.

Before the Cornell project anthropologists, economists, and politicians had usually argued that Indians faced nearly insurmountable social, cultural, and psychological barriers to adapting to modern ways. Holmberg suggests that the project heavily discounted if it did not definitively invalidate this argument: "If granted respect, the Indian will give respect. If allowed to share in the making of decisions, he will take responsibility and pride in making and carrying them out." [21] One of the important changes that took place in Vicos was the expansion of schooling and adult education. Thus one of the most dramatic redistributions of resources was that of information. In addition, the threat of coercion was greatly reduced.

How can we assess the productivity of these new distributions of resources? The productivity of economic resources is easiest to determine. In 1958, the first year after "independence," production on the hacienda doubled even though the labor force working in agriculture had been reduced. Further improvement was recorded in 1959. Certainly improved economic incentives were a major factor contributing to this increase.[22] The wider dissemination of information probably also contributed to it; laborers came to know improved production techniques and could attribute greater meaning and purpose to their work. Possibly the reduction in threats of coercion encouraged more diligent and efficient labor. The previous exploitative use of force may have had negative consequences for productivity. We cannot determine how important the redistribution of status and authority were to the boost in economic output, but reports indicate that these resources also contributed.

In the case of Vicos, it seems likely that reduction of the vast differential between high and low status increased the output of esteem and deference. Under the previous social stratification, the patrón and his family were given great deference, if not genuine esteem, while the Indians received very little of either, and that from one another. Under the new stratification, the esteem and deference for the hacienda's aristocracy declined greatly, and members of the much larger group, in part because their self-respect had been increased, exchanged greater esteem and deference. Raising the status of the many more than offset the decrease in the status of the

[21] Holmberg (1960:97).

[22] Holmberg notes that more often than not, increased economic benefits introduced under the previous conditions were channeled through traditional values and social systems and thus intensified the old imbalances. See Holmberg (1960:98).

few. The new social stratification was a more productive one from the point of view of the Indians, though obviously not from that of the *patrón*.

Perhaps the most basic change to take place in the Vicos community was the radical redistribution of authority. The right to participate in decisions affecting the community was more widely and evenly shared than ever before. Whether the right to speak in the name of the community became more effective and productive as a result of the reallocation of authority is a matter to be determined over time. At the time of "independence," the contributions of the newly enfranchised seemed to increase compliance with authoritative decisions. True, the threat of coercion was reduced so that obedience could not be secured with this resource, but the increase in legitimacy accorded to authoritative decisions appeared to more than make up for the decline in coercion. For one thing, social pressure could be employed to secure compliance. Once the Indians rather than the *patrón* exercised authority, withdrawal of esteem and deference proved to be an effective sanction against members of the Indian community who did not comply with authoritative decisions. To consider the consequences of authority reallocation in another way, we would say that the "publicness" of issues increased, thereby eliciting more resources to back up the exercise of authority.

If we distinguish political information from information in general, we could say that a wider and more equal dissemination of information generally contributed to greater productivity in Vicos. Greater education and use of communications media facilitated this change, which was not so much a redistribution as a dramatic increase for all who would take advantage of its availability. We have no idea of what the distribution of political information was in Vicos after the withdrawal of the project, or what its consequences were, but the productive ramifications of changes in the allocations of other resources we feel sufficiently demonstrate our contention.

EQUALIZATION OF RESOURCES.

The analytical assumptions of welfare economics would probably lead us to the conclusion that the most productive distributions of wealth, status, and authority would necessarily be egalitarian ones.[23] We are not here advocating unequal distributions of resources, either in general or in particular

[23] Even if political resources could be equalized at some point in time, they would not remain equal over time any more than economic resources redistributed equally could remain equal in subsequent economic interaction.

cases. We merely stress the fact that different distributions of economic, social, and political resources, and of information and force, have varying productive consequences when seen and judged from the perspective of the entire community or from that of a regime or a particular sector. Those who have or can mobilize political power may be expected to try to reshape or restratify the political community to suit their particular values.

Let us demonstrate briefly why egalitarian distributions of resources need not necessarily be conducive to the greatest welfare of all members of the political community taken in the aggregate. Such welfare cannot be determined objectively, but only in terms of particular preferences, time horizons, and estimates of marginal utility. We will first consider the most tangible of resources, economic goods and services. As long as tastes differ, welfare is not optimized by equal shares of all goods and services produced. More important, over time such an equal distribution may provide inadequate incentive for production, and the absolute level of satisfaction may decline. In a low-income country especially, an egalitarian distribution of income may not contribute to future welfare. It is well established that wage-earners save and invest a smaller proportion of their income than those persons who, possessing other factors of production, receive higher incomes.[24] To the extent that capital accumulation is the key variable in economic growth, income equalization might well slow down economic growth. One of the most heated issues in the politics of developing countries, over which there is room for legitimate disagreement because any conclusion is determined by particular preferences and values, is the time horizon within which income and welfare should be maximized.

We cannot offer concrete evidence that an egalitarian social stratification is less productive of esteem and deference than one less so, yet the fact that status is valued not only in absolute terms, but in relative terms as well, suggests that this would in fact be the case. If all persons receive equal es-

[24] See Lewis (1949:53). H. S. Houthakker has conducted a detailed econometric study of differentiated savings and investment rates. In this study Houthakker found that although the aggregate elasticity of saving was 0.8 (for every one per cent increase in total income, savings increased by .8 per cent), the figure for income from employment and transfers was 0.4, and the figure for other personal income was 1.2. Thus the marginal propensity to save from wages and transfers was much lower than that for income from property and entrepreneurship. If half of national income accrues to owners of non-labor factors of production, and income increases at the same rate for both labor and non-labor factors, the latter will contribute three times as much to saving and capital formation. To reallocate income from the latter to the former would surely lower the aggregate elasticity of saving estimated by Houthakker as 0.8. See Houthakker (1965:216–217).

teem and deference, the value of what they receive is likely to depreciate. Unlike economic goods and services, which might be increased more or less indefinitely, status—like authority—is relational, defined in terms of superior-subordinate relationships. Persons usually want more prestige than others, not just more prestige per se. It thus could be that an egalitarian social stratification would increase the volume of status at the same time that the value of status produced declined. Since status helps to differentiate ourselves from others, identical status for all has little meaning.

Equalization of authority may increase the legitimacy to exercise authority and thus increase compliance and the productivity of the polity. However, it is also likely to reduce the ability of government to use coercion as a means of enforcement. Thus to the extent that opinions differ on the proper use of authority, and other power means to ensure compliance are in short supply, the productivity of authority will decline. In the extreme, egalitarian authority is ineffective and even non-existent. If all can speak equally in the name of the state, none can do so effectively. Indeed, the more widely shared authority is, the more its productivity may decline.[25] The most productive distribution of income, status, authority, information, or force in a community will depend upon the prevailing relationships within that community.[26] Extreme inequality may be relatively unproductive, but so may be extreme equality.[27] Political economy does not prescribe any particular allocation for universal application, although analysis would probably show that greater productivity would in many cases result more from egalitarian than inegalitarian distributions of resources. In our

[25] Frederick W. Frey does not use a model like ours in his attempt to analyze Turkish political development, but when he tries to account for variable political power relationships he comes across the problem we raise here. See Frey (1963:324); see also Parsons (1957).

[26] The distribution of force in a society may be a major source of social order, as Etzioni has suggested (1960:xv–xvii). Insofar as it permits or encourages greater productivity of other resources, the particular distribution of force may be said to be productive as well. Productivity may result from a balance (or imbalance) between the regime's capacity for coercion and the ability of others to employ violence. Or it may result from approximate parity in the physical strength of all sectors so that none can attempt to take advantage of others without suffering serious and deterring losses.

[27] Consider the case of information. To distribute all available information equally would probably be "counterproductive." The costs would not only exceed the benefits, but a reduction in production might result. Specialization of roles is in part a means of distributing information for greater productivity. Specialization in education to take advantage of special abilities and different levels of intelligence also distributes information unequally but to good effect.

model we aim at providing analytical tools that will enable a statesman or anyone else engaged in politics to estimate what changes in the prevailing allocations might lead to more valued resource outputs.

Our consideration of the productive implications of alternative resource allocations has shown that resource management cannot simply aim at some optimal use of resources based on existing resource positions or the preferences of regime and sectors. Policies must aim at particular desired allocations of income, status, authority, information, and force. This holds true even if the regime is primarily oriented toward maintaining the status quo, since unless the political market is in a condition of stagnation, measures must be taken to protect the status quo from erosion or subversion. Management of regime resources solely on the basis of present judgments of productivity and present power relations would very likely lead the statesman into political cul-de-sacs or into the snares of anti-statesmen. Therefore, having discussed problems of political resource management in their more or less present-oriented, optimizing context, we shall turn to the more future-oriented concerns of resource accumulation in order to expand upon the production possibilities of a political community.

VII

POLITICAL RESOURCE ACCUMULATION

The new wave [of West African political entrepreneurs] accomplished its initial aim with very meager means. They used bicycles, a few trucks, or very occasionally an automobile. They sometimes had some private funds, but relied mainly upon a small band of dedicated men. The organizations they created were at first very limited: some form of executive composed of the co-founders, a larger group of correspondents, with contacts among various voluntary associations. . . . They did not ask for much: most important of all, a willingness to agitate in the marketplace, to greet vociferously a passing European official, sometimes the payment of a small membership fee in exchange for the promise that grievances would be set right and of a place in the new society, and very soon afterwards, a vote.

Aristide Zolberg [1]

In West Africa nationalist leaders faced the necessity of accumulating sufficient political power to oust the ruling colonial regimes and occupy the authority roles themselves. To accomplish their goals, they had to draw upon all the various political resources. More than goods, services, and money were needed, though these were basic. Status had to be withdrawn from the European rulers and the status of African leaders had to be exalted. Information had to be gathered through a widespread organizational network, and this same organizational structure was needed to exercise authority within the movement. The decisive resources for achieving independence, however, were violence and legitimacy. To gain authority, African leaders had to be able to threaten violence against the colonial regime and to carry out their threats if demands for self-government were ignored; they also had to discredit the legitimacy of the colonial rulers. Though the

[1] Zolberg (1966:13).

support given by Africans to the colonial regime was not great, it had to be withdrawn and transferred to the prospective indigenous leaders.

To secure the resources they needed, African nationalists had to respond to the grievances of the indigenous sectors. As Zolberg points out, many of the grievances were related to economic factors such as shortages and high prices of imported consumer goods, fluctuation in the price farmers obtained for their cash crops, low wages, and bad housing conditions.[2] The nationalists' promises to set right popular grievances thus entailed the reallocation of economic resources. In addition, nationalists promised greater status—"a place in the new society"—and a share in authority through extension of the franchise. Presumably indigenous leadership would also mean a reduction in coercion. Insofar as self-government would increase educational opportunity, Africans would enjoy many benefits through acquired information and skills.

In any community both the statesman and anti-statesman are faced with the need to accumulate political resources to achieve their respective goals. The statesman will devote a share of his resources to political investment, while the anti-statesman will undertake political capital formation. If the processes of resource accumulation are unfortunately less verifiable than those of exchange, they are nonetheless real. Certainly the colloquial language of politics points to the existence of such processes. We hear talk of "capitalizing on an opponent's mistakes," making a "profitable" decision, making a political "investment," and so forth. Yet because social scientists have given little serious and systematic attention to these processes, we cannot offer as much documentation and illustration as we would like.

Capital Formation

Both acquiring and maintaining authority require *political capital formation.*[3] Aspirants for authority either conserve the resources and currency needed to occupy or reshape authority roles or borrow them from other sectors. All sectors have, at least potentially, some interest in the statesman who exercises authority, as they will want to ascertain what areas his au-

[2] Zolberg (1966:13).

[3] Both statesman and anti-statesman undertake what may be thought of as political capital formation. Here we consider how the anti-statesman goes about it. The techniques most commonly available to the statesman are those of political investment.

thority legitimately encompasses. If the statesman comes from a particular sector and shares its interests, or if he is in some way associated with a sector and is amenable to its interests, that sector will have an advantage when resources are allocated authoritatively. On the other hand, a sector whose position is distant from the regime's core combination may benefit from contributing to an anti-statesman's accumulation of political capital. Usually the further a sector is from the core combination, the more it stands to gain and the less it has to lose from following such a course.

A contender for authority needs various resources. He usually needs money to acquire goods and services; he certainly needs information; and he often needs violence to use against the regime or other contenders. Most of all he needs support, which will enable him to secure needed resources at the appropriate time. Support may be expressed in votes and will confer authority if political competition is channeled through an electoral system. If there are no electoral opportunities, support is all the more necessary because of the amount and variety of resources needed for non-electoral competition. Currency given to an anti-statesman may have relatively little direct cost for sectors until it is redeemed for their various resources such as goods and services, status, and information.

An anti-statesman must campaign for authority. It is interesting that the term "campaign," first used to describe a military effort to gain dominance over opponents on the field of battle, has been adopted for use in other fields as well. Many anti-statesmen are able to wage electoral campaigns, perhaps coupled with the political equivalents of sales campaigns or advertising campaigns. Others choose or are forced to wage military or quasi-military campaigns for authority. By winning away what would have been contributions to the regime, by acquiring clearly superior political power in terms of resources (and particularly legitimacy and the currencies of allegiance and support), and/or by the use of force, an anti-statesman may be able to oust the incumbent. While he is seeking authority, he has no control over the authoritative allocation of resources and thus cannot compensate sectors that give him working capital except by disbursing what resources he has. He also has no control over the resources of non-supporting sectors. To secure political capital, the anti-statesman offers pledges of influence, prestige, money, and no coercion. These currency IOU's are bonds issued in recognition of sector contributions.

Those sectors that aid the anti-statesman expect to improve their future resource position and their ability to enjoy greater prosperity, security, respect, ideological influence, or whatever they most desire. If they did not think the anti-statesman could and would help them to achieve their ends, they would continue giving resources to the regime. The resources and currencies the anti-statesman receives from sectors are mostly in the form of loans, carrying implicit (or explicit) calculations of interest to be accrued.[4] The less likely it is that an anti-statesman can wage a successful campaign for authority, the higher the price he will have to pay for resources, or the higher the interest he will have to pay on the loans he receives. If he is not successful in assuming authority, he must default on these loans and will not be able to honor the currency IOU's pledged to the sectors. In addition to the risk of default, another factor conditioning the price or interest he must pay is the cost sectors must undertake for making loans to the opposition and reducing their contributions to the regime. Any statesman is likely to retaliate against a sector that supports his opponents by reducing the positive benefits it receives from his regime and even sometimes by using coercion against it to reduce if possible its aid to the opposition.

By considering the factors that make political capital formation more or less costly to an anti-statesman, we can clarify an important distinction between political inflation and hyper-inflation, and between political deflation and depression. As long as the activity within the political market is oriented toward using or influencing the authority of the regime, the imbalances between supply and demand produce inflation or deflation. If the supply of authority is kept too limited for the demand, or if the supply available is ineffective or overpriced, sectors will increasingly agree to or seek the exercise of authority by a different regime. Both hyper-inflation and depression reflect states of the political market in which the statesman's authority is not highly valued by the important sectors.

As a rule, political inflation means sector deflation, a decline in the purchasing power of sector resources. During periods of political inflation, political capital formation should, all other things being equal, be less expensive for an anti-statesman. But as in economics, other factors affect the level of resource supply and demand. A regime enjoying controlled political inflation is in a very strong resource position. Under such conditions loans to an anti-statesman are quite risky for sectors receiving positive benefits from exchange with the incumbent regime. Because of the regime's affluence, what authority it does share is effective for sectors' purposes, and sector disposition to shift support is likely to be low.

A situation of political deflation would suggest that the accompanying sector inflation would make capital formation expensive. The assumption

---

[4] We consider the application of the economic concept of "interest" to political analysis later in this chapter.

would be that the regime is more dependent on sectors during a time of political deflation and would thus be more willing to compensate them generously for their resources. This may not be the case, however. If the demand for authority is less than the supply, possibly sectors do not consider that authority to be very effective. As long as there are no challengers to the regime, sector deflation may accompany political deflation. Sectors may have little choice but to make the best arrangement they can with those in authority. Under such circumstances the costs of capital formation for a single anti-statesman entering the field of competition would be quite low. We can see that the number of competitors for regime authority is an important consideration in determining the cost of political capital formation. As in business, the higher the profits to be gained, the greater the probable number of entrepreneurs that will become active.[5] If during political inflation a number of anti-statesmen emerge and compete for sector resources, sector deflation may quickly be converted to sector inflation. If the price of sector resources is bid up, the resulting dominant core combination will be narrower than it would have been if the price of sector resources had remained at a lower level.

At the extremes of political inflation or deflation the costs of political capital formation become less. In a situation of hyper-inflation, the regime can no longer channel and control the demand for authority. Regime costs of remaining in authority mount, especially in terms of coercion. The resulting situation is quite similar to the extreme of political depression. The statesman becomes quite dependent on sectors for whatever contribution they can and will make toward keeping him in authority. In effect, hyper-inflation leads to depression for the regime as a result of a reduction in the sectors' desire to participate within the regime or to influence regime decisions. At this point sectors stand to gain most by supporting a new regime. If a regime is discredited, a relatively normal and free market condition may emerge as several or many political entrepreneurs seek to put together a core combination of sectors providing adequate political power to acquire and exercise authority.[6]

[5] Speaking of West African politics after 1945, when the British colonial regimes had increased the areas in which Africans had authority, Zolberg observes that "in order to be successful, organizations had to mobilize support from much larger bodies of people and compete with an increasing number of political entrepreneurs drawn into the game once the risks of punishment had practically disappeared and the rewards had become more tangible." Zolberg (1966:19).

[6] In politics "discredited" means that a leader is without political credit. He cannot get resources except those for which he pays "cash on the barrel-head."

Ousting an incumbent regime requires more than the acquisition of re-sources by an anti-statesman. The resource position of the statesman must be undermined as well. Sectors that feel deprived by the scarcity or over-pricing of authority may transfer allegiance and support to the anti-statesman and withdraw legitimacy status from the regime in authority. Even if the anti-statesman can mobilize violence from his supporters, his efforts are usually not effective unless the statesman's ability to coerce is somehow reduced.[7] For the anti-statesman to succeed, he must not only have resource superiority, but he must also drive his entrenched political foe into bankruptcy so that the regime no longer has sufficient resources to stay in authority in the present.

When an anti-statesman begins his campaign for authority there is often no way of knowing how much political capital he will need to accumulate. It will be necessary for him to estimate the regime's resources both at pres-ent and in the future, but his political skills may compensate for meager resources or may squander plentiful ones. As the power differential be-tween the contenders narrows, it should become easier to analyze the strengths and weaknesses of each as they compete for support, legitimacy, status, information, force, and economic resources. A regime's vulnerability is always a topic of interest and speculation. Some analysts consider legiti-macy the crucial resource staving off bankruptcy, while others focus on the "hard" resources—economic, coercive, and informational. When a regime must resort to coercion to remain solvent, it often begins to lose what sup-port and legitimacy it has left. However, many coercive regimes have sur-vived prolonged crises. A decline in demand for regime resources and for authority in particular does not necessarily signal the demise of a regime. With skillful use of the resources at hand, a statesman may still increase his own political capital by establishing new policies, mobilizing new sec-tors, or by borrowing resources from abroad that may be expended more freely than those borrowed from the sectors.

Since polities, like economies, are usually open systems, other countries may provide resources upon which a statesman and/or his opponents can rely. A regime trying to resist the political onslaught of an anti-statesman may be able to secure economic, military, informational, and other re-

[7] Huntington has observed, as have others, that a revolution needs defections from the established army in order to succeed militarily. See Huntington (1962:23–32). Katharine Chorley (1943:23) maintains that insurrection can-not be successful against a professional army operating with all its technical re-sources at full strength. Certainly these generalizations are supported by the events of the Bolshevik revolution in 1917 and more recently of Castro's revolu-tion in Cuba. In fact, we can think of few exceptions to the rule.

sources to maintain its solvency. However, nearly as often, foreign governments or sectors give aid to anti-statesmen. Any study of political capital
formation must consider the money, status, legitimacy, information, or
force coming from abroad that assists or resists the anti-statesman's efforts
to gain authority.

If the anti-statesman succeeds in his aim and attains authority, he faces
new problems. He must demonstrate his ability to govern effectively, a feat
that requires sufficient political resources to exercise the responsibilities of
government. If he cannot meet the demands of significant sectors, he may
find his own resource base eroding. Indeed, at the outset he may have to
permit fairly generous exchange rates if he wishes to gain the support and
contributions of sectors that withheld support during his campaign. Thus
initially the new statesman may need more resources than his predecessor
did to achieve the same incidence of compliance. He would need more
economic resources, more information, and most frequently, more coercion.

In protracted political struggles, the eventual outcome depends not so
much on who possesses the greatest amount (or the best "mix") of political working capital, but on who can develop the most productive political
infrastructure. Infrastructure is the result of invested political capital.
Huntington points out that in revolutionary military campaigns, the opposition must create a state within the state in order to maintain its military
force. It sets up its own parabureaucracy, collects taxes, runs schools and
courts, prints newspapers, polices the area under its control, and so forth.
The success of the opposition hinges on its capacity to maintain such a
state. The government in authority must destroy the political infrastructure supporting the insurgent forces if it hopes to crush the opposition.[8]

How authority is transferred to a successful political entrepreneur would
depend on the infrastructure and parameters of the political community
and on the propensities of the regime and its opponents for using force,
negotiations, and so forth. If there are electoral methods of competition, in
which votes are indicators of support and a majority or plurality of votes
entitles a contender to assume authority, the transfer may be relatively non-
violent. In situations where other means of acquiring authority are not
available, violence may be used to oust leaders of a regime from positions
of authority. When an unpopular regime is removed in this way, the successors may enjoy considerable support, allegiance, and legitimacy. To the
extent that the previous regime was popular, however, the new regime will

[8] Huntington (1962). See also Chalmers Johnson (1964:62–63, 67) for a
discussion of military mass insurrections and the required rebel infrastructure.

have to rely on coercion until it has proven its staying power and is accorded enough legitimacy to secure compliance with less expenditure of
coercion.

The process of political capital formation is essentially the same in all
countries. To be sure, the characteristic mixture of resources will vary from
community to community, depending on the institutions, customs, and
values of each. In one instance, legitimacy may be more important than
violence. Indeed, violence may effectively disqualify a contender for authority. In another, traditional social status may be more crucial than any
other resource. It is important that an analysis of regime changes not be
institution-bound.[9] The study of political economy should facilitate a more
truly comparative analysis of the transfer and consolidation of authority
by treating with the sources, amount, types, and combinations of political
capital accumulated and used to gain control of state institutions.

Mobilization of Sectors

For both the statesman and the anti-statesman, one of the most significant
means of accumulating political resources is sector mobilization.[10] At
times there are sectors of the population that are not organized to produce
political resources or enter into political exchange.[11] Some sectors may par-

[9] Majority support registered in an election does not assure that the victor
has legitimacy or even much support. Votes may be secured just as effectively
by money, threats, or social deference; they are often secured through party
programs or ideological appeals. The perverse usages of "plebescitarian" democracy demonstrate that elections may be more "undemocratic" than machinery
in which sectors lobby and compete non-electorally for decisions favoring their
interests.

[10] Apter uses the term "mobilization" to denote a type of political system
that aims at rapid development by relying on a hierarchical authority structure,
"consummatory" values, and the use of coercion. See Apter (1961) and
(1965). We prefer to use the term with reference to specific sectors, though we
know that the consequences of "mobilization" according to either definition
could be similar.

[11] For example, parents may constitute an unmobilized sector even though
they participate in the political process as peasants, merchants, or army officers.
If parents come to see that they have an interest in acting politically as a group,
they will make demands and will usually increase the total of resources they are
willing to contribute to the regime. To make demands, they may or may not
have to transfer resources they previously used as members of another sector for
use by the newly mobilized sector. Depending on the circumstances, a statesman may be able to get increased resources by mobilizing parents.

ticipate in the national political market but contribute less than they are potentially able to. If a potential sector is unmobilized, there are usually good reasons why.[12] The effective demand for its output may not be great enough or the price it can command may not be high enough to cover costs. Or complementary inputs may be lacking. Or there may not be sufficient infrastructure to make participation efficient. Mobilizing a sector generally requires some expenditure, though sometimes mobilization may only be a matter of getting an unmobilized sector to take advantage of new demand for its potential output. Often at least some expenditure or investment must be made to establish a communications network so that the sector will recognize its interests and act upon them.

The distinction between expenditure and investment is pertinent to evaluating the resources used for mobilization. If the payoff is long-term or uncertain, the resources spent on mobilization may properly be considered an investment. If the payoff is short-term and more certain, the resources spent are more appropriately considered expenditure. Stimulating unmobilized sectors to increase their production may yield sufficient returns to warrant the statesman's investment in this area even if he were to incur budget deficits in the short run. In this case he may make promises or loans to sectors that can be paid off in the near future. The decision to invest in an unmobilized sector may be only secondarily related to direct profitability. Often the opportunity costs of leaving a sector unmobilized and susceptible to appeals by regime opponents may justify certain expenditure and investments to place the sector in question within the regime's political ambit. We would call this pre-emptive, or sometimes co-optive mobilization. Of course, sectors may mobilize themselves for reasons of their own ideologies or interests.

The profitability of expending certain resources to mobilize a potential sector cannot be determined without assessing what and how much of certain resources are needed by the regime or by an anti-statesman. If support is needed for particular purposes and its value to the statesman rises, hitherto unprofitable investment in certain sectors may become advantageous. Or if contributions of coercive force are desired, investment in one sector becomes profitable but investment in another does not. Some sectors have greater potential than others for furnishing certain resources. A populous

[12] In discussing the economics of land resettlement, W. Arthur Lewis notes that if land is vacant, there is usually a good reason for it. It is either unproductive or requires considerable investment or the current market value of its output is too low. The analogy with political mobilization is evident. See Lewis (1954b). Mancur Olson, Jr. considers under what conditions it pays for groups to organize for political activity. His is a thoughtful effort to estimate the relative costs and benefits of mobilization. See Olson (1965).

sector might produce votes or support; another sector could employ its capacity for violence against an undesirable sector; still another might give social status to the regime. The benefits from mobilization expenditures would be weighed by statesman and anti-statesman alike in terms of the marginal value of the increases in resource contributions such mobilization would bring about.

Some sectors may be mobilized relatively cheaply. Mobilization may merely involve helping members to organize so that they can receive benefits from acting as a collectivity. Some sectors do not even need organization to participate in the political process. Members of such sectors may be educated to the advantages of participation, or the statesman may raise certain issues that make it advantageous for the sectors in question to become politically active. In any case, mobilization will involve some cost to the regime or the anti-statesman. Merely raising an allocative issue may require giving up some influence or economic resources. The sectors that cost least to mobilize are those that hardly function or need not function as collectivities. The statesman can predict the production consequences of such sectors even if the members' relations with the regime are individualistic. However, mobilization of such sectors may necessitate considerable other expenditures by the regime.

Some sectors are inherently difficult or expensive to mobilize. Investing social status in a group like the "untouchables" in India would probably be a large and long-term investment, which a statesman might undertake for either of two reasons. He might judge that his investment would pay large dividends of support in the long run, and that he might well need such a "harvest" in the future. Or his ideological preferences might lead him to make this investment in an effort to change the stratification of the community. In his opinion, achievement of an altered stratification would be more valuable than the net loss of support he would incur. The upgraded sector would increase its support, but other sectors might well reduce their support to the statesman. The cost of mobilizing a sector extends beyond an initial investment. Once a sector is organized and seeks to further its own interests, its members will make demands on the regime (or anti-statesman) as the price for their continued support and other contributions. Landless laborers who have been organized to support a regime's land reform policy and decrease the regime's dependence on landowners in rural areas are likely to make demands for status and economic resources that will be costly for the regime to meet. Thus the cost of mobilization must be considered over time, with the maintenance costs figured along with the original capital expenditure.

Deciding whether or not to use certain of the regime's scarce resources to mobilize a sector requires careful analysis and estimates of the ratio of benefits to costs. Consider, for example, the choice of whether or not to invest resources to upgrade the pariah entrepreneur sector. Such a sector is probably already participating in the political market, so that the statesman is faced not with mobilization pure and simple, but with bringing the sector closer to the core combination. A statesman needing financial support or increased economic production to curb inflationary pressures may consider investing resources in this sector. Sector members will probably desire social status and some influence on economic policy. Indeed, they may argue that they cannot boost industrial and commercial output without being granted some influence over tariffs, wages, and business taxes. But this influence will be expensive for the statesman to give up. Such an action might run counter to his goal of more indigenous and collectivized production. What is more, if he accepts support from and tries to give status to pariah entrepreneurs, other sectors already active in politics may reduce their support and other contributions to the regime. In such a situation, the cost and benefit calculations to be made are complex, but certainly any statesman faced with such a choice makes them, at least intuitively. He must assess the resources to be spent and recovered in terms of their marginal value. If a regime were low on money and needed to increase the growth of gross national product, investment in pariah entrepreneurs would be more advantageous than it would be if the regime needed support to maintain its political solvency.

Ironically, a regime that is affluent in resources is better able to afford mobilization because the marginal value of the resources it expends is less. However, such a regime also has less incentive to mobilize sectors. The marginal value of support, money, status, or legitimacy to be gained by mobilization is less than it would be to a more impoverished regime.[13] Perhaps one of the considerations weighing in the balance is the opportu-

[13] Another way of assessing the profitability of mobilizing various sectors is to use Riker's rule for the formation of "minimum winning coalitions" in politics (1962). According to Riker, the participation of additional sectors in exchanges with the regime will usually diminish the privileged position of those previously included sectors. They would try to prevent the mobilization of new sectors by putting pressure on the statesman. However, Riker's rule must be modified in light of reality. The statesman's goal is not simply to gain authority but to use authority for affecting the nature of the political community. Effecting changes, in contrast to just maintaining a position, requires more resources than the minimum implied by Riker's model. Riker's measure of productivity is the maximization of "consumption" by sectors, whereas we have taken as our criterion for productivity the maximal achievement of the statesman's goals.

nity costs the regime may incur if a statesman leaves certain sectors unmobilized. The opposition might well seek to mobilize such sectors for its own political benefit, capitalizing on the issues that interest the unmobilized. Of course, the opposition too might decide to invest in mobilization of certain sectors in order to pre-empt regime gains from these sectors in the future.

We cannot make blanket prescriptive statements about the advisability of mobilizing sectors. The assets or liabilities depend on the specific sector in question and on the resource position and the needs of the statesman or anti-statesman, as well as the marginal utility attached to specific sector resources at the present and in the foreseeable future; the presumed propensities of the sector; the expenditures and investment necessary for mobilization; the likely supply and demand relationships after mobilization; and the opportunity costs involved. Estimates may be crude, but without them the statesman cannot accumulate resources intelligently. Errors in judgment about whether or not to mobilize may assist the anti-statesman in his political capital accumulation.[14]

Saving

To save resources or currencies, a regime or sector withholds them from political exchange and does not consume, expend, or invest them for some period of time. The most common purpose for saving resources is to create a reserve for future use. In addition to this purpose, there are others. Saving may simply be a bargaining tactic; a sector or regime may restrict the supply of a resource available for exchange in order to raise the resource's value. The effectiveness of saving for this purpose depends on how significant the withholding sector or regime is as a supplier of the particular resource. Saving may also be simply speculative when a sector or regime thinks the value of its resource will appreciate vis-à-vis that of other resources in the future. Presumably all decisions to save a resource are motivated by the expectation of gaining greater value from the resource in the

[14] In an article on the effort by Dominican "constitutionalists" to end military rule in the Dominican Republic and reinstate the regime of Juan Bosch, James Petras (1966) describes the unmobilized sector of "unemployed youth" and the consequences of its mobilization for politics in the Dominican Republic. He provides an excellent analysis of the duel between statesman and anti-statesmen on the left and right, giving special emphasis to the resources of coercion and violence, economic and social status privileges, and the injection of resources from abroad, especially from the United States.

future than could be obtained by using the resource in the present.[15] In such cases we can conceive of increased future value as representing an implicit accrual of interest over time. Measurement of such an interest rate does not seem possible at present, but we accept in principle the validity of interest on political resources.[16]

In political economy there are two forms of saving. The first and simpler form is analogous to saving in the sense common in economics: resources that can be kept in a stock may be conserved rather than consumed or expended in some other way. Thus economic goods or information may be saved or hoarded, often to advantage. On the other hand, economic services, which are flow resources rather than stock resources, cannot be saved in this conventional sense. The same is true of status and legitimacy, which like services are flow resources and cannot be saved by recipients.[17] There is another type of saving that is decided upon by the producer of a resource rather than by the recipient. A sector or regime almost never produces resources at maximum output. It usually withholds some of the amount of status or legitimacy it could grant to others because it judges the cost of expenditure to be greater than the benefit. For one thing, increasing the supply of status or legitimacy usually depreciates the value of that already accorded, for which certain resources are being gained in exchange. For another, both status and legitimacy, once they are granted, may be used in turn by the recipient to make claims on other resources held by the grantee. Thus the decision to produce or not to produce is quite similar to the decision to save or not.

This particular kind of saving is especially pertinent to the resources of authority and force, and to their currencies, influence and threats. If a statesman did not "save" some or most of his authority from exchange,

[15] There is a difference between a sagacious sector or regime and a frugal one. The latter may simply have a higher propensity for saving which may result from a high valuation of future security. A sagacious sector carefully calculates the expected returns from saving and consumption using its estimation of present and future marginal utility to compare value at both times. Regimes, of course, may also be sagacious or frugal, or may be spendthrifts.

[16] We will consider the implications of political interest in the next section.

[17] Status and legitimacy can in effect be saved in the form of their currencies, prestige and support, just as services can in effect be "saved" through accumulation of money. Currencies as claims on resources may be converted into resources at some future time instead of in the present. Thus a decision to save currencies amounts to a saving of resources. Of course, the amount of resources to be gained from a particular currency in the future is usually less definite than the amount to be gained if the currency were converted into resources in the present, so there is a risk factor involved.

that authority would be greatly depreciated and made ineffective. He could spend his authority in many ways, but it is most valuable to him if husbanded carefully. By according a certain sector some influence over authoritative decisions governing a particular area, the statesman could get a certain amount of resources from that sector. But by reserving this authority for himself for the time being, he counts on being able to secure more resources of value to him over time than he could if he were to expend his authority in the present. When held by sectors, influence is a currency quite suitable for saving. Claims to influence authority are commonly saved until the most opportune, i.e., profitable, moment.

Similarly, most coercion and violence are saved at any one time. For one thing, as we noted in Chapter III, the expenditure of force frequently results in high costs, as the affected party may retaliate or may withdraw certain resources. For another, the expenditure of violence or coercion in increasing amounts may depreciate the value of the resource being employed, resulting in diminishing marginal returns. Thus saving these resources is usually advantageous. There are many threats a regime or a sector could make against others, but for the same reasons that force is not expended profligately, threats are not made as often as they could be. They are likely to yield more resources if saved and used discriminatingly.

It may be asked whether political economy proposes a marginal propensity to save that has consequences for the growth of output through a "multiplier effect" similar to that postulated and observed in macroeconomics. It is clear that some sectors have higher and others have lower marginal savings rates. Rates vary according to the sectors' valuation of present versus future satisfactions. To the extent that resources are saved and withheld from political exchange, the effective volume of resources possessed by others is less than it might be. A significant increase in the proportion of certain resources saved by sectors would have a depressing effect on the regime's resource position or on the state of the political market. Similarly, an increase in the proportion of resources withheld by the regime would restrict supply and reduce the total volume of exchange. (However, the total value exchanged might not be much changed because of the inflation of the price of regime resources.)

An increase or decline in the amount of authority shared by the regime may expand or contract political exchange by more than the value of the change in authority shared, but this increase or decline does not seem to be directly related to sector savings ratios. If there is a reduction in regime or sector savings ratios, the regime or sector will offer more resources in the political market. Thus there seems to be some kind of a "multiplier effect" in politics: the less the savings or withholding from the political market, the greater the volume of resources exchanged and the greater the output of the polity as a whole. Nevertheless, we do not propose a political "multiplier" that would be equal to the reciprocal of the marginal propensity to save. One could be postulated, but the quantitative techniques for testing and estimating it are not at hand. In addition, there is reason to believe on theoretical grounds that a multiplier effect would work differently in the political market than it would in the economic market.[18]

Interest

The colloquial usage of the term "interest" in politics gives us an idea of what is involved in the more formal meaning we attach to the word. To have an interest in a decision means to be affected by that decision, to stand to gain or lose by it. Might we not then by extension think of interest in politics as the accrual of value to a resource held by a regime or sector as a result of favorable decisions or exchanges? An "interest group" has a stake in the outcome of a particular decision, action, or policy. It has resources that will be increased or decreased in value, enlarged or lost, depending on what is done or decided. Because of the "interest" that might accrue, it is worth the group's effort and expenditure to protect or advance its interest(s).

When a regime comes into authority as a result of political capital formation, the sectors that lent it capital usually receive more favorable allocations of resources. As long as the anti-statesman-turned-statesman continues to rely on these particular sectors for his basic flow of resources and currency, the contributions of these sectors are valued more highly than

[18] In economics, the marginal propensity to save applies to a nearly endless chain of homogeneous transactions. Exchanges in political economy are not comparable, since sectors and regime are not identical as customers. In political economy, then, such a propensity would have to take a somewhat different form. Because saving in the political process includes withholding from production as well as non-consumption of resources produced, there is not in politics the same depressing effect on the level of demand that results in economics when monetary savings not made available for future exchange constitute a "leakage" and have a depressing effect. Resources are not produced jointly among sectors, so there are no extra-sectoral factor payments involved. Thus if a sector withholds legitimacy or information, an imbalance between the purchasing power of sectors and the resources available will not necessarily result. If a sector decides to withhold some amount of a resource, it may unbalance supply vis-à-vis demand, but there appears to be no mathematical relationship between the proportion saved and the subsequent effect on demand.

those of other sectors.[19] These sectors receive more for their support from the new statesman than they did from his predecessor. However, the new statesman probably cannot meet all their demands. He cannot do so in part because their demands have become more costly now that their resources have appreciated in value. Perhaps more important, if he were to try to meet such demands unreservedly, he would reduce contributions from other sectors and raise costs of enforcement. Unless it is widely accepted that "to the victor belong the spoils," official favoritism beyond some tolerable level will be retaliated against by disadvantaged sectors.

DEBT.

It does not take a model of political economy to point out the fact and significance of *political debt*. We have already seen how certain debts President Sukarno of Indonesia contracted during his campaign for authority limited his freedom of choice once he acquired power and cost him resources that different economic policies might have yielded. Statesmen may or may not be able to reduce their obligations once in office. The burden of debt depends somewhat on the state of the political market at the time of capital formation, on whether, for example, sector inflation raises the rate of return that must be promised. A government's economic debts are usually quite clear, though they are sometimes obscured for political purposes. The amount of a government's political debt and the identity of its creditors may be veiled to minimize adverse repercussions from sectors not receiving interest payments. When a regime borrows economic resources from certain sectors because it lacks enough to achieve certain ends, the use to which such resources are put is frequently of a public nature; such loans are incurred on behalf of the polity or at least in the name of the state. But the borrowing of political resources may specifically serve the needs of certain favored sectors. Other sectors will be less willing to help repay these loans.

When sectors give aid to an aspirant for authority, there may be no stipulated agreement that repayment will yield the creditor returns of greater value, though the idea of such returns is usually implicit in a sector's deci-

[19] Such considerations are made in marginal terms. If the statesman depends heavily upon his core combination for support, this support has high value. Additional support coming from more peripheral sectors is less useful to the statesman than his basic support. If he dispenses with any support, it will be support "at the margin." At the same time we must remember that support from the core combination may be more expensive than support from peripheral sectors, so that the statesman has some incentive, if the costs of core combination resources get too high, to shift or reshuffle the base of support.

sion to give assistance. A successful competitor for authority can and frequently does transfer his debts to the polity as a whole.[20] Indeed, it is this possibility that motivates sectors to aid an anti-statesman in his campaign against an incumbent regime. While statesman and anti-statesman may make loans to a sector and its leaders upon occasion, the direction of aid is usually the reverse.

The attitudes of statesmen toward debt repayment in general and toward certain debts in particular will vary. Some obligations may interfere with the attainment of policy objectives and others may not. Some may even promote a statesman's value preferences by transferring resources to a favored creditor sector. Debt management is a problem for the statesman only when it makes the achievement of valued ends more difficult. Difficulties may arise over the direct costs of "servicing" his debt or the indirect costs of other sectors objecting to and retaliating against his use of the polity's resources to pay off "partisan" debts. Here we are particularly concerned with the former.

The statesman may be anxious to repay loans so that he will be freer of interest obligations and can shape his policies with less influence from certain sectors, however much he may otherwise sympathize with these sectors. The principal difficulty he encounters is the often implicit nature of political loans. Only when quite definite terms are agreed on in advance— when what is commonly called a "deal" is made—can the statesman know with certainty what constitutes satisfactory repayment and whether he has met and terminated the creditor sector's claims. It is more common for support or other aid to be given without explicit terms for repayment.

Indeed, resources may be given, loaned, or withheld without prior consultation. For example, a sector may withhold information and taxes from a regime that is struggling with opponents and then consider this a "debt" once the anti-statesman comes into authority. Even if no agreement was made, expectations of repayment of equal value with interest were nonetheless created. A statesman may find that he has alleged debts of which he knows nothing, owed to sectors that will consider him ungrateful or worse if these debts are not honored. To fail to repay these alleged debts may cause the disappointed sector to withdraw its support and other positive contributions. The sector may even undertake sanctions against the regime, perhaps resorting to violence. After independence the Moroccan Rif Berbers were offended when their substantial military contribution to the

[20] In politics it is at least tacitly accepted that a political leader who succeeds in occupying the authority roles can in effect nationalize his debts. His manner of repayment may be subtle or blatant, but as long as he remains in authority, his preferences will be decisive in making authoritative allocations.

independence struggle was not followed by greater governmental assistance in the form of schools, jobs, communications, and the like. They subsequently refused to pay taxes, boycotted the government marketplaces, and sought to disengage themselves from the national political system.[21] However, the very ambiguity of political debts, while it may be responsible for misunderstanding and even sector retaliation for disappointed expectations, may still be used by the statesman to his advantage. If no deal was made or definite terms agreed upon, it may be difficult for a sector to prove or insist that the debt was not repaid by certain favors from the regime. In particular, a politically weak sector, desiring future favor from the statesman, is not in a position to protest effectively a statesman's decision that a debt is paid.

When repaying a debt, a statesman might give a creditor sector influence over one particular area for an indefinite period of time, as a kind of "lump sum" payment. Or he might arrange for a favored sector to have a standing amount of credit with the regime, sort of a revolving credit arrangement in which he would have some discretion as to what would be procured with this credit. Or he might repay the principal with interest on an installment plan, so that at the end of a certain period the debt would be liquidated. Some statesmen may cancel or invalidate a debt at some point in time, even before any interest is given. They may do so with impunity when dealing with a weak sector, but not when dealing with a stronger one. However, cancellation of debts, especially without paying any interest, usually lowers the statesman's credit rating and makes future borrowing from the sector impossible or at least much more expensive. Once a statesman has not honored his debts, the risk of default is judged by sectors to be greater. Conversely, a reputation for "straight dealing" with sectors is a potential asset and may help a leader secure resources more readily and cheaply in time of need.

If a statesman has diversified and expanded his base of support after taking office, he may have developed sufficient alternative sources of resources to afford arbitrary action with his creditors. Or he may run a deficit political budget in an effort to mobilize other sectors, attempting to generate enough new political resources to maintain his solvency.[22] How a statesman handles his problem of paying interest on and repaying his debts is a

[21] Geertz (1963:124).

[22] If the statesman breaks off his relations with some sectors, he may find others glad to come to his aid, expecting some interest to accrue to them, to be sure. The regime may or may not form as close a relationship with these sectors as it did with those initially in the core combination, but the new exchange relationship will be more mutually beneficial than the previous one between the regime and these sectors.

critical problem in resource management and depends on the means used for resource accumulation. Political interest, though less quantifiable than economic interest, must be considered in the calculations of any regime that undertakes to incur or has incurred obligations to sectors.

INTEREST RATES.

As we noted in our discussion of political monetary policy in Chapter VI, there is no generalized interest rate that can be manipulated by the regime. The interest rate paid to sectors that furnish the regime or its opponents with resources often depends very much on particular circumstances such as how much advantage the sector receives from the incumbent regime and how likely the anti-statesman is to capture authority. Yet we can imagine an average interest rate that varies according to the state of the political market. Depending on whether sector inflation or deflation is greater, the average interest rate for borrowing resources will be higher or lower. As in economics, this variable rate may operate somewhat as a countercyclical factor. In the case of political inflation, the relatively lower interest rate resulting from sector deflation will encourage more political entrepreneurs to enter the field, thereby making the political market more competitive and probably lowering the price of authority.

There is one variable we have not incorporated into our discussion because it is less demonstrable than other variables we are discussing. It is the level of employment of factors of production, or more simply, the level of production as a proportion of potential output. In times of political deflation, production for political exchange is reduced. If we follow the economic analogy through, we conclude that the opportunity costs of employing factors will be lower during these times than during times of political prosperity and full political employment. Given these lower opportunity costs incurred by sectors for lending resources to an anti-statesman, the rate of interest obligation an anti-statesman would have to incur to secure these resources would be correspondingly lower.

If an anti-statesman does indeed succeed in accumulating enough political capital to topple a prosperous regime, his interest obligations to the sectors that aided him will be greater than they would be if he had raised his capital in less politically prosperous times. These higher servicing charges may considerably reduce his flexibility in carrying out his political plan, since relatively fewer resources will be uncommitted. Such reduced flexibility may lead him to broaden his base of support. Gaining additional support, and hence a greater supply of resources, will necessitate depreciating or reducing his obligations to the few advantaged sectors.

A high rate of political interest thus commonly reflects a relatively full employment of political factors of production and probably also a relatively high price level of political resources. Both a high price for a resource and a high rate of interest for borrowing result from conditions of high demand. When interest rates are generally high, the statesman too must pay high rates of interest on borrowed resources. His rates may be somewhat reduced, however, because under these conditions he is an excellent credit risk. He is less likely to be ousted and thus to have to default.[23] In times of political deflation when the rate of political interest is low, it would seem that the statesman would be able to borrow resources relatively inexpensively, but this is not usually the case. Under these conditions the statesman is a poor risk, and sectors will as a rule insist on exchanges that yield them a *quid pro quo* for their resources. Indeed, not unless offered quite a high interest rate will they agree to lend resources to the regime, and even then they are likely to require collateral or security such as influence or authority over areas of interest to them. Thus it may be that a statesman finds it most difficult to get loans at the time he needs them most, at a time when it is relatively easier for his opponents to get loans of political resources.

Investment

For the sake of simplicity, we have framed our analysis of political motives and political success in terms of maximization of resources. Thus it is important for us to emphasize the variety and validity of a statesman's chosen goals in our consideration of political investment. We do not assume, and few political leaders would assume, that maximum resources or maximum control are inherently desirable. At best they are means to achievement of ends for a particular political community. Within the political community there is probably (and properly) no unanimity about ends. Ends are selected, modified, reordered, and implemented in the course of the political process. Political leaders with various aspirations and designs for the community contend for the authority to further their respective values and ideologies. Political investment plays an important part not only in the ac-

[23] Of course, if a statesman borrows too often and too much, creditors will begin to lose confidence in his ability to manage the affairs of state. A statesman who lives beyond his political means is likely to be regarded suspiciously by sectors that stand to lose resources as a result of his profligacy. A sector's opinion of course depends on the uses to which borrowed resources are put. Sectors will often view borrowing for consumption unfavorably, while they usually regard enterprising investment as a venture worth backing.

quisition of authority through capital accumulation, but also in the exercise of authority through ensuring possession of sufficient and increasing resources.

An investment differs from other expenditures in that the full return from an exchange is delayed until some time in the future. Thus there is some uncertainty as to whether or not there will be a return, or if so, how much it will be.[24] Not all resources are equally suited for each kind of investment, as will become evident when we consider political and administrative infrastructure more extensively. Authority invested in the management of a state manufacturing enterprise may yield economic resources, but certain political information invested in this way might be totally unproductive. In order to have a more productive polity, whether from the point of view of the statesman or from that of the sectors, a variety of investments is probably necessary. With greater resources at his disposal in the future the statesman should be better able to achieve his goals, while with more resources the sectors should be able to meet a larger proportion of their needs and desires. The incentive for a statesman or an antistatesman to make investments, and for sectors to provide resources saved from other uses for use in investment, is the anticipated gain in value, i.e., "interest" in the political sense discussed above.

Investment by either a regime or sector may yield returns in the form of increased efficiency or effectiveness of political interaction. A statesman, thanks to improved political infrastructure, may be able to achieve the same incidence of compliance with less expenditure of resources. Similarly, a sector may take advantage of political infrastructure to wield a given amount of political power on the strength of fewer resources. Both may achieve the same result—or output—with reduced resources—or inputs. Political investments may also be used to increase the productivity of regime or sector resources. If we say that a regime or sector achieves greater output with the same input as before, we do not mean simply or necessarily that it secures a greater volume of resources, but rather that it has greater ability to achieve desired ends as a consequence of certain investments.

[24] We reiterate here the view that the distinction between investments and expenditures is more a matter of degree than kind. Education, for example, may be either expenditure or investment, depending on the perspective employed and on the particular time horizon and uncertainty of return involved. If it primarily increases satisfaction, now and in the future, it is usually considered consumption, while if it raises productivity, it may be considered investment, even if the return is quick.

TYPES OF INVESTMENT.

Perhaps the most tangible and familiar investments are *investments in political and administrative infrastructure*. We will consider these in some detail in the next chapter. In addition to infrastructure investments, we feel that there are three other major types of investment.[25] *Stability investments* are allocations aimed at reducing potential and probable opposition to the regime in authority. These investments may involve coercion or threats as well as economic resources, and would aim at containing the demands of sectors able to disrupt the polity, for example, secessionist groups, radical trade unions, or the urban unemployed. Less specific stability investments would be any investments that are intended to improve the regime's future resource position. These in all probability increase the regime's power and hence its ability to maintain political stability. Any measures creating expectations that reduce an anti-statesman's potential for success, for example, determined anti-inflationary measures or displays of "big power" support from another country, are conducive to stability.[26]

Because the resource of legitimacy differs in several respects from other political resources, it is useful to think in terms of *legitimacy investments*. Implementing certain educational programs, upgrading the status of authority roles, or ideologically justifying certain exercises of authority may yield greater legitimacy for the regime and its policies. By making legitimacy investments, a statesman should be able to secure compliance with given policies with less expenditure of other resources such as coercion. Such investments aim at inculcating acceptance of civil authority and at discouraging sectors from feeling they have a right to make authoritative allocations without the permission of civil authorities. One form of legitimacy investment involves sharing authority. For example, a central government that hitherto reserved for itself the power to command certain economic resources through taxation may confer this right to tax on some local government units. Such a measure is likely to reinforce acceptance of

[25] These three types are discussed at greater length in Ilchman and Bhargava (1966).

[26] The measures Huntington suggests to slow the processes of mobilization or politicization may be considered stability investments. Some of the investments that follow from a scheme of requisites for "nation-building" may in fact be destabilizing, since they increase the number and effectiveness of demands made on regime resources. Consolidation of major political forces into a single party to reduce intra-elite competition would be a stability investment in our terms. See Huntington (1965).

the central government's right to allocate authoritatively in other areas. The greater legitimacy accorded to the regime enables the regime to reduce its use of coercion.

Though their returns may be difficult to measure, investments intended to affect behavioral parameters may be quite profitable. In Chapter IV we suggested that greater social and political solidarity contribute both to stability and legitimacy for the regime.[27] *Solidarity investments* are aimed at securing emotional commitments to the state. To the extent that persons are encouraged to transcend sectoral identifications and to value the prevailing political, social, and economic stratifications, solidarity will be increased. If our conceptualization seems abstract, we need only consider the consequences of increases in patriotism or national loyalty for a statesman's ability to secure compliance.

More generically, political investment includes all expenditures that offer the likelihood of increased future productivity or efficiency but require that certain resources and current advantage be risked and possibly decreased. Perhaps arbitrarily, we would consider expenditures that are made without calculation of benefits or without reasonable chances of gain not investments but *political gambles*. These have a time-honored place in the conduct of politics but are beyond the scope of analysis and prediction. Political investments may involve risks, but they have ends in view that are judged commensurate with expected costs.[28]

RETURNS ON INVESTMENT.

We would classify as returns on any particular investment both the *increased resources* that accrue to a regime or a sector and the *resources saved* in securing compliance with decisions or preferences. Before investing any resource saved or withheld from current consumption, a statesman or other political leader may consider, on the basis of past experience or reasonable examination, which of various alternative uses is likely to return the greatest benefit net of present benefits foregone. An investment should not merely be aimed at securing maximum increases in the amount of regime

[27] See pp. 116–117.

[28] An example of a calculated risk that failed, in part due to unforeseeable circumstances, is Stolypin's proposed program of agricultural reforms in Russia before the Bolshevik Revolution. Fainsod says that Stolypin's move to break up the *mir* and build a class of sturdy peasant proprietors "represented a bold and intelligent effort to provide a bulwark against revolution, but the slowness with which the reforms were executed and their virtual suspension during World War I largely robbed them of their intended effect." Fainsod (1966:248).

resources. Rather it should be aimed at securing the greatest increases in those resources most valued for achieving certain political objectives at or over a particular period of time.

It should be apparent that most political investments, like most economic investments, are not once-for-all efforts. As a rule, certain *maintenance costs* are involved. In order to establish the *net* return on a particular investment, those expenditures (investments) for the upkeep of, say, an anti-inflationary campaign or a national cultural festival must be deducted from the return. Once the net return on an investment is estimated over time, the equivalent of a rate of interest can be computed as well. However crude the calculations, the interest to be accrued must be considered in connection with any investment decision. If the estimated net return is not greater than the probable value to be gained from simply saving the resources involved, investment would be unwise. Indeed, if no sufficiently profitable investment opportunities are available, a regime or sector may get the greatest value from its resources by consuming or exchanging them in the present.[29]

At any particular time we can try to assess the *marginal efficiency* of political capital, whether of particular kinds of capital or of accumulated political capital in general. Marginal efficiency is determined by the state of political technology and the possible production functions, to borrow two concepts directly from economics. In economic analysis it is said that for a given state of the arts, the marginal efficiency or marginal productivity of capital will decline over time as the volume of investment increases. This relationship appears to hold for political economy as well, underscoring the need for political entrepreneurship. Innovation in the state of the political arts can continually change the political production functions, recombining political factors in such a way that production is more efficient and the level of production is raised.

Entrepreneurship

Political resource accumulation is not an automatic process or phenomenon. Only the will, drive, and activity of political entrepreneurs will bring it

---

[29] We do not think it useful to consider in our discussion the notion of *discounted value* of future resources. Given the lack of possible quantification at this stage, such a consideration would be frivolous. The future value of resources is considered in terms of *anticipated marginal value* to the regime at some particular point in time.

about, whether through capital formation, mobilization, saving, or investment. In particular, innovation in political investment is the key to break-
throughs in political productivity; political entrepreneurs are those who
find new combinations of, uses for, and sources of factors of political production.[30] If it were not for the fact of scarcity, entrepreneurship would
lose much of its meaning. In business the son of a multimillionaire may
have entrepreneurial abilities, but it is not really skill that makes for his success, though lack of skill may make for failure. The political entrepreneur is
one who by improving the state of the political arts raises the marginal efficiency of capital. Imagination and initiative frequently enable him to increase his power, in or out of office, by acquiring greater political resources.
Of course, the political environment facilitates or militates against his success. Many political as well as economic entrepreneurs go broke because
there is no demand for their "product." The political market may be as
ruthless as the economic market in ruining the casual, premature, careless,
or uncalculating entrepreneur.[31]

Successful political leaders in this or any other century have been entrepreneurs, but our evaluation of them as entrepreneurs depends on the extent to which they improved on the initial endowment of resources and
infrastructure with which they had to work. Thus Roosevelt might rank
higher than Churchill as a war leader, and Stalin might well rank higher
than either because he was in the midst of a political, social, and economic
revolution when he was required to redirect and exploit the resources of his
polity for purposes of national defense. The two political leaders of this

[30] In recent years the concept of political entrepreneurship has come to be
widely accepted. The resemblance of political enterprise to economic enterprise
is great enough for social scientists to have adopted the metaphor without having the conceptual tools of political economy that give the idea more analytical
substance. Apter makes the resemblance quite clear in his introduction to a
consideration of non-western government and politics. See Apter (1963b:649).
He defines a political entrepreneur as someone who can "organize a following in
order to gain access to state resources." Apter (1965:71). As we have seen, Zolberg finds this conception useful in his analysis of West African politics
(1966).

[31] Apter seems to stress the environmental factors affecting success or failure,
though not to the exclusion of factors of will and determination. He suggests
that the "kind of politics [that] emerges depends in no small measure upon the
nature of the social and economic raw material that exists, the degree of cultural strain, and the institutional framework, antique and modern, which is the
inheritance of a new nation." Apter (1963b:649). We would agree with
Apter's emphasis on the influence of the political environment, but we are looking for means of exploiting this environment or minimizing its limiting effects.
This is what political entrepreneurs do.

century who have probably had the greatest impact on the politics of other countries are M. K. Gandhi and V. I. Lenin. Both were imaginative and forceful entrepreneurs but had quite different goals for a "good society." The select, highly disciplined Bolshevik party, ready and willing to use violence, contrasts markedly with the equally influential national congress-type party that Gandhi fashioned to employ non-violent means to achieve political goals. Both Lenin and Gandhi aimed at substantial restratification of the economy, society, and polity. Each articulated an ideology of change and national goals. It is worthwhile briefly to compare them as political entrepreneurs in order better to demonstrate the analytical approach of political economy.

The statesmen against which each worked are of less interest to us than the sectors each mobilized in his campaign for authority. Lenin was ideologically committed to the proletariat as the agent of political, social, and economic revolution. When it became clear to him that this sector had insufficient resources for success, he turned to the peasantry, for the most part because it furnished the bulk of recruits to the critical sector, the army. Yet the peasantry was not part of the core combination, but was only within the ideological bias. Lenin would have been quite satisfied for the peasantry to disappear over time as the result of what he considered inevitable economic transformation. Gandhi, on the other hand, valued the Indian peasantry. It represented the Indian virtues he prized and hoped to perpetuate. He was generally in sympathy with the lower castes that comprised the large but underprivileged sectors. The status he offered them led to growing support and willingness to follow Congress strategy. Because the workers could play a critical role in urban areas, they were part of Gandhi's core combination, but were less favored because they were tainted with "modernity." Non-cooperation, the denial of legitimacy status to the colonial regime, proved as potent a political weapon as the Leninist reliance on strategic violence against the old regime.

Of interest to us are the attitudes of both men toward nationalism, a political parameter of sorts. While Gandhi utilized and intensified this incipient orientation to action to get various sectors to offer resources without direct or immediate compensation, Lenin rejected it. In its place he attempted to substitute proletarian internationalism. The lesser political profitability of this strategy compared with that of exploiting the strong nationalistic sentiments existing in Russia became clear within a decade. Stalin chose to play down the international aspects of Communism in favor of "socialism in one country," a policy that proved to yield needed resources at a crucial time in the transformation of the Soviet polity.

Related to Gandhi and Lenin's different attitudes toward nationalism were their differing approaches to the problem of nationalities. Both Russia and India incorporated many diverse ethnic, linguistic, and religious groups. Lenin sought to gloss over these differences, promising the nationalities that a Communist regime would end Tsarist exploitation and white Russian cultural chauvinism. During the struggle for power, some of the nationality groups contributed greatly to the Bolshevik effort. The returns they received were meager. After Stalin's accession to authority, a consistent policy of cultural integration—in the name of respect for cultural diversity—led to increasing national homogeneity. Gandhi made relatively few particularistic appeals, preferring to draw on common Indian or nationalistic identifications for support. It seems unlikely that he would have moved toward cultural integration as Stalin chose to do in the Soviet Union. Nehru, Gandhi's successor, attempted to forge a common nationality for India, but with limited success. The perils of ethnic strife that India faces today may be attributed in part to Gandhi's unwillingness to force the pace of integration.

There is some difficulty in comparing the effectiveness of these two leaders because Gandhi never had a chance to show what entrepreneurial skills he possessed as a statesman. Lenin showed considerable flexibility once he acquired authority. The New Economic Policy is recognized as a masterful strategy to maintain economic production during a time of political consolidation. Lenin's justification for the NEP—"one step backward, two steps forward"—must rank as one of the most politically profitable slogans ever coined for mobilizing resources.[32] Though he did not live to see his preferred stratifications firmly established, he had effectively lain the political groundwork for this transformation.

We do not necessarily propose Lenin and Gandhi as heroes, though certainly political leaders in developing countries have borrowed much in the way of investment strategies from either or both. Our concern is for the leader who is not a Lenin or a Gandhi, the leader who lacks their innovative capabilities and opportunities. It is he who most needs the guidance that political economy attempts to provide.[33] Any statesman, even one

[32] The idiom "to coin a political slogan" is apt. One of the other slogans most profitable for mobilizing political resources is that of the American revolutionaries: "no taxation without representation." Translated into the language of political economy, the slogan calls for no economic resources without authority of equal value in return.

[33] Almond and Powell are also very much concerned with the statesman's need for guidance, though they formulate their analysis in terms of capabilities rather than resources. We appreciate their orientation toward this problem. See Almond and Powell (1966:329).

with little ambition except to remain in authority, must make some stability investments. Few will neglect opportunities, at least the most obvious ones, for making legitimacy investments or for investing in the profitable parameters of patriotism or reduced sector reliance on violence in political bargaining. Every investment, of course, need not tax a statesman's entrepreneurial talents. Some investments are marked by their more routine qualities. However, a statesman's most ambitious investments are usually made in the area of political and administrative infrastructure. The costs, returns, and risks of infrastructure investment are probably the greatest and thus most require further analysis.

VIII

POLITICAL AND
ADMINISTRATIVE INFRASTRUCTURE

The effective breakdown [in the Congo] of the colonial tradition of highly centralized administration and the disintegration of the colonial provinces rendered essential a painful reconstruction of the whole community on new bases. This has been achieved at the high price of immediate loss of efficiency and the invalidation of much of the administrative legacy of Belgian rule. The process is irreversible, however, and eventually may amortize the administrative cost in producing a governmental framework which can more easily obtain a consensus for its operation.

M. Crawford Young [1]

Statesmen in underdeveloped countries must be concerned both with accumulating political capital and creating infrastructure. While short-term pressures may dictate the priority of working capital, long-term occupancy of authority roles—or indeed maintenance of roles that in the long run will be worth occupying—impels statesmen to consider the fixed capital of politics as well. For this reason, we will now turn to a discussion of political and administrative infrastructure. The idea of infrastructure applied to politics is not new. When political and social scientists began to think about the state as an organization for the achievement of various ends, it was natural for them to identify certain processes as indispensable to political production. Shils, Eisenstadt, Almond, and others have drawn the analogy between political and social and economic overhead capital in order to differentiate types of institutions and processes. Their argument was that some institutions and processes facilitate politics while others are the stuff of politics. We might note that while the most ambitious project

[1] Young (1964:579).

yet undertaken in the field of comparative politics was intended to treat the various political "functions" comprehensively, it in fact described forms of political and administrative infrastructure.[2]

The contribution political economy makes to the study of such infrastructure is to draw and use the analogy between political and economic infrastructure in a way that permits evaluative judgments to be made. Almond and Powell's "capabilities" are analogous to infrastructure, but insofar as these are treated in functional terms, there is no way of determining for any regime to what extent a capability is or must be fulfilled. Nor are "nation-building" studies more useful for guiding choices. They provide no means to judge which institutions and processes are more necessary than others if all desirable changes cannot be implemented. Nor do these studies advance a means of evaluating the extent to which any institution or process is required to sustain "nationhood." Political economy, on the other hand, focuses on assigning priorities and estimating the adequacy of certain infrastructure, though each judgment is situational and depends on the goals of a specific regime. Our concept of political and administrative infrastructure follows naturally from our concepts of political resources, capital accumulation, and political investment.[3]

The Characteristics of Political and
Administrative Infrastructure

The characteristics of infrastructure are such that a simple definition of infrastructure is not very instructive. Therefore, we will proceed to discuss

[2] We will refer frequently to the Studies in Political Development sponsored by the Committee on Comparative Politics, originally under the chairmanship of Gabriel Almond. This well-known series relates bureaucracy, communications, education, political culture, and political parties to political development. Volumes in this series include Pye (1963); LaPalombara (1963a); Ward and Rustow (1964); Coleman (1965); Pye and Verba (1965); and LaPalombara and Weiner (1966).

[3] Blau's use of the term "institutionalization" is similar to our use of the term "infrastructure": both terms refer to formalized procedures that perpetuate organizing principles from generation to generation. According to Blau, establishing formal procedures requires an investment of resources, and preserves and rigidifies patterns of social conduct and relations. Institutions, he says, impose historical limits on social structure which in turn exert structural constraints on individual conduct. They preserve social arrangements for the production and distribution of social facilities, contributions, and rewards. Furthermore, says Blau, they perpetuate authority and organization to mobilize re-

the characteristics of both political and administrative infrastructure and then, perhaps more instructively, we will consider specific institutions, structures, and processes that belong in each category. The distinction between political and administrative infrastructure is neither dichotomous nor invariable. Political infrastructure is primarily used in the mobilization of support and resources for acquiring and maintaining authority; to use the language of Easton, Deutsch, and Almond, its primary function is providing inputs for a regime's policy allocations. Administrative infrastructure, on the other hand, is necessary for the exercise of authority; it is responsible primarily for the implementation of policy allocations, in other words, for handling regime outputs.[4]

To deal adequately with the various forms of political and administrative infrastructure would require a whole book or a series of volumes. Thus our treatment of infrastructure in this chapter is admittedly more suggestive than definitive. In our treatment of political infrastructure we discuss regime political parties, auxiliary organizations, opposition parties, elections, ideologies, and development plans. Under the heading of administrative infrastructure we discuss public bureaucracies, the army, police, and intelligence organizations. Economic capital, education, and communications systems are also considered as political infrastructure, though they conform to economists' definition of infrastructure as well. What, we must ask, do these disparate institutions, structures, and processes have in common? In varying degrees, by regularizing roles, exchanges, and valuations that determine political interaction, they make political production more efficient. In this context "efficiency" means that a goal can be accomplished with reduced inputs or expenditures of resources, or that more goals can be achieved with the same inputs as before. In either case there is some improvement or innovation in political technology; a gain in efficiency must be preceded by some new means of acquiring resources, combining them, substituting them, or utilizing them.[5]

sources and coordinate collective actions. See Blau (1964:273–277). When Huntington writes of "institutions" as a mark of political development, he is referring to what we call political infrastructure. See Huntington (1965).

[4] To be sure, the distinction we are making is sometimes more analytic than concrete, as some infrastructure may have both political and administrative functions.

[5] Almond and Powell observe that rulers in bureaucratic societies were able to rely on one of the great political "inventions" in history. Bureaucratic regimes were better able to regulate behavior in their own society, to expand their territory, to increase their own resources, and to pursue autonomously other political goals. See Almond and Powell (1966:45). Rustow cites the many novel

Basically, infrastructure economizes on the use of political resources by increasing *predictability* or *mobility*. The establishment of certain exchange relationships, whether mutually beneficial, legitimated, or coerced, provides for predictability in the amount and kinds of resources available to maintain other relationships. When benefits, sanctions, norms, or simply expectations are established with respect to a given pattern of political competition or exercise of authority, compliance may be achieved with the expenditure of fewer resources because political activities and attitudes can be more reliably predicted. Infrastructure contributes to the increased mobility of resources in much the same way that transport systems contribute to greater efficiency of economic production. Political production is made more efficient by institutions, structures, and processes that facilitate movement of resources between sectors and regime. Infrastructure is used to gain support, enforce authoritative decisions, gather information, deploy coercion, and confer status at less cost than would be the case if established patterns did not exist. We also would mention two less basic functions of political infrastructure, that of enabling a regime better to cope with demands,[6] and that of controlling resources by linking peripheral political, social, and economic markets to the central markets.[7]

It may appear that there is little difference between the use of political resources for infrastructure and the use of such resources for other political purposes. The distinction between expenditures for infrastructure and other expenditures is certainly less definite in political than in economic analysis. Nevertheless, we can distinguish uses of resources for infrastructure from other uses. In the first place, expenditures for infrastructure con-

devices introduced into Turkish politics by the "Young Turks." He says that cabinet responsibility, elections, active journalism, partisan clubs, and military interference in politics brought into being a more productive polity. See Rustow (1966:117).

[6] Although Easton does not write in terms of infrastructure as such, his conceptualization is similar to ours. He writes that "channelling mechanisms such as parliaments, interest groups, parties, or responsive administrative organizations did not just emerge as ways of absorbing, communicating and processing demands. They were social inventions, gradually worried through, to deal with specific sources of tension, one of which involved the increasing rate of demand input and the need to devise ways of handling it." See Easton (1965:121).

[7] Education, communications media, and ideology are kinds of infrastructure that can facilitate "nationalization." Deutsch (1961) expresses the concern that "social mobilization" will increase demands on the regime and thereby reduce its capacity (resources) for achieving goals. Infrastructure can, however, be adapted so that such "mobilization" has the beneficial effect of causing a net increase in regime resources.

stitute investments, since costs precede benefits by some amount of time. In exchanges costs and benefits are more or less concurrent. Second, infrastructure investments rather than *being* exchanges instead *create* exchange relationships that are maintained over time. These relationships provide greater net benefits for the regime than would be the case if the investments had not been made and the relationships not established.

However, spending resources for infrastructure investments, like other expenditures, involves costs. First, a regime must reckon with the *direct costs* resulting from the expenditure or commitment of resources. When a law is passed or promulgated, for example, the regime's use of authority is bound in certain ways. This restriction may amount to an insignificant or a considerable cost, depending on whether passing the law furthers or hinders the achievement of regime objectives. In addition, there are the *maintenance costs* that a regime must bear over time, such as the expenditure of coercion or the issuance of threats to keep the law effective. *Indirect costs* of infrastructure are also important. Insofar as sectors find the law onerous, they may reduce the support they give to the regime or may withhold resources such as information or legitimacy. Sectors often impose indirect costs on a regime because the establishment of infrastructure has lowered their status or authority, or because they believe the newly established infrastructure will be contrary to their interests in some general way.

In addition to direct, indirect, and maintenance costs, *opportunity costs* are invariably involved in investment choices. Resources invested for one purpose cannot be used for other purposes. Building certain infrastructure could starve some existing political relationships and thus entail considerable costs for the statesman in the long run. Moreover, each investment choice has an impact on other choices already taken. As we will suggest below, some investments decrease the effectiveness or raise the costs of other investments already made. Though many costs, and benefits as well, must be assessed in judging the net productivity of political and administrative infrastructure investments, the various consequences of each can be enumerated and their value assessed in resource terms.

The use of political resources for infrastructure is most closely related to choices to induce social and economic change and to remain in authority in the future. The use of scarce resources to build political and administrative infrastructure requires saving resources from current consumption to invest for future gain. These resources are then not immediately available for use in coping with present social and economic change or remaining in authority in the present. As is the case for all choices oriented toward the future, the element of contingency in infrastructure investments is high. The statesman must take account of the imputed costs of uncertainty. He must consider the possibility that there will be no return realized from his investment because the intended relationships are not established or because the structure may be used by others for their own political profit and to his own political loss.[8]

All regimes need not invest the same amount in infrastructure. Some have natural advantages. Just as an extensive system of natural waterways may spur economic development, political development may be facilitated when the population speaks a common language (Tanzania as opposed to Uganda), or is ethnically homogeneous (Tunisia as opposed to Morocco), or lives contiguously (Cambodia as opposed to Indonesia), or is used to participating in some form of local government (India as opposed to Iran). *Natural infrastructure* is the infrastructure inherited from previous generations that is not the result of deliberate actions by regime or sectors. Such infrastructure may reduce the cost of assessing sectoral demands or of securing compliance, or it may provide institutions or values that can be modified or reoriented to serve the regime's purposes. The costs of government for regimes with natural advantages are relatively less than the costs confronting other regimes.[9]

[8] Let us give a hypothetical example of the kind of calculation required to take such contingencies into account. If the possible benefits from establishing, say, a farmers' organization were symbolically 200 units of support, but the probability of achieving the maximum benefit were only 50 per cent, the anticipated benefit would be discounted to 100 units. If the possible cost resulting from the organization's being captured by the opposition were 200 units of support, and the probability of capture occurring were 25 per cent, we would deduct an additional 50 units, leaving an anticipated net benefit of only 50 units. Would this investment be profitable? It would probably produce benefits of legitimacy, information, and reduced violence, but these would have to be weighed against the costs of economic resources to be invested as well as against the costs of granting some influence, sharing some authority, or perhaps of sharing some political information. If the statesman intended to promote a program of agricultural development, the support and legitimacy he gained would be of more value to him than it would be if he were concentrating on developing the industrial sectors of the economy. The net benefits from such an investment have to be figured in terms of the marginal value of the inputs and outputs to a particular regime, and this value depends on the particular regime's resource position and goals.

[9] Two examples of how common language and culture can lower the costs of pursuing policy goals are presented by Mouly (1966:20) and Rossillion (1966:51) in their consideration of rural development programs in the Central African Republic and in Mali.

One of the most significant forms of natural political infrastructure is a *social stratification* based on norms that sanction intervention in the social market by authority figures. To the extent that the political and social stratifications are congruent, a highly inegalitarian and hierarchical social stratification biases political exchanges to the advantage of those occupying authority roles. The power of monarchs has not rested solely or perhaps even primarily on their use of coercion. Monarchs who dominated the social stratification were able to manipulate the status market to their political advantage. Because so many exchanges were affected by an individual's status, the power to elevate or demote persons in terms of status was a major source of monarchs' political power.[10] Generally, when the prerogative of authority figures to alter status declines, so does their political power.[11]

Related to the social stratification but analytically separate from it is the political culture of a community. Widely shared values and meanings associated with the competition for and exercise of authority usually make politics and government more "economical" by making them more predictable. By calling political culture natural political infrastructure, we do not mean to say that political culture evolves without human intention or intervention; rather it is inherited by each generation of political participants as a sort of "natural endowment" and is usually subject to only marginal changes in any given period of time unless norm-altering events affect the lives of most members of the community.

Many elements of a society's culture may have political implications or

[10] When British missionaries and emissaries made their way to the kingdom of Buganda in what is now Uganda, they found that the king, the *Kabaka*, occupied an unusually powerful position in the society. Factors contributing to his power were the absence of status groups apart from the royal family and the fact that great honor and wealth were associated with the subordinate authority roles to which persons were appointed by the *Kabaka*. Since he could remove persons at will and the offices were not necessarily hereditary, the *Kabaka* controlled social mobility. This particular form of social stratification readily served his political ends. Once other means of acquiring status (and wealth and authority) were introduced, the *Kabaka's* power declined. See LeVine (1963:290–291); also Fallers (1959), Richards (1960: Chap. II), and Apter (1961).

[11] This relationship between decline in control over social status and decline in political power is evident from Tocqueville's account of the decline of the *ancien régime* in France. See Tocqueville (1955). To be sure, a decline in control over status may be due more to changes in sector attitudes toward what roles and persons deserve esteem and deference than to changes in the authorities' ability to confer the symbols of status and prestige. For a general theoretical discussion of social stratification and the political community, see Bendix (1960).

potential political consequences, but there is no necessary connection between these elements and the political process. They are analogous to a country's natural advantages in mineral endowments, which have economic value only when exploited for economic purposes. Cultural values, traditions, and role expectations may be exploited by political participants to further certain political ends, but unless so exploited they are not political, just as unexploited minerals are not economic. Despite our analogy with mineral endowments, we do not consider political culture a resource. Rather we consider it infrastructure because it facilitates the production and exchange of resources or at least increases the predictability of resource flows. For example, cultural norms such as deference for persons in authority positions or avoidance of conflict can be utilized by a statesman to secure compliance more economically in various circumstances.

Exploitation of political culture may itself require making some investments, perhaps in a political party or an official ideology. Yet certain aspects of political culture may make such investments cheaper for the statesman. If, for example, there is a tradition of persons coming together at a community level to cope with collective problems, establishment or extension of local government will cost less. Statesmen and other political participants who have very long time horizons might consider making investments to alter the norms dominant in a political culture in a more favorable direction. The payoff, however, would be distant and uncertain, and for this reason changes in the parameters of political culture are seldom deliberate. They are nonetheless significant for the conduct of politics and the exercise of authority.

Some statesmen may have advantages in constructing or extending political infrastructure because they can utilize pre-existing infrastructure. Upon achieving independence, an existing nationalist movement can be reshaped as the regime's political party for channeling sector resources into regime programs. A redefinition of roles would be involved, but a major new investment would not. We need only compare post-independence India with Ceylon to note the difference such advantages can make.

Whether building on pre-existing infrastructure or beginning with new forms of infrastructure, a regime needs to take account of maintenance costs. To neglect infrastructure often amounts to *disinvestment*. Thus the requirements of existing infrastructure often dictate the uses to which a regime puts its available resources. A system of local government must be continually nourished with grants of authority and money if it is not to decline in its efficiency for containing demands, providing information, and yielding compliance. The range of infrastructure choices that a statesman may seriously consider is also limited by the fact that much infrastructure is dependent on other infrastructure already being in existence or coming into existence at approximately the same time. For maximum effectiveness in helping the regime achieve its goals for the polity, a system of local government, for example, should probably not be set up or extended before a political party building support for the regime's program has been established throughout the countryside. Similarly, unless there are already in existence institutions for law enforcement such as courts and police, the effectiveness of laws will be minimal.

Thus a consideration of *complementarity* and *sequencing* is critical for the subsequent political profitability of infrastructure investments. As is the case with economic investments, political investments are often most productive if combined into a package of infrastructure additions such as an integrated set of increments in a country's laws, police, and courts. Benefit-cost ratios are raised by external economies that result when other investments share some of the initial or maintenance costs or when investments are undertaken in certain sequences. An effective bureaucracy requires making a considerable prior investment in education in order to produce highly trained manpower. If all of the cost of an educational system from primary school to university were weighed against the bureaucracy's contributions to the regime's resources, the investment in education would not be considered economical. But since other infrastructure—local governments, parliament, radio and television, economic enterprise, and the legal system—also rely on the output of the educational system, investment in educational infrastructure usually proves profitable.

The occurrence of *external economies* points to the multiple uses of infrastructure and also to what Hirschman calls *linkages*, both forward and backward.[12] Some forms of infrastructure provide outputs that are in turn required as inputs for other forms. Thus establishing one form is likely to create some pressure for establishing other forms. The effect of linkages on complementarities, sequences, and externalities makes calculation of benefits difficult and often imprecise, but political economists must try to unravel the connections if they would improve their understanding of the consequences of political infrastructure.

One kind of infrastructure investment may have negative as well as positive effects on another. We have mentioned external economies; in some cases there may be *external diseconomies*. Zolberg describes how in West Africa political parties have been invested with certain authority, even at the local level. Conflict between party and local bureaucratic officials has arisen, and in some cases the incidence of compliance with regime deci-

[12] Hirschman (1958: Chap. VI).

sions has been reduced as a consequence of the parallel infrastructure.[13] In certain cases there may even be some degree of incompatibility between infrastructures so that one negates the other's benefits. Regimes in Ghana and Algeria were overthrown by military coups after those regimes had created paramilitary infrastructure that threatened to reduce the army's monopoly on coercive force. For both Nkrumah and ben Bella, a second investment in paramilitary organization proved politically unprofitable.[14]

Many investments are neither mutually exclusive nor complementary. There may be situations in which investments are viewed as alternatives to one another. In terms of securing desired compliance, certain investments may be *functional equivalents*. For example, a strong bureaucracy and police may serve as alternatives to the maintenance of an effective political party. Rustow suggests that Nasser's regime is pursuing such a course of investment in Egypt.[15] Nasser has made several attempts at establishing a party but has not at any time invested an adequate amount of authority or other resources to make the party effective. It should be possible for a political economist to ascertain the consequences, costs, and limitations of choosing one set of infrastructures for investment and maintenance rather than another.

Our discussion of alternative investments raises the question of *indivisibilities*. Investments are often "lumpy"—that is, half a steel factory or half a road will yield no benefits—and an entire project must often be undertaken at one time. Indivisibilities may be less marked in political investments, though the example of Nasser's political party cited above suggests the extent of their effect. Apparently a party cannot be productive with only a minimal investment of authority in its operation. Possibly a very small army will be unproductive. It may be large enough to topple a regime but not large enough to wield coercion effectively against any significant sector in the population. Such was the case of the 650-man army in Dahomey.

In political investment there may also be a phenomenon similar to what

13 Zolberg (1966:125–126).
14 Little has been published on the Algerian coup, but reports from Algeria at the time indicated army dissatisfaction with the attempt to create special units that would be loyal to the President and party rather than to the regular army command structure. For views of members of the Ghanaian army on Nkrumah's establishment of a special Presidential Guard, see Alexander (1965:102) and Afrifa (1966:100). On the other hand, Paz Estenssoro, President of Bolivia during the 1950's, demonstrated that investments in paramilitary organization may be politically profitable under certain conditions. See Lepawsky (1957) and Patch (1960).
15 Rustow (1966:130).

is called in economics the *acceleration principle*.[16] As our discussion of sequencing suggests, some kinds of infrastructure investments may be prerequisites for making others. For example, before an investment in newspapers for communication would become profitable, a regime would need to invest in education to raise the extent of literacy. However, to achieve a certain net investment, a considerably larger gross investment is often required, and certain destabilizing consequences may result from making the necessary larger initial investments. Developing a school system for a limited purpose such as raising literacy to a level that makes newspapers an effective means of communication means expanding the output of certain resources, in this case trained manpower to become teachers. Letting this capacity for training persons become idle when regime demand for the output of the educational system slackens may have serious repercussions for the political community. Reducing the level of net investment may induce a larger reduction in the gross level of investment. Insofar as an investment has forward- or backward-linkages, some acceleration effects are probable.

Decisions on infrastructure investments are complicated by the fact that an institution or collectivity may serve both as infrastructure and as a sector. A bureaucracy is infrastructure insofar as it carries out the interests of the regime, accepting the regime's allocations of rights and duties. But civil servants commonly make claims for amended rights and duties as well. To the extent that they do so, the bureaucracy is engaging in politics and acting as a sector. Our distinction between sector and infrastructure is analytic. However, a statesman is usually well aware of the dilemmas inherent in this distinction and will seek to increase the infrastructural and reduce the sectoral characteristics of a certain group or organization. He will want

[16] In order to raise the output of economic product X by some amount through investment, there must first be some investment in the capital goods industry to increase the output of machinery with which to produce X. Thus the gross investment is greater than the net investment to produce X. Once the additional machinery has been produced by the capital goods industry, unless the new, higher rate of investment is maintained, the industry will have redundant capacity and will have to reduce its operations. The disparity between net and gross investment causes what is known as the "accelerator effect." Any increase or decrease in net investment has a magnified impact on the level of gross investment. This magnification of impact accounts for the repercussions of "crash" investment programs, whether political, social, or economic. These programs create additional productive capacity which is idled if the rate of increased investment ever falls off. Considerable political benefits are to be derived from expansion of investment, but serious negative repercussions are likely to result from contraction.

a group or organization to be mediating for him, gathering resources, or making their transfer easier, but the group's actions along these lines are sometimes beyond his control.

The statesman is also faced with the possibility mentioned earlier that infrastructure may be used by other political leaders to further their particular objectives. Some infrastructure is more and some less vulnerable to capture by anti-statesmen or sectors. Communications media, even if they were developed to serve the regime, are commonly used by statesman's opponents.[17] Of course, sectors or opposition movements may invest in their own communications media as well. As a rule, primary education is less subject than higher education to exploitation by a regime's opponents. Political parties are usually easier to control than the auxiliary organizations intended to align sectors with the regime's program through quasi-party affiliation. The institution usually thought to be most subject to the statesman's control is the bureaucracy. However, the capture of government agencies or departments by sectors is common throughout the world.[18]

We may consider, as the statesman occasionally does, the costs of and benefits that would result from the nullification or destruction of certain infrastructure. If a statesman wishes to eliminate such infrastructure, his options are to starve it of needed maintenance expenditures or to expend resources directly to disturb and interrupt certain exchange relationships crucial to its existence. Of course, if this infrastructure has become self-sufficient over time, the first option is not really available to the statesman. If he seriously wants to eliminate the net costs accruing from this infrastructure, he must choose the latter course.

Whenever the costs of existing infrastructure exceed the benefits, a statesman is well advised first to try to discover ways of making that infrastructure yield net benefits. Such a course will to be sure often require certain investments. If, however, the statesman concludes that no plan of his can produce net benefits, he will take steps to disestablish the infrastructure. It is often the case that the older a party or other infrastructure is, the more difficult it is to suppress.[19] By saying this, we are recognizing the fact that infrastructure, through its participants, may develop "vested interests"

[17] For example, some of the infrastructure investments in modernizing Turkey were clearly not subject to the control of the modernizers. Rustow reports that the railroads and telegraphs established in Turkey could be used either to communicate liberal ideas or to repress them. See Rustow (1966:116).

[18] Such capture by core combination sectors is, of course, less costly than that by sectors in the stability group.

[19] LaPalombara and Weiner (1966:23) offer this proposition with respect to political parties.

in its own survival. Participants may be able to impose high costs on a statesman wishing to dismantle a party or newspaper or constitution. If persons occupying infrastructural roles develop no interests of their own, presumably the infrastructure could be destroyed at any time at the same cost to the regime.

Because we have adopted in our analysis the perspective of the statesman, we have presented our analysis in terms of regime investment decisions. However, sectors can and do invest in infrastructure. For example, sectors more often than regimes invest in interest groups and newspapers. Often it is sectors rather than a regime that make the major investments in a political party. A regime seldom makes direct investments in an opposition party, though such an investment by it or by others invariably costs the regime something. Seldom does an infrastructure investment benefit only the investor. As is the case with economic infrastructure, with political infrastructure there are usually returns in the form of external economies that benefit others, whether sectors or regime. Those investments with the greatest external economies contribute most to the productivity of politics, but neither regime nor sector will make an investment unless its direct benefits from that investment outweigh the costs.

We have not tried to make general prescriptive statements about particular types of infrastructure because there has not yet been sufficient empirical analysis to determine the costs and benefits of the various types, either in general or in particular cases. Comparative studies will probably be useful in developing general statements about different types of infrastructure. At present we can only give a hypothetical example of the kind of analysis we have in mind. If we were to aggregate and abstract the costs and benefits of investment, say, in local government, we might come up with the following relationship between costs and benefits as the scale of investment increases: [20]

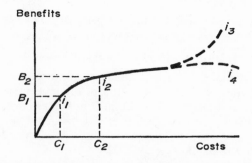

[20] At present this aggregation and abstraction is not very practical and is only suggestive. Many different resources make up costs and benefits. There are

It may be that local government when first instituted has rapidly rising benefits vis-à-vis costs. Generally speaking, it would thus be advisable to invest up to point i_1. Beyond this point costs would be rising relative to benefits. Yet if a statesman felt that he needed to reach the level of benefits b_2, he might nonetheless invest up to c_2. At higher levels of investment it is uncertain whether there would be increasing returns to scale (i_3) or diminishing returns (i_4).

We do not know the general shape of this benefit-cost curve for local government or whether the curve for local government would be the same as the curve for communications media. What is more, the curve for local government in a particular polity will probably vary from the general curve derived from comparative analysis. Investment decisions would presumably be taken at the margin, meaning that a statesman and political economist could determine as they proceeded whether or how far the political relationships of the particular system diverged from those they would expect on the basis of the general propositions that had been developed. General estimates would be most helpful when totally new investments were being considered and incremental decisions could not be made. It is worth noting that some of the work in conventional political science before the last decade was concerned, albeit imprecisely, with questions that touched upon the political productivity of various forms of infrastructure. Studies concerned with constitutional engineering, with relationships among different political institutions (executive, legislative, judicial), and with bases of electoral systems (two-party, single-party, multi-party) were in effect trying to assess the productive consequences of alternative infrastructural arrangements for achieving certain political ends.[21] We think that if the terms of analysis had included consideration of political resources and exchange, the conclusions of such studies would have been more broadly comparative and more meaningful to those who make choices about such arrangements.

If political scientists have not treated constitutions, elections, parties, and the like as political infrastructure, it is no wonder that they have not tried systematically to examine what economists regard as infrastructure in

no transitive exchange rates among resources, and consequently costs and benefits are not denominated in common terms. Nevertheless, a statesman could and would judge different combinations and amounts of resources yielded by a certain local government structure as more valuable or less valuable to him than other combinations and amounts yielded by other kinds of local government infrastructure.

[21] For a survey of such studies, see Eckstein and Apter (1963: Parts III, IV, and V). It is unfortunate that the more recent contributions to the study of comparative politics should not have built upon and developed the implications of such traditional political studies for the analysis of political productivity.

terms of its political productivity. It is widely understood that a regime lacking economic resources is likely to be a weaker regime than one better endowed economically. There should be detailed consideration of the political costs and benefits of economic investments in directly productive activities such as factories and farms; in social overhead capital such as transportation, power, and telecommunications; and in social services such as education, housing, and health facilities. Politicians recognize the political benefits accruing to a regime that makes economic investments, but they are confronted with the problem of deciding how much is enough, or how much of what kind of investment is most productive politically as well as economically.[22] In particular, the education system and media of mass communication have extensive political ramifications. We therefore consider them in greater detail later in this chapter.

In developing an investment strategy, the statesman must begin by considering what resources he has available or can make available for investment. Though it might be politically profitable to invest in expanded education, he might nonetheless lack the financial or manpower resources to do so. Indeed, given his resource constraints, his only option may be to make investments in other infrastructure that yields lower returns. Although some optimum amount and combination of infrastructure may theoretically exist for a polity, the statesman has to consider how to improve his own political position. He will try through successive decisions to approach a more productive position for his regime without necessarily being concerned about a theoretical optimum, although on the other hand, some idea of what an optimum configuration of infrastructure would be would probably better inform his incremental decisions.

[22] In terms of net political benefits, what are the advantages of stimulating private enterprise as compared to those of undertaking direct state investment in industries or agriculture? Allowing new productive capital to be provided and owned by private persons rather than by the state will alter the relative costs and benefits as far as the regime is concerned. The regime will need to expend fewer of its own economic resources, but in addition to having less control over economic production it will lose some control over the allocation of status within the society.

With respect to social services, if private agencies are allowed to provide housing, education, or health services, regime costs will be considerably lower, but the regime will also have fewer benefits at its disposal to distribute in order to maintain its political resource position. In developing countries many regimes that are quite short on economic resources will nonetheless invest heavily in providing social services because they are as short or even shorter of political resources. To allow these activities to pass into private hands could lead to regime bankruptcy.

The calculations necessary to assess the productivity of different investments in infrastructure appear to be very complex. In practice, however, there are three factors that will simplify the statesman's considerations. First, a statesman is aware of some hierarchy of goals. If he is not, there is little the political economist can do for him. Certain kinds of infrastructure are more productive than others for achieving various goals. For remaining in authority in the future, a political party is usually more productive than laws and legislatures. Elections may indeed be counterproductive to this end, at least if there is no effective party to aid the statesman. To cope with demands for social and economic change, the bureaucracy and police may need to be strengthened. To induce change, on the other hand, education and communications media may be more effective. Remaining in authority in the present requires expenditure of resources for consumption and precludes investment.

Second, a statesman will have certain resource scarcities that are more acute than others when it comes to satisfying his goals. If he lacks information, it may be productive for him to invest in an intelligence system, or interest groups, or opposition parties. If he lacks legitimacy and support sufficient to carry out his political plan, this may necessitate greater investments in a regime party, in elections, and in an official ideology. If, as is the case with so many regimes in developing countries, economic resources are crucially scarce, implementation of an economic development plan may seem one of the wisest priorities. Other investments—in education and bureaucracy, for example—often cannot be expanded more adequately to serve the statesman's needs unless increased economic resources are available.

Third, the statesman, when weighing investments in infrastructure, will consider the propensities of sectors. To the extent that certain sectors have a propensity to use violence in political exchange, a greater investment in infrastructure such as police and army is called for. If, on the other hand, significant sectors have a propensity for bargaining, electoral and parliamentary infrastructure will probably be more productive for achieving the statesman's goals. In general, the more sectors are willing to accept deferred gratification, the more leeway a statesman has for making future-oriented investments at the price of current consumption. Also, the more sectors desire more material gratifications, the more investments yielding goods and services or coercion are likely to be politically profitable.

We have not tried to develop a general strategy of infrastructure investment. First, the empirical basis is lacking. Second, strategies would have to be tailored to the existing level and configuration of infrastructure in a political community as well as to the needs of the particular regime. Elaborating such strategies should be possible, however, and would, we think, represent an advance over the analysis of investment strategies in terms of providing "capabilities." We believe that "unbalance" is a salient leading concept in investment strategy. Though coordination is relevant and important, the very notion of strategy involves timing for the most productive deployment of limited resources. If there were no resource scarcity, there would be no need for strategy, and all productive investments could be made simultaneously. Because statesmen in developing countries do not have sufficient resources to achieve all their ends, strategies of investment aim at selectively allocating available resources over time among various investment opportunities. Those investments that if made prior to others facilitate or make the others more likely are preferred. Not just the greatest constant increase in the volume of resources produced should be sought, but that sequence of increases that achieves the greatest value of outputs within a specified time horizon.

At the end of this chapter the reader will find a table that summarizes the different types of resource investments, returns, or savings that might be expected for the various types of infrastructure. Because the tabular summarization will be clearer once the reader has considered the specific descriptions of infrastructure we present below, we do not wish to present the table at this point. Considerable research might go into the refinement of such a table.[23] Of special significance for our consideration is the extent to which the outputs of some infrastructure are or may be used as the inputs of other infrastructure. The close study of linkages should make it possible for the statesman to make more discriminating judgments about whether or in what manner his regime may best follow a balanced or an unbalanced investment strategy. The statesman must, for example, determine whether the coordination or synchronization of investments to take advantage of complementarities and external economies is more important to productivity than the timing or sequencing of investments. Careful consideration of timing may allow a statesman to take advantage of forward- and backward-linkages and to induce other investments as a consequence of the growth of "leading sectors" of political and administrative infrastructure.

[23] To some extent the entries in this table are derived from statements about political parties, education, bureaucracy, and communications in the Committee on Comparative Politics series on political development. Although it may seem fanciful, we can imagine the construction of an input-output table with modal coefficients as a guide to political investment decisions.

Given the fact of linkages among infrastructures—the fact that an output of one form of infrastructure may be the input of another—it should be possible to develop an input-output matrix for the infrastructure of a political community. If all resources were produced by infrastructure, those outputs that were used as inputs for other infrastructures could be treated as "intermediate products," those outputs used in policies treated as "final demand," and at least a figurative input-output matrix for infrastructure could be worked out. Since sectors are the major source of resources, a comprehensive matrix would, of course, be based on sectors and would for analytical purposes treat as sectors such infrastructures as the bureaucracy and police. Such an intersectoral matrix could be used to represent the overall structure of the political community in the way that an input-output matrix can be used to represent the structure of an economy. With less complex research it should be possible to estimate coefficients of inputs and outputs for particular infrastructure in particular communities. At present the best we can do is to discuss in general terms the inputs and outputs of particular types of infrastructure, taking into account the special characteristics of each particular type. This method, we think, is already an improvement on the way parties, constitutions, and other political structures have been treated to date.

Political Infrastructure

REGIME POLITICAL PARTY.

The most patently political form of infrastructure is party organization. Political scientists have paid a great deal of attention to parties and have recognized their productive and economizing characteristics. While the contributions to the volume *Political Parties and Political Development* [24] illuminate many of the infrastructural characteristics of parties, we think that some elaboration in terms of our model is instructive. We will first consider the infrastructural contributions and costs of parties supporting a regime. In another section we will discuss the infrastructural contributions and costs of opposition parties.

[24] LaPalombara and Weiner (1966:3). The editors define a political party as an organization that has continuity over time, manifests some amount of local organization, is determined to capture and hold power, and seeks popular support through electoral processes. They single out the common functions of parties as the organization of public opinion, the communication of demands to the center of government power and decision, and political recruitment.

A political party is an organization created for the purpose of mobilizing sufficient resources to acquire authority and/or exercise it once it is achieved. In many ways the party is the equivalent in the political market of the corporation in the economic market. It can survive its members, who have limited liability; members may gain more than the value of their contributions, but stand to lose no more than they contribute. By making possible the mobilization of many times more resources than any individual could raise, parties have made possible a revolutionary advance in political production similar to the economic revolution that ensued from the organization of corporations.

We prefer not to regard parties in "functional" or reified terms. It seems to us misplaced emphasis to speak of a party recruiting persons for authority roles. Rather we would say that aspirants for such roles strive for them through party organization. The outcomes of political interaction are more usefully examined and explained in the latter context. The creation and maintenance of party organization require investment of resources, whether by persons in authority or persons seeking authority. Only those who judge the probable returns to be of greater value than the cost of the resources invested will make such an investment. Parties may sometimes take on a life of their own, surviving after their political productivity has drastically declined and when a regime is no longer interested in them. Their survival is not to be explained in functional terms, but rather in terms of the net benefits—material, psychic, or otherwise—perceived by contributors. Splinter parties in many developing countries produce nothing more than a little status for party leaders, but even this may be enough to ensure their continuation. We are not concerned here, however, with any but political parties intended to support the ruling regime.

What benefits can a political party bring to the statesman and to his regime? According to the contributors to *Political Parties and Political Development,* a party system is one of the best instruments for gaining legitimacy for a regime. In addition, they say, parties gain support for the government and do so more effectively than either the army or bureaucracy. They suggest that a party yields allegiance as well as support and that it can increase a regime's authority.[25] A party produces information by commu-

---

[25] See LaPalombara and Weiner (1966:408, 410). Wallerstein observes, with reference to Tanzania, that if a party may reduce the amount of authority wielded by sectors, such a reduction may benefit the statesman. Binder makes a similar point when he states that the party Nasser established in Egypt reduced the participation of the urban political elite, which had previously made the greatest political demands. See Wallerstein (1966:207) and Binder (1966:218).

nicating sector demands to the central authority through the party mechanism. By providing sectors with a means for making demands or for gaining some influence over the exercise of authority, a party may reduce the amount of violence employed in a polity and/or reduce the amount of coercion necessary to gain compliance. A party can usually elicit contributions of goods and services. And it may be possible for a party to increase the amount of status exchanged among and within sectors though more frequently party organization is used to reallocate status among sectors.[26]

What are the costs of creating or maintaining a political party? [27] What resources are invested or expended over time as maintenance costs, and what complementary investments are advisable? For one thing, unless there is some kind of electoral system, parties are less productive of support and legitimacy. Thus to spur production of resources, the extension of suffrage is required.[28] Indeed, unless some authority is invested in the party, permitting it to make or influence authoritative decisions, there is little incentive for sectors to participate in it or contribute to the regime.[29]

[26] Binder observes how social and political stratifications were altered through the mechanism of the parties Nasser successively brought into being in Egypt. Peasants, for example, were deliberately given greater status and influence than they had previously enjoyed. Moreover, it was evident that the party electoral system introduced by Nasser worked to confirm the status and influence of the rural middle class, thereby proportionally reducing the status and influence of urban sectors. When the Arab Socialist Union later adopted functional representation, urban influence was increased again. At the outset of Nasser's efforts to create a regime party, industrialists were favored for their anticipated contribution to economic development. Subsequently the regime decided on a more socialistic course, and industrialists were downgraded within the party. See Binder (1966:224–226, 230–233, 238–240).

[27] For simplicity's sake we discuss investment in a regime political party as though one were being started *de novo*. In practice investment decisions concern expansion, maintenance or reduction of the size and power of an existing party. Only occasionally, as in Egypt, do such decisions entail whether to establish a party or not. See Binder (1966:228–229).

[28] La Palombara and Weiner (1966:9).

[29] Binder reports that when Nasser established parties in Egypt, influential members of the new parties wanted real participation. Nasser, however, was not willing to share authority, and all important decisions were reserved for the regime. According to Binder, "membership or even officeholding in the National Union did not convey much political influence, but given the close control over the distribution of political values in Egypt this is the only manner in which participation of outsiders is possible." Binder (1966:218–221, 229). A political economist would say that Nasser, by keeping the supply of authority strictly limited, has raised the value of influence and thus lowered the cost of getting resources from persons seeking it. Usually a regime has to give up more

Sharing authority with a party usually involves considerable costs for the statesman or anti-statesman, although some contribution of resources is of course expected in return for grants of authority or influence.

Nkrumah's efforts to upgrade the status of the CPP in Ghana, discussed in Chapter III, illustrate a regime's investment of status in a party. The status of party officials was increased when regional commissioners were given ministerial rank and the secretary-general of the CPP was given the title of ambassador. In the neighboring Ivory Coast, writes Zolberg, the most significant aspect of the 1965 Congress of the PDCI was "a serious attempt to restore the party to its place of eminence in the country." [30] Status invested in a party not only makes the party more effective, but also makes it more attractive. Moreover, the status accruing to individuals on the basis of party membership usually increases contributions to the party or reduces the cost of securing these contributions.

It is clear that some amount of economic resources must be invested in a party. Seldom are parties self-supporting financially on the basis of membership dues or contributions. Maintaining branch organizations at the regional and local level is expensive, due to the costs of communication and salaries and of surveillance and control. One of the most tangible investments a regime may make is in party headquarters and ceremonies, which contribute to a party's status in the eyes of many people. Zolberg tells of a campaign in Mali to build new party headquarters:

> When their country's very survival was at stake, and the economy almost came to a standstill, the leaders of the *Union Soudanaise* appealed to the population of the capital to contribute their labor and scarce resources to the construction of a new party headquarters. *La Maison du Parti*, built in 1960, is a tangible symbol of the prominence of the party in the political life of Mali.[31]

Economic expenditures such as allowances and gratuities, which build up support for the party over time, also constitute investments.[32]

The amount of political information required to maintain a party is hard

authority than Nasser has to make its party effective as a means of getting resources and political currency. Indeed, the effectiveness of Nasser's parties is questionable. Rustow suggests that in Egypt the bureaucracy and police may be much more productive for the Nasser regime than political parties. See Rustow (1966:130).

[30] Zolberg (1966:100–101).

[31] Zolberg (1966:100, 103–104). For a general discussion of parties, see 93–106.

[32] Rustow reports how the Turkish Unionists, once they gained full control of government, used their powers of patronage and economic regulation to

to predict. There must be a standing commitment on the part of the regime to share at least some information concerning regime intentions or problems with party leaders. If the party is acting only as infrastructure, the cost of information passed on to the party is not great. However, to the extent that party leaders do not see their interests as identical with those of the regime, this commitment may involve costs. It is not clear whether and how much coercion must be invested in a party. As a rule, coercion is probably not a very effective resource to invest for this purpose, yet when a statesman judges that a party can be effective only with total participation, coercion may be employed. Whether coercion invested through party channels is productive of legitimacy and support is usually questionable, however, and a decision to employ coercion in connection with party organization needs to be weighed very carefully.

It is apparent that a party's effectiveness as infrastructure depends in part on the extent to which that party provides incentives for sectors to contribute to the achievement of regime objectives. Because there is some cost to sectors when they contribute resources and currencies to a regime through its party, the regime must provide some compensation in the form of status, influence, information, or income. President Nyerere's characterization of his Tanganyika African National Union party as a "two-way, all-weather road by which government could reach the people in every village, and the people could reach the government" [33] specifically emphasizes the exchange of information between regime and sectors, but this two-way road facilitates other exchanges as well. Party infrastructure will be productive to the extent that it enables both regime and sectors to gain more value than they give up to each other. The reciprocal relationships entered into by party members and leaders are more important than any "functional" relationship of the party to the rest of the political system. Thus even well-organized parties are commonly limited in their effectiveness to achieve a statesman's ends. They cannot be manipulated by a leader for just any purpose, as most party leaders know.[34]

A totalitarian party may under some conditions be the most productive

build up a strong network of party organization. By using the government's vastly increased powers of economic regulation, they encouraged the growth of a Muslim-Turkish business class. Indeed, the capital raised by a surcharge on bread supported the party leaders' Tradesmen's Association. Rustow (1966: 117–119).

[33] Nyerere cited by Emerson (1966:274).

[34] Binder describes the diminishing returns to Nasser's regime in Egypt that resulted when attempts were made to gain legitimacy and support by manipulating a regime party without making substantive contributions to party members in return (1966:228).

kind of party in terms of the volume of compliance with regime decisions, but such a party is usually quite inefficient, as the ratio of inputs to outputs is relatively high. The cost of such a party is very high, far higher than many statesmen could afford even if they desired such a party. In the first place, large and continuing expenditures of coercion and threats would be required to secure compliance, since no authority or influence would be shared. The cost of securing information would be high because individuals would make less information known publicly when coercion was used widely. Controlled mass media could keep undesired information from flowing but would not elicit as much information from sectors as "open" mass media. Such a situation would prove expensive, not just in terms of economic resources, but in terms of sector information foregone.[35] In general, to maintain a totalitarian party, tremendous amounts of economic resources have to be expended on party activity and organization. Heavy expenditure of all kinds would probably be justified through ideology on the grounds that all power and authority should rest solely with the party and regime leadership. If such an ideology persuaded people to accord the party some legitimacy, the party could rule with proportionately less coercion; still, legitimacy produced by such expenditures would be much more expensive than legitimacy given more voluntarily as a consequence of electoral competition.

While investments in infrastructure are seldom once-for-all, political parties require continuing maintenance investments, as Zolberg's discussion of West African parties makes clear. In West Africa party leaders have had to make continuing efforts to revive enthusiasm for the party, reduce the corruption of officials, and preserve the orthodoxy of the party line. To maintain the party and make it more effective, women's, youth, student, farmer, labor, and other auxiliary organizations have had to be created, at some expense to the regime and sectors. Educational programs have been necessary. Greater status and economic resources have had to be made available. What is more, internal reorganization has been common. There has been formation and reformation of local branches, restructuring of relations between regions and the center, and changing and replenishing of the central party organs. In an effort to gain greater support and legitimacy, resources from certain sectors and leaders disadvantaged by reforms have had to be foregone.[36]

[35] Apter describes this situation when he speaks of the reciprocal relationship between rule through information and rule through coercion. The more of one, the less of the other. See Apter (1965:40 ff.).

[36] See Zolberg (1966:93–106).

The scope of party organization and participation raises important considerations about costs and benefits. A regime must determine how wide a coalition of sectors and what coalition of sectors will yield the greatest net benefits. Often parties attempt to present themselves as the broadest possible aggregation of interests; however, this presentation need not be true in fact. Each sector included within the rubric of a party makes some claims on the regime's resources. Sartori points out that in Italy the price of support from the Roman Catholic Church is daily interference in the exercise of authority at all levels.[37] In Latin America, according to Scott, middle-class parties have found the support of organized labor quite expensive. To reduce their political costs, they have often turned to the unorganized city masses or the rural population. *Acción Democratica*, the regime party in Venezuela, has found itself unable to contain the divergent interests of its urban and rural supporters.[38]

The particular base of support on which a party draws is a crucial factor in determining whose interests will be served. After 1945 it became apparent to the Ghanaian middle-class elite that to oust the colonial regime and acquire authority in its own right it needed a broader base of support. As Emerson puts it, the elite decided it needed "the battering ram of the illiterate masses." To this end it recruited Kwame Nkrumah to reorganize the United Gold Coast Convention Party and mobilize the less privileged sectors.[39] The new base, however, proved too broad and unmanageable. Nkrumah bolted the UGCC with a majority of its members following him to form the Convention People's Party, the dominant Ghanaian party from 1951 to 1966. In the Ivory Coast, on the other hand, the nationalist party relied on a different base of support. Instead of depending on workers and farmers, it drew in the resources of the cocoa planters, civil servants, and chiefs, and primarily served the interests of those sectors. The regime has opened the country to foreign capital and has not deprived France, the former colonial ruler, of high status.[40] President Houphouet-Boigny prefers these policies, but he probably could not follow them if his support came from the kind of coalition on which the CPP rested.

If the statesman wishes to facilitate modernizing changes, the costs of including traditionalist sectors in a party coalition are likely to be considerable. In Ghana the price of gaining support for the CPP from the tradi-

[37] Sartori (1966:143).

[38] Scott (1966:343, 347). Riker's principle of the optimality of a minimum winning coalition applies here (1962).

[39] Emerson (1966:279).

[40] Emerson (1966:280–281).

tional chiefs was the preservation of much of their authority at the local level. In Guinea Sekou Touré's single party, ideologically probably the most militant in Africa, includes the traditionalist sectors. Either the party cannot rule without including them, or Touré has judged that compliance can be secured at less expense by including them. The costs of including them are considerable nonetheless. Zolberg writes that "in a society where for many of the ethnic groups kinship and political structure coincided . . . after six years of intensive effort, the party, far from transforming society, had come to reflect . . . persisting traditional features." [41] Wallerstein claims that bringing traditional leaders into the party "revalorizes" them and that the costs of extending party organization to the local level are to be measured in terms of effect on long-range goals.[42]

The importance, i.e., productivity, of a political party as infrastructure depends in part on the presence of other infrastructure. Complementary infrastructure may make a party more productive in terms of the volume of resources gained, though when other infrastructure is lacking or weak, a party may be more productive in terms of the marginal value of the resources it secures. When there is no strong or established bureaucracy, a party's contributions to a regime are likely to be more crucial to the regime's success in achieving its goals than they would be if other infrastructure existed. Conversely, where other infrastructure exists, a party will probably be relatively less important and productive in marginal terms. Wallerstein has asserted that party precedence in Africa is only formal and that access to the military is more important. He made this assertion after the Algerian coup but before the wave of military coups that have ousted more than ten regimes.[43]

[41] Zolberg (1966:103).

[42] Wallerstein (1966:209–210).

[43] Wallerstein pointed to the ease with which ben Bella, despite his nominal control over the FLN party, was ousted by his Defense Minister who had power over the military. In Senegal President Senghor thwarted an attempted coup by his Prime Minister, Dia, in 1963. Though Dia had strong support from elements of the party, Senghor had the support of the military. See Wallerstein (1966:205, 211). Nkrumah's vaunting of the slogan "The CPP is Ghana, and Ghana is the CPP" was rendered null and void by the action of the army and police in 1966. Very few Ghanaians defended the CPP during or after the coup. Ruling parties in Sierra Leone, Nigeria, Burundi, Dahomey, Upper Volta, the Central African Republic, and most recently Mali have been toppled by military action. Probably few ruling parties could prevent a coup if army leaders were intent on ousting a government, but some parties might be able to make a coup exorbitantly costly to an army. The amount of support that a party mobilized for a leader would surely figure in the calculations of potential coupmakers. See Mazrui and Rothchild (1967).

AUXILIARY ORGANIZATIONS.

To get the greatest return from investments in a political party, a states-man may make complementary investments in what are often called auxil-iary organizations. These include women's associations, trade unions, farmers' councils, youth organizations, and the like. Given the expenditure of resources for party organization and activity, additional investment in auxiliary groups may yield proportionately greater returns. However, as Wallerstein points out, investments in auxiliary groups may prove politi-cally unprofitable or less profitable than anticipated. Such groups can be captured and made centers for criticism of government policy; conse-quently they can draw away support from government programs.

Auxiliary organizations pose the same dilemma for the statesman that a regime party does. The more tightly controlled they are, the more certain it is that the resources they mobilize will be channeled for the benefit of the regime. Yet if they are very tightly controlled by the regime, they will satisfy sector demands less and thus will elicit fewer sector contributions. The important issue for the statesman to determine is the net productivity of different degrees of control over auxiliary organizations. If he is not greatly dependent on their resources, he can better afford to allow these organizations some independence with the expectation that they will have a greater gross volume of resources at their disposal. If, on the other hand, he needs certain minimum contributions for the maintenance of his regime, he will have to try to control these organizations closely. At this point we can neither offer a resolution of this dilemma nor offer decision-rules for investment in auxiliary organizations. Empirical research is needed to determine how to raise the net productivity of auxiliary organ-izations for regimes.[44]

OPPPOSITION PARTY.

A statesman should not simply regard an opposition party as an alternative regime or as a sector making claims on the polity's resources. In many ways he can make use of it as political infrastructure. The infrastructural charac-teristics of an opposition party are clear from Apter's characterization: "A

---

[44] Wallerstein notes that when such groups are captured and draw away support from government programs, any regime move to counter this capture will probably reduce the activity of the organization and thus its contribution to the regime. But the net contribution to the regime would presumably be in-creased by such a move. See Wallerstein (1966:208–209).

political opposition is neither a luxury nor a danger. If it performs its function well, it can be of crucial service both to the government of the day and to the people of the nation." Apter suggests that if the opposition exercises discretion, discipline, and self-control, it will be a safety-valve for discontent, provide "information" that the government needs if it wishes to avoid sitting on a powder keg, and offer useful alternatives to government policies.[45] However, while the statesman might need to invest few economic resources, status, or information in an opposition party, he would still have to reckon on indirect costs. An opposition party might well reduce his support. It might also reduce his legitimacy, though he might try to use his permission of organized opposition as grounds for his own legitimacy and that of his program.[46]

The benefits of permitting an opposition party to function vary. Apart from the legitimacy to be gained thereby, the most important benefit of permitting an opposition party to exist is a gain in information about sector preferences. Moreover, as Apter suggests, an opposition party may develop alternative policies or programs that the regime will see fit to expropriate. Yet another benefit may be some reduction in the political violence used against the regime or in the amount of coercion that must be expended to achieve compliance. This reduction is due only in part to the effects of legitimacy. When dissident sectors have an opportunity to make their claims through a party structure, they have less need to use violence as a means of pressing their demands.

Against the benefits he receives from permitting opposition, a statesman weighs the costs he is likely to incur in terms of a reduction in the number of objectives he can achieve. He may receive or save resources as a consequence of permitting opposition, but such gains still may not enable him to achieve certain goals. After Ataturk's death, the modernizing regime in Turkey departed from his strategy and permitted an opposition party to form, since the cost of continuing to suppress organized opposition would probably have been too great for the regime to sustain. The consequence was that in free elections, the new party achieved a majority in parliament

[45] Apter (1963c:57); see also Apter (1962).

[46] Apter's distinction between an opposition based on "interest" and one based on "values" may help us understand whether an opposition increases or decreases the regime's legitimacy. If an opposition is based on interest, conflict is over policies and legitimacy should be increased by the fact that the conflict is open and openly resolved. If, on the other hand, opposition is based on values, there may be no way in which opponents can accord legitimacy to the regime and its policies. Thus this latter kind of opposing party entails greater costs whereas the former kind may yield net benefits.

and ousted the regime that was building on Ataturk's program of change.[47]

ELECTIONS.

Political parties are likely to have little purpose or productivity unless there are elections of some sort. We have suggested that even unfree elections may yield at least some legitimacy. While the relationship remains to be substantiated by research, it may be that the amount of legitimacy and support gained through elections is in some way proportional to the degree of competitiveness of the elections. The same relation may hold for the production of information, another important output of elections. Or it may be that the resources gained through elections are somewhat proportional to the possibility that authority can indeed be transferred to a new regime. The costs a statesman incurs when undertaking elections exceed the possible loss of authority. His goals for the polity are at stake. Elections may hinder his achievement of a more desired state, since if a statesman is reelected by a reduced majority, this evidence of reduced support will diminish his power to implement programs. Observers of politics in developing countries agree that by and large elections strengthen local and often parochial sectors; yet even so, they may yield more to a regime than they cost.[48] As Weiner observes, elections in India, while increasing caste-ism, communalism, and provincialism, have gained *allegiance* for the political system as communal politics have paid off for the various sectors. Thus although elections manifest great conflict in India, they are productive for the polity and regime.[49]

LOCAL AND REGIONAL GOVERNMENT.

From the quotation that opened this chapter, Young's observation on the productive consequences of further decentralizing the structures and powers of government in the Congo, we can see that local and regional government may serve as political and administrative infrastructure.[50] Es-

[47] Rustow discusses why the Republican Party invested in an opposition party and what costs resulted. Rustow (1966:122–123).

[48] See Binder (1966:237–238); Emerson (1966:288); Rokkan (1966: 262).

[49] Weiner (1965:210).

[50] Inasmuch as local and regional governments involve the devolution of authority, they are primarily political infrastructure. To the extent they serve to implement central government decisions, they are also administrative infrastructure. The designation is not important; the activities are.

tablishment of local and regional government commonly reduces the costs of securing compliance from sectors, but involves costs for the central government as well. While the net benefit may accrue to the regime, sectors also benefit from local and regional government and thus contribute to its productivity.[51]

For the most part, creation of local and regional government units involves the investment of authority. Units receive the right to speak in the name of the state on a certain range of questions. The power of taxation is an especially valued right, often contested between central and local authorities because of the value of economic resources to be gained. In addition, the central government may have to share its own revenues with local and regional governments to make these units effective. To enforce local decisions the central government may have to use its coercive force; to fail to do so may seriously depreciate the regime's investment of authority. Investments of status and information will be relatively less than those of other resources. Despite these costs, the benefits accruing from investment in local and regional government may be considerable. In the case of the Congo, regional government in particular produced legitimacy for the central government. Weiner observes that in India the creation of states based on a common language yielded support and allegiance.[52] That local and regional governments produce valuable political information is also evident. Furthermore, the experience of the Congo showed that the maintenance of local government could reduce political violence.[53] How these costs and benefits balance depends on the particular situation, but the experience of virtually all countries is that local government institutions reduce the cost of governing.

[51] Zolberg's discussion of local and regional government gives a more extended account of the infrastructural characteristics of local and regional government organizations, though not in terms of political economy. Zolberg (1966:114–119).

[52] Weiner (1965:230).

[53] We would note here that local or regional governments may or may not be empowered to establish their own police forces to provide an independent source of coercion. As a rule, local constabularies may be quite effective in reducing non-political violence, but they are often less adept at or less concerned about quelling political violence. Establishing local and regional government may reduce the central government's monopoly on coercion. Such a reduction usually depreciates the value of the regime's coercive power, even though the total amount of coercive force available may have increased. Local police may not do the bidding of the central authorities. For this reason, most central governments wish to keep control over all police.

It may be said that local and regional government is wasteful of economic resources in countries where these resources are especially scarce. Some will ask whether the benefits to be received justify this expenditure of money. A conference on local government in Africa grappled with the question and concluded:

Theoretically, the question now is whether Africa can afford the luxury of liberty [at the local level] at the price of squandering its meager resources in administrative waste. Practically, the answer is that African governments must go on giving local authorities a measure of freedom to preserve stability. At the same time, drastic steps will have to be taken to improve their efficiency.[54]

In the opinion of conference participants, local government constituted a stability investment. We would concur.

The costs and benefits of local government cannot be weighed only in terms of immediate and foreseeable expenditure or receipt of resources. We must also consider how the creation of local government affects certain of a regime's goals for the polity. For example, a statesman concerned with democratization and greater popular participation in government might well invest in local government even if his resource returns were not great. If, however, national integration is one of the statesman's objectives, investment in local government may have limited productivity. Young observed that in the Congo, "the deliberate use of ethnic pride in several key provinces may well succeed in legitimating the province at the cost of further complicating the task of developing meaningful loyalties to the polity as a whole." [55] Similarly, if modernization of economic, social, and political relations is desired, local government may slow progress toward this goal.[56]

Certain objectives may be facilitated through the creation and modification of local or regional government units. It may even be possible for a regime to shift the balance of political power through reorganization of local or regional government, as the British colonial regime did in Sierra Leone. The establishment of an Assembly for the rural hinterland sur-

[54] See the report issued by the Cambridge University Overseas Studies Committee, *Summer Conference on Local Government in Africa* (1961:5–7).

[55] Young (1964:566).

[56] For studies of this phenomenon in India, the Philippines, and Sierra Leone, see, respectively, Bendix (1964:215–298); Riggs (1964:367–396); and Kilson (1966:215–216).

rounding Freetown increased the influence of the more conservative rural sectors in the Protectorate at the expense of the more mobilized and militant urban sectors. This move, says Kilson, gave the hinterland "more political weight." [57]

Establishing or restructuring regional governments may also weaken certain sectoral interests that make claims on the central government. Gowon's decision to divide up the four regions of Nigeria into twelve states had the effect of reducing the power of the Hausas and Ibo's. Furthermore, by giving other ethnic sectors more control over the exercise of authority in their areas, Gowon was able to engender support. It should be apparent that the size of regions is important.[58] Fesler points out that Diem personally stopped a plan by his political lieutenants to merge the provinces of South Vietnam into larger units. Diem reasoned correctly that the merger plan would only create larger areas and amounts of resources for the Viet Cong to capture.[59] His aides' plan of investment in regional reorganization was shelved as unprofitable because the probable losses outweighed the possible gains. As long as he had sufficient economic and personnel resources, Diem stood to benefit more from decentralized regional government than from some more aggregated arrangement.

One advantage of having a viable system of local and regional government is that divisive issues not essential to national security can often be delegated to it. If this is the case, claims on the resources held by the central government may be reduced. More important, dissatisfied sectors are less likely to penalize the central government by withholding resources from it; instead, dissatisfaction is deflected to lesser authorities.[60] We suggested this tactic in Chapter IV when discussing bargaining strategies. It is not without costs but may reduce those costs likely otherwise to be incurred.

[57] Kilson (1966:154).

[58] The overwhelming size of Northern Nigeria, which contains half the country's population, is a major source of Nigeria's present difficulties. James Fesler stresses that the size of subordinate governmental units is important for carrying out the policies of the center. Would the Supreme Court of the United States, he queries, have been as willing to rule as it has in recent years on desegregation if there were only one regional government for the South instead of a number of separate state governments? See Fesler (1962:127).

[59] Fesler (1962:130).

[60] Fesler (1962:128). We would note that as we have discussed it, decentralization involves *devolution* or *delegation* of authority to other and not necessarily subordinate governmental units. What Fesler describes as field administration involves *deconcentration* of administrative authority.

IDEOLOGY.

In previous chapters we have often spoken of the ideologies of statesmen, anti-statesmen, and sectors. These value preferences or hierarchies are basic to the daily conduct of politics. However, we also wish to consider the infrastructural qualities of ideology. When a belief system is no longer used merely to guide the choices of those who formulated it but is promulgated to affect others' choices as well, it becomes in effect political infrastructure.

An ideology is a statement, more or less explicit, about a preferred allocation of resources or about valued political, social, and economic stratifications.[61] It may approve of the status quo or it may seek more or less far-reaching changes, but in any case it involves a statement of what *ought* to be the distribution of resources. Ideology represents a promise of how resources will be expended to maintain or strive for certain allocations and stratifications. Resources are not so much invested as they are mortgaged for the future. The political benefits that may result from ideology are not unfamiliar, though they have seldom been described in terms of political resources and currencies. Clearly a regime or movement presenting an ideology may thereby gain legitimacy, support, and allegiance from sectors. Resources so gained may be used to secure compliance in various

[61] From this conception it is clear that we do not accept the proposition that there is or need be an "end of ideology." As long as resources continue to be scarce, not all preferences can be satisfied. Persons and groups will develop normative statements of what and whose preferences ought to be fulfilled. Although the scarcity of economic resources can be ameliorated, demands for status and authority cannot be. We concur with Geertz's critique of the doctrinaire abhorrence of ideology so common in present social science and with LaPalombara's rejection of the "end of ideology" thesis. See Geertz (1964) and LaPalombara (1966:5–16). While we would not accept Daniel Bell's thesis, especially his epilogue, we do accept his definition of ideology as a world-view, belief system, or creed held by a social group about the arrangements in society, justifying certain arrangements as morally right. We also agree that in an ideology ideas are converted into social levers. On the other hand, we cannot agree that what gives ideology its force is its passion. Promises and rewards are what give ideology its force and its passion. We would not, as Bell does, attribute ideology's power to launch and sustain social movements to its simplification of ideas and its claim to "truth." Commitment to action predicated on ideology stems from the rewards and satisfactions anticipated by individuals. As often as not, quite altruistic motivations lead sectors to support the promises held out by an ideology and to contribute to the fulfillment of its preferred allocations. See Bell (1960: esp. 367–375).

ways, possibly to acquire economic resources and violence for use against others or to reduce violence against the regime.[62]

There are several means by which resources are mobilized through ideology. Ideology defines and prescribes time horizons for activity: rewards are scheduled over time and required expenditures described. It sets priorities in simplified form and establishes an ordering of preferences, thus creating some predictability of choices and actions. It coordinates and synchronizes action, suggesting the most productive sequencing of actions. To some extent it also simplifies actions, making explicit various connections of cause and effect. Politics without ideology, if such a thing were possible, would be much less economical than it is at present. We do not mean to imply that all ideology is to be found in manifestos or clear programs. Even when relatively implicit, ideology nonetheless orders politics.[63]

In its articulated form, ideology is a relatively recent political innovation, but when used implicitly, it is as old as politics itself. Medieval Christendom is an example of an implicit ideology that sanctioned certain political, social, and economic stratifications, and channeled flows of resources. Resting on religious tenets and values, it gave legitimacy to a particular political division of labor and allocation of authority. In contemporary times ideologies are utilized more as deliberate instruments for political, social, and economic change. They have, to use Geertz's words, made "autonomous politics possible, by providing authoritative concepts that render it meaningful." [64]

Because ideology is commonly conceived of in "idealistic" terms, the costs of ideology are not as clearly perceived as they might be. This is to say that "ideas" are not the independent variables, but rather that the allocations of resources for which they stand are. For a regime to commit itself to a definite allocation of future resources is often costly. Deutsch has called attention to such costs with reference to the Soviet regime,

[62] See Emerson (1954:140) and Matossian (1958:217–228).

[63] Along with the Geertz essay cited above, we think one of the most useful discussions of ideology is presented by Fallers (1963).

[64] Geertz (1964:63). Ideology is formulated and articulated in terms of symbols. We do mean to imply that these symbols are in some way unreal. Their reality is what they stand for, what preferred allocations are advocated or rationalized. Thus we would accept only in part Edelman's suggestion (1964:40) that symbols are the "only means by which groups not in a position to analyze a complex situation rationally may adjust themselves to it, through stereotypization, oversimplification, and reassurance." An element of simplification need not make ideology irrational. People are presented by political entrepreneurs with certain ends. To the extent that these ends are valued, contributions will be made toward their achievement.

which has relied so heavily on its Communist ideology.[65] In effect the statesman invests authority in an ideology. His freedom of choice thus becomes limited by that ideology. He cannot always use his authority to act in the most politically profitable way at a particular moment. The ideology that mobilizes resources for his regime also specifies to some extent how, when, and for what purposes those resources will be used.

If a political leader seeks to mobilize or reallocate resources through the reallocation of status, he may need to use or develop an ideology to do so. Exaltation of the yeoman farmer, the industrial worker, the party activist, the black-skinned, and the progressive, or vilification of the petty bourgeoisie, neo-colonialists, and foreign merchants is most effective in the context of an ideological statement about the preferred stratifications for the community. Those rewarded with status may make contributions to the regime more willingly; those chastised, if not driven into open opposition, may try to protect themselves by greater contributions.[66]

The reallocation of status through ideology involves costs. Costs will vary, of course, depending on whether sectors suffer status losses in absolute or relative terms. It costs an African political leader little to proclaim the ideology of *Négritude* because this ideology raises the status of Africans at the expense of whites. On the other hand, where the educated elite is exalted by leaders in the drive for modernization, the status of illiterates is depreciated. Illiterates may seek compensation for this loss by insisting on educational opportunities for themselves or their children. Or they may be willing to support an anti-statesman who praises them and their status for their "authenticity" or traditionality.

ECONOMIC DEVELOPMENT PLAN.

A regime's economic development plan represents a promise or projection of future resources to be made available to sectors in some particular allo-

[65] Deutsch (1954).

[66] Apter is especially concerned with the problem of moral meanings inherent in ideologies. Ideologies, he says, make explicit the moral bases of action, linking particular actions and mundane practices to wider sets of meanings; in addition, they provide moral bases for social manipulation resorted to by leaders to accelerate development and can be used to build authority and minimize antipathetic cultural strains. Apter clearly considers the productive consequences of ideology, especially in the legitimization of authority, but unfortunately gives little consideration to costs. See Apter (1964a:16–18, 22–23). We find little that is useful in Pye's analysis concentrating on the factor of "identity." Resources promised, expended, allocated, explain more, we think, than does "identity." See Pye (1962).

cation. The promise is intended to elicit from sectors the economic and other resources necessary to achieve the plan's goals. The political import of an economic development plan should be clearly understood. As Green says, "basically, an economic development plan must be, *and be seen to be*, a quantitative programme designed to create conditions in which national socio-political objectives can be attained." [67] It is useless and counterproductive, he contends, to challenge the basic goals and aspirations that lead a government to propose a plan: "A political climate of serious concern for attaining economic development is a precondition for any plan's success, and a plan which clearly promotes socio-political goals is equally a precondition for such a climate." [68]

A political economist like W. Arthur Lewis appreciates well the political implications of economic development planning. Of interest is his rationale for deciding on a Ten-Year Plan rather than a Five-Year Plan:

> The third advantage of long-term planning is purely political. When the call goes out for projects, every area and every interest puts in its claim. The result is a demand for public services far in excess of available resources. In order to retain support, the Government will be anxious to show that it recognizes the legitimate needs of all the people. It cannot put everything into the Plan, but it can put more than twice as much into a Ten Year Plan as into a Five Year Plan (since resources should be larger in the second five years than in the first five years), and so it can provide twice as much pleasure. The importance of such political considerations must not be underestimated, since the people are more likely to acquiesce in the payment of the high taxes which development requires if they see that their needs are recognized, than if the Plan does not mention schemes which they value, or mentions them only to put them aside. [69]

Lewis makes the infrastructural characteristics of a plan especially clear when he discusses a plan's productive capability for securing economic resources from domestic and foreign sectors. [70] A plan, he points out, may be unproductive or even counterproductive if it is not carefully calculated in economic *and* political terms. All things considered, a plan made with acumen should be a reasonably good investment.

[67] Green (1965:251).
[68] Green (1965:252).
[69] Lewis (1966:149).
[70] Lewis (1966:152–153).

The fulfillment of an economic development plan requires the input not only of economic resources, but of political resources as well. Albert Waterston notes this in his comprehensive analysis of development planning. He emphasizes how important political commitment (we would say the investment of authority by the regime and of legitimacy-qua-support from the sectors) is for the success of a plan. Yet the problem by now familiar in our political economy analysis arises once more. The more a regime needs the benefits of a development plan, the less effective the plan may be. Waterston goes so far as to suggest that only a strong, stable government can succeed in economic development planning. In the absence of stability or solvency, the most advanced form of planning will not contribute much to the country's development.[71] We think it most useful to see a plan in terms of what it contributes to a regime's political solvency, since solvency is a *sine qua non* for development, rather than to view politics primarily in terms of what it can contribute to the fulfillment of a plan.

OTHER POLITICAL INFRASTRUCTURE.

It has not been our intention to analyze the forms of political infrastructure in detail. Rather we have suggested how different institutions might be analyzed as infrastructure. Our hope is that these institutions will be studied in depth as infrastructure to ascertain specifically what investments are involved in establishing and maintaining them, how much of the various resources are required, and what net benefits might be gained from such investments. Other forms of political infrastructure deserving attention are *interest groups, legislatures, constitutions*, and *legal systems*. The reader may refer to the table at the end of this chapter for an enumeration of the inputs and outputs of these forms of political infrastructure. Such a tabular presentation will, we hope, give impetus to the kind of research that will make it possible to give substantive advice on political investment decisions.

[71] Waterston (1965:6, 340–343). By summarizing variations in political and economic inputs in terms of a government's "will to develop," however, the reasons for such variations are not clear. Not all sectors have an equal interest in economic development; more important, a particular pattern of development affects the various sectors differently. The net contributions of sectors are what a government needs to make any "will to develop" effective, but these contributions themselves depend on the shape of development programs.

Administrative Infrastructure

PUBLIC BUREAUCRACY.

Like political parties, public bureaucracies may be analyzed both as infrastructure and as sectors. Given the resource-exchange model on which political economy is based, the infrastructural functions of administration should be obvious. The regime allocates many of its resources, combined into policies such as education, public health, housing, and licenses and permits, through the agency of public bureaucracies. On the other hand, many of the resources necessary for the maintenance and success of the regime must be acquired by public servants from sectors in the form of compliance (taxation, census, conscription, and so forth). Moreover when the regime intervenes and mediates in intersectoral exchange by enforcing rights and duties of some sectors vis-à-vis others, public servants are often engaged in these activities.[72]

When public servants perform the tasks assigned them by the regime, bureaucracy approximates our definition of infrastructure. Bureaucracy is a fundamental investment aimed at reducing the cost of putting policies into effect. The existence of a bureaucratic network endowed with authority to command and penalize permits the regime to interact more directly with the sectors and to accelerate the movement of resources. The execution of tasks by the bureaucracy allows for greater stability and predictability of political exchange. Through bureaucracy the regime's supply of economic goods and services, information, legitimacy, and other resources and currencies is rendered more reliable. Without this network, continuous policy implementation and the acquisition of resources would indeed be expensive. Substitute infrastructure such as political parties might not fulfill these functions as inexpensively or as well as public bureaucracies would. If the economic costs of maintaining a bureaucracy are higher than those of maintaining a party, the political costs are likely to be lower.

The costs of administrative infrastructure, however, are likely to be high in any case, not only because of the expected direct costs of establishing and maintaining any form of infrastructure, but also because public bureaucrats often act as sectors. Insofar as public servants participate in the claims-making process, acting as claimants for themselves or for favored sectors, they are acting as sectors. Indeed, insofar as public servants re-open

[72] See Eisenstadt (1963b).

the allocation of rights and duties to new claims through their activity of implementing laws, they are competing with the regime itself.[73] The sectoral characteristics of bureaucracy have been the preoccupation of many contemporary social scientists writing about developing countries.[74] While the prevalent view on this issue is the result of a common prejudice towards the role of public servants and therefore cannot be considered universally relevant to decisions on strategies of political development, there is in the current literature on bureaucracy much that would be of interest to the advisor to statesmen.[75] Especially valuable are the arguments of LaPalombara, Riggs, and Eisenstadt that a statesman should invest in the countervailing infrastructure of political parties and perhaps associational groups, and Spengler's argument that a statesman should rely more on the private sectors to enforce rights and duties.[76]

Changing the ratio between the infrastructural and sectoral characteristics of a bureaucracy is likely to be one of the statesman's major objectives. Distinguishing between the two kinds of characteristics permits insight into the phenomena of corruption and sabotage. In the case of corruption, public servants short-circuit sector resources that are intended for the regime and use them for their own personal advantage. Sabotage, more often marked by political than personal objectives, is a form of sectoral activity in which public servants re-open previously assigned rights and duties to claims by favored sectors for alterations or exceptions. Both corruption and sabotage have more or less extreme forms. Public servants, for example, may threaten a regime by a slowdown of activity, stopping short of open confrontation and sabotage. Corruption is not limited to bribery; favoritism displayed by bureaucrats toward certain sectors diverts resources from other ends intended by the statesman. Every statesman is forced to accept a degree of both sabotage and corruption; the costs of eliminating them— of transforming public servants into completely neutral administrative infrastructure—are too great to be undertaken. Nonetheless, sabotage and corruption can and have bankrupted regimes.

There are many factors that affect statesmen in their task of making the public service more infrastructual than sectoral in character. If the public service is highly stratified, and the leading positions are filled by members

[73] These distinctions and others are developed more fully in Ilchman and LaPorte (in press).

[74] See, for example, LaPalombara (1963b) and (1963c).

[75] For alternative views of bureaucracy, see Bendix (1964:105–142).

[76] LaPalombara (1963c); Eisenstadt (1963c); Riggs (1963); and Spengler (1963).

of those sectors that provide the leaders of the regime, corruption in the lower ranks of the hierarchy is more likely to be a problem than sabotage in the top ranks. On the other hand, if the leading positions in the public service are recruited on an agency basis rather than on an elite basis, there is less need for policies to neutralize bureaucrats as a sector than for policies to forestall collusion with the sectors affected by the agency. Finally, divisions within the administration that are based on programs and other value orientations might result in "sectoral" struggles within the bureaucracy and between otherwise faithful instruments of the statesman's purposes.[77]

Decisions to create, extend, or neutralize arms of the public service are costly for any regime; however, no regime has benefited by avoiding them. Shared authority, economic resources, status, and information need to be combined in various ways and amounts to institutionalize and control administrative activity and make it effective for regime purposes. The regime may also have to use threats and coercion to ensure more neutral responses from public servants.[78] An additional cost is the considerable amount of sector resources that must probably be foregone as a result of the alienation arising from delays, red-tape, and officiousness.[79]

The chief question confronting the statesman is how much administrative infrastructure is enough. Here he receives little assistance from contemporary public administration or political science. No studies have succeeded in relating types and extent of structure to output of resources.[80] But more important, no study of what is needed for administrative infrastructure can be undertaken without considering the statesman's needs. His goals, his resource scarcities, and his assessment of sectoral demands and propensities determine the level of administrative activity he deems necessary in the present and in the future. How much is needed will vary from community to community. Some statesmen may rely on inherited advantages: a colonial civil service of high calibre; an extensive network of field offices established by previous regimes; or a widespread agreement on political neutrality among civil servants. Other statesmen may have alternative structures that diminish the need for administration such as a cohesive and decentralized party system. At present too little is known about the consequences of such variations for productivity and/or about what productive effects could be achieved with marginal improvements. We

[77] See, for example, Ilchman (1967) and Ilchman (1969).

[78] Such was the course practiced in the wake of Ayub Khan's accession to power in Pakistan in 1958. See, for example, Wint (1960).

[79] See Eldersveld (1965).

[80] On this question, see Ilchman (1968).

look forward to empirical research on these questions, being satisfied that public bureaucracies can best be understood in infrastructural terms and analyzed in terms of the flow of resources.

ARMY.

As in the case of bureaucracy, characterizing the army or the military as administrative infrastructure does not remove it from the realm of politics or mean that it cannot serve as political infrastructure. In recent years, political scientists have paid considerable attention to the military, both as a sector and as a regime.[81] We have made frequent references to the military in our discussion so far. That an army has interests peculiar to its members is clear. We can, and the statesman must, consider its ideology, its propensities, its time horizons.[82] Here, however, we wish to discuss the infrastructural characteristics of the military, and this we need do only briefly.

As infrastructure the military produces coercion for use against foreign sectors or against dissident sectors. By its employment of coercion, or sometimes just by the fact of its existence which presents an implicit or explicit threat of coercion, the military reduces the amount of violence employed by sectors, usually a service of value to the regime. If intelligence functions are part of the military establishment, the military may produce valuable information as well. The resources the regime invests in the military are primarily economic resources and status; military establishments are usually quite jealous of economic and social perquisites. Direct costs of resources foregone from sectors may be loss of legitimacy and perhaps information, if and when coercion is used. Support in general may be decreased as a consequence of the military's production of other resources.

One concern of a statesman making investments in an army will be how to maximize its infrastructural and minimize its sectoral characteristics. For one thing, by separating the intelligence function, the army's actual or po-

[81] Three books deal specifically and extensively with the military in developing countries: J. Johnson (1962); Janowitz (1964); and Finer (1962). Pye did an earlier comparative study of the political role of the military; see Pye (1961).

[82] Janowitz (1964) gives considerable attention to the ideology of the military as a sector and as a regime. An interesting and imaginative study of the military's propensities, surveying and testing the full range of propositions thus far formulated about its propensity to intervene in politics, is Putnam (1967). Rustow (1963) in a less mathematical way tries to develop propositions about military intervention in the Middle East.

tential power will be somewhat reduced. For another, the less the statesman has to rely on the army's coercion, the less political power the army
will have and the less likely it will be to overthrow him.[83] To break the
military monopoly on coercion, many statesmen have invested in people's
militias and other paramilitary organizations. As we noted above, such investments have not always been politically profitable. Another method is to
employ the technique of control by political commissars developed by the
Bolsheviks and advanced by the Chinese Communists. Here an investment
of manpower over and above that invested in the army itself may prove
productive for the statesman's ends. More than any other type of infrastructure, the military has been the subject of the kind of research that
could most easily be interpreted and analyzed in the terms of political
economy.

OTHER ADMINISTRATIVE INFRASTRUCTURE.

After our discussion of the military, the infrastructural characteristics of
police and intelligence organizations should be evident. Relatively little attention has been paid by social scientists to the police in developing countries,[84] but the importance of police, especially in crisis situations, is evident from the major contribution made by the police in Nigeria after the
July, 1966 coup. Though the Nigerian army was in chaos and the regions
were politically separated, the police continued to operate as a national organization and kept the peace. There was no significant increase in lawless-
ness among the civilian population, even though there was no agreed-upon
national government and the future of regional governments was uncertain.

Intelligence organizations and special security forces are also a kind of
administrative infrastructure. While the police produce a major contribution of coercion as well as some information, these units primarily produce
information but also some coercion. Both require investments of economic
resources, though police usually require more of these. If intelligence units,
secret police, and the like cost the regime less in terms of investment of
money, they cost more in terms of support and legitimacy foregone. In addition, their existence may reduce the amount of information gained voluntarily from the sectors.[85] Both police and security forces may of course

[83] See Rustow (1963).

[84] One of the exceptions is Crawford Young's study of politics in the Congo
(1964: Chap. XVI).

[85] An interesting discussion of high-cost information regimes is presented by
Apter (1965).

act as sectors, but they have tended to be less political than the army. We consider them as administrative rather than political infrastructure because they do not undertake the task of mobilizing or controlling support.[86]

Communications Media

Any consideration of political infrastructure should include some analysis of communications systems. The volume *Communications and Political Development* suggests many of the infrastructural qualities of communications networks, both physical or interpersonal.[87] We would emphasize that communications systems exist in any society, and not only to serve political purposes. They may, however, be used for political ends and may even be constructed or modified so as better to serve the political purposes of a regime or sector. The idea that communications systems have infrastructural characteristics is not new. Ithiel de Sola Pool argues that "a mass media system which reaches all strata of the population is part of the social overhead capital for the creation of a nationwide arena of action." [88] We are specifically interested in the political implications and consequences of such systems. It is to these that Pye refers when he states that there can be no politics spanning the nation without a network of communications capable of enlarging and magnifying words and choices of individuals.[89] One basic purpose of investing in communications media is enlarging subsistence social and political markets and linking them to a central market, thus facilitating the process of nationalization, and often politicization.

It would be a mistake to think of modern communications systems as necessarily superior to traditional systems. Persons usually attribute greater reliability to information transmitted through familiar, interpersonal channels than to information received through the mass media. On the other

[86] Our characterization of bureaucracy, army, and police as administrative infrastructure is not absolute. As we suggested earlier, the distinction between political and administrative infrastructure is often chiefly analytical. Administrative infrastructure may at times aid leaders in acquiring and maintaining authority rather than just in exercising it.

[87] Pye (1963). Many similar observations could be made about transportation systems. These are usually constructed for economic or social purposes but may lower costs of securing compliance nonetheless. Wittfogel (1957) suggests cases where transportation networks were built with specifically political ends in mind. We leave the reader to consider for himself the political infrastructural qualities of transportation systems.

[88] Pool (1963a:285).

[89] Pye (1963:6).

hand, the information transmitted through the mass media can be much more easily controlled by a regime to suit its ends. Usually the regime has little control over traditional channels. Pye suggests that the development of communications is for the most part less dependent on investing in modern, urban-based mass media systems than on adjusting informal rural systems to each other and to the mass media system.[90] His position stems from the recently acknowledged importance of informal opinion leaders in communications theory. The "two-step flow of communication" through intermediaries is even more important in developing countries than it is in the U.S., where most studies have been made.[91]

We do not agree with Pool's observation that the communications development policies in most countries have been relatively apolitical. His argument is that with the exception of most Communist regimes which have deliberately used the mass media for exhortation and mobilization, regimes have treated the media more as educational instruments, even when aiming at furthering economic and social development.[92] Pool's argument neglects the fact that an "apolitical" communications policy that permits, for instance, laissez-faire use of radio, television, and newspapers is in fact political in that it apportions use of communications media to those sectors that have the economic resources to pay for such use, or status to command it. Regime choices of one communications policy or another have political consequences for the community.

A more concrete investment policy may be worked out for communications systems as infrastructure than for the types of political and administrative infrastructure already discussed. Schramm has, for instance, already worked out an inventory of capital and personnel investments.[93] His inventory does not make explicit the political and social resources also required, but these may be figured out as well. Pool has set forth four major questions to be decided in formulating a communications policy: How much of the scarce resources of a government should be invested in the mass media? What roles should be assigned to the private and public sectors? How much freedom or control of the mass media is desired? At what cultural level should media appeals be made, or to whom should the media appeal?[94]

We will first consider the economic requisites of an investment policy

90 Pye (1963:27).
91 Pool (1963a:285–286). See Katz and Lazarsfeld (1955).
92 Pool (1963a:284).
93 Schramm (1963:44–45).
94 Pool (1963b:234).

for communications systems. Lerner makes the case that the level of development of the mass media is closely associated with the level of economic development. He argues that whether leaders of a country are pursuing a Hamiltonian, Stalinist, or Gandhian development strategy, they cannot much exceed the normal limits on mass media development set by the level of economic capacity.[95] Aside from economic resources, few other resources need be invested directly. There are nonetheless other costs involved in establishing mass media such as newspapers or radio stations. While communications systems themselves may not "speak in the name of the state," they may permit an anti-statesman to advocate different uses of authority and thus to solicit support for his alternative policies. Newspapers, which may be important instruments for a regime to use in gaining support for its programs, are often a base for regime opponents.[96] Moreover, an improved communications system may make it easier for opponents to transmit certain political information detrimental to the regime.

The benefits that may accrue from investment in mass media are considerable. A communications policy may increase the legitimacy of the state. At the same time, it will probably mobilize support for the regime from larger numbers of persons.[97] Pool declares that mass communication confers status on certain groups.[98] We think that it is not useful to think of the mass media primarily in terms of their capability to indoctrinate, as does Frederick Yu. However, we would agree with Yu that use of the media may well reduce the necessity of securing compliance by coercion.[99]

One presumed benefit of investing in modern mass media is an increase in the modernity of a society; however, such an increase does not necessarily result. Mosel points out with reference to Thailand that modern

[95] Lerner (1963:336–337).

[96] Passin (1963:100) cites examples from India and Japan.

[97] Pye (1963:229–230).

[98] Pool (1963b:252). He suggests that politicians may be the greatest benefactors of this capacity of the media to confer status. The press in particular gives politicians a national code of standards by which to confirm or enhance their status.

[99] Yu (1963:259). Using the example of contemporary China, Yu speaks of indoctrination reducing the necessity of "ruling by naked force." This is a dramatic metaphor, to be sure, but the media are seldom as omnipotent as Yu implies. Sectors may be persuaded, sometimes on spurious or deceitful grounds, to act against what they formerly perceived as their interests, but brainwashing is hardly involved, even in China. Ideology is involved, and its effectiveness may be considerably increased by a well-developed mass media system. For a discussion of the limited effectiveness of mass media in developing countries, see Pool (1963a:285, 290).

media may perpetuate old roles rather than revise them.[100] There are some who would propose that modernization can be accelerated by stimulating demand for modern goods and services through the mass media and that increased demand in turn stimulates investment and modern production. Pool points out that such a view assumes that the barrier to modernization is insufficient popular awareness of the benefits of modernization. Insufficient awareness of benefits, he argues, is not the barrier, but rather the lack of means for obtaining these benefits. The need is to curb rather than to stimulate consumer demand. According to Pool, the media would aid economic development only if they could encourage productive thrift.[101]

Kemal Ataturk employed an imaginative political strategy for the use of communications systems. After he acquired authority he exploited, rather than lamented or attacked, the bifurcation of communications networks in Turkey. He conducted no drive to mobilize the masses, who were hardly touched by the mass media anyway. Instead, he concentrated on extending and consolidating a modernist beachhead within the ruling elite. After the bulk of the elite was modernized, he then moved to the greater task of mobilizing the peasant sectors. One means of reducing the power of opponents to block or slow his drive for secularization was to decrease their ability to communicate. He did so in part by prohibiting the teaching of Arabic and Persian languages and the maintenance of religious schools. The school system and the press communicated the government's view on all questions.[102]

Three considerations should be borne in mind in planning a communications investment strategy. First, the statesman should consider making complementary investments to increase the profitability of expanding the mass media's coverage. Pool notes that government policies need not only to be supported by the mass media, but also need support from informal processes of communication.[103] A regime party or auxiliary organizations may provide local opinion leaders to interpret the content of the mass media to sector members. One of the major complementary investments to augment the mass media is an investment in education. Literacy is required to make newspapers into effective means of communication and persuasion. In addition, the content of other forms of mass media may become more intelligible following at least some minimum of formal education. Lerner's account of the social transformation of Balgat, Turkey,

[100] Mosel (1963:185).
[101] Pool (1963a:288).
[102] Frey (1963:313–317).
[103] Pool (1963b: 233).

provides dramatic evidence of the productivity of complementary investments. Little mobilization occurred when the only means of communication from the outside world was via the radio, which had to be interpreted by the traditional village leader. Once, however, political parties, bus transport, and other infrastructure for communication and transportation were introduced, the village was quickly modernized.[104]

The statesman should also consider making alternative investments for achieving a given purpose. In Guinea, as a matter of policy, the government prevented the establishment of any newspapers.[105] Touré understood full well that newspapers might impose future political costs on his regime. Instead, he chose to attempt communication with sectors through the nationalist party he had developed during the struggle for independence. In principle at least, the party could reach into any community in the country and all sectors were represented within it. One of the advantages of this communications policy was an increase in the value of party membership, as membership became a means of securing information that would otherwise be available in other countries through the mass media. Pool notes that while it is extraordinary for a country to attempt modernization without allowing a press, this policy could prove to be a profitable one for Touré—at least for the immediate time period.

Finally, the statesman should give special attention to innovation in communications policies and investments. A number of governments have judged it politically profitable to adapt traditional forms of communication to modern media. In Thailand, for example, popular "verse editorials" have been developed. In addition, modern publicity and transportation have increased the effectiveness of government-sponsored dance-dramas with an anti-Communist theme.[106] These forms of communication are based on traditional language and values, and perhaps the medium is the message. Such imaginative use of communications should be an example to statesmen and political economists.

Education

Investment in educational systems, like investment in communications systems, need not be undertaken with political intentions. However, such investment may nonetheless result in unintended political consequences and

104 Lerner (1958: Chap. I).
105 Pool (1963a:283).
106 Mosel (1963:184, 208–209).

costs. Since education may serve as political infrastructure, it deserves some discussion here. The contribution of education to political development has already been recognized and discussed, though not in as explicitly political terms as we would propose.[107] Investment in human resources has become a subject of much interest, and economists and educators have tried to estimate the rates of return on such investments.[108] The net benefits of basic or primary education yielding little more than literacy have been compared with those of secondary or post-secondary technical education, or with those of higher or liberal education. Like the statesman, we would be as or more concerned with education for citizenship. Where Coleman says that education produces support for society, we would say that it produces allegiance.[109] Moreover, we would say that to the extent that an educational system teaches the alleged virtues of the regime and its policies, such a system can produce valuable legitimacy and support.

Educational systems, like communications systems, require a major investment of economic resources. Indeed, education is the largest single expenditure in many government budgets.[110] In developing countries a regime can seldom afford compulsory universal education, but if it could, it might have to expend some coercion to enforce school attendance. Yet because of the nature of the educational process, coercion is likely to be unproductive or even counterproductive. When the government tries to determine what courses of study shall be given priority and requires students to take certain courses, it exercises its authority and thus may risk losing support from students who feel themselves deprived in some way. We can describe the costs deriving from an educational system in broader terms. Education frequently perpetuates what is called the "elite-mass gap" as well as religious, regional, and other cleavages. Bonilla reports specifically on the intersectoral conflict education produces in Brazil,[111] but such conflict is common throughout the developing areas. Geertz goes so far as to say that conflict over education is to communal sectors what the strike is to the struggle between labor and management.[112]

A regime that favors certain kinds of changes may reap various broad

[107] See the contributions in Coleman (1965).

[108] Schultz (1961); Harbison and Myers (1964:3–14).

[109] Coleman (1965:23).

[110] At present governments spend between 2 and 4, but as high as 7 per cent of gross national income on education. As much as 30 per cent of their local budget may be expended on education. Harbison and Myers (1964:45–48, 217).

[111] Bonilla (1965:219–220).

[112] Geertz (1963:124–125).

benefits from education. For one thing, the nexus between education and status and wealth that is common in most countries may be broken by a program of mass education. Coleman and Passin both note that education may bring about a change in the class standing of privileged sectors.[113] Education may also ameliorate interparty conflict. Passin notes that in Japan, "old boy" social ties help to unite radical and conservative politicians who have serious ideological differences.[114] Education may be used by a regime to affect the political culture of a community. Over time the educational system may alter what we have called parameters. It may curb the readiness to use violence as a means of making political claims, encourage greater acceptance of the political division of labor, and strengthen the disposition to work out political conflicts through bargaining and negotiation rather than through conflict.[115]

The returns of investment in education are often long-term. Such investment may incur large economic costs in the short run with little immediate benefit; however, providing the statesman is in a position to make the investment and is willing to adopt a long time horizon, education offers one of the most effective means of restructuring the political community. Coleman makes it clear that there is at least as yet no single recommended strategy for formulating an educational program to increase economic growth or to decrease political instability; yet he indicates that the ideology of statism common in developing countries gives governments an adequate opportunity to try to control the educational system. Aside from this ideology, he says, there are few guideposts for planning.[116] The political ramifications of education are clearly a subject for extensive and intensive research by political scientists and educationists.[117] There is a great need to determine the political and social costs and consequences of educational investments as well as to establish the conditions under which different educational development strategies are most effective for achieving certain objectives. Political economy should facilitate such research.

[113] See Coleman (1965:300, 228). Mass education in the USSR, Japan, and the Philippines dramatically opened up new channels for mobility.

[114] Passin (1965:303).

[115] Bonilla (1965:213).

[116] Coleman (1965:526).

[117] One of the few such studies is that by David Abernethy on the political implications of introducing free universal primary education in Western and Eastern Nigeria (1969).

IX

THE APPLICATION OF
POLITICAL ECONOMY

If to do were as easy as to know what were good to do, chapels had
been churches, and poor men's cottages princes' palaces.

William Shakespeare, *The Merchant of Venice* [1]

Joseph Tussman once argued that "it would be irresponsible folly to teach
the wielders of authority merely the arts of power." [2] Many students of
politics, whether they consider themselves theorists or empiricists, may
concur with Professor Tussman's judgment. Tussman's words underscore
the distinction between power and authority, but they also raise this question: Shall those who occupy authority roles learn how better to use the
resources at their disposal to pursue their ends more effectively? Tussman's
assumption is that those who possess authority will act irresponsibly if
given an opportunity.

We make no such assumptions. Constructive and valuable objectives
may be and are achieved through political exchange. We believe that it is
not our place either to set up a hierarchy of goals for others or to catechize
others on their obligations, as Tussman would have us do. If political
power is used irresponsibly it can be curbed, but only by those who are possessed of a sophisticated understanding of political exchange. The fact that
some leaders may use their power selfishly or destructively does not deter
us from our concern with the plight of Colonel (now General) Gowon
and others like him. If the wielders of authority in developing countries
lack an effective understanding of the arts of power, they cannot achieve
valued ends—theirs or those of their constituents. Indeed, they may by default advance the interests of those sectors that benefit from a situation in

[1] I, ii, 13.
[2] Tussman (1960:17).

which public interests are faintly perceived or faint-heartedly promoted.

Political economy is an open book. Not only the statesman may study and practice it, but his opponents and various sectors as well. If it is true that certain political leaders act "irresponsibly," a better understanding of the political process should facilitate the defeat of such political leaders and the emergence of more "responsible" leadership.

Political Economy and Public Policy

Policy is the use of resources by those in authority to achieve preferred ends. In the past when social scientists have taken an interest in matters of policy, they have usually conducted research *on* policy. This research orientation has resulted mainly in *ex post facto* analysis and has been marked by a fastidious preoccupation with historical details. We believe that those dissatisfied with either the uncertainty or inconsequence of much social science research are or should be interested in research *for* policy.[3] By this we mean an *ex ante* orientation for research with the objective of improving political choices about to be made or modified. One justification for following such a course would be that statesmen need and seek advice in formulating their policies. It is often thought that by virtue of their training, social scientists should be more knowledgeable and objective advisors than less disciplined observers. Yet it has been our argument in this book that social scientists can at present contribute little of value to the making of policy choices. What then prompts our concern for the study of policy from the point of view of political actors? The study of political economy may be a way of reconciling social scientists' concern for public policy with their aspirations to advance social science.

[3] For one of the first major attempts to apply social science methodology to the study of policy choices, see Lerner and Lasswell (1950). Lasswell's introductory essay sets noble and thoughtful goals for social scientists, but not even his collaborators pick up or follow through on substantive issues. Lasswell repeated his call for attention to policy in 1956. In his rationale for the study of policy, he combined a curious deprecation of politicians as "tricksters" with an appreciation of political constraints. No visible reorientation of political science resulted from Lasswell's exhortation, perhaps because his own work did not reflect an interest in analytical variables that were subject to policy control or readily measurable. See Lasswell (1956), as well as his article on the Vicos experiment (1965a). Yehezkel Dror has recently stated the case for the development of a profession concerned with the methods and substance of policy. See Dror (1967:197–203).

POLICY RESEARCH AS THE VERIFICATION OF
SOCIAL SCIENCE THEORY.

In our view, policy research is not restricted to making practical and hope-fully beneficent contributions to government and public life. It may be the best way of developing and testing social science theory. As Boulding has suggested, the most essential element of the scientific process is *prediction*. He writes:

> Experiment . . . is not essential to the scientific process; predic-tion, however, in the sense of an exact image of the future, is essential. When the future is fulfilled the image of the present can be compared with the past image of the future, and if there is a divergence between the two something has to give. . . . A failure of prediction is a sign of error, though success in prediction is not necessarily a sign of truth. The method of science, however, is essentially a mutation-selection process by which erroneous images are continually eliminated. The more error is eliminated, the more, one hopes, there is an asymptotic approach to truth.[4]

Until a hypothesis or generalization is put to the test of application, its veracity or validity is only presumed. Historical or cross-sectional studies can only furnish us with ideas of how variables interact. However interest-ing a correlation may appear, it becomes relevant only when some causal relationship can be demonstrated by reliable prediction of consequences.

For social scientists who aim at developing predictive capabilities as a test of their theories, policy research offers opportunities for verification otherwise unavailable. Behavioral scientists more than social scientists may be able to make studies under experimental conditions, but the validity of such work still rests on demonstrating through prediction that real-world relationships can be extrapolated from laboratory findings.[5] In order to deal with situations affected by policy choices, social scientists must de-velop their theories through empirical tests in the most difficult and exact-ing, and ultimately the only productive laboratory, the "real world."

Yet policy research is not "experimentation" in the usual sense of the word. Policy researchers do not induce governments to manipulate inde-

---

[4] Boulding (1966:13–14).

[5] A provocative discussion of the methodological and theoretical deficiencies of much experimental work in the behavioral and social sciences is offered in Fairweather (1966).

pendent variables in experimental fashion. Rather they attempt to use their knowledge by predicting the consequences of the alternatives being considered by those in authority, or by suggesting other alternatives not yet considered. The requirements of policy themselves make for cumulative development of theory and the successive improvement of models. After policy choices have been made, policy researchers attempt to determine what consequences in fact ensued from the course chosen, what costs were incurred, and what alternatives or modifications might better have achieved the desired ends. Such analyses should verify or amend the models from which the predictions were made.

Thus we would consider the aim of policy research to be the development of increasingly reliable models of social change and social control. Three aspects of policy research are particularly pertinent to this effort. First, by adopting the perspective of government policy-makers, policy research deals with relevant time periods, those with which governments must deal. While a distant time horizon may offer social scientists the protection of hedged or uncollected bets, to use Almond's metaphor, it is a luxury in which governments cannot indulge. What is more, it is a luxury that social scientists should not wish to afford. Efforts at prediction and the verification of hypotheses are only meaningful if made within given and limited periods of time.

Second, policy research considers government policies in terms of an "open" political system. Even at the national level of government, choices can seldom be evaluated without reference to the constraints imposed and the possibilities offered by factors outside the particular political system being considered. We feel that policy research should be especially concerned with the opportunities and costs of importing economic, social, and political resources. Social science research that ignores exogenous variables is all too often biased a priori. To assume the constancy of exogenous variables or to treat such variables in *ceteris paribus* terms is in effect to assign them zero value.

A third, more complex aspect of policy research, but one essential to the discernment of causal connections, is the necessity of differentially distinguishing the general and particular effects of policy choices. The problems involved are well illustrated by Charles Lindblom. In an article on policy analysis he states that because economists have made a general case for the use of the price system for purposes of allocation, and against the use of direct controls, they thereby too often presume the efficacy of the price system in treating any particular policy problem. He points out that this presumption is not always appropriate. He adds that economists or other social scientists have too often made a general case for planning without considering the particular cases in which planning is more or is less productive.[6]

Our point is that explanation of cause and effect must proceed at two levels, the general and the particular. General prescriptions represent first approximations. Particular descriptions represent more detailed and relevant statements. The first are *ceteris paribus* statements; the second take into account what is not *paribus*. Without the first, organizing our knowledge is less efficient, yet if we stop with the first, our findings are worth little. We would not, then, choose one level over another to evaluate the reliability of theoretical statements. Policy research should contribute to the scientific understanding of causation at both levels.

The model of political economy should make possible the marriage of policy research and social science. By attempting both the analysis and prediction of the outcomes of choice, it deals with the empirical world in a search for useful knowledge. The different elements of the model—sectors, stratification, propensities, exchange, strategies, infrastructure, and the like —correspond to the elements in any calculation of the effects of policy, yet they also relate to much of the work done in different social science disciplines.

EXPLANATION IN SOCIAL SCIENCE: SOME COST-BENEFIT CONSIDERATIONS.

We would propose that social scientists should proceed on the assumption that some optimal amount of ignorance exists on any particular subject. Unfortunately, the assumption now common in social science is that the best explanation is the one based on the most encompassing universe. We mean by this that the explanation of social phenomena is sought in hypothetical constructs derived from macro-historical or macro-sociological data or from pervasive personality factors. The chain of causation that is thereby constructed is lengthy and not always explicit. Consequences are necessarily contingent and probabilistic.

To explain social phenomena we can attempt to trace the chain of causation back many links, but the more remote the presumed cause is from the observed effect, the greater and the more significant the intervening variables become. These variables are too often made to function as *dei ex machina* for weak theories in social science. Too seldom are they recognized as causes in their own right. We are not seeking to banish from so-

[6] Lindblom (1958:299).

cial science efforts at all-encompassing explanations. We acknowledge the potential contribution of such explanations to an improved understanding of the social universe, but we feel that the more encompassing an explanation is, the less testable, the less verifiable, and the less certain it is as a causal explanation, and thus the weaker it is as a basis for prediction and choice.[7] We would not dispute the fact that the nature of the problem at hand determines how complex and encompassing an explanation is needed. Neither would we deny that speculative or heuristic models may eventually prove fertile. However, we would argue that good theory is more likely to result from inquiries that deal with tangible problems in terms of proximate causes and effects than from those that define problems in terms of more remote connections.

While we would agree with those who plead for some general theory against which to set the findings of scientific inquiry, we must emphasize that a theory's utility and validity should be judged in terms of its power to explain and predict the consequences of *real* problems. The statesman who castigates "theory" is not against the application of knowledge to problem-solving. However, he must deal with ascertainable causes and verifiable consequences. While he does not dignify his working knowledge of cause and effect with the appellation of "theory," theory it nonetheless is. If social scientists adopt his perspective and try to verify and systematize relationships between choices and consequences, they will probably learn more that is valid and reliable than they would if they continued to treat knowledge as a "free good" in the economist's sense.

Because of this apparent "propensity" of social scientists to search for the most encompassing universe of explanation, we suggest the idea of ascertaining the boundaries of optimal ignorance. The converse—the aim of ascertaining optimal knowledge—is equally valid, but in practice it is interpreted as a call for maximum knowledge. In this escalated form, the aim of reaching optimal knowledge does not raise sharply enough the issue of

---

[7] Medical science in its early years had similar problems in arriving at reliable explanations of illness and cures. Before physicians could discriminate among diseases or were free to learn about the body through dissection, they propounded the theory that four body fluids determined man's health and temperament. Imbalance among the four humours—blood, phlegm, black bile, and yellow bile—caused pain and disease. The theory lost favor when the study of cellular pathology was developed. Social science based on the study of "functions"—coincidentally four: adaptation, integration, goal attainment, and pattern maintenance—may be scientifically at the stage of Hippocrates and Galen. Social scientists need to develop "cellular" theories of interaction and causation that deal with proximate rather than remote effects.

costs and benefits. Too often it simply serves as a justification for more research. It gives the benefit of any doubt to further study and adds to the
impetus for ever more encompassing explanations. Acceptance of the notion of optimal ignorance signifies a consciousness of the costs of augmenting knowledge. The costs include not only or primarily research costs—
salaries, travel, support, publications—but also the intellectual lost opportunity costs of pursuing optimal or maximal knowledge, i.e., of foregoing
explanations with greater predictive power. A scientist who works with the
rule of optimal ignorance as his guide will focus on proximate causation
and press back the borders of explanation one reliable step at a time.[8] This
kind of social science is what the statesman and others in authority or seeking authority need.

EXAMPLES OF EFFORTS AT EXPLANATION.

Let us briefly consider two policy problems facing many leaders in developing countries and look at the kinds of advice social scientists might offer in
an attempt to deal with these problems. These problems illustrate the
difference between the "optimal knowledge" and "optimal ignorance" approaches to explanation.

STIMULATING ENTREPRENEURSHIP AND INVESTMENT IN INDUSTRIES.
Suppose that a statesman wished social scientific advice on how best to
stimulate entrepreneurship in small industries as part of a Five-Year plan;
to whom should he turn? A number of social scientists have dealt with this
problem. Four government strategies might be formulated on the basis of
the theories of four scholars: David McClelland, Everett Hagen, Albert
Hirschman, and Gustav Papanek.

Achievement Motivation.   One of the most elaborately conceived and
executed studies of the psychological factors causing or accompanying economic development is McClelland's work, *The Achieving Society*.[9] In this
study McClelland attempts to measure achievement motivation as a psychological drive, called "need for achievement," or in abbreviated form, n
Achievement. In societies that developed rapidly in the past and in ones
presently trying to develop he finds that n Achievement correlates significantly with economic achievement and especially with entrepreneurial

[8] The requirements and discipline of policy research should lead to the construction of more meaningful research designs. Multiple and linked hypotheses
could replace single-hypothesis studies. See Platt (1964).

[9] McClelland (1961).

activity. Variation between societies and within societies in terms of the amount and distribution of n Achievement he explains in various ways.

McClelland attaches primary importance to child-rearing practices, especially those that encourage mastery over the environment at an early age and promote confidence in a child's ability to manipulate his environment. He proposes various other factors that influence the need for achievement. Specifically, McClelland suggests that n Achievement varies inversely with father-dominance in the home. In addition, he finds that the drive for achievement correlates with Protestant religious values and other forms of "positive mysticism." The expression of need for achievement in popular myths and children's stories he finds to be a plausible source of high n Achievement in a population. McClelland suggests that ultimately, the most powerful force behind the growth of entrepreneurship is "ideological conversion" to economic development. There is no substitute for ideological fervor, he says, but this conclusion verges on tautology and does not necessarily follow from his data or his basic theory.

A statesman who tries to apply McClelland's explanation of the origins of entrepreneurship will find that the theory offers very few effective or assured policy measures. It would be very difficult to intervene in child-rearing practices without the state "expropriating" children at an early age. Reducing father-dominance poses similar difficulties; perhaps the statesman could draft fathers into the national service to remove them from the home environment. Forced conversion to Protestantism would be a very costly investment, especially in Muslim, Hindu, or Buddhist communities, and there seems to be no way that a regime could foster "positive mysticism." One of the cheapest investments proposed by McClelland would be to rewrite children's stories to increase their emphasis on achievement motivation.

A major problem with McClelland's theory is that a regime would have to wait at least a generation to see any substantial payoff. Furthermore, many of the variables analyzed by McClelland are largely beyond the statesman's policy control. Most important, there is in McClelland's theory no certainty of any causal connection between the activities undertaken to raise n Achievement and subsequent entrepreneurial activity. Indeed, it might be suggested that increases in n Achievement are as likely to lead to political aspiration and conflict or social unrest as to economic initiative. McClelland himself is careful to make clear that correlation does not mean causation, though he still infers that increased economic activity will result from increased n Achievement. On the basis of the evidence presented, few statesmen would follow McClelland's strategy for accelerating economic growth.[10]

Rebellion against Traditional Society. Economically underdeveloped societies value certain roles, institutions, and accomplishments to a greater extent than do societies enjoying greater economic prosperity. In his search for theories of social change leading to economic development, Hagen suggests that historically, new personalities, roles, and values making for greater productivity have stemmed from the attitudes and activities of deviant minorities.[11] For persons to abandon traditional ways and undertake new tasks that modernize their society, argues Hagen, they need to have little personal stake in traditional arrangements. He develops the concept of "withdrawal of status respect" as an incentive to change, tracing over several generations a psychological path of retreatism, rage, erosion of values, repression of needs and retreat into fantasy. At some point, he says, out of retreatism come creativity and the emergence of values conducive to economic growth. As examples of minorities that supposedly traversed this path he gives the Jews, the Old Believers in Russia, the Parsis in India, the overseas Chinese in Asia, the Antioqueños in Colombia, and others.

Hagen's work, like McClelland's, provides little in the way of policy instruments to use for deliberately increasing entrepreneurship. A statesman would hardly seek to stimulate entrepreneurship by stigmatizing or persecuting a minority group, though he might do this for other reasons. In addition, increments in entrepreneurship could not be expected by this method in less than 100 years. Hagen places great emphasis on child-rearing practices, but these are insufficiently accessible to alteration by the government. Placing children in institutions for special rearing would presumably not have the effect Hagen desired. Since personality, the factor supposedly the most important for effecting entrepreneurship, is basically determined in the preschool years, formal education would not be useful as a policy instrument. Indeed, the only short-term measure we can imagine would be to build colleges of business in areas where disadvantaged minority groups reside.

Such measures as Hagen proposes would appear unprofitable to a statesman wishing to accelerate economic growth. The statesman cannot afford

[10] The most practical suggestion McClelland offers is that governments do more subcontracting to private business. This suggestion, however, would involve the manipulation of economic incentives rather than the reshaping of personalities.

[11] This thesis, based on comparative historical studies as well as psychological theory, is most succinctly stated in Hagen (1960:185–187). It is elaborated more fully with greater empirical and theoretical detail in Hagen (1962a).

to wait the several generations implied in Hagen's theory before receiving any payoff on his investment. He would probably find it quite costly politically to build educational institutions for minority groups or to subsidize the economic activities of minorities. However, the most important consideration for us is that the correctness of the theory has as yet not been determined. The theory has not been put to any test and perhaps cannot be tested.[12] That some pariah sectors have been successful in the past does not necessarily indicate that these sectors can or should be the basis for future economic development. Indeed, Hirschman points out that many deviant minorities—homosexuals and ex-convicts, for example—"have not shown particularly strong entrepreneurial inclinations." [13]

Unbalancing Investments. The strategy of economic development advocated by Hirschman relies heavily on the stimulation of entrepreneurship.[14] However, Hirschman pays little attention to personality or institutional factors. He expects that strategic public investments in social overhead capital and/or directly productive activities will elicit private decisions and activities that take advantage of the newly created opportunities for profit. This strategy he believes will be more effective than one that leaves investment entirely to private decisions or to government action through central planning. Following Hirschman's plan, a regime seeking to encourage investment in small industries would perhaps invest in industrial parks to lower the fixed capital costs to budding entrepreneurs, or in roads to lower transportation costs, or in factories that have strong forward- and backward-linkages of supply and demand for others' products. Here is indeed a work of social science that deals with limited factors and is intended to guide and be tested by policy. The extent to which Hirschman is correct about the effect of strategic unbalancing government investments on the incentives of private individuals to invest can be demonstrated within some reasonable time period. It should be possible to establish *which* kinds of unbalancing investments yield the most private investment under certain

12 Hagen speaks of the principle of "relative social blockage." This principle has an untestable Toynbeean quality about it—minorities should have just enough status withdrawal (challenge) so that they will become innovators in activities not valued by the traditional culture (response). McClelland is critical of the tautological character of Hagen's theory, not appreciating that his own theory has the same defect. According to McClelland, children are supposed to learn "mastery" in their early years by having various tasks set for them by their parents. The tasks should be difficult and challenging, but not too difficult to solve. One cannot know except by definition "how much" is "enough."

13 Hirschman (1962:37).

14 Hirschman (1958).

circumstances, and *how much* each kind yields. When connections between investments and outputs are reliably established, behavioral or cultural variables affecting both of these might usefully be explored and tested.

Economic Incentives. One of the most instructive studies of entrepreneurship and the contribution it makes to the development of industry has been conducted by Papanek with reference to Pakistan.[15] In this study Papanek attempts to account for the factors that boosted industrial output during the fifties and early sixties. The explanations of entrepreneurship found in social science literature, most of which relate to personality determinants, he finds unconvincing in light of the Pakistani experience. He finds the most pertinent explanation for the rapid development of industrial entrepreneurship to be powerful economic incentives.

The extremely high rate of industrial growth in Pakistan since 1947 was encouraged by a number of factors. The partition of Pakistan from India meant that the products of Indian industry were kept out. The price and output of jute, Pakistan's leading export, rose greatly during the Korean War, but fell as rapidly after the war. Imports of some foreign goods practically disappeared. All this meant that the opportunities for profit from domestic industry were greatly increased. Traders especially shifted their resources from trade to industry. Papanek explains the traders' "over-representation" in the new entrepreneurial sector in terms of their familiarity with the economic market. Not all groups were equally exposed to the same incentives.

Though some of the factors contributing to economic expansion in Pakistan were fortuitous, the decisive factors seem to have been certain government policies that helped to channel capital into industrial development. Strict control of capital transfers abroad prevented the export of domestic capital. Fear of impending land reform made land a poor investment. Industrial investment brought returns as high as 100 per cent in one year. Import regulations of the government favored investment goods over consumption goods, especially over luxury items. Generous depreciation allowances were given as well. It is true that "deviant" minorities played an important economic role in Pakistan's expansion. Five small "communities" (quasi-castes) that constituted only one per cent of the population contributed almost half of the entrepreneurial sector. Grossly underrepresented were the Bengali Muslims, who constituted 50 per cent of the population but only 4 per cent of the entrepreneurial sector. Yet "other Muslims"—40 per cent and 44 per cent, respectively—contributed the largest single group of entrepreneurs and were proportionally represented. The

[15] See Papanek (1962).

previous concentration of the entrepreneurial sects in trading activity was probably more responsible for their industrial enterprise than were personality factors. Papanek notes that for all their economic innovation, Pakistani entrepreneurs were not social innovators.

It may be objected that Papanek does not "explain" why entrepreneurship took place, why certain groups were so active and others so inactive in industrial enterprise. Hagen in particular objects that Papanek does not deal with or show any change in personality. We would not agree that Papanek explains too little. Rather we would suggest that by attempting to offer a more encompassing explanation, it is Hagen who does not explain enough.[16] As an explanatory variable, personality appears to be less significant than the more proximate variables of economic conditions and government policy. It is evident that Hirschman and Papanek offer more relevant and reliable guidance to the statesman seeking to stimulate industrial entrepreneurship than McClelland and Hagen do. Yet for coping with different policy problems, McClelland may have something to offer. If a regime were concerned with how it could best develop a more productive educational system, it might consider in what way the system might as a side-effect raise the level of entrepreneurship. In this context some of McClelland's findings might be useful. The test of their truth value would, however, not be the number of correlations offered in *The Achieving Society*, but the changes that an educational system altered according to McClelland's theory could bring about.

REDUCING BUREAUCRATIC CORRUPTION. One problem with which many statesmen wish to deal is the prevalence of corruption within their bureaucracies. There have been many evaluations made of bureaucratic corruption in developing countries, some more concerned with its moral implications and others more concerned with its consequences for bu-

[16] Hagen (1962b:59–61). Hagen admits that it is not certain how long a time will pass before groups discriminated against will become innovating groups—perhaps four to eight generations. Furthermore, he concedes that "new personality may not cause a conspicuous change in behavior until it has burst through external barriers and creates new economic opportunities, a slowly budding process which may suddenly burst into bloom." This is no explanation at all, but only speculation. Hagen acknowledges (1962a:240) that a change in economic conditions is commonly the force initiating economic growth. He prefers, however, to try to explain why certain groups respond positively to these incentives. His theory offers no explanation for the largest group of Pakistani entrepreneurs, the "other Muslims." Moreover, Hagen neglects to deal with the fact that without favorable economic conditions, there would be no certainty that members of minority groups would become entrepreneurial. Thus "explanation" within Hagen's frame of reference breaks down once it gets beyond the variables subject to government control.

reaucracy's productivity. Various measures for assessing the costs and consequences of corruption have been put forward.[17] We would like to compare the policy implications of the studies conducted by Fred Riggs and Joseph Nye.

Creating a Pluralistic Polity. Riggs believes that inasmuch as bureaucratic corruption is caused or facilitated by the values and behavior of a "prismatic" society, it will be reduced when such a society develops toward a more "diffracted" state.[18] In his terms bureaucracy is "heavy-weighted" and able to dominate other political, social, and economic groups. When this condition prevails, he says, there are no checks on bureaucrats to prevent them from seeking their own self-interest and accepting or extorting bribes. As developing societies become more differentiated, says Riggs, a plurality of competing groups, especially parties and interest groups, will arise. Most important, differentiation will result in "constitutive" politics in which a strong legislature will be able to subordinate the bureaucracy to majority will. If a statesman were to seek advice from Riggs on how to reduce corruption, he might be told that corruption was a function of the level of development his society had reached, that his regime was in a "prismatic trap," and that little could be done to change the situation until the society at large became more differentiated.

Presumably, according to Riggs, a statesman faced with bureaucratic corruption would be well advised to make political investments in an opposition party or two and in interest groups that could check the bureaucracy's selfishness and compel it to serve collective interests. We feel that such a strategy for reducing corruption would probably not be worth the candle. Not only would it involve great expenditure of resources, but it might well foreclose the possibility of the statesman's achieving his other political ends. The political competition resulting from such investments could well thwart his program or even lead to his ouster. Of course, the statesman does not know whether Riggs' strategy would yield the desired results even if all the necessary investments were made. Given the configuration and intensity of demands in a developing country, creation of additional channels for making political demands might well lead to paralysis of the political market, to a political stalemate, or to immobilism.

[17] The most extensive consideration of corruption is that by Wraith and Simpkins (1963). A succession of articles have offered various analyses of the problem and remedies for it. See Braibanti (1962); Leff (1964); Leys (1965); Bayley (1966); Greenstone (1966); and Dwivedi (1967). Two of the better treatments of the various issues are Riggs (1964) and Nye (1967).

[18] Riggs (1964:222–237, 260–285).

Under conditions of increased pluralism, bribery might turn out to be the only way in which any government authorizations or decisions could be implemented. Thus Riggs' prescription could lead to increased rather than reduced corruption, at least in the short run. Riggs' assurance that corruption in the long run would be diminished would carry little weight with a statesman, since more commonly than other mortals, statesmen in the long run are dead.

Calculating Costs and Benefits. Rather than simply assuming that any and all corruption is "unproductive," Nye lays out an analytical scheme for assessing the possible benefits and costs of different kinds of bureaucratic corruption.[19] He suggests conditions for ascertaining whether the benefits of corruption may exceed the costs. He points out that corruption varies, according to whether it affects the higher or lower levels of the bureaucracy, whether modern (universalistic) or traditional (ascriptive) inducements are used, and whether the deviation from formal duties is excessive or not. Corruption may benefit a regime or nation by facilitating or encouraging economic development, national integration, and/or the improvement of governmental capacity. On the other hand, it may cost the regime much in terms of waste of resources, greater political instability, and/or reduced governmental capacity. Nye comes up with a corruption cost-benefit matrix, estimating the probability of desirable or undesirable consequences under certain conditions.

The frame of reference presented by Nye offers an orientation to the problem of corruption that differs substantially from those that Riggs and others have put forth. With it we begin to analyze whether corruption brings net gains or losses, or rather under what conditions it results in either. If we determine that costs exceed benefits, we can, according to Nye, assess at which level, with what inducements, or to what degree corruption is costly to a regime. The means Nye suggests to correct the situation, such as paying higher salaries, not posting officials in their home area, making penalties harsher, or encouraging professionalization, are appropriate to particular situations and would not require the large-scale changes that Riggs proposes. The consequences of making no change or of making a particular change in policy could and would under Nye's scheme be examined to determine just who was benefiting and how much. The correctness of any hypothesis about costs and benefits would be subject to test. For these reasons, we feel that the approach outlined by Nye is more appropriate for social science than Riggs' approach, and is better for policy research

[19] Nye (1967). Leff (1964) and Greenstone (1966) had previously argued that corruption could be productive for economic and political development.

as well. Until more convincing empirical work demonstrates Riggs' proposition, we would not accept his idea that corruption is a necessary function of a "prismatic" society, or that it can be eliminated by increased pluralism.

ASSESSING AND CHOOSING STRATEGIES: IMPLICATIONS FOR SOCIAL SCIENCE RESEARCH.   Our consideration of alternative explanations of the origin of entrepreneurship and different approaches to dealing with bureaucratic corruption points up the importance of relating social science inquiry to the problems of social change or social control. Of course, the dimensions of the problem at hand and the time horizons of persons dealing with the problem will determine the utility of different levels of explanation. We have urged that social scientists give special attention to costs when formulating strategies for change. The benefits anticipated from

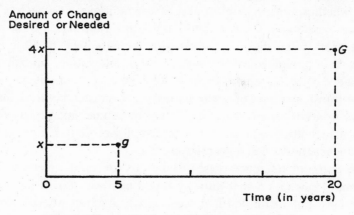

Figure Four: Goals of Strategies a and A.

short- and long-run strategies must be assessed comparatively in relation to the various costs that are estimated.

Let us suggest this sort of calculation graphically (Figure 4). We will consider two strategies. The short-run strategy will be designated as *a*, the long-run strategy as A. The former represents the analyses of Papanek and Nye, the latter those of McClelland and Riggs. These strategies aim at goals g and G, respectively. For the sake of illustration, we consider *a* and A to be roughly proportional with respect to the amount of change sought and the time within which change is to occur. However, those resources expended and those gained or saved are not necessarily proportional.

Because strategy *a* (Figure 5) aims at less ambitious change than does strategy A, and because its causal connections are more definite, the costs

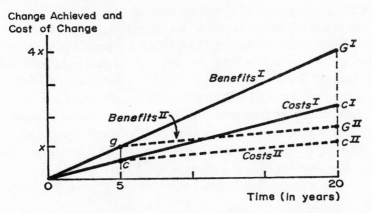

Figure Five: Alternative Benefits and Costs of Strategy a.

and benefits of strategy *a* are more or less proportional and ascertainable. When goal *g* is achieved, the regime may wish to persist with the same measures. If a situation of constant returns to scale exists, goal G^I could perhaps be achieved in twenty years. If not, we might expect some continued gains over time, but they would be proportionally less. If there are not diminishing returns, the net benefits of strategy *a* would be G^I minus c^I. Diminishing returns would lead to long-term gains of, say, G^{II} at the cost of c^{II}.

With strategy A (Figure 6) we are faced with a more difficult problem, that of estimating costs and benefits over a longer period of time. If benefits and costs were proportional (suggested by cost and benefit paths I), goal *g* would be reached in five years and goal G in twenty years; there

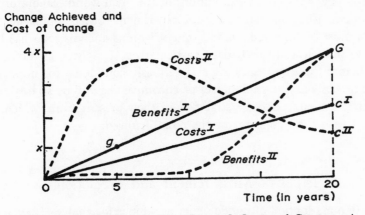

Figure Six: Alternative Benefits and Costs of Strategy A.

would be no reason, if we had to choose between strategies *a* and A, why we should not prefer the latter. However, we suggest that because of the magnitude of change required, strategy A would follow benefit path II—sort of a logistic curve—and would have the very high initial costs indicated by path II, though these costs might be lower in the twentieth year than would be the case if path I were followed. Thus if a statesman desires to increase industrial entrepreneurship or reduce bureaucratic corruption by some amount within approximately five years, he should choose strategy *a* (Papanek or Nye) which would yield *x* results with costs amounting to somewhat less than benefits. If strategy *a* could reach goal G of 4*x* change in twenty years, so much the better, but we do not assume proportionality for either strategy *a* or A.

A statesman desiring a change of 4*x* might for good reasons want to choose strategy A (McClelland or Riggs), but if he needed to reach goal *g* within five years this strategy would not help him. If he were willing and able to wait twenty years and to pay costs indicated by path II in Figure 6, he would have lower maintenance costs in the long run. However, he still might not be able to choose strategy A if he did not have the required resources for a massive investment in the short run, during which time there would be only low returns.

We would express some concern for caution should a statesman be willing and able to adopt strategy A. The resources it requires are valuable, in that there are usually many competing demands for their productive use. If the anticipated result is not realized, great waste of resources is the consequence. It may be argued that we will never know whether strategy A will yield 4*x* results within twenty years or what the cost would be unless we try the strategy, but here the limitations of the "real world" laboratory become evident. First, to make such an experiment, other approaches and programs must be foregone. Second, more rigorous analysis than has been performed on such strategies to date, particularly *cost* analysis, should be performed before these strategies are ever seriously considered for implementation. The costs and possible losses of encompassing A-type strategies are too great to embark on these strategies in their present form, which was developed with little concern for the costs involved.

Some Issues of Measurement and Prediction

Implicit in our adoption of public policy as a focus for analysis is an acceptance of the view of political science expressed by Sartori:

If political scientists have something different to say from the historians, and something more to say than the social determinists, this is because we are interested in predictions; and we are interested in predictions not because we advocate an anticipated fatalism but because we want to find out how much of the so-called inevitable is evitable—if we wish to avoid it.[20]

We have already expressed our concern for the predictive power of any social science analysis, having cited above Boulding's emphasis on prediction's central role in social science endeavors. Once prediction becomes a major concern, however, problems of measurement and motivation come to the fore. What is to be measured, and how? In an area of activity as complex as the political market, what behavioral assumptions improve prediction, or indeed make it possible?

So far we have done little in this book to propose indicators that might be used to measure the amounts and flows of resources. Our omission has not been due to oversight. As yet we have not had the opportunity to develop and test indicators empirically, although we are engaged in such efforts. Rather than suggest untested indicators that are not intrinsic to our model, we have only observed in passing how, for example, votes and money may indicate support, material symbols may denote status, or civil disobedience may manifest withdrawal of legitimacy. We recognize the problems confronting us in applying the model of political economy to real-world situations in a fully satisfactory way, but our chief consolation and encouragement is that calculations such as those called for in our model have been and are being made by statesmen and others. Moreover, we feel that various alternative approaches to the analysis of politics in developing nations, though they have not hitherto provided significantly useful frameworks for analysis of public choices, would be strengthened by adoption of the elements of political economy. A look at four of the leading approaches will demonstrate, we think, the particular analytical significance of political resources. Though we have not resolved the various problems involved in the measurement of political resources, we feel that these resources merit the critical attention of political scientists working with any one of the many analytical approaches.

[20] Sartori (1966:166). Sartori prefaced this judgment with the opinion that "we should pay more attention to the manipulative aspects of politics, whereas we have recently yielded too much to the social-determinist and also to a somewhat cultural-determinist point of view. If we attempt to explain everything in terms of political culture, then we are likely to reach the conclusion that what happens is, or was, inevitable. But we do not need a political science to find that out."

THE SIGNIFICANCE OF POLITICAL RESOURCES.

We will first consider the study of *political culture*. Though this approach offers many insights into patterns of political interaction, it contributes little to an understanding of the outcomes of such interaction unless it incorporates an analysis of political resources. It makes little difference for the polity that a sector holds alienated values unless that sector has resources with which to affect regime policies. But even assuming that the sector has resources, say, considerable violence, at its disposal, the consequences of the sector's political activity will depend on many other factors. What resources do other sectors and the regime possess? What are the demands and propensities of other sectors? What are the regime's goals, and how do the sector's demands correspond to these? What is the regime's elasticity of demand for no violence? How much coercion can the regime employ in response to sector violence, and at what cost? What violence might other sectors use in retaliation against the dissident sector, or what economic and other sanctions could be threatened or used against this sector? These many factors are more decisive in affecting political consequences than the attitudes of persons toward politics and political actors. The study of political culture may complement political analysis, but to comprehend the consequences of political attitudes and values, an analysis embracing the factors of political economy is needed.

A second approach is based on the study of political *capabilities* suggested by Almond and Powell. This approach may be useful in analysis of developing countries, especially when it is used to deal with what we would call political and administrative infrastructure. However, "extractive" or "symbolic" capabilities do not handle at all adequately the costs incurred by the regime. A regime's extraction of resources from the sectors requires many and varied expenditures and investments. While we appreciate the fact that Almond and Powell's notion of capabilities expresses what we have described as the "flow" of resources, we feel that unless the resources themselves are named and measured, little is gained for analysis. By thinking in terms of exchange rather than capabilities, analysis becomes less monolithic.

The manipulation of symbols involves important costs for a regime. Ideological commitments or nationalistic values entail significant costs in that they represent various uses of resources now and/or in the future. Unlike Almond and Powell we cannot treat status reallocation simply in terms of symbolic capability because the consequences of such reallocation are manifested in terms of altered resource flows, not just symbols. The manipulation of status relations for political ends needs to be viewed in terms of changes in allocation and production, and not just as psychic gratification.

We find the analysis of political change and development in terms of *crises* less useful than other approaches because of its unavoidable *post hoc* nature. Such analysis has as little to offer in the way of explanation and prediction as the Toynbeean challenge-response conundrum. The crisis approach posits that if a problem arises, it must be solved; if one that is expected does not arise, it must have been solved somehow. It thus neglects the fact that—in politics at least—problems and crises are made, not born. A participation crisis only occurs when sectors excluded from authority demand a share of it or an influence on it and have the resources to make their demand effective. As long as a sector lacks the resources or the will to make effective demands, any of its demands for participation may be inconsequential for the rest of the community. However, once resources are at hand and are accompanied by the desire to use them politically, a "crisis" arises. How the crisis is resolved depends on the same kinds of considerations suggested above with reference to political culture; what are sectors' resources and propensities, and what are the regime's resources and goals? Crises of legitimacy, integration, and participation can, we think, best be understood within the analytical framework offered by political economy. Without such a framework solutions, with or without crises, have a deterministic character that reduces the scope for human choice.

We would regard as productive many studies of various political *institutions*. Expressed in terms of established or changing patterns of exchange, such studies can contribute to an improved social science as well as to policy research. However, there is in such studies a common tendency toward reification of institutions against which we would argue. Consideration of "conditions" for the establishment or maintenance of institutions is especially misleading, as tautological fallacies abound in such discussions of requisites or prerequisites.[21] What does it mean to say that a bureaucracy is "prematurely" established? What help is an explanation offered in terms of a bureaucracy's inability to achieve its goals because of insufficient sup-

[21] A discussion of the conditions under which different types of political parties "emerge" or are "modernized" is offered by LaPalombara and Weiner in their introduction to their volume on political parties (1966:19–42). In this discussion social conditions seem to be *dei ex machina* that explain variations in party development. The right conditions lead to certain patterns of development. Without these conditions development does not occur. Such a formulation of social determinism leaves little room for the impact of political choices and the outcomes of political competition.

portive attitudes or a lack of institutional congruence? Are we not more likely to understand when and how a bureaucracy is effective by looking at the configuration of interests around it, the resources available to it and how these are employed, and the interplay of power?

The establishment of a more effective bureaucracy from either a regime's or a sector's point of view depends on the reallocation of status, wealth, and authority as well as on changes in the distribution of information and coercion. While a "functional" analyst of bureaucratic development emphasizes the beneficent systemic consequences of greater differentiation, the political economist assumes at the outset that some sectors stand to gain and some to lose. He wants to know the *net* costs and benefits for the regime and the sectors affected. Effective bureaucratic performance does not depend primarily on "mature" personalities of bureaucrats, but on the cooperation (compliance) of sectors affected by bureaucratic decisions. Generally, if powerful sectors stand to gain from establishing an effective bureaucracy, one can take root and flourish despite great "cultural backwardness." [22]

From the foregoing discussion it is clear why we think the concepts of resources and exchange improve the various approaches now current in the study of comparative politics. Without these concepts the intentional and non-predetermined nature of political activity is sidestepped. That cultural or institutional parameters exist is clear, but these set the stage for political activity. It should also be clear that they are not eternally fixed. Parameters should be understood—and measured—in terms of their impact on the political power of various regimes and sectors as these attempt to achieve goals through exchange of political resources. The centrality of resources exchanged to any analysis of politics makes the measurement of these resources a logical priority for political scientists. Yet measurement is no easy task. If it were, an effective means of dealing with it would probably have been found by now.[23]

[22] The bureaucratic empires of antiquity stand as mute exceptions to many of the generalizations made by contemporary social scientists about social and political change and development. See Eisenstadt (1965) and Wittfogel (1957).

[23] As we have indicated, a number of political scientists have approached the analysis of politics in developing countries with some terms and concepts akin to those of political economy. We would make note of the works by Apter (1964b); Binder (1965) and (1966); Frey (1963); Kilson (1964) and (1966); Levine (1965); Rosberg and Nottingham (1966); Rustow (1965) and (1966); Young (1964); and Zolberg (1964a), (1964b), and (1966). One study that has come to our attention corresponds particularly to the analytical

SOME ASSUMPTIONS OF POLITICAL ECONOMY.

Political economy posits five assumptions that simplify the problem of developing measures of resources and exchange.[24] First, we assume that political behavior and choices can basically be explained in terms of resources, all of which flow from the activities and attitudes of individuals.[25] To be sure values, norms, historical factors, random occurrences, and so forth are important elements affecting political developments, but we assume that only what is manifested within some definite time period and impinges upon political exchange requires measurement and analysis. To try to encompass all conceivable factors would make predictive analysis impossible. A second assumption we make is that political men choose and act with the intention of furthering their preferences and goals. The concern often expressed about the "irrationality" of political men we find misplaced. The "rationality" or "irrationality" of political actors becomes largely a matter of perspective, depending on the vantage point from which choices and acts are viewed. Choices constrained by resource scarcity or derived from preferences for certain kinds of allocation should be dealt with on their own terms rather than be judged "irrational" by some external standard.

modalities and concerns of political economy; see the monograph by Jaguaribe (1967) on political strategies for national development in Brazil.

Two recent articles suggest to us some ways in which statistical methods may be used to estimate some of the relationships in political economy. Sten Sparre Nilson has tried to explain periods of political stability in terms of supply and demand relationships. Most intriguing are his equations relating levels of government expenditure with votes received over time. Robert D. Putnam, using the statistical technique of path correlation, imaginatively tries to account for and predict the *propensity* of military sectors to intervene in civilian politics. See Nilson (1967) and Putnam (1967).

[24] These assumptions carry with them the problems that accompany any simplification, but all models are based on simplifications, and we wish to be quite clear about those we include in our model. Only empirical work will show whether these simplifications are productive or not.

[25] Indeed, all resources could be treated as activities if we were to consider status and legitimacy solely in terms of manifested social or political deference (apart from attitudes of esteem) and to regard information solely in terms of the act of transferring it from one person to another. Though we do not consider ourselves disciples of Bentley, we appreciate his view that "if we can get our social life stated in terms of activity and of nothing else, we have not indeed succeeded in measuring it, but we have at least reached a foundation upon which a coherent system of measurement can be built up." Bentley (1908: 202).

Third, we assume that political analysis is improved by the deliberate disaggregation of the political community in terms of sectors, an assumption that permits us to differentiate among interests and to assess the impact of these interests on the political process. Useful as some measure of "gross national power" might be, we do not choose to deal in these terms. Rather we would view and value resources from the particular perspective of a regime or sector, thus avoiding the need to construct an intersubjective and absolute standard of value. When the different flows of resources are separated and attributed to the appropriate sectors, we assume that resources will be more readily measurable than they would be if we were to treat them in the aggregate.[26] A fourth assumption is that most estimations of value can be made in marginal terms, these being easier to ascertain than the average value for a particular resource.[27] Alterations in the value of resources at the margin reflect changes in supply or demand that are themselves reasonably ascertainable.

A fifth assumption is that problems of measurement that are insoluble in the abstract will become more tractable when put in terms of comparative value, i.e., some amount of x is worth more than some amount of y to a particular regime or sector.[28] We recognize that often valuations cannot be arrived at mathematically because there will be too many unknowns. However, when estimates or approximations must be made, it will be considerably less risky to treat the value of certain consequences or probable outcomes in terms of the value preferences of a regime or sector than to weigh one value absolutely against another (or against all others).

We are mindful of Marshall's warning, cited in Chapter II, about the shortcomings of analyses measuring some factors when other factors remain unmeasured or unmeasurable. Political economy is a model of the

[26] As should be apparent, we have avoided the misleading and oversimplified distinction between "elite" and "mass" so common in social and political science. In our view this distinction does not disaggregate interests sufficiently; moreover, it glosses over the critical consequences of conflicting groups and interests within each category.

[27] This focus on marginal change can be related to some of the analytical work by Lindblom and others who stress an incremental approach to valuation of policy changes. See Lindblom (1965) and Braybrooke and Lindblom (1963). As few decisions can be made de novo, some kind of incrementalism is unavoidable. We agree with Lindblom that the value or effects of marginal changes are more easily measured than average values or affects.

[28] See Pennock (1966) for a survey of literature on calculating political values. Additive calculations of the net benefits of policy alternatives are possible to make without numerical intercession. Combinations of valued ends that would be hard to compare in the abstract can be weighed in practice.

real world, and its validity depends on its utility in evaluating and predicting the outcomes of choice. We think that the significant factors of politics have been included and integrated in the model, so that if resources can be measured and valued, predictions can be made. If useful predictions can be made, we would infer that some of the less tangible aspects of politics, such as ultimate values or psychological needs, are in effect incorporated into the analysis with resources, propensities, or other elements of the model serving as proxies.

POLITICAL MAN AND INTENTIONALITY.

We return now to the issues of motivation and the predictability of behavior in politics. It may be asked whether political actors make calculations of value as explicitly or self-consciously as our model implies they do. If they do not, how then can political scientists accurately measure political phenomena or dissect political intentions? Implicit in our discussion of political economy has been a model of "political man" that offers a behavioral guide to the study of politics. It may have seemed that our *homo politicus* was a twin of *homo economicus*, simply buying cheap and selling dear.[29] As we have often stated, the end of political activity is the attainment of goals—qualitative preferences that may often be ill-expressed or ill-achieved in quantitative terms. Political resources are, however, means for achieving this end, and as a rule we assume that having more of these means is preferable to having less. In this sense the operating assumption of maximizing behavior is useful, but it is only an approximation.[30]

[29] The simple notion that economic man buys cheap and sells dear is itself a caricature. It is more appropriate to say that in seeking to maximize his utility, economic man usually aims at maximizing his income. To the extent that money can secure goods and services yielding utility (satisfaction) and to the extent that the economic market is non-discriminatory, income maximization is a reasonably rational goal. But money cannot buy everything, as the saying goes. If, for instance, the utility from additional labor or investment is less than that from more leisure or consumption, economic man will not try to increase his income. Only to the extent that command over greater resources yields satisfactions greater than the costs of attaining them (satisfactions foregone) does economic man seek more resources.

[30] In the political market the constraints of monopolized authority and the inequality of competitors make maximization of political resources in quantitative terms less relevant as an operational rule for making political choices than the criterion of maximization is for economic decision-making. The value of resources is always equivalent to what the resources can yield in terms of preferred relationships or allocations.

Economic theory permits better prediction as persons more closely approximate the model of "economic man" in their calculations and behavior. Similarly, we would say that political economy becomes more applicable as more persons choose and act as "political men." We are not saying, however, that all men act politically or that those who do so act politically all of the time. Rather we are saying that however crudely or intuitively, it is done, enough persons understand the political process and channel their own activities and those of others accordingly to make prediction possible and refinable on the basis of the behavioral model we posit. To make predictions we would assess a sector's or regime's *resources* and its *values* as expressed in its ideology and time horizons. We would also take into account its *propensities*, its *strategies* and *tactics*, its use of available *infrastructure*, and the way in which others use these same factors to impinge on its achievement of goals. The more our understanding and measurement of these elements are improved and refined, the better the predictions that should result.

The calculation of value that persons make in the process of political exchange determines whether, all resources considered, they are "better off" with respect to some chosen time horizon or not. Whether they make such calculations explicitly or not is a moot point. Some persons use whatever resources are at their disposal as well as the resources of others whom they involve in order to gain some measure of control or influence over the use of authority. These persons are considered the most "political." But others who do not calculate explicitly nevertheless act in an "interested" manner, and it is possible to make predictions about how they will act by analyzing their resources, interests, propensities, strategies, tactics, and infrastructure, even if *they themselves* do not explicitly calculate these. It is difficult to predict the choices or actions of a man who is "uneconomic" or "apolitical." If a man has no sense of the constraints imposed by limited resources and has no hierarchy of values, his choices are random and prediction breaks down. Yet predictions of the ramifications of these choices for others in the community may still be made and verified. As economic theory has advanced, attention has had to be given to the behavior that does not correspond to the simple behavioral model. Similarly, political economy will have to consider how to deal with those who do not calculate as predictably as the model implies.

Controversy over the "rationality" of political or economic man is, we think, unresolvable. We would prefer to see the discussion recast in terms of *intention* and the wisdom of choices. To say that a political actor chooses irrationally is to argue that he desires a certain goal yet acts counter to his desire. Imperfect knowledge is part of the human condition. Little is gained by castigating as "irrational" decisions that fail to achieve desired goals because of faulty information. Neither is it useful to ascribe to prejudice, bias, optimism, or pessimism those choices that appear to thwart announced ends. Such labeling contributes nothing to an analysis of why and how what appear to be self-defeating means were chosen. Insofar as goals are spelled out, political economy attempts to find the most effective means available to achieve them. If goals are inchoate or unclear, our model cannot aid in their articulation and ranking except to estimate what the respective costs of achieving them will be. Political economy does not pass judgment on the goals of a political actor or try to specify goals for him. It strives to be an aid to calculation, but it is no substitute. The more we recognize the complexity of the ends political actors pursue, the more we realize that "rationality" is not a useful issue. The accomplishment of intentions through the reconciliation of costs and benefits is an ongoing activity and the central aim of political economy.

Political Ethics and Political Economy

Some readers may consider this book to be in the tradition of Machiavelli. The common judgment of immorality that brought his work into ill-repute may in part be responsible for turning succeeding political scientists away from the problems and arts of government. Some have turned to passing "ethical" judgments on what *should be* the consequences of government, others to describing what *have been* the consequences. Too few have concerned themselves, despite all the talk about politics being "the art of the possible," with what *could be* achieved through government. This last implies a concern with power, its uses, its costs, its consequences. We would contend that a real concern for ethics cannot avoid questions of power, and that specifying valued ends without determining the costs of their means is in its own way unethical. We concur with Spitz in his judgment that:

Short of death, there is no way to escape power. Men may bemoan some of the consequences of its possession, but possess it someone will. Joined to a good cause, power is a meritorious tool. Joined to a bad cause, power becomes an instrument of discomfort and even, perhaps, of tyranny. But power by itself is neutral; what matters is not the fact of power but its uses, and this becomes largely a problem of determining who controls whom, and for what purpose.[31]

The statesman in our model is not the Prince, though he might be one. In this book we are not giving advice on what the wielders of authority should do as much as offering a model for understanding the political process. With our model we think that the social scientist should be able to give advice on means to achieve valued ends. We are not as concerned about whether the statesman triumphs over his enemies (in many polities our sympathies would be with the "enemies") as we are with an improvement in the efficiency of the political process for achieving collective ends. We do not assume that there are certain ends on which all members of the polity agree except, of course, at the most abstract level. Rather we assume that there are collective ends on which enough persons agree to combine their resources to advance these ends through politics and government.

As we have repeatedly pointed out, political economy could serve the interests of an anti-statesman or a sector equally as well as it could serve the interests of the regime. Indeed, we might say that it is probably those who are most disadvantaged or exploited who least understand the political process, and it is they who have most need of a model of politics. It might be argued that those in the core combination do not need the illumination that political economy might provide, for they understand the political process already, at least intuitively. Sectors that have some resources and know how to use them politically are able to make the authorities take them into account and to wield some political power. We could have written this book from the perspective of the anti-statesman or a sector or a bureaucrat or a local authority. Insofar as the conception of politics we offer here has validity, it can be applied explicitly to these other perspectives, but our restricted focus on the statesman's choices has been a matter of exposition rather than a matter of ethics. For those concerned with questions of ethics, a more valid objection might be that our model posits no hierarchy of values, contains no ends, and makes no judgments other than the stipulation that political resources should not be wasted. We have carefully considered this objection, but remain unmoved. If we are to contribute to an understanding of politics in developing countries, we think that we do no service to ourselves or others by importing our own values into the model itself and imposing a logic external to the system. With the model it should be possible to impute the costs and consequences of policy

[31] Spitz (1964:1).

choices, after which ethical and intelligent judgments could then be made.

At present social scientists have the estimable task of evaluating the productivity of past or projected policy changes from the particular perspective of a leader, a party, a sector, or an individual. If some do not find this a satisfying task, they may suggest and rank a set of valued ends for a community and work out policy measures for that community that would increase welfare for the different sectors by some margin at some cost. Those political actors who value these ends and are willing to bear the cost may find such analysis a guide to policy. However, for social scientists or social philosophers to suggest ends or policies without regard to costs is in our view to be irrelevant if not irresponsible. We would have little sympathy with either the view that a social scientist should advise nobody or the view that he should advise anybody and everybody. Just as political participants have values, so too do political scientists. We would not expect political scientists to work against their own preferences, but we would hope that the intellectual tools they have to work with would be serviceable and would permit prediction and assessment of costs as well as consequences.

POLITICAL RATIONALITY.

In any discussion of ethics, the question may be raised as to what positive value we should assign to politics. The exercise of state power is often regarded as devious, distorting, or demeaning. Attention is focused on Lord Acton's caveat about power's corrupting influence. Sometimes, the argument may be made that the exercise of political power interferes with individuals' rational pursuit of valued ends in the economic and social markets; political decisions and motivations are consequently regarded as irrational. In this regard we appreciate the argument that some have made in favor of "political rationality" as a valuable and even preferable kind of calculation, not at all necessarily unethical in its moral implications.[32]

Students of ethics are correct in minimizing the importance or the rationality of efficiency or economizing as an end in itself. Efficiency has value only as a means to other ends and its value is equal to that of the ends it permits to be achieved. The political process may be seen as a

[32] This position is argued persuasively in Wildavsky (1966:307–310). Wildavsky cites with approval Paul Diesing's writings on the subject of "political rationality." See Diesing (1962).

means of achieving collectively more goals valued by individuals and groups than might be achieved without the existence of a political market. That authority may be used against the interests of some or many is beyond doubt, but that societies reap net benefits from the existence of a public realm is also evident. The ubiquity of politics and authority roles attests to these benefits.

We would recall Weber's distinction between *formal* and *substantive* rationality.[33] His analysis showed that explicit and formal calculations to determine the best means to achieve given ends (i.e., formal rationality) do not ensure that the ends will in fact be achieved (i.e., substantive rationality). Nor may the achievement of substantive ends be contingent on formal-rational choice of means.[34] We would argue that political activity with its intervention in the economic and social markets constitutes an effort to achieve collective substantive rationality at the expense of individual formal rationality, i.e., individual selection of means to achieve desired ends. If individuals with their own calculations and means cannot reach these ends, they may through the institutions of collective action approach them more closely.

The ethical justification for politics is not that politics makes government serve some "general will" or "the public interest." We would not argue, as some do of the economic market, that the political market arrives at or even necessarily tends toward some optimum level of production for satisfying human needs and wants. Rather the justification for the political market is that more needs and wants are satisfied through it than could be satisfied in its absence. The institutions of government and politics that are upheld by political rationality make feasible the achievement through collective action of ends that could not be reached privately.

Some sectors may be disadvantaged or exploited through the political process. Some may desire that the extent of the public realm be reduced. However, the question that causes political debate and conflict is not *whether* government should exist, but *how much* government, and government serving *what ends?* The ethical issue is practically and ultimately not the use of power but to what uses power shall be put. Similarly, debates as to "whether" there should be economic or social planning serve no useful purpose. There is already political intervention in the economic and social

---

[33] See Weber (1947:35ff.).

[34] The implications of this Weberian distinction for economic and social planning have been explored by Harry Eckstein with empirical reference to the difficulties of planning the British National Health Service. See Eckstein (1956).

markets, if only for the purpose of upholding existing allocations. A legitimate consideration is whether there should be more intervention or not. Clearly there is no question as to whether there should be political planning or not. The issue is how we may improve the substantive political rationality of those making or influencing choice.

ETHICS AS CHOICE.

The centuries-old and frequently acrimonious debate about man's freedom of will has often obscured the issue of choice and its consequences, an issue now raised so pointedly by the various schools of existentialist thought. Those who subscribe to the position of radical freedom of will or radical determinism of choice will find little of interest in political economy. However, those who are struggling to discover a position between the extremes may find our model of choice within constraints suggestive.

Perhaps we can delineate the realm of ethics by referring to theological notions of what constitutes "morality." According to these notions, morality is conceivable only if man is free and able to act or choose immorally. If man were perfect, he would not choose wrongly or immorally, so ethics would not be at issue. If man's future were predetermined, he could not really choose, so again ethical considerations would be irrelevant. If there were no scarcity, there would be no need for choice. Indeed, man's imperfection or selfishness may derive from the condition of scarcity. All this is to say that ethical concerns can be raised only where men are able to and must make choices. Thus we see a juncture between the study of ethics on the one hand, and the study of social science or policy research on the other. Both are ultimately, if not always immediately, concerned with human choice under conditions of scarcity. Although often unclear about it, both deal with the costs and consequences of choice. If social science can clarify what these costs and consequences are, lay or professional students of ethics can better make judgments about their value.

Such an assertion raises the age-old question of what shall be the relation of men of knowledge to men of power. If, as we believe, the human condition is one in which men choose with certain degrees of freedom, one of the tasks of the men of knowledge may be to increase the degrees of freedom for any or all who must make choices. Finding new options with greater results for the same cost, or with the same results for less cost, is no small contribution. To identify these options should remain the task of social scientists, and this task will be facilitated if social scientists increase their understanding of the phenomena with which they deal. Too often it seems that social scientists and students of ethics concern themselves with what Weber might have called "formal ethics." As with formal rationality, formal ethics would suggest that if a man's intention is good or pure, he is not responsible for the result; but a formally ethical act or choice satisfies only the actor or chooser, and then perhaps not even him. It has been said, though we know not by whom, that it may take the work of ten men to undo the harm done by a man who was *only* good.

Weber has suggested the distinction between the "ethic of ultimate ends" and the "ethic of responsibility." The believer in the former, he says, "feels 'responsible' only for seeing to it that the flame of pure intentions is not quenched." But, he cautions, "no ethics in the world can dodge the fact that in numerous instances the attainment of 'good' ends is bound to the fact that one must be willing to pay the price of using morally dubious means or at least dangerous ones—and facing the possibility or even the probability of evil ramifications. From no ethics in the world can it be concluded when and to what extent the ethically good purpose 'justifies' the ethically dangerous means and ramifications." [35] We are in no position to decide for others what ethical standards of judgment to adopt. Our concern with political economy has been motivated by the all too frequent gap between intentions and results. Good intentions in themselves do not make acts and choices ethical. Unintended consequences are as much a part of the results of acts and choices as are the intended ones. Enabling persons and groups better to achieve intended results should help to orient ethical judgments toward substantive rather than formal criteria.

Political economy does not set political ends, nor does it clarify ends in the sense of ordering or ranking them. What it does attempt is to facilitate the calculation of costs. Political choices and political acts are not "free"; neither are they determined. But we are less concerned with those who mistakenly advocate a determinist theory of politics. Their mistake is less seductive than the error of those who suggest that politics is only a matter of will. Those who ignore the costs of politics mislead; ultimate irresponsibility is theirs. More important, they are in no position to understand or to contribute to the productivity of politics. It has been our hope to show social scientists the productivity of politics and especially to encourage them to contribute to the realization of public purposes. It is our intention to attempt such a contribution ourselves. May the new generation of social scientists, wherever they may be, find intellectual excitement and rewards in such engagement with public problems and public choices.

[35] Weber (1958:120–128).

REFERENCES CITED

Abernethy, David B.
  1969 The Political Dilemma of Popular Education: An African Case.
Afrifa, Colonel A. A.
  1966 The Ghana Coup, 24th February 1966.
Alexander, Major-General H. T.
  1965 African Tightrope: My Two Years as Nkrumah's Chief of Staff.
Almond, Gabriel A.
  1960 A Functional Approach to Comparative Politics. In: The Politics
        of the Developing Areas, Gabriel A. Almond and James S. Coleman,
        eds., 1960:3–64.
  1966 Political Theory and Political Science. American Political Science
        Review 60 (December, 1966):869–879.
Almond, Gabriel A. and James S. Coleman, eds.
  1960 The Politics of the Developing Areas.
Almond, Gabriel A. and G. Bingham Powell, Jr.
  1966 Comparative Politics: A Developmental Approach.
Almond, Gabriel A. and Sidney Verba
  1963 The Civic Culture: Political Attitudes and Democracy in Five
        Nations.
Apter, David E.
  1961 The Political Kingdom in Uganda: A Study in Bureaucratic Nation-
        alism.
  1962 Some Reflections on the Role of a Political Opposition in New
        Nations. Comparative Studies in Society and History 4 (January,
        1962):154–168.
  1963a Ghana in Transition.
  1963b Non-Western Government and Politics. In: Comparative Politics:
        A Reader, Harry Eckstein and David E. Apter, eds., 1963:647–656.
  1963c The Role of the Political Opposition in New Nations. In: Africa:
        The Dynamics of Change, Herbert Passin and K. A. B. Jones-
        Quartey, eds., 1963:56–70.
  1964a Introduction: Ideology and Discontent. In: Ideology and Dis-
        content, David E. Apter, ed., 1964:15–46.
  1964b Ghana. In: Political Parties and National Integration in Tropical
        Africa, James S. Coleman and Carl Rosberg, eds., 1964:259–315.
  1965 The Politics of Modernization.

Bachrach, P. and M. S. Baratz
　1962　Two Faces of Power. *American Political Science Review* 56 (December, 1962):947–952.
Ballard, John A.
　1966　Four Equatorial States. In: *National Unity and Regionalism in Eight African States*, Gwendolyn M. Carter, ed., 1966:231–327.
Banfield, Edward C.
　1958　*The Moral Basis of a Backward Society.*
　1961　*Political Influence.*
Bayley, David
　1966　The Effects of Corruption in a Developing Nation. *Western Political Quarterly* 19 (December, 1966):719–732.
Bell, Daniel
　1960　*The End of Ideology.*
Bendix, Reinhard
　1960　Social Stratification and the Political Community. *Archives européennes de sociologie* 1 (1960:2):181–210.
　1964　*Nation Building and Citizenship.*
Bentley, Arthur
　1908　*The Process of Government.*
Berger, Morroe
　1957　*Bureaucracy and Society in Modern Egypt: A Study of the Higher Civil Service.*
Bernhard, Richard C.
　1960　Mathematics, Models, and Language in the Social Sciences. National Institute of Social and Behavioral Science, *Symposia Studies Series*, No. 3:1–5.
Binder, Leonard
　1965　Egypt: The Integrative Revolution. In: *Political Culture and Political Development*, Lucien W. Pye and Sidney Verba, eds., 1965:396–449.
　1966　Political Recruitment and Participation in Egypt. In: *Political Parties and Political Development*, Joseph LaPalombara and Myron Weiner, eds., 1966:217–240.
Black, Cyril E.
　1966　*The Dynamics of Modernization: A Study in Comparative History.*
Blanksten, George
　1959　Political Groups in Latin America. *American Political Science Review* 53 (March, 1959):106–127.
Blau, Peter M.
　1964　*Exchange and Power in Social Life.*
Bonilla, Frank
　1965　Brazil. In: *Education and Political Development*, James S. Coleman, ed., 1965:195–221.
Boulding, Kenneth
　1961　Knowledge as a Commodity. National Institute of Social and Behavioral Science, *Symposia Studies Series*, No. 11:1–6.
　1962　An Economist's View: A Review of *Social Behavior: Its Elementary Forms* by George C. Homans. *American Journal of Sociology* 67 (January, 1962):458–461.

1966   *The Impact of the Social Sciences.*

Braibanti, Ralph
1962   Reflections on Bureaucratic Corruption, *Public Administration* 40
(Winter, 1962):365-371.

Braybrooke, David and Charles Lindblom
1963   *A Strategy of Decision: Policy Evaluation as a Social Process.*

Bredemeier, Harry C. and Richard M. Stephenson
1962   *The Analysis of Social Systems.*

Bretton, Henry
1962   *Power and Stability in Nigeria: The Politics of Decolonization.*
1966   *The Rise and Fall of Kwame Nkrumah: A Study in Personal Rule
in Africa.*

Buchanan, James M. and Gordon Tulloch
1962   *The Calculus of Consent: Logical Foundations of Constitutional
Democracy.*

Cambridge University, Overseas Study Committee
1961   *Summer Conference on Local Government in Africa.*

Chorley, Katharine
1943   *Armies and the Art of Revolution.*

Ciriacy-Wantrup, S. V.
1952   *Resource Conservation: Economics and Policies.*

Clark, Terry, ed.
1968   *Community Power and Community Structure.*

Coleman, James S., ed.
1965   *Education and Political Development.*

Coleman, James S.
1967   The Resurrection of Political Economy. *Mawazo* 1 (June, 1967):
31-40.

Coser, Lewis A.
1956   *The Functions of Social Conflict.*

Curry, R. L., Jr. and L. L. Wade
1968   *A Theory of Political Exchange: Economic Reasoning in Political
Analysis.*

Dahl, Robert A.
1956   *A Preface to Democratic Theory.*
1957   The Concept of Power. *Behavorial Science* 2 (July, 1957):201-215.
1961   *Who Governs? Democracy and Power in an American City.*
1963   *Modern Political Analysis.*

Dahl, Robert A. and Charles A. Lindblom
1953   *Politics, Economics, and Welfare: Planning and Politico-economic
Systems Resolved into Basic Social Science Processes.*

Dahrendorf, Rolf
1958   Out of Utopia: Toward a Reorientation of Sociological Analysis.
American Journal of Sociology 64 (September, 1958):115-127.
1959   *Class and Class Conflict in Industrial Society.*

Deutsch, Karl W.
1954   Cracks in the Monolith: Possibilities and Patterns of Disintegration
in Totalitarian Systems. In: *Totalitarianism*, Carl J. Friedrich, ed.,
1954:308-333.

1961   Social Mobilization and Political Development. *American Political Science Review* 55 (September, 1961):493–514.
1963   *The Nerves of Government: Models of Political Communication and Control.*

Deutsch, Karl W. and William J. Foltz, eds.
1963   *Nation Building.*

Diamant, Alfred
1966   Political Development: Approaches to Theory and Strategy. In: *Approaches to Development: Politics, Administration and Change,* John D. Montgomery and William J. Siffin, eds., 1966:15–47.

Diesing, Paul
1962   *Reason in Society: Five Types of Decisions and Their Social Conditions.*

Dobyns, Henry F.
1965   The Strategic Importance of Enlightenment and Skill for Power. *American Behavioral Scientist* 8 (March, 1965):23–27.

Doughty, Paul C.
1965   The Interrelationship of Power, Respect, Affection, and Rectitude in Vicos. *American Behavioral Scientist* 8 (March, 1965):13–17.

Downs, Anthony
1957   *An Economic Theory of Democracy.*

Draper, Theodore
1965   The Dominican Crisis: A Case Study in American Policy. *Commentary* 40 (December, 1965):33–68.

Dror, Yehezkel
1964   Muddling Through: "Science" or Inertia? *Public Administration Review* 24 (September, 1964):153–157.
1967   Policy Analysts: A New Professional Role in Government Service. *Public Administration Review* 27 (September, 1967): 197–203.

Dwivedi, O. P.
1967   Bureaucratic Corruption in Developing Countries. *Asian Survey* 7 (April, 1967):245–253.

Easton, David
1953   *The Political System: An Inquiry into the State of Political Science.*
1957   An Approach to the Analysis of Political Systems. *World Politics* 9 (April, 1957):383–400.
1965   *A Systems Analysis of Political Life.*

Eckstein, Harry
1956   Planning: A Case Study. *Political Studies* 4 (February, 1956):46–60.

Eckstein, Harry and David E. Apter, eds.
1963   *Comparative Politics: A Reader.*

Edelman, Murray
1964   *The Symbolic Uses of Politics.*

Eisenstadt, S. N.
1961   *Essays on Sociological Aspects of Political and Economic Development.*
1963a   *The Political Systems of Empires.*

1963b   Problems of Emerging Bureaucracies in Developing Areas and
New States. In: *Industrialization and Society*, Bert F. Hoselitz and
Wilbert E. Moore, eds., 1963:159–174.

1963c   Bureaucracy and Political Development. In: *Bureaucracy and Political Development*, Joseph LaPalombara, ed., 1963:96–119.

Eldersveld, S. J.
1965   Bureaucratic Contact with the Public in India, *Indian Journal of
Public Administration* 11 (April–June, 1965):216–235.

Emerson, Rupert
1954   Paradoxes of Asian Nationalism. *Far Eastern Quarterly* 13 (February,
1954):131–142.

1960   *From Empire to Nation: The Rise to Self-assertion of Asian and
African Peoples.*

1963   Nation Building in Africa. In: *Nation Building*, Karl W. Deutsch
and William J. Foltz, eds., 1963:95–116.

1966   Parties and National Integration in Africa. In: *Political Parties and
Political Development*, Joseph LaPalombara and Myron Weiner,
eds., 1966:267–302.

Esman, Milton J.
1966   The Politics of Development Administration. In: *Approaches to
Development: Politics, Administration and Change*, John D. Montgomery and William J. Siffin, eds., 1966:59–112.

Etzioni, Amitai
1960   *A Comparative Analysis of Complex Organizations on Power, Involvement and Their Correlates.*

1966   On the Process of Making Decisions. *Science* 152 (May 6,
1966):746–747.

Fagen, Richard R.
1966   *Politics and Communication.*

Fainsod, Merle
1963   Bureaucracy and Modernization: The Russian and Soviet Case. In:
Bureaucracy and Political Development, Joseph LaPalombara, ed.,
1963:233–267.

Fairweather, George
1966   *Methods for Experimental Social Innovation.*

Fallers, Lloyd A.
1959   Despotism, Status Culture, and Social Mobility in an African Kingdom. *Comparative Studies in Sociology and History* 2 (October,
1959):11–32.

1963   Equality, Modernity and Democracy in the New States. In: *Old
Societies and New States*, Clifford Geertz, ed., 1963:158–219.

1964   Social Stratification and Economic Progress. In: *Economic Transition in Africa*, Melville Herskovits and Mitchell Harwitz, eds.,
1964:113–130.

Fesler, James W.
1962   The Political Role of Field Administration. In: *Papers in Comparative Administration*, Ferrel Heady and Sybil Stokes, eds., 1962:117–
144.

Finer, S. F.
  1962   The Man on Horseback: The Role of the Military in Politics.
Fischer, Joseph
  1965   Indonesia. In: Education and Political Development, James S. Cole-
         man, ed., 1965:92–122.
Foltz, W. J.
  1963   Building the Newest Nations: Short-run Strategies and Long-run
         Problems. In: Nation Building, Karl W. Deutsch and William J.
         Foltz, eds., 1963:117–131.
Foster, George
  1962   Traditional Cultures and the Impact of Technological Change.
Frey, Frederick W.
  1963   Political Development, Power, and Communications in Turkey. In:
         Communications and Political Development, Lucien W. Pye, ed.,
         1963:298–326.
Friedrich, Carl J.
  1950   Constitutional Government and Democracy.
  1963   Man and His Government: An Empirical Theory of Politics.
Geertz, Clifford
  1963   The Integrative Revolution. In: Old Societies and New States,
         Clifford Geertz, ed., 1963:105–157.
  1964   Ideology as a Cultural System. In: Ideology and Discontent, David
         E. Apter, ed., 1964:47–76.
Ghana, Central Bureau of Statistics
  1966   Economic Survey, 1965
Glassburner, Bruce
  1962   Economic Policy-making in Indonesia, 1950–57. Economic Develop-
         ment and Cultural Change 10 (January, 1962):113–133.
  1963   The Role of Economic Interests in the Indonesian Politics of the
         1950's: A Rejoinder. Economic Development and Cultural Change
         11 (January, 1963):177–180.
Green, Reginald H.
  1965   Four African Development Plans: Ghana, Kenya, Nigeria, and
         Tanzania. Journal of Modern African Studies 3 (1965:2):249–279.
Greenstone, J. David
  1966   Corruption and Self-interest in Kampala and Nairobi. Comparative
         Studies in Society and History 7 (January, 1966):199–210.
Hagen, Everett E.
  1960   The Entrepreneur as Rebel Against Traditional Society. Human
         Organization 19 (Winter, 1960–61):185–187.
  1962a On the Theory of Social Change.
  1962b Discussion of "The Development of Entrepreneurship" by Gustav
         F. Papanek. American Economic Review 52 (May, 1962):59–61.
Harbison, Frederick and Charles A. Myers
  1964   Education, Manpower, and Economic Growth: Strategies for Human
         Resource Development.
Harsanyi, John C.
  1962   Measurement of Social Power for N-Person Reciprocal Power Situa-
         tions. Behavioral Science 7 (January, 1962):81–91.

Hirschman, Albert O.
  1958   *The Strategy of Economic Development.*
  1962   Comments. In: *Development of the Emerging Countries: An Agenda for Research*, Robert E. Asher, et. al., 1962:37–44.
  1963   *Journeys Toward Progress: Studies of Economic Policy-making in Latin America.*
Hobbes, Thomas
  1862   *The English Works of Thomas Hobbes*, Vol. 6, Sir William Molesworth, ed.
Holmberg, Allan
  1960   Changing Community Attitudes and Values in Peru: A Case Study in Guided Change. In: *Social Change in Latin America Today*, Richard N. Adams, ed., 1960:63–107.
  1965   The Changing Values and Institutions of Vicos in the Context of National Development. *American Behavioral Scientist* 8 (March, 1965):3–8.
Holt, Robert T. and John E. Turner
  1966   *The Political Basis of Economic Development: An Exploration in Comparative Political Analysis.*
Homans, George C.
  1950   *The Human Group.*
  1957   Social Behavior as Exchange. *American Journal of Sociology* 63 (May, 1958):597–606.
  1961   *Social Behavior: Its Elementary Forms.*
Hoselitz, Bert F. and Ann R. Willner
  1962   Economic Development, Political Strategies and American Aid. In: *The Revolution in World Politics*, Morton A. Kaplan, ed., 1962:355–380.
Houthakker, H. S.
  1965   On Some Determinants of Saving in Developed and Underdeveloped Countries. In: *Problems in Economic Development*, E. A. G. Robinson, ed., 1965:212–224.
Hunter, Floyd
  1953   *Community Power Structure.*
Huntington, Samuel P.
  1962   Patterns of Violence in World Politics. In: *Changing Patterns of Military Politics*, Samuel P. Huntington, ed., 1962:17–50.
  1965   Political Development and Political Decay. *World Politics* 17 (April, 1965):384–430.
Ilchman, Warren F.
  1967   *New Time in Old Clocks: Productivity, Development, and Comparative Public Administration* (Comparative Administration Group Occasional Paper).
  1968   The Unproductive Study of Productivity: Public Administration in Developing Nations. *Comparative Political Studies* 1 (July, 1968): 227–249.
  in
  press   Productivity, Administrative Reform, and Anti-Politics: Dilemmas for Developing States. In: *Theoretical Problems of Administrative Reform in Developing Countries*, Ralph Braibanti, ed.

Ilchman, Warren F. and Ravindra C. Bhargava
1966 Balanced Thought and Economic Growth. *Economic Development and Cultural Change* 13 (July, 1966):385–399.
Ilchman, Warren F. and Todd R. LaPorte
in press *Comparative Administration: Synthesis and Analysis.*
Jacobson, Norman
1964 Causality and Time in Political Process: A Speculation. *American Political Science Review* 58 (March, 1964):15–22.
Jaguaribe, Hélio
1967 Political Strategies of National Development in Brazil. *Studies in Comparative International Development*, Vol. III, No. 2.
Janowitz, Morris
1964 *The Military in the Political Development of New Nations.*
Johnson, Chalmers A.
1964 *Revolution and the Social System.*
Johnson, John J., ed.
1962 *The Role of the Military in Underdeveloped Countries.*
Katz, E. and P. Lazarsfeld
1955 *Personal Influence.*
Kilson, Martin
1964 Sierra Leone. In: *Political Parties and National Integration in Tropical Africa*, James S. Coleman and Carl G. Rosberg, eds., 1964:90–131.
1966 *Political Change in a West African State: A Study of the Modernization Process in Sierra Leone.*
Kunkel, John
1961 Economic Autonomy and Social Change in Mexican Villages. *Economic Development and Cultural Change* 10 (October, 1961):51–63.
Lamont, W. D.
1955 *The Value Judgment.*
LaPalombara, Joseph, ed.
1963a *Bureaucracy and Political Development.*
LaPalombara, Joseph
1963b An Overview of Bureaucracy and Political Development. In: *Bureaucracy and Political Development*, Joseph LaPalombara, ed., 1963:3–33.
1963c Bureaucracy and Political Development: Notes, Queries, and Dilemmas. In: *Bureaucracy and Political Development*, Joseph LaPalombara, ed., 1963:34–61.
1966 Decline of Ideology: A Dissent and an Interpretation. *American Political Science Review* 60 (March, 1966):5–16.
LaPalombara, Joseph and Myron Weiner, eds.
1966 *Political Parties and Political Development.*
Lasswell, Harold
1936 *Politics: Who Gets What, When, How.*
1956 The Political Science of Science. *American Political Science Review* 50 (December, 1956):961–979.
1965a The Emerging Policy Sciences of Development: The Vicos Case. *American Behavioral Scientist* 8 (March, 1965):28–33.

1965b   The Policy Sciences of Development. *World Politics* 17 (January, 1965):286–309.

Leff, Nathaniel
1964   Economic Development Through Bureaucratic Corruption. *American Behavioral Scientist* 8 (November, 1964):8–14.

Lens, Sidney
1966   Editorial. *Liberation* 11 (September, 1966):3–4.

Lenski, Gerhard E.
1966   *Power and Privilege: A Theory of Social Stratification.*

Lepawsky, Albert
1957   Revolution and Reform in Bolivia: A Study of the Root and Branch of Public Administration in a Developing Country. In: *Toward the Comparative Study of Public Administration*, William J. Siffin, ed., 1957:219–252.

Lerner, Daniel
1958   *The Passing of Traditional Society: Modernizing the Middle East.*
1963   Toward a Communication Theory of Modernization. In: *Communications and Political Development*, Lucien W. Pye, ed., 1963:327–350.

Lerner, Daniel and Harold Lasswell, eds.
1950   *The Policy Sciences.*

LeVine, Robert
1963   Political Socialization and Cultural Change. In: *Old Societies and New States*, Clifford Geertz, ed., 1963:280–304.

Levine, Donald
1965   Ethiopia: Identity, Authority, and Realism. In: *Political Culture and Political Development*, Lucien W. Pye and Sidney Verba, eds., 1965:245–281.

Levy, Marion J., Jr.
1952   *The Structure of Society.*
1966   *Modernization and the Structure of Societies.*

Lewis, W. Arthur
1949   *The Principles of Economic Planning.*
1954a   Economic Development with Unlimited Supplies of Labor. *The Manchester School*, May, 1954. Reprinted in *The Economics of Underdevelopment*, A. N. Agarwala and S. P. Singh, eds., 1963:400–449.
1954b   Thoughts on Land Settlement. *Journal of Agricultural Economics* 11 (June, 1954):3–11.
1965   *Politics in West Africa.*
1966   *Development Planning: The Essentials of Economic Policy.*

Leys, Colin
1965   What is the Problem About Corruption? *Journal of Modern African Studies* 3 (August, 1965):215–230.

Liebenow, J. Gus
1956   Responses to Planned Political Change in a Tanganyikan Tribal Group. *American Political Science Review* 50 (June, 1956):442–466.

Lindblom, Charles
   1958 Policy Analysis. *American Economic Review* 48 (June, 1958):298–312.
   1959 The Science of "Muddling Through." *Public Administration Review* 19 (Spring, 1959):79–88.
   1965 *The Intelligence of Democracy: Decision-making Through Mutual Adjustment.*
Lipset, S. M.
   1960 *Political Man: The Social Bases of Politics.*
March, James G.
   1965 An Introduction to the Theory and Measurement of Influence. *American Political Science Review* 49 (June, 1955):431–451.
   1966 The Power of Power. In: *Varieties of Political Theory*, David Easton, ed., 1966:39–70.
March, James G. and Herbert A. Simon
   1958 *Organizations.*
Marshall, T. H.
   1965 *Class, Citizenship and Social Development.*
Matossian, Mary
   1958 Ideologies of Delayed Industrialization: Some Tensions and Ambiguities. *Economic Development and Cultural Change* 6 (April, 1958):217–228.
Mazrui, A. A. and Donald Rothchild
   1967 The Soldier and the State in East Africa: Some Theoretical Conclusions on the Army Mutinies of 1964. *Western Political Quarterly* 20 (March, 1967):82–96.
McClelland, David
   1961 *The Achieving Society.*
McClosky, Herbert and John E. Turner
   1960 *The Soviet Dictatorship.*
Mills, C. Wright
   1956 *The Power Elite.*
Mitchell, William C.
   1958 The Polity and Society: A Structural-Functional Analysis. *Midwest Journal of Political Science* 2 (November, 1958):403–420.
   1967 The Shape of Political Theory to Come: From Political Sociology to Political Economy. *American Behavioral Scientist* 11 (November–December, 1967):8–20.
Mosel, James H.
   1963 Communications Patterns and Political Socialization in Transitional Thailand. In: *Communications and Political Development*, Lucien W. Pye, ed., 1963:184–228.
Mosher, Frederick C.
   1954 *Program Budgeting.*
Mouly, J.
   1966 The Young Pioneers Movement in the Central African Republic. *International Labor Review* 93 (January, 1966):19–28.

Nilson, Sten Sparre
  1967   Measures and Models in the Study of Stability. *World Politics* 20 (October, 1967):1–29.
Nkrumah, Kwame
  1968   *Dark Days in Ghana.*
Nurkse, Ragnar
  1957   *Problems of Capital Formation in Underdeveloped Countries.*
Nye, J. S.
  1967   Corruption and Political Development: A Cost-Benefit Analysis. *American Political Science Review* 61 (June, 1967):417–427.
Olson, Mancur, Jr.
  1963   Rapid Economic Growth as a Destabilizing Force. *Journal of Economic History* 23 (December, 1963):529–552.
  1965   *The Logic of Collective Action: Public Goods and the Theory of Groups.*
Paige, Glenn D.
  1966   The Rediscovery of Politics. In: *Approaches to Development: Politics, Administration and Change,* John D. Montgomery and William J. Siffin, eds., 1966:49–58.
Papanek, Gustav F.
  1962   The Development of Entrepreneurship. *American Economic Review* 52 (May, 1962):46–58.
Parsons, Talcott
  1951   *The Social System.*
  1954   *Essays in Sociological Theory* (revised edition).
  1956   Suggestions for a Sociological Approach to the Theory of Organizations. *Administrative Science Quarterly* 1 (June and September, 1956):63–85, 225–239
  1957   The Distribution of Power in American Society. *World Politics* 10 (October, 1957):123–143.
  1964   Some Reflections on the Place of Force in Social Process. In: *Internal War: Problems and Approaches,* Harry Eckstein, ed., 1964:33–70.
  1966   The Political Aspect of Social Structure and Process. In: *Varieties of Political Theory,* David Easton, ed., 1966:71–112.
Parsons, Talcott and Edward A. Shils, eds.
  1951   *Toward A General Theory of Action.*
Parsons, Talcott and Neil J. Smelser
  1956   *Economy and Society: A Study in the Integration of Economic and Social Theory.*
Passin, Herbert
  1963   Writer and Journalist in Transitional Society. In: *Communications and Political Development,* Lucien W. Pye, ed., 1963:82–123.
  1965   Japan. In: *Education and Political Development,* James S. Coleman, ed., 1965:272–312
Patch, Richard W.
  1960   Bolivia: U.S. Assistance in a Revolutionary Setting. In: *Social Change in Latin America,* Richard N. Adams, ed., 1960:108–176.

Payne, James L.
  1965a *Labor and Politics in Peru: The System of Political Bargaining*
  1965b Peru: The Politics of Structured Violence. *Journal of Politics* 27
         (May, 1965):362–374.
Peacock, Alan T. and Jack Wiseman
  1961 *The Growth of Public Expenditures in the United Kingdom.*
Pennock, Roland
  1966 Political Development, Political Systems, and Political Goods. *World
         Politics* 18 (April, 1966):415–434.
Petras, James
  1966 The Dominican Republic: Revolution and Restoration. *Liberation*
         11 (September, 1966):5–11, 38–39.
Pfaff, Richard
  1963 Disengagement from Traditionalism in Turkey and Iran. *Western
         Political Quarterly* 16 (March, 1963):79–98.
Platt, J. R.
  1964 Strong Inference. *Science* 146 (October 16, 1964):347–352.
Pool, Ithiel de Sola
  1963a The Role of Communication in the Process of Modernization and
         Technological Change. In: *Industralization and Society*, Bert F.
         Hoselitz and Wilbert E. Moore, eds., 1963:279–295.
  1963b The Mass Media and Politics in the Modernization Process. In:
         Communications and Political Development, Lucien W. Pye, ed.,
         1963:234–253.
Putnam, Robert D
  1967 Toward Explaining Military Intervention in Latin American Politics.
         World Politics 20 (October, 1967):83–110.
Pye, Lucien W., ed.
  1963 *Communications and Political Development.*
Pye, Lucien W.
  1961 Armies in the Process of Political Modernization. *Archives euro-
         péennes de sociologie* 2 (1960:1):82–92.
  1962 *Politics, Personality and Nation Building: Burma's Search for Identity.*
Pye, Lucien W. and Sidney Verba, eds.
  1965 *Political Culture and Political Development.*
Redfield, Robert
  1950 *The Village That Chose Progress: Chan Kom Revisited.*
Richards, A. I
  1959 *East African Chiefs: A Study of Political Development in Some
         Uganda and Tanganyika Tribes.*
Riggs, Fred
  1957 Agraria and Industria. In: *Toward A Comparative Study of Public
         Administration*, William J. Siffin, ed., 1957:23–116.
  1963 Bureaucrats and Political Development: A Paradoxical View. In:
         Bureaucracy and Political Development, Joseph LaPalombara, ed.,
         1963:120–167.
  1964 *Administration in Developing Countries: The Theory of Prismatic
         Society.*

1968   The Dialectics of Developmental Conflict. *Comparative Political Studies* 1 (July, 1968):197–226.

Riker, William A.
1962   *The Theory of Political Coalitions.*

Rokkan, Stein
1966   Electoral Mobilization, Party Competition and National Integration. In: *Political Parties and Political Development*, Joseph LaPalombara and Myron Weiner, eds., 1966:241–266.

Rosberg, Carl G. and John Nottingham
1966   *The Myth of the Mau Mau: Nationalism in Kenya.*

Rosenstein-Rodan, Paul
1943   Problems of Industrialization of Eastern and Southeastern Europe. *The Economic Journal* (June–September, 1943). Reprinted in *The Economics of Underdevelopment*, A. N. Agarwala and S. P. Singh, eds., 1963:245–255.

Rossillion, C.
1966   Civic Service and Community Works in Mali. *International Labor Review* 93 (January, 1966):50–65.

Rudolph, Lloyd I.
1965   The Modernity of Tradition: The Democratic Incarnation of Caste in India. *American Political Science Review* 59 (December, 1965): 975–989.

Rustow, Dankwart A.
1963   The Military in Middle Eastern Society and Politics. In: *The Military in the Middle East: Problems in Society and Government*, S. N. Fisher, ed., 1963:3–20.
1965   Turkey: The Modernity of Tradition. In: *Political Culture and Political Development*, Lucien W. Pye and Sidney Verba, eds., 1965:171–198.
1966   The Development of Parties in Turkey. In: *Political Parties and Political Development*, Joseph LaPalombara and Myron Weiner, eds., 1966:107–133.

Sakata, Yoshio and J. W. Hall
1956   The Motivation of Political Leadership in the Meiji Restoration. *Journal of Asian Studies* 16 (November, 1956):31–50.

Sartori, Giovanni
1966   European Political Parties: The Case of Polarized Pluralism. In: *Political Parties and Political Development*, Joseph LaPalombara and Myron Weiner, eds., 1966:137–176.

Scalapino, Robert A.
1964   Ideology and Modernization: The Japanese Case. In: *Ideology and Discontent*, David E. Apter, ed., 1964:93–127.

Schmidt, Hans O.
1962   Foreign Capital and Social Conflict in Indonesia, 1950–1958. *Economic Development and Cultural Change* 10 (April, 1962):284–293.

Schramm, Wilbur
1963   Communication Development and the Development Process. In:

Communications and Political Development, Lucien W. Pye, ed., 1963:30–57.

Schultz, Theodore W.
  1961 Investment in Human Capital. *American Economic Review* 51 (March, 1961):1–17.

Scott, Robert E.
  1965 Mexico: The Established Revolution. In: *Political Culture and Political Development*, Lucien W. Pye and Sidney Verba, eds., 1965:330–395.
  1966 Political Parties and Policy-making in Latin America. In: *Political Parties and Political Development*, Joseph LaPalombara and Myron Weiner, eds., 1966:331–368.

Selznick, Philip
  1949 *TVA and the Grass Roots: A Study in the Sociology of Formal Organization.*

Shils, Edward A.
  1961 *Political Development in New States.*

Sibley, Mulford Q., ed.
  1963 *The Quiet Battle: Writings on the Theory and Practice of Non-Violent Resistance.*

Sklar, Richard L.
  1965 Contradictions in the Nigerian Political System. *Journal of Modern African Studies* 3 (1965:2):201–213.

Smythe, Hugh H. and Mabel M. Smythe
  1960 *The New Nigerian Elite.*

Spengler, Joseph J.
  1963 Bureaucracy and Economic Development. In: *Bureaucracy and Political Development*, Joseph LaPalombara, ed., 1963:199–232.

Spitz, David
  1964 *Essays in the Liberal Idea of Freedom.*

Stinchcombe, Arthur L.
  1965 Social Structures and Organizations. In: *Handbook of Organization*, James G. March, ed., 1965:142–193.

Tocqueville, A. H. D. de
  1955 *The Old Regime and the French Revolution.*

Truman, David B.
  1951 *The Governmental Process.*

Tussman, Joseph
  1960 *Obligation and the Body Politic.*

Uphoff, Norman T. and Warren F. Ilchman
  1968 *The Time Dimension in Institution Building.* Inter-University Research Program in Institution Building.

van de Kroef, Justin
  1955 Economic Development in Indonesia: Some Social and Cultural Impediments. *Economic Development and Cultural Change* 4 (January, 1956):116–133.

Vasquez, Mario C.
  1965 The Interplay Between Power and Wealth. *American Behavioral Scientist* 8 (March, 1965):9–12.

Waldo, Dwight
 1948 *The Administrative State: A Study of the Political Theory of American Public Administration.*
Wallerstein, Immanuel
 1966 The Decline of the Party in Single-Party African States. In: *Political Parties and Political Development*, Joseph LaPalombara and Myron Weiner, eds., 1966:201–214.
Ward, Robert E.
 1965 Japan: The Continuity of Modernization. In: *Political Culture and Political Development*, Lucien W. Pye and Sidney Verba, eds., 1965:27–82.
Ward, Robert E. and Dankwart A. Rustow, eds.
 1964 *Political Modernization in Japan and Turkey.*
Waterston, Albert
 1965 *Development Planning: Lessons of Experience.*
Weber, Max
 1947 *The Theory of Social and Economic Organization*, translated by A. M. Henderson and Talcott Parsons.
 1958 Politics as a Vocation. In: *From Max Weber: Essays in Sociology*, translated and edited by H. H. Gerth and C. Wright Mills, 1958:77–128.
Weiner, Myron
 1965 India: Two Political Cultures. In: *Political Culture and Political Development*, Lucien W. Pye and Sidney Verba, eds., 1965:199–244.
Whitaker, C. S.
 1967 A Dysrhythmic Process of Political Change. *World Politics* 19 (January, 1967):190–217.
Wildavsky, Aaron
 1964 *The Politics of the Budgetary Process.*
 1965 Private Markets and Public Arenas. *American Behavioral Scientist* 9 (September, 1965):33–37.
 1966 The Political Economy of Efficiency: Cost-Benefit Analysis, Systems Analysis, and Program Budgeting. *Public Administration Review* 26 (December, 1966):292–310.
Wilkie, James W
 1967 *The Mexican Revolution: Federal Expenditure and Social Change Since 1910.*
Wint, Guy
 1960 The 1958 Revolution in Pakistan. In: *South Asian Affairs*, St. Antony's Papers, No. 8, 1960:72–85.
Wittfogel, Karl
 1957 *Oriental Despotism: A Comparative Study in Total Power.*
Wraith, Ronald and Edgar Simpkins
 1963 *Corruption in Developing Countries.*
Young, M. Crawford
 1964 *Politics in the Congo: Decolonization and Independence.*
Yu, Frederick T. C.
 1963 Communications and Politics in Communist China. In: *Communi-*

cations and Political Development, Lucien W. Pye, ed., 1963:259–297.

Zolberg, Aristide

1964a   One-Party Government in the Ivory Coast.

1964b   Ivory Coast. In: Political Parties and National Integration in Tropical Africa, James S. Coleman and Carl G. Rosberg, eds., 1964:65–89.

1966   Creating Political Order: The Party-States of West Africa.

1968   The Structure of Political Conflict in the New States of Tropical Africa. American Political Science Review 62 (March, 1968):70–87.

AUTHOR INDEX

SUBJECT INDEX

Administrative Infrastructure. *See* Infrastructure, Administrative

Allegiance, as currency for legitimacy. *See* Legitimacy

Allocation: of resources, 29-30, 61-62, 98, 137, 239; linked to production, 28, 59, 104-105; cause and effect of stratification, 61-62; effects of marginal changes in, 53, 105, 107, 125-126, 138; productivity of different allocations, 20, 59-60, 66-67, 160, 173-179. *See also* Policy; Productivity; and Stratification

Anti-statesman: relevance of political economy to, x, 29, 57, 257, 282; as competitor for occupancy of authority role, 31, 71, 77, 79, 100, 113, 117, 136-137, 161, 172, 219, 251. *See also* Political Capital Formation

Appreciation, Political: as increase in value of currency, 72, 84, 155-157; as change in value of resource, 140n, 191, 195. *See also* Depreciation

Army: as infrastructure, 157-158, 217, 223, 247-248; as sector, 12, 41, 44, 247-248; examples of political consequences of, 4-6, 126, 143, 147, 158-159, 185, 205, 217, 232

Authority: as resource, 5, 81-86; as right to speak in name of state, 81; derived from occupancy or estab-

lishment of authority roles, 18-19, 81; regime monopoly on, 33, 82, 159; objective of remaining in, 33-37 *passim.*; problems of remaining in, 185, 190n, 206-207, 210, 223; productivity of, 81-82, 111-112, 176, 178; relation to power and legitimacy, 81, 86, 111-114, 141, 256; influence as currency for, 84-85, 92-93, 102, 128, 130, 156, 162, 193; delegation or decentralization of, 82-84, 133-134, 152, 163, 174, 236-238; cooptation 136, 152n; saving of, 193; symbols of, 90; examples of exchange for status and wealth, 110-111; relation to political inflation and deflation, 140-149 *passim.*; in developing countries, 86, 112-114; acquisition by anti-statesman, *see* Political Capital Formation. *See also* Authority Roles; Legitimacy; and Power

——— Roles, 18-19, 80, 81, 141, 180, 208. *See also* Political Division of Labor

Auxiliary Organizations: as infrastructure, 213n, 219, 230, 233, 253

Bankruptcy, Political, 15, 37, 47, 113, 148, 185, 245. *See also* Solvency

Bargaining, Political, 44, 118-136 *passim.*, 163, 170; not always explicit,

DATE DUE

GAYLORD			PRINTED IN U.S.A